The Poetry of T.V. Reddy:
A Critical Study of Humanistic Concerns

Edited by
Dr. P.V. Laxmiprasad

Modern History Press

Ann Arbor
Michigan – USA

The Poetry of T.V. Reddy: A Critical Study of Humanistic Concerns
Edited by Dr .P.V. Laxmiprasad
Copyright © 2018 by P.V. Laxmiprasad. All Rights Reserved.

2nd Printing June 2018.

Library of Congress Cataloging-in-Publication Data

Names: Laxmi Prasad, P. V., Editor
Title: The poetry of T. V. Reddy: A Critical Study of Humanistic Concerns / edited by Dr. P. V. Laxmiprasad
Description: Ann Arbor : Modern History Press, 2017. | Includes bibliographical references and index
Identifiers: LCCN 2017053452 (print) | LCCN 2017056544 (ebook) | ISBN 9781615993734 (ePub, PDF, Kindle) | ISBN 9781615993710 (pbk.: alk. paper) | ISBN 9781615993727 (hardcover: alk. paper)
Classification: LCC PL4780.9.N39585 (ebook) | LCC PL4780.9.N39585 Z83 2017 (Print) | DDC 894.8/2717109--dc23
LC record available at https://lccn.loc.gov/2017053452

Published by
Modern History Press
5145 Pontiac Trail
Ann Arbor, MI 48105
Michigan USA

www.ModernHistoryPress.com
info@ModernHistoryPress.com

Toll free (USA/CAN): 888-761-6268
Fax: 734-663-6861

Contents

Preface	iii
1 – Angst of an Aging Heart: Surveillance of Subjectivity in the Select Poems of T.V. Reddy's *Golden Veil* by Sheeba S. Nair	1
2 – Wails of Grief and Waves of Peace in T.V. Reddy's *Quest for Peace* by D. Gnanasekaran	7
3 – T. Vasudeva Reddy, the Poet in his Poetry: A Study of *Golden Veil* by DC Chambial	13
4 – Speaking through Images: A critical Study of T. V. Reddy's Poetry by Abida Farooqui	22
5 – Chronicles of Life and Times: Exploring T.V. Reddy's Poetry by C.A. Assif	27
6 – A Critical Exploration of the Pastoral Panorama of T. V. Reddy's Poetry by K. Padmaja	33
7 – Rainbow or Mirage? Life beyond and behind Golden Veil by Santosh Ajit Singh	41
8 – Exploring the 'Ultimate Truth': A Study of Golden Veil by T.V. Reddy by Vijaya Babu, Koganti	50
9 – Poetry as Social Commentary: A Thematic Study of T. Vasudeva Reddy's Quest for Peace by Arabati Pradeep Kumar	56
10 – Portrayal of Nature in T.V. Reddy's Melting Melodies: A Study by Palakurthy Dinakar	66
11 – Poet as Man Speaking to Men: An Appreciation of T. V. Reddy's *Melting Melodies* by S. Karthik Kumar	74
12 – T.V. Reddy: A Study of his Poem "Life is a Desert" by D.C. Chambial	81
13. A Critical Study of T.V. Reddy's Thousand Haiku Pearls by G. Srilatha	85
14 – A Collage of Random Images: The Abysmal, the Angst and the Social Responsibility in T.V. Reddy's Poems by Anju S Nair	94

15 – Rapturous Notes of Melancholy in T. V. Reddy's When Grief Rains
    by S. Malathy   100

16 – T.V. Reddy's Gliding Ripples –An Overview
    by Lily Arul Sharmila   106

17 – Social Consciousness in the Poetry of T.V. Reddy's Golden Veil
    by V. Suganthi   112

18 – Nature, a Healing Heaven: An Ecological Reading of T.V. Reddy's Golden Veil
    by R. Janatha Kumari   118

19 – Ecological Concerns in T.V. Reddy's collection of poems *The Broken Rhythms*
    by Sr. Candy D Cunha   125

20 – Echoes of Native Ethos: A Study of Indian Sensibility in T. V. Reddy's *Echoes*
    by Gobinda Sahoo   130

21 – Manifestations of a Fractured Soul in T. V. Reddy's Pensive Memories
    by J.S. Divya Sree   137

22 – T.V. Reddy's Quest for Peace and T.S. Eliot's The Waste Land: A Comparative Study
    by Poonam Dwivedi   142

23 – Nature: "Fairest Eve in Eden" in T.V. Reddy's Thousand Haiku Pearls
    by Prof. K. Rajamouly   159

24 – Social Consciousness in T.V. Reddy's poem *Quest for Peace*
    by Neelam K. Sharma   171

25 – India Seen through the Eyes of T.V. Reddy: A Study of *The Broken Rhythms*
    by Prof. Ramesh Chandra Mukhopadhyaya   176

26 – Poetic Iridescence of T.V. Reddy
    by Prof. A.K. Choudhary   183

27 – The Vicissitudes of Life: A Critical Analysis of *Fleeting Bubbles*
    by Prasaja VP   189

28 – Exploring Paradoxes and Contradictions of Postmodern Life in *Echoes*
    by Arti Chandel   194

29 – Angst and Despair: Existential Concepts in the Poems of T.V. Reddy
    by Anantha Lakshmi Hemalatha   200

30 – Echoes of the Sublime in T.V. Reddy's *Sound and Silence*
    by Dr. K. Rajani   206

About the Poet   215

About the Contributors   217

About the Editor   220

Index   221

Preface

Poetry is the expression of overall life on the vast canvas of universe. In fact, it is an established art practiced by poets all over the world. India has had a long history of poetry in Sanskrit down the ages. Later, colonialism in India gave a new language, English for the expression of sentiments, sensibilities and reaction of Indians. Poetry in the ancient India was considered to be the language of Gods and Goddesses. Indian English Poetry made its debut in the last one and a half decades and has continued to impress the readers throughout the world. It has been generally divided into three phases - (i) the imitative, (ii) the assimilative and (iii) the experimental.

The period from 1850 to 1900 is the imitative phase when the Indian poets were purely romantic poets whose main inspiration came from the British Romantic poets: Wordsworth, Scott, Shelley, Keats and Byron. The period from 1900 to 1947 is the assimilative period when the Indian poets tried to assimilate the romanticism of the early nineteenth century British poets and 'the new' romantics of the decadent period for expressing the consciousness of the Indian renaissance between fervent nationalism and rapid political changes which ultimately paved the way for freedom from the British in 1947.

The first phase of Indian poetry marked the period of literary renaissance in India. Romantic spirit attracted the poets like Henry Derozio, Michael Madhusudhan Dutt, Manmohan Ghose, Kasiprasad Ghosh. Toru Dutt alone emphasized on India and her heritage by putting into verse a large number of Indian legends. The poets of the second phase, still romantic in spirit were Sarojini Naidu, Tagore, Sri Aurobindo Ghose and Harindranath Chattopadhyaya. The poetic output of these poets was prolific. Nationality, spirituality and mysticism were different from English romanticism. Aurobindo with his search for the Divine in man and Tagore with his quest for the Beautiful in man and Nature turned out to be Philosopher-poets. Sarojini Naidu was noted for verbal melody as she was under the influence of the English poetry as well as the Persian and Urdu poetry. As a lyricist, she is best remembered as "the nightingale of India". The appeal of emotions embedded in nationalistic, philosophical, spiritual or mystical elements reached a wide readership in the country. The poetry of Toru Dutt, Sri Aurobindo, Tagore, and Sarojini Naidu represented the best voice of the contemporary Indian time-spirit.

The ethos of Post-independence phase of Indo-English literature is radically different from the first two phases. Modern age in Indian English Literature began virtually in 1947 with the partition of India, the tensions and emotions of Indian psyche. Thus, the post-independence era of hope and aspiration was soon replaced by an era of questioning. The national identity gave Indian writers a new confidence and spirit to work on the present and the past and of themselves. It can be accessed from the works that while the pre-1947 poets borrowed from the romantics, Victorians and 'new' romantics of the decadent period, the post-1947 poets borrowed from the modernist poets like W.B. Yeats, T.S. Eliot, Ezra Pound and W.H. Auden.

The later phase of Indian English Poetry (IEP) is of two phases: i) Modern ii) Post-modern. The modern poetry is the result of experimentation or the process of modernization which includes urbanization, industrialization, independence, social change and revolution in system, and a mass educational awareness. Modern poetry deals with concrete experiences in free verse. The major post-independence Indian English poets are Nissim Ezekiel, Dom Moraes, AK Ramanujam, P. Lal, R. Parthasarathy, Gieve patel, Arvind Mehrotra, Pritish Nandy, Kamala Das, K.N. Daruwalla, Shiv K Kumar, Jayanta Mahapatra, Dilip Chitre, Eunice De Souza, Meena Alexander, Agha Shahid Ali and Vikram Seth. Contemporary Indian Poets in English are, without doubt, D.H. Kabadi, I.K. Sharma, I.H. Rizvi, T.V. Reddy, DC Chambial, PCK Prem, R.K. Bhushan, R.K. Singh, Manas Bakshi, K.V. Raghupathi, Nalini Sharma, and others.

Two important pre-conditions had to be met before Indians attempted to write poetry in English. First, the English language had to be indianised to express the reality of Indian situation. Secondly, Indians had to be sufficiently Anglicised to use the English language to express themselves. IEP has historical significance from another dimension. In 1835, Viceroy Macaulay laid the foundations of modern educational system to promote European science and literatures among the Indians through the medium of English language. The result was that English as a language settled in India, as later in other British colonies and a privilege of passport and visa to take IEP beyond Indian boundaries. Still, the tension between the alienating language and the Indian sensibility has been as old as Indian Poetry in English itself.

Among the contemporary Indian English Poets, T.Vasudeva Reddy (better known as T.V. Reddy in literary circles) is a prominent poet in English with a large bulk of poetry to his credit. Basically, he is a poet of social criticism besides being a predominantly rural poet. As one who hails from rural area near Tirupati in Andhra Pradesh, India, T.V. Reddy has depicted the rural scenes besides the contemporary issues in his own style mostly by metre and rhyme, and by using imagery, satire and irony as his poetic tools. Writing about common scenes and people in countryside is a rare phenomenon in Indian English Poetry. Not many poets have depicted rural life in their poetry. Only a few poets like I.K.Sharma, DC Chambial, PCK Prem, and P. Raja have written several poems about rural life. Of these, T. V. Reddy occupies a permanent place as a rural poet. He is deeply committed to his village. Poems such as " The Sparrow", " Penance for Cow", " Thirsty Field", " The Wood is Calm", "The Lake at Night", deal with common scenes in Indian village. " Fortune Teller", "Toiling Ants", "Naked Tree", "The Train", "Travel by Bus", "Women of the Village", "The Indian Bride", "The Housewife", " An Old Woman", "The Kalyani Dam", "The Fort", "The Coconut Tree", "The Tiller", "A Pair of Sparrows" are examples of poems under rural element. His rural element reminds the readers of Mahatma Gandhi's quote that "India lives in the countryside". In fact, all the collections are known for rural sensibility. Critics estimate him that the poet has had a strong passion for poetry for the last three and a half decades. His interest sustains him even now.

To quote, K.V.Raghupathi, poet and critic, "T.V. Reddy's poetic growth spanning over three decades is one of involution. Strangely much contrary to what happens in most poets' career, he has moved from being intensely subjective, contemplative and philosophical in his first collection to social in his later collections. Clarity of thought, lucidity of expression and imagery are the hallmarks of good poetry. In poem after poem, T.V. Reddy's diction moves like a fluid, yet his is simple and direct endowed with impressive imagery" (*The Rural Muse: The Poetry of T.V. Reddy,* ed. K.V. Raghupathi,5-7). As such, he articulates human struggles and unrest, social as well as psychological and depicts a sort of restlessness that is the order of modern times. He protests against the social evils and ills. He paints his experiences in words with different images which make them remain in the memories of the readers. Words in his poetry dance to the tune of thoughts and create sounds, but in absolute silence. The natural flow of the lines, the remarkable ease and felicity of expression are striking features of his poetry. The poet takes the readers into the soul of India. People become alive in his poetry. Natural rhymes affect their taste and interest. Though a sense of grief and despair looms large in his earlier collections, a note of optimism marks his later collections.

Preface

This critical volume on the poetry of T.V. Reddy consists of thirty well-researched papers by scholars and professors across the country. To begin with, Sheeba S Nair is an eminent critic to work on *Golden Veil*. Her paper entitled "Angst of an Ageing Heart: Surveillance of Subjectivity in the Select poems of T.V. Reddy's "*GoldenVeil*" focuses on subjective touch to poet's personal experiences, moods and passions. Life's hardships help the poet achieve consensus with reality and mould him to undergo ageing with tolerance. She concludes that the collection of poems mentally prepare everyone to face the challenges of old age. Gnansekaran is another distinguished critic who has studied *Quest for Peace* for a brilliant analysis. His paper is entitled "Wails of Grief and Waves of Peace in T.V. Reddy's *Quest for Peace*. He remarks that T.V. Reddy is a selfless social critic and has a philosophical bent of mind. He gathers all his strength to anchor himself at a certain vacuum and uses the vacuous space to place himself close to the source of peace. He sums up that avarice; power-mongering, indulgence in sex, social inequality and all kinds of ethical erosion should be replaced by waves of peace. Only then, peace will prevail in the world. DC Chambial is another eminent critic to work on *Golden Veil* and finds that the poet has emerged as a champion of the poor, a representative of rural India holding human ethics to his heart and a detractor of the present polity. He envisages his original ideas about love for nature and hope. Next, Abida Farooqui, through her scholarly paper entitled "Speaking through Images: A Critical Study of T.V. Reddy's Poetry" observes that the most striking feature of his poems is the conveyance of sense through images. With a characteristic deftness, he incorporates the ordinary into his poetic fabric. Abida concludes that the poet is cryptic, at times satiric and at others pessimistic and dejected and still, hopeful and optimistic. The poet has this knack to blend the ordinary with the extraordinary.

C.A. Assif is another reputed critic to trace the chronicles of life and times in the poetry of T.V. Reddy. He finds that the poet has post-modern sensibility as dwells in the realm of what we call everyday life. Assif concludes that Reddy has attempted to depict some of the perennial issues of the age and thereby tried to chronicle his life and times. K. Padmaja is another eminent critic to explore the pastoral panorama in the poetry of T.V. Reddy. In fact, rural element is the most dominant theme of his poetry. Almost, all his collections carry poems with rural sensibility, scenery and predominantly form the bulk of his poetry. "A Critical Exploration of the Pastoral Panorama of T.V. Reddy's Poetry" is the title of her paper. Padmaja concludes that T.V. Reddy depicts idyllic nature, the rustic people and villages as well as the lasting damage done to nature by humans and the destruction of villages and the livelihoods due to urbanization. All these present sweeping panoramic view of the rural life encompassing a huge canvass of poetry.

Santosh Ajit Singh, an eminent critic, evaluated the collection *Golden Veil* and observes that the collection captures the quintessential spirit of life. Life is a relentless pursuit of the eternal truth that is the driving force behind all existence. T.V. Reddy makes a strong case for re-working notion of life. She concludes that the poet has dwelt upon emotions to pen down his musings on life. "Rainbow or Mirage? Life beyond and behind the Golden Veil" is the title of her paper which throws light on the life in all its hues and myriad forms. K.Vijaya Babu is another distinguished critic who has evaluated the collection *Golden Veil* for the ultimate truths. He termed the collection as something that projects the poet's kaleidoscopic view of the colorful feelings and emotions of his heart as a sensitive poet and as a keen observer of the world. The poet conveys a few ultimate truths to realize the loss man has undergone in his sojourn. Further, Vijaya Babu observes that the poet asks us to identify the loss of relationships between man and nature, and man and man, and man and society. Man has to realize that relationships are central to human existence. Next, A. Pradeep Kumar, an established critic, through his paper entitled "Poetry as Social Commentary: A Thematic Study of T.V. Reddy's *Quest for Peace*" reveals that T.V. Reddy is a social commentator and predominantly a true Indian nationalist. The collection remains largely distinctive of Indo-English poetry as it contains elements like social satire targeting the social problems like terrorism, corruption, environmental pollution, defective education system, filthy politics, unethical print and electronic media, VIP culture in temples and finally degenerating ethical and moral values. The poet champions the cause of social evils through the collection.

P. Dinakar is a critic who worked on the collection *Melting Melodies*. "Portrayal of Nature in T.V. Reddy's *Melting Melodies*" is a critical study for exploring nature scenes. He observes that the poet very succinctly views nature from different dimensions. Every line of collection is embedded with nature and its gifts. Dinakar finds that T.V. Reddy's collection provides a serene atmosphere in the minds of the readers. Nature continues to inspire poets even in the Post-modern world where other burning issues hold the nerves. It has profound impact on the poet and his surroundings made their presence in the collection. S. Karthik Kumar, another distinguished critic, takes up the collection *Melting Melodies* for a critical appreciation. He finds that the poet has become the representative voice of the millions of people and in a way; he is the ambassador of their concerns through creative faculty. Universal anxieties affect his poetry and the poet speaks to men as the speaker or the spokesperson. Karthik finds that the collection is replete with themes ranging from love to politics. Society is the main focus through which the poet examines all sorts of relationships. His poetic sensibility, according to Karthik, is so keen that anything he comes across in everyday life becomes a source of poetry. The ordinary becomes extra-ordinary in his hand.

DC Chambial in his brilliant second paper titled "T. V. Reddy: A Critical Study of his Poem "Life is a Desert" writes that life seems to have taught him so many lessons coupled with struggle to express and establish himself in his academic as well as social life. He sums up that the poet used iambic pentameter but does not delve on rhymes. Alliteration has been effectively employed in the poem. G. Sri Latha is another eminent critic to evaluate T.V. Reddy's *Thousand Haiku Pearls*. She writes that the poet criticizes the present social conditions as chaotic due to never-ending crime rates. The focus of the collection is more on education, politics and society. Her observation is more pertinent in the context of modern day education where it has shifted from holistic education to materialistic life. Total reforms in the modern life are the only way to purify the maladies of world and thereby envisage a life of peace and inner calm. Arti Chandel is another eminent critic to explore paradoxes and contradictions in the collection *Echoes*. The poet, as she observes, uses paradox, contradictions, and oxymoron as effective tools to expose, ridicule and satirize contemporary man and his actions. His aim is nothing but correction. Arti cites certain poems which reveal universal truths through a series of contradictions and inherent paradoxes. Attachment in detachment and detachment in attachment are the two sides of the same coin.

Random images get their due share in the poetry of T.V. Reddy. Anju S Nair traces out certain random images from the collection *Fleeting Bubbles*. "A Collage of Random Images: The Abysmal, The Angst, and The Social Responsibility in T.V. Reddy's Poems" is the title of her paper through which she presents invoking ideas of modern man and his plight. It is what she describes material and intellectual life in the barren world. A man loses his senses when he is caught in a state of forlornness. The isolated, secluded, and pitiable condition of man who yearns for solace depicts the state of helplessness. S. Malathy is another distinguished critic to work on the collection *When Grief Rains*. Her paper entitled "Rapturous Notes of Melancholy in T.V. Reddy's *When Grief Rains*" presents the warp and woof of human dilemma and complexity. It not only depicts the amount of grief by the poet but also the pain of the people around him. Malathy sums up that the collection shows T.V. Reddy as the poet of his fellow living-beings. It is an exhilaration that his readers enjoy as the poet excels in his art of highlighting even tiny specks of life.

Lily Arul Sharmila has taken up the collection *Gliding Ripples* for an overview. She writes that the poet has unified ideas, promulgated truths and universalized his long-cherished ideals. This is where T.V. Reddy is successful as a poet of universal concerns. Anantha Lakshmi Hemalatha is another critic who has studied T.V. Reddy's collections for existential concepts like angst and despair. She observes that the poet's art gains everlasting magnitude as it borders on the living conditions of human beings. The mystery of continued existence is permanent and unending.

V. Suganthi has taken up *Golden Veil* and explored the theme of social consciousness. The righteous world is no more now and it is now replaced by corrupt world where there are no moral values. The poet presents social milieu in the collections and as a poet, voices his concerns towards the better world. He awakens the world against the wrong-doings. Suganthi rightly remarks that the poetry of T.V. Reddy is quite relevant and responsive to the society. Nature continues to dominate the poetry and T.V. Reddy in particular, whose poetry strongly echoes the impact of nature. R. Janatha Kumari through her brilliant paper entitled "Nature, A Healing Heaven: An Ecological Reading of Golden Veil" explores the profound impact of nature on the universe. She observes that the collection is rather a beautiful portrait of colorful, soothing and lovely nature in spicy and elegant verses. It is, according to Janatha Kumari, a lullaby for the readers to lull ourselves in the lap of the Mother Nature. His poems exhibit his ample love and appreciation for nature. Nature is supreme and for T.V. Reddy it is more than a mere worshipping of nature but to go deep into the secrets of universe.

"Ecological Concerns in T.V. Reddy's *The Broken Rhythms*" is a brilliant paper by an eminent critic Candy D Cunha who has worked substantially on Eco-literature. The select poems she has studied are about the wounded earth and with which the poet painted them in the form of poetry. The children of the earth have turned against her and have exploited her and further, have stripped off her green garment, making her to feel in absolute shame. Her ecological concerns target the man-machine world and the immoral practices and natural destruction of the beautiful inn that God has created for us.

Gobinda Sahoo is another critic who has critically evaluated the perspectives of Indian ethos in the poetry of T.V. Reddy. He deals with the echoes of native ethos, the reflections of Indianness. India is a land of diversities and the poet's sensibility gets reflected in the poetry. It is his love and passion for the country that is reflective of typical Indian sensibility. The imagery and idiom, issues and illusions, philosophy and location s of India have received ample expression in the poetry of T. V. Reddy. Gobinda concludes that the poetry of T. V. Reddy bears multiple notes of Indianness with echoes of native ethos which can be called as one of the striking themes of his creation.

J.S. Divya Sree has studied *Pensive Memories*, a poetry collection by T.V. Reddy and traces out certain manifestations of a fractured soul. Divya writes that almost all the poems in the collection contain that element of suffering of man at physical, emotional and spiritual levels. She concludes that his keen observation of nature, speculation in life, harsh criticism of social institutions and use of alliterative verse makes him stand apart from his contemporary poets. A.K.Choudhary, after a careful analysis of his poetry, expresses that "Like Jayant Mahapatra Reddy makes an earnest attempt in exposing the social and political hypocrisy of the Indian masses that made a treasury of the raw materials for versification in English poetry."

Prasaja VP is another critic who has examined *Fleeting Bubbles* with her critical perspective interpreting the vicissitudes of life reflected in the poems. She finds that the collection is a representation of multifarious lives in this mini world. As the title signifies, it is a delineation of the transient and ephemeral nature of life. She concludes that though pain and sufferings permeate his poetry, many of them have a hopeful tone.

Poonam Dwivedi has taken up a comparative study for her critical evaluation. She compares T.V. Reddy's *Quest for Peace* with T.S. Eliot's *The Wasteland*. T.V. Reddy's invocation of the ancient anecdotes to resurrect the dead souls living in the present day world is to be found everywhere in the poem just as there is the focus of T.S. Eliot on the ancient tale of fertility rituals vis-à-vis modern thought and religion in the guise of Fisher King. The mythical aphorism remains the spine of the thematic structure of both the poems of significant length. Both the poets have dealt with Post-modern chaos, despair, disappointment and frustration in the poems. "Peace" in Vedantic term means

"*Shantih*". The poet voices for a better world to prevail on earth though there are political, social, and regional and religious barriers.

The paper by Poonam Dwivedi has relevance and context in the backdrop of the happenings around the world. K.Rajamouly is another critic to work on Haiku. He writes that nature is so beauteous and bounteous for T.V. Reddy that it attracts his deep attention towards its charms and rhythms, beauty and music. He as a poet and man loves to live and move in nature and become one with nature. His love for nature is not only due to his temperament but also to the background of his native region. He was born and brought up in a village surrounded by green fields and groves, hills and forests, rills and rivers. It is natural that his main focus is on nature and man in nature. One of the nucleus themes of his poetry is nature, "Fairest Eve in Eden".

Ramesh Chandra Mukhopadhyaya has examined the collection and observes that *The Broken Rhythms* is a significant book of poems on many counts. Firstly it holds out a mirror to life as it is in India. "Thousand pages of Indian economics and Indian sociology cannot teach us the truths about the social and economic predicament in India better than the handful of poems in *The Broken Rhythms*". "India Seen through the Eyes of T.V. Reddy" is the title of paper that the critic has found Indian dimensions in his poetry. Neelam Kumar Sharma found *Quest for Peace* for social consciousness. He concludes that *Quest for Peace* by T.V Reddy is a great piece of art containing social satire in it. Every satirist is at heart a reformist. *Reddy* also wants to reform the society by pinpointing the vices and shortcomings in it with the help of his moral responsibility, civic sense and practical wisdom. Undoubtedly he has been very successful in accomplishing his self-imposed mission.

K.Rajani in her perceptive article "Echoes of the Sublime in T.V. Reddy's *Sound and Silence*" speaks about the voice of the sublime in T.V. Reddy's poetry and finds the echoes of the sublime in abundance in Reddy's sonnets. She remarks "Reddy's sonnets are a mine of delectable music springing from the constant beat of the rhythm and such expressions are beyond count in his poetry and in fact music is the breath of his poetry. Dr. Reddy's poetry is a marvelous blend of sound and sense springing from profound silence. In his poems that deal with social or satirical theme, nature or spiritual theme we find an undercurrent of the sublime voice whose echo lingers long in our minds."

Thus, the poetry of T. V. Reddy is the poetry of life in all aspects and angles. He is not just a poet of nature but also a poet of rural India and at the same time a poet who has experienced the world around him. He is a passionate observer, and these reflections have found a place in the form of verses. A profound philosopher, a poet of rural sensibility, and equally a poet of universal concerns, T. V. Reddy is, I reckon, the representative poet from India whose contributions will be remembered in the world.

Dr. P.V. Laxmiprasad
English Literary Critic and Editor
Karimnagar, Telangana, INDIA

1 Angst of an Aging Heart: Surveillance of Subjectivity in the Select Poems of T.V. Reddy's *Golden Veil*

Sheeba S. Nair

Subjectivity is a major philosophical concept which comprises in itself the consciousness and experiences of an individual related to his/her reality and truth based on his state of being. In other words, it can be simplified as an entity's specific perceptions, experiences, expectations and understanding of a reality which may be biased based on the understanding of a subject. To most of the creative writers, more specifically poets, literature is an expression of their hearts, expectations, plaints, grief, despair, disappointments and so on. To T.V. Reddy, the creative and meritorious poet par excellence, poetry springs out of his personal experiences reflecting and refracting his different moods and passions. They are, in fact, interpreters of his 'own self' and soul. This quality of his writing extends a subjective touch to his poetic pieces, making their reading the most endearing experience. Though personal, they do endorse the objective reality through an individual's identity and experiences and can never be dismissed or overlooked as the idiosyncrasies of an individual.

"Time and tide wait for none" is a well known maxim that reminds the human beings of the transient nature of their life. Still, the general human tendency is to ignore this greatest truth and live as though they are eternal and immortal beings. Especially, the youth gloat over their strength both mental and physical and display interests in wielding power; they live believing that they are the power centre of the universe. But passage of time proclaims how ephemeral human life is, particularly the bloom of youth or the salad days traverse from one's life at breakneck speed. It is so swift that it would have crossed one's life before one comes to realize. With passing time, the power structure of human life also undergoes a change. They may experience a state of decentering, a quick jetting from centre to margin which shatters their identity and existence. Hence, from *puranic* time onwards there is a hunt for *amrita*, a divine portion that confirms immortality. Research still progresses though human beings who have not yet succeeded in attaining immortality and it makes life desperate. It leads to disappointment, frustration, despair etcetera and these feelings could be evinced in the poems of T.V. Reddy in the collection *Golden Veil*. Though the collection includes poems on variety of themes, it is extensively about ageing which pours down the spirit of the poet or the narrator. Furthermore, it sheds light on the poet's personal life and his experiences.

Golden Veil begins with a poem "In the Shell of Solitude" which undrapes Reddy's ailing heart. The poem is highly subjective as it records the poet narrator's reserved nature and preference for solitude. The poet confesses that he is "Unused to Hawkish hues of dash and drive / I prefer to stay in the sober shell of solitude" (9). The personal pronoun employed in the verse extends an authentic touch to the poem, permitting the readers an access to the otherwise reserved heart of the poet which is encircled deliberately by "the stony wall" (9). The poem on the whole is set in a confessional note. The poet admits that "I am from birth shy and timid, / True, I do not know why … I can't transform my mute cells" (9). Though desperate, he admits that he has to be bold and it could be possible only with the grace of the almighty, "Bereft of it these lives and lines can't blaze" (9). "In the Shell of

Solitude" concludes on a positive note in spite of its gloominess by recording that if a common man shows courage he can turn into a legend and it is in the individual who has to decide whether he "has to live" or "crawl as a lone lizard" (9).

The confidence and the hope that Reddy expressed in the first poem of the collection *Golden Veil* soon vanishes giving room for frustration and desperation. The strength he displayed even while living a secluded life in his youth deserts him and he feels completely desolate. He experiences loss of identity and that drives him to equate him to that of an insignificant cast-off napkin that is old. The plaintive tone of the poet marks the frustration of the old man who feels, "We old men nowadays are like old napkins / to our fast earning kids and wealthy kith and kin, / trash thrown out as waste and useless tins and pins, / used tissues disposed and dumped in dustbins" (10). Though the above lines are highly subjective in nature, objective representation of the changed social scenario could not be dismissed. Very subtly, Reddy refers to the materialistic nature of the modern youth who pays no attention or reverence to the old who were once looked upon as a source of knowledge and guidance.

"Old Napkins" is not just a recantation of the poet's afflicted heart. It is more a didactic poem than a plaintive one. It shows how the young hate the old for remonstrating while they go astray. They are impatient and impertinent. Still, the poet feels that they should be properly guided though they detest. The poet moralizes "If elders fail to advise, children will sink and stink" (10).

A streak of similarity could be evinced in Reddy's poem with that of Shelley's "Ode to the Westwind". Besides being subjective, both the poems enunciate the troubled life of the poets and the way both conclude on a rhetorical note. While Shelley expresses hope that all his sufferings will come to an end as winter will surely be replaced with spring, Reddy's closing lines invoke the reader's mind regarding the inevitability of pruning and weeding the young minds in the proper way. The brilliantly simple and uncomplicated comparison through which Reddy conveys the vital truth or message demands special attention and appreciation: "when cattle graze in another's rice field / a strong stick does the angry farmer wield; / when leaves and buds are infested by pest, / till pesticides are applied do we simply rest?" (10). The 'Indianness' in these lines cannot be dismissed either.

The philosophical nature of Reddy's poetry evokes comparison with not only Shelley's poems but with Robert Frost too. "Choose the Right Path" reliably alludes to Frost's "Road not taken". Both the poems are subjective and articulate the need to take a decision at a point of time. While Frost implies the decision that one has to make in the youthful days, Reddy insinuates an experienced or grown up man's struggle to decide on the path to pursue. The line "My travel continues from dawn to noon" (16) marks the time the poet has spent on this earthly abode and "No shade, I walk in severe scorching heat" (16) again refers to the hardships that the poet has undergone in his life, yet he is hopeful though he has not yet reached his destination, "I hope to reach it soon" (16). While Frost writes of

> Two roads diverged in a yellow wood,
> And sorry I could not travel both
> And be one traveler, long I stood
> And looked down one as far as I could
> To where it bent in the undergrowth; (Frost, "The Road not Taken")

Reddy presents the same in the Indian scenario: "Beneath the peepal tree I stand, I stare at the split, / The path splits in two, my tired feet stand still" (16). While both Frost and Reddy speak about the difficulty of making choice, Reddy differs in articulating not just about the need to make a choice but also about the troublesome nature of the life that he has lived so far which makes him lament that his "throat dries up, reluctant are my feet" (16). However, both mention the general human tendency to choose the "easy one, the pleasant cozy one" (Reddy 16) as "instant fruits and sweet comforts it dreams to reap" (16). Though the road with "a feast of festive lights teeming with tempting sights"

(16) attracts him over the highly dangerous "winding craggy hill", he like Frost chooses the less travelled difficult path in "Search of Truth, an uphill task, leads to lasting bliss" (16) and the explanation that Reddy provides with for choosing the difficult path as "We are not sheep to graze and relish the ephemeral kiss" (16) also justifies Frost's words "And that has made all the difference" ('Road not Taken').

Reddy's "Soon the Sun does Set" is a highly philosophical poem where the poet comes in consensus with the bitter truth that he cannot escape old age. He commences with the acknowledgement that indeed youth is the most attractive phase in one's life but he advises the readers not to panic before the racing time: "Be brave to turn a new leaf, never be meek / No use in recollecting the youthful days" (17). The metaphor of sun is used by the poet to ram home the strength and radiance of a youth but soon he reminds that sharp and bright sun "would set, retire hurt and gory" (18) for as rightly recalled by the poet "You can't ride on the crest of the racing tide / Each has his moment and then a jerky slide" (18). Never once does Reddy cast off his philosopher's robe in this book *Golden Veil* and that expounds the wealth of his experience, mostly bitter.

The subjective nature of the poem makes the readers deduce that the poet is nearing his old age: "The sun is past the meridian line, rays are slant/ Soon he would set without heat, rage and rant" (18). The poet does not forget to express the conflict between the mind and body which one experiences in the old age: while "your mind thinks you are still young and stronger" (18), your body realizes "you can walk no longer" (18). The concluding lines record the effort the poet takes to convince his mind which is still youthful and looks shuddered at the ageing body. He consoles his own exasperated self: "You are tired, my child, you are grown too old; / No use in groaning and gasping for bad breath" (18). Though he mentions about the awaiting death, he likes to look at it as "The old frame... laid to rest with a formal wreath" and is hopeful that "The sun has set for good with the hope of rest" (18). Despite being melancholic in tone, the poem extends the greatest philosophy of life with utmost sincerity and simplicity and it alludes to the thoughts of the greatest philosopher G.B. Shaw who averred "Do not try to live forever, you will not succeed".

The troubled life and its problems are recorded faithfully in the poem "No More Tears". The poet recounts how he has spent almost all his feelings at the far end of his life which has left him with "No more drops of tears to fall / No more words or thoughts to call" (20). He laments that not only tears and thoughts have eluded but love and peace too. The passing years deprive a man of everything jocund and bright and he can dream of "No more light or delight, no more my love" (20). What envelops him is the darkness, "the eerie darkness" and it waits to fill his life "as a dark cloud or a sable shroud" (20). "No More Tears" though accents a happy note, it in fact discloses the passionless life one is compelled to undergo in one's old age.

The angst of Reddy's poetic heart is well expressed in the poem "Forget Me Not" which takes the poem from pathos to anxiety and apprehension. It is addressed to his wife to whom he pleads not to forget him even after his death. A typical fatherly concern marks the rest of the poem: "Children are too tender and young / Many thorny years to be strung" (21). It also reminds the readers about the difficulty of this mundane life yet, it is very dear to all especially one who has a beloved. He confesses his lady that "The moment you hold my feeble hand / I feel I am still safe on this fluid land" (21). The fleeting nature of time is insinuated once again here and the poet cautions "you can't arrest this moment" (21).

The rest of the poem portrays the poet to be a typical Indian who is not swayed or shattered by the fact that he is approaching his end. Though he expresses his anxiety of being forgotten in the course of time, what ails him the most is the anxiety he feels for his wife and children. Hence, he extracts promises from his wife that "Now or later you should not lament / Look after the kids and see them fly /..../ Let not your heart yield to tears or fears" (21). The concluding lines inform us that the poet has come to accept his fate and confesses that "At the call I would fly to the unknown sphere / from where none can come back alive here" (21). Nevertheless, he takes solace that though he dies and the world may forget his existence, still he leaves his beloved "who remembers me waits with loving eyes" (21) and that it is the greatest achievement he has accomplished in this earthly abode.

Though at the end of rumination, the poet tries to arrive at a poised state, he is often troubled by the annihilated identity he experienced in his old age. Being a poet, Reddy pours out his troubled conscience as and how he feels. The poems in the collection *Golden Veil* bear testimony to it. His sincere attempt to accept the reality often deserts him and he laments aloud pensively and helplessly, "I am vexed ... / Aggrieved with the age, with the stage/ I am a retired man, an old decrepit man" (24). His grief leads him to empathize with himself: "What more can I do? Where would I be acceptable" (24) conveys his helpless state. The irony of life also gets verbalized in the midst of the poem. When the young people look forward to the holidays to enjoy, the poet at the old age complains about the unending holidays he has and he is perplexed not knowing how to celebrate it; he feels unwanted everywhere except "in parks and on less trodden pavements / and near the temples and less known ashrams" (24). He continues contrasting his purposeless old age with the highly active and meaningful life he led once when he "served with feet on wheels/ till wheels fell victims of wear and tear" (24). It dawns on him that he is incapable of resuming that active life or 'take another novel route" (24). So he decides to condescend before the supreme creator, "Before the journey ends with lust and rust" (24) because He alone can "make this piece of life real" (24) and meaningful. The transient nature of life and the way to salvation can never be better expressed than this.

There are several poems in the collection *Golden Veil*, like "Pyres and Fires", and "End of Arch" which spell out the listlessness and anguish one experiences in old age. Nevertheless, the poet tries to maintain equilibrium in each of the poems by realizing that "Truth is a bitter pill – when we long to live long / we know without peace we die all along" ("End of Arch", 50). He reminds us often how foolish it is to pine about old age and its problems; still, anxiety does not leave the poet. He confesses –

> I know I am reasonably old
> Truth is no one likes to become old
> But it is a thing that can't be avoided;
> Like everyone else I too wish to be young,
> Young in mind, young in bone and tone; (54)

However, the passing years leave his body and mind wearied and dull. Loneliness becomes his only companion and hence he bemoans "How long should I bear this enforced estrangement / .../ Past has deluded while the future seems to elude" (55). His mind tries to recoup through "memories of erased images of the past" (55). Still, he frequently rationalizes that past has no relevance and "What matters now is the now and this moment" (55). Though lonely and deserted, the poet hopes to "stand firmly" with the understanding that whatever he has achieved so far "bursts as bubbles" and he assuages that he does not care to live or worry if whatever he has achieved "fails to recharge and illuminate the crux of the now;" (55). He gives vent to his frustration by saying if all his younger days and its achievements are not going to help him in spending the old age happily and peacefully, "Then let this fragile unremarkable perishable body / dissolve in the unsolved mystery of five elements" (55). The above lines proclaim the shattered spirit of the poet at his old age.

The symbol of the sun has been employed throughout the book *Golden Veil*. The title itself refers to the golden rays of the sun which is the source of energy to all living being including humans. The rising sun is used by the poet to refer to his sunny youthful days when he too looked so full of energy and spirit like the planet sun. However, the poet being old and his poems being very personal and subjective often refer to the image of the setting sun which alludes to his physical weakness and his disappointment and vague acceptance of the approaching death which seems imminent. Similar is the theme that one could trace in the poem "To Rest in Peace". The initial lines articulate the sunset period of his life when he experiences weakness which he pens as follows: "The setting sun looks weak and yellow bent too low/ He shines before he sinks in his last glow to fade" (48). Death that awaits one is compared to that of darkness that "waits as a quiet prowling wolf to invade" (48).

The great philosophy that death is a great leveler is suggested by Reddy who expounds the truth that the darkness of death falls on every living being: "All the power of mind or scepter can't revive the breath / From the fatal moment there is no escape, no defense. / At the final call none can resist the clasp of cold death". (48). The Shakespearean philosophy of the world as a stage and its human beings as its actors is also presented with a little acclimatization. Reddy calls the humans as "toys, players in a masquerade" (48). The ever approaching or watchful time is something that is indispensable about which he writes as: When time tolls none can cross the line of barricade / From the unseen book of life, torn is the last pitiful page" (48).

As usual with his poems, the poet tries to accept the reality and concludes the poem "To Rest in Peace" with a philosophical observation: "Life is a race, rough and tough; let us move with grace / Let us dream and die, die and dream to rest in peace" (48). The concluding lines do reflect the listlessness or the disappointments that one encounters in his old age. The life which appeared very much in his grip while young, slips away from him as he grows old and it is something frustrating and hard to be reconciled with. Yet, it is a bitter reality which Reddy has brilliantly articulated in the poem "To Rest in Peace".

The poems like "Let Me Stand Erect" and "Grow Old We Must" explicate a stance that a human in his/her senescence should take. The poem "Let Me Stand Erect" as usual begins with the issues especially loneliness and negligence that trouble old people. The aged become so unwanted in the youthful circles. The loss of roots that the poet experiences, makes him lament: "Neighbours wish to see me fall and fade / In fact in their hearts they kick me out" (37). The choice of words conveys the degree of negligence that the society displays towards the old who make their existence very hard and he writes that through "troubled waters I wade" (37). Yet, he recuperates all his energy to prolong his life and challenges those who disregard and disrespect him: "The more they ignore the stronger is my will" and when they "wait on pins to hurl me in academic gloom/ .... / When they wish my doom, by God's will I bloom / When they long to see my quill and will broken/ I move and march with an unruffled mind unbroken"(37). Soon he explains that he has no intention to ignore or pass over them; all he wishes is to remain "cool and calm, simple and fire-proof" (37). The path as Reddy confesses is very trying and tiring and the tale of hardships he faced during his early days or after his marriage probably from the neighbours of his village is expressed as follows:

> From patches of thatch quietly I march to stand
> Stormy winds of stress and strain I withstand
> From pensive past rooted in pain and penury
> I march through varied shades and scars of injury;
> From the clouds of rage and envy I emerge like a star (38)

The poet confesses candidly that it is his writing skills that help him to resurrect from his worries and sufferings. Whenever he is dejected or disappointed, he pours them down on a piece of paper which eases his soul and body and helps him soar "above the clouds of regrets and total neglect" (38). It saves him from being doomed and strengthens him to face the inevitable death with the courage and hope that he has succeeded in making his progeny remember him through "a few humble lyrical notes to recollect" (38). This is a consoling thought which makes his life meaningful and satisfactory.

"Grow Old We Must", the poem with which I wish to conclude my article, is all about Reddy's perception of life. The tone again is confessional where he states whether one likes it or not one has to grow old. He adds that we may gloat that we are young now but he reminds "Though not now, tomorrow meet we must" (96). So he deduces that we should welcome it with a bold heart as we cannot evade it. He extends the idea by saying that not only human beings but everything in nature plants, planets too undergo this change as it is "Nature's law we must accept till the day of doom" (96) and everything fades with the passage of time. He notifies that "Beauty.... / Glory we lose, which we often fail to keep / Strength we lose, it goes with braying age" but he adds all these loses will be compensated with the "spiritual growth" which one should aspire to pursue. If we are able to achieve that, then we will understand that "We are born to die, so why should we weep?" (96).

The concluding five lines are highly consoling to people in senescence and they bring with them echoes of Tennyson's thought that "Old age hath yet his honor and his toil" ('Ulysses'). Quite like Tennyson, T.V. Reddy surmises "Old age has its honor with all its wrinkles unkempt / .. . . / All passions spent, mellowed mind moves sober and slow/ with rainbow charm it has the soft sunset glow" (97). These words do not simply eulogize ageing but explicate how the plaintive attitude of the poet which the readers experienced in the beginning of the book *Golden Veil* has undergone tremendous change in its course. Life's hardships help the poet achieve consensus with reality and mould him to admit ageing with magnanimity and tolerance. Reading Reddy's poetry is a great learning experience; it teaches the young as well as *old* to greet old age without anxiety and exasperation. It must be said as a concluding remark and observation that the book *Golden Veil* is not just an expression of the poet's personal feelings, it is a thought-provoking set of poems preparing everyone for the most inevitable and indispensable old age.

Works Cited

Frost, Robert. "The Road Not Taken." *Selected Poems*. Edited with introduction by Ian Hamilton. 1973. Harmondsworth, England: Penguin books, 1975. Print.

Reddy, T.V. Golden Veil. New Delhi: Authors Press, 2016. Print.

Shaw, George Bernard. https://www.brainyquote.com/authors/george_bernard_shaw/

Shelley, P.B. "Ode to the West Wind". Shelley. Poems, OUP, *The World's Classics*, 378. Print.

Tennyson, Alfred. "Ulysses". *Tennyson's Poetry*, 2nd edition, Ed. Robert W. Hill Jr., W.W. Norton & Co., 1999.Print.

2 Wails of Grief and Waves of Peace in T.V. Reddy's *Quest for Peace*

D. Gnanasekaran

The overall assessment I have gained by reading T. V. Reddy's long poem *Quest for Peace* (2014) is that he is a selfless social critic and has a philosophical bent of mind. It is said that a microorganism has evolved into man and the evolutionary process appears to have taken million of years. A good many million years may have passed by since man started his quest for peace, mainly inner peace. Inner peace is no doubt an extension of outer peace. Golden periods of creative output have been the byproduct of peace and harmony in society at large. Rollo May states in *Man's Search for Himself* that anxiety strikes us at the core of ourselves; it is what we feel when our existence as selves is threatened. Reddy is one who has a certain anxiety in the interest of all humans.

Seers, saints and seekers of truth have tried down the ages to understand the meaning and purpose of human life on this planet but woefully made only partially successful attempts and confessed to the fact that peace in human life is highly elusive. They have located the most possible source of peace and convinced themselves of their hard-found solution that peace dwells within and one should make one's conscience clear and cleanse one's soul to make it the dwelling place of the ubiquitous God or some Greater Being incomprehensible to the ordinary human mind. However, man perennially toils in pursuit of peace, peace of mind.

Human existence is a series of predictions and expectations and also a series of disappointments and unexpected quirks of fate. These two series continually intersect and get interspersed with each other. One may argue that fatalism is the failure of reason and blindness to realities and reactions, and may also favour man's helplessness in the overall scheme of things on earth, call it predetermined or predisposed. So we are totally at a loss and nonplussed about the answer to the question: Why are we born and why are we to die leaving behind the fruit of all our labour and loved ones? When one thinks of this state of affairs in the continuum of life, he turns inward, looks within and begins his quest for peace. Many questions crop up while we are fretting and strutting upon the stage since in the end all our sound and fury fades into insignificance all of a sudden. T. V. Reddy is one such human embarking on the long endless voyage in the direction of the abode of peace through his effusions of poetic expressions. Mostly Reddy's lines loosely fall under the genre of heroic couplet with end-rhymes.

T.V. Reddy's poem is aptly titled *Quest for Peace* and runs to 1665 lines falling under seven segments. In fact, this is a long uninterrupted meditation on the essential emptiness of human life and a momentary stay in the midst of chaos and of continuous flux and emotional commotion. Reddy gathers all his strength to anchor himself at a certain vacuum and uses the vacuous space to place himself very close to the source of peace, because the very source of peace is the spring of vacuum. He is at ease at his best for peace but like his ilk in the past, he makes an abortive attempt to reach his destination, where he can derive inner strength and enjoy the bliss of peace. However, we are all praise for his poetic attempt after all.

In the beginning itself, Reddy states his mission. The statement is unambiguous and speaks eloquently of an arduous task:

> For this single soul's ceaseless flight
> this is a brief linear landing place for rest
> to refuel its teasing tank with inherent right
> and refresh with clean air free from pest. (1-4)

The fabled ancient eastern hilly place, Kedarnath, which "relished once the Lord's supreme grace" (8), is a symbolic location where he locates himself and extravagantly indulges in self-introspection and retrospection to strive to experience peace a bit against the backdrop of the inevitable existential conflict. Born into this world, one has to be confronted with unavoidable unrest and forced to feel the urge to seek a locale of rest and peace.

A comparative understanding intrusively makes its appearance as Reddy is still conscious of the corruption both physical and moral all around much worse than in the past. He bemoans the corruption that has expanded its domain even in this "sacred spot … on the earth." Hundreds of people, "exiled by the metropolitan pell-mell" get set "to deconstruct their cultural remains/on planned ways and sanctioned lines" (12, 21-22). Only "a sorely slighted miniscule minority/ with positive thoughts" "coolly venture to reconstruct in a cool way/ … the sole inheritance of ageless sages" (33-36).

After a brief statement of his purpose, Reddy has spoken about the ills of today's society, political, social, economic and moral by cataloguing them throughout the poem, sometimes repetitively. He looks at certain realities from his perspective and is free to describe India as a democracy "crushed under fish-catching reservations" and "exploitation of capitalism" (63). On the one hand, we acknowledge his enthusiasm to identify the missing links and menacing embroils and on the other, we see him wish to "free this city from heat and hunger" (84) like a self-appointed comrade-cum-good Samaritan with communist leanings. Reddy enlists all the realities soaked in ugliness and speaks at length to reason out why peace is absent amidst humanity at present. He is able to see that "now a third force rises from slums /and announces its emergence with drums" (98-99).

Reddy goes non-stop to give a dreary picture of India today, not the shining India, not the incredible India but the shunned India. In the name of ultra-modern civilization and cosmopolitanism, we promote uncivilized behaviour and happily march back to primitive savagery: "mercury of morals to bottom level slopes and dips/crowded bars, rising stars, tempting lips and zips" (123-24). He is thus ruthless in his criticism and nothing unacceptable from his point of view escapes his vigilant eyes. Schools mushroom like "money-minting factories and college teachers always count arrears "unmindful of students' needs and careers" (152-53).

Reddy is very restive and finds it hard to digest all sorts of misdemeanors and ill-conceived mindsets. "Books strangely appear as untouchables at last" (189). He cries as if from a roof top that "our tired bodies badly need fresh vitamins (176) and our bankrupt souls "need garlic pearls of morals, more moral pills" (195). He concludes the first segment with the earnest appeal to every one of us: "let us fortify and energize our heart's enclosures" (205-6). "To survive the nomadic onslaughts of erasures, / "our great *Upanishads* see the glow of God in all/while the corrupt pundits caused the murky fall" (293-94), "hurling people into an iron trap of illusion" (317).

Reddy undauntedly proceeds further to list out the deficiencies that are spotted among us Indians and he does it repetitively, maybe, with the intention of reinforcing his anguish and agony to ding all this into our unwilling ears and defiant mental faculties. Sometimes the repetition is jarring and hard to relish beyond a certain degree. Our national policies also come into the crossfire between his well-meaning sensibilities and serious criticism: "Decades of stale and impotent and false non-alignment/breeds steady decay and fears of new alignments" (361-62). Reddy is not exaggerating when he says: "Theatres and liquor shops are overcrowded/while values and ethics are flouted and clouded" (381-82). Unproductive schemes of Government make "men and women, hitherto hard in field work, /now sit under the thick green tamarind tree,/spend in idle gossip and all work they shirk" (421-22).

Reddy's exposé here is very honest to the core and is expressive of his pain and grief. Another true picture emerges from his pen as an example of his bold plain-speaking: "Easy waiver of loans to billions of rupees/wrecks our paralyzed nation's feigned peace/makes our leaders and gang leaders rich/while honest payers pay and lose the pitch" (443-46). He takes a dig at the press today: "newspapers have sunk into personal pamphlets,/for hitting opponents to the hilt ever outlets,/indulging in out-dated barren pun and rhymes" (494-96).

Reddy reiterates his purpose again at the beginning of the third segment. He turns nostalgic and repentant. He wishes to renovate his sinking heart with the material of his own aesthetic art: "in uneasy cohabitation my days I waste/breathing spicy fumes of borrowed taste" (547-48). As a result, faith in sheer fear and doubt flies from him, seeing the shy unchanging coward in him. He is quite compelled to see through all shady and shabby affairs of human life: "A high pedestal now occupy market values/while in ignoble exile go our moral values" (604-05). Like the Scholar-Gipsy of Matthew Arnold, this MBA-Gipsy finds himself at the crossroads where one road has already faded into oblivion and the other is yet to come into view.

Most of us barter our "sins with a prayer too simple/burn in flames of camphor all our vices/and loot afresh others' wealth and spices" (711-13). People thus supposedly find an easy solution to rid their conscience of cumulative sins but they can't be unburdened so easily. It is only a wishful thinking and an exercise in self-deception. Though late, he says, a simple beginning has to be made. Indians at large should "realize the concept of collective good/where people should work and deserve food/and live in a righteous atmosphere of peace" (736-38). No doubt, peace accompanies pure conscience and purer thoughts.

Reddy firmly believes that "supreme symbols of liberty and human powers/fail to give some peace and make our search false" (764-65). He attempts to seek peace in the midst of "the rich sylvan scenic beauty of Char Dham, the four sacred Himalayan seats of Parandham, the quiet enchanting snowy silver heights" and the Gangetic thrills (758-61). Like Shelley who wishes to be a bird, Reddy wishes to "fly like a bird from tree to tree,/and tour the sky with wide wings fully free/and make an aerial survey of land and seas/woods and mountains as nature's child (813-16). "The terrible boundless blue expanse" (832), "the smiling sand and shining shells/that lay like fallen leaves at autumn's response" and "diagrams on the damp slate of sand" (838), "tiny fish", "gulls and herons running for easy prey", "ducks wading in waters calm and clear" (842) etc are the sources for Reddy to seek peace and pure joy. Many more such images abound in Reddy's verses and they widen his poetic vision and enhance readers' enjoyment.

Reddy's anguish grows more intense when he sees the supposedly serene places being desecrated by mindless behavioral absurdities and evil-propelled activities. While reckless youth for fun try to molest, there is none to heed (886-87). The long lawn is covered with dewy pearls but search for peace slowly leaves in whirls (888-890. Naked truth and harsh realities ooze visibly through Reddy's verses: "Qualified youth thrown on idle Indian roads/like famished birds fly to the American shore" (891-92) and "in the fertile land they try to find fresh roots" (894). Reddy's hovering eyes whir past the Indian subcontinent and cover the entire world as far as degradation in any form occurs. The crashing of the imperial World Trade Centre that fell to terrorists is a snapshot through his poetic lenses. Even the richest nations are far from peace. The question that has been haunting the poet for some time of late is: "Where can I find peace full of cool breeze?" (914)

Reddy is one with Wordsworth towards the close of the fourth segment. He wants to find peace in the lap of Nature. The following lines typically echo Wordsworthian sentiments:

> When majestic wind, their true task master
> blows, beats, treats, waves and whips them
> they rustle and bustle, toss, tear and dance
> as if they are in a windy whirling trance
> like a fully drunken man on the busy street
> drowned headlong in liquor with his feet
> or the wide-hooded hissing cobra bright
> dancing to the tune on gourd pipe light
> of the primitive old tribal snake charmer
> who gets a little rice from the poor farmer. (930-39)

In the above passage, the imagery reflects nativity and juxtaposes the magnificent manifestations of nature and the man-made devastations of our culture, aping the West. Rudyard Kipling once said that "East is East and West is West and the twine shall never meet". His boastful West has eroded the East in the 21st century and it is a sort of post-colonial neo-colonialism. The West has enslaved the East differently in the post-millennial context. His comparisons are fresh and down-to-earth. His masterly strokes of imagery bring forth summer heat and chilling winter vividly and aesthetically:

> The sun shoots like whetted arrows
> while summer hangs like Damocles' sword
> winter wails like a poor kidnapped child
> going fast to school on a busy traffic road
> by teenaged gang for lusty luxuries wild. (961-65)

He superbly wields his poetic camera to capture the middle class syndrome and doesn't spare the dictatorial private colleges which "flourish fast with fresh foliage/and extract work from dawn to dusk" (1017-18). Life today in its many-sided complexity is succinctly pictured beautifully by Reddy, of course, with a tinge of sadness. When the poet is feeling high of the feats of the great Cholas of South India, he begins to drink

> ... the ancient glory in cool Cholas
> to forget in graded sips the present pain
> which is our sole inheritance from Cain. (1042-45)

Christian tenets cohere with Hindu ideologies to forge a bond among human beings regardless of geographical, religious and racial boundaries. Again like the Scholar-Gipsy, we stand with a divided aim and a sense of uncertainty. Reddy observes:

> From the chaotic present let me shrink
> though of unknown future I dare not think. (1089-90)

Touching upon the burning issue of environmental hazards, the poet is aggrieved at "the endless game of cutting trees/to burn piled bricks to build growing cities" (1112-13). Modern man lives among concrete jungles and the real jungles where the wild are supposed to have their habitat are dwindling in size, paving the way for a man-animal conflict. Reddy's pen takes a wider survey and brings every facet of modern existential edifice under the scanner. His heart bleeds helplessly, rather impotently when humans' self-invited disasters multiply.

At the end of the fifth segment, Reddy is much firmer now about his avowed task of establishing peace all around:

> I want to live and move in this sphere
> with ethical values in clear atmosphere

> with people neither bad nor always sad;
> Let us try to make this restless earth
> a livable place of peace, love and mirth.
> Before we make unawares our sudden exit,
> let us do some good even in small digit;
> before it is too late, let us soon awake
> or our acts and gestures become fake. (1139-47)

God may be extolled in multiple forms but basically we are children of one Supreme Soul or *Paramathma*:

> One who preaches hate and kill is no God
> for peace and love stands always true God. (1187-88)

We have to weed out the negatives in due course and "the urgent need of the hour is right action;/if you fail by mischance, your fall is certain" (1211-12). We have to "maximize the fruits of existential moment/without getting panicky as a child in a convent" (1239-40). After all these agonizing cries alternated with words of self-confidence and determination, Reddy raises the question in self-doubt at the beginning of the seventh segment: "Is search for peace a wild goose chase? (1147). He is aware that "search for peace is a tantalizing fiction" (1356). To him, "peace is a blessed of state of mind" (1357) and one who is content has peace of mind (1359).

In a bid to foresee a peaceful India in the near future, Reddy feels that "today's children are our wealth and bulwark,/let us guide them with ethics and truth stark" (1389-96). What the Vedas and the Buddha, Christ and the Mahatma have said rings true even today. Reddy simply follows in their footsteps. He prescribes the remedy in a nutshell:

> Where bombs and bullets fail to conquer
> a little love will do with a kind generous act
> pregnant with power flinty hearts to stir
> to bring peace and smiling joy with tact. (1391-94)

He is a pragmatic and a no non-sense man. "Fate of peace is like a mad man's dress in rags,/in sheer fear and global chaos it limps and lags. (1550-51). He is very candid and reiterative when he says:

> We can't expect from the sky any miracles
> with impure hearts obeying devil's oracles
> How long should we look up the sky and want
> for the ascent of a good leader to show us light
> or the fancied descent of an ethereal angel bright
> to come and cleanse and set the chaos right. (1564-69)

External peace is the manifestation of the internal peace. So he exhorts us to "not be narrow and religion-bound" and establish "a common faith in peace and love" (1574) and "ennoble and lift us to reach the ultimate" (1581). He sounds the clarion call at last boldly and fervently:

> Unless intense moral light dawns bright on all
> we cannot escape from the foul inevitable fall. (1642-43)

Avarice, power-mongering, unregulated indulgence in sex, social inequality and all kinds of ethical erosion should go and they ought to be replaced by waves of peace. By doing so, one hopes that *'shanti'* will definitely reside within every one of us cutting across regional, political, religious and ideological divides.

Works Cited

Kipling, Rudyard. *The Ballad of East and West.* Web. https://learnodo-newtonic.com/rudyard-kipling-famous-poems/

May, Rollo. "Man's Search for Himself". Web.https://www.amazon.in/Man's-Search-Himself-Rollo-May/dp/0393333159/

Reddy, T.V. *Quest for Peace.* New Delhi: Authors Press, 2013. Print.

3 T. Vasudeva Reddy, the Poet in his Poetry: A Study of *Golden Veil*

D.C. Chambial

T.V. Reddy has been in the arena of writing poetry since 1982 when his first book, *When Grief Rains*, appeared from Samkaleen Publications, Delhi. It has been over 35 years and in these years he has incessantly pursued his skill in creative and critical writing and has published 10 volumes of his poems. The first eight have been published in one book – *The Rural Muse: The Poetry of T. Vadsudeva Reddy* (2014) edited with elaborate introduction by Dr. K.V. Raghupathi. His two latest volumes—*Thousand Haiku Pearls* and *Golden Veil* appeared in 2016, besides his two novels—*The Vultures* (1993) and *Minor Gods* (2008), and two books of criticism on the British novelist: *Jane Austen: The Matrix of Matrimony* and *Jane Austen: the Dialectics of Self-Actualization in her Novels,* both published in 1987 from two different publishers, besides a book of Grammar, *Advanced English Grammar & Composition* (1996). His recent book *A Critical Survey of Indo-English Poetry* (2016) is a great contribution to the critical evaluation of Indian poetry in English. All this reveals his multifaceted character and a disciplined writer of verses. My thesis, in the present paper, is to study his latest book, *Golden Veil* (2016), for salient features.

The very first poem, "In the Shell of Solitude" (9), begins with the protagonist's affirmation that he prefers privacy than the crowded noisy life. The reader is apprised of his (protagonist's) misfortunes: "Winds of destiny push me to the stony wall", which is hard for the protagonist to break: "I fail to break the wall and swallow the gall"; unable to find solutions, due to his inherent hesitant nature, to these troubles, he evaluates himself weak. He, for the time being, loses faith in God: "I can't expect any help from the seeing Lord". He decides and declares that he has been diffident from his birth and now wants to give up this timorousness and become bold. But by the end of the poem he seeks blessings of the "higher Grace" without which, he maintains, these lines will not burst into flames to show his strength to the world. The poem ends with a moral that one needs be bold in life otherwise he will have to suffer throughout his life: "Courage often makes a common man a legend / or one has to live and crawl as a lone lizard" (2-21). This poem is based on the dictum from *Brihadaranyaka Upanishad*: तमसो मा ज्योतिर्गमय (Lead from darkness to light). His *mantra* for success in life is: Be bold and give up all diffidence and timidity. At another place he, in "Soon the Sun does Set" (18), advises to avoid dilly-dallying practice in life to succeed in life: one has to "be brave to turn a new leaf, never be meek" (3). While meekness makes one diffident, boldness or bravery gives energy to tackle all problems that come in one's way.

After having advised to be bold, the poet, in "Old Napkins" (10), meditates upon the neglect of aged parents and disregard to their suggestions. The well off children—"the fast earning kids"— consider old parents useless things: "We old men nowadays are like old napkins". The protagonist opines that no one thinks about their feelings. He is of the view that erring children must be told what is right and what is wrong when they go astray or exhibit an inclination to do so. If, ever, the old people dare chide the children, their mothers call old people cruel. However, the persona advises that

"Correction at the initial stages is the only way" to mend their ways and need strong chiding from the elders: this, in fact, is the way to prevent them from going off course from human ethics. To corroborate his point, he cites example from agriculture: "When leaves and buds are infested by pest, / till pesticides are applied do we rest?" (15-16) to keep them healthy and free from the pests that cause harm to the plants. Similarly, if children are not instructed at the appropriate time, they are sure to go off track and "sink and stink"—learn bad habits that may, in the course of their lives, prove fatal not only to them but also to society. The thesis of the poem is that aged people are not useless but useful: they have the experience of their lives to sift right from wrong and good from bad that can help develop good habits and manners in the younger generation. Their advice deserves to be followed.

This advice to the younger generation leads his imagination to focus on Polity. In "Need of the Hour" (12-13), the poet/protagonist argues that the hard earned freedom is imprisoned by our corrupt polity to "hoist selfish agenda". They are least bothered about the masses and the country. They seek power by buying "caste, communal and reserved votes / with their corrupt sacks of wealth". In the present times, corruption rules: "from top to bottom offices stoutly stink and stench, / law makers are our law breakers to suit their ends". Honest people are branded as fools; "only those who hate and cheat, grab and rob rule" (18). In this environ of complete corruption and moral debility, the poet/protagonist muses:

> ... Burying ethical frame of mind and spiritualism
> By the new found weapon of pseudo-secularism.
> We eagerly look to a true leader with clean wand
> to save this most abuse and misused ancient land;
> another avatar of Narasimha is the need of the hour
> to establish dharma and end corrupt secular power (27-32)

The poet terms the present age as the age of *adharma*; and he prays to God to emancipate it from present rulers, "corrupt secure power", in tune with what Lord Krishna says:

> Yadaa yadaa hi dharmasya glaanirbhavati Bhaarata,
> Abhyuthaanamadharmasya tadaatmaanam srajaamyaham.
> Paritraanaaya sadhoonaam vinaashaaya cha dushkrataam,
> Dharmasamsthaapanaarthaaya   sambhaami yuge yuge.
>   (*BhagavadGita* 4.7-8)

His faith in *Dharma* and the *Gita* is also apparent in the last poem of the book, "Eternal Ethics" (100). It is a prayer to "*Sanatana Dharma*". He laments the degradation of human ethics enshrined in our scriptures:

> Noble concept of ethics falls to abysmal depths here.
> Flames of wrongs and heinous crimes rise high
> Fanatic fools and ruthless terrorists butcher and loot
> Lives of the righteous roll in poignant cry   (4-7)

He also holds that under such conditions, when all human ethics is thrown to the winds and fanatics and terrorists seem to control the stage, only the knowledge of "*Gita* alone can save the world and the chaos uproot." The man, "biped beast" has become the emblem of "vices, lies and crooked deeds". The hatred for the man is manifest in the phrase, "biped beast". The poet prays to God for protection:

> O Lord, with thy trident protect us from chaos untold
> Universe exists on Thy sole strength, order and fair play.
> Thou art the glory of the Lord that holds the universe

The Poet in his Poetry: A Study of Golden Veil

Without thy base and breath world would be a curse. (11-14).

These lines, unambiguously, portray him as a staunch believer of Lord, who "holds the universe"—controls the cosmos—for the liberation of present world "from [ubiquitous] untold chaos" and for the restoration of order in anarchy and "fair play" in our actions.

Similarly, the poem "Waiting for an Avatar" (98-99) is as powerful a poem as Yeats's "The Second Coming". Both poems wait for the birth of a God that will deliver the world from its chaos. In this chaos, "The upright lose faith, the corrupt snatch all the gains" (Reddy), or "The best lack all conviction, while the worst / Are full of passionate intensity" (Yeats). Here, Reddy also hopes that contrary to present politicians, who are lost in money making and exploiting the common man, such a political leader will be born who will work for making the nation strong:

> Let us await a true leader, free from vicious greed,
> with the spirit of sacrifice for the nation to be strong
> to wake up the nation from snares and nightmares
> and drive out the dark negative forces as the rising sun. (22-25)

These lines also reveal the poet's wish that under such leader, "free from vicious greed", the country will break loose of all hurdles and negative forces that do not let her "fly free". The people, under centuries of alien rule, have become submissive and lazy. He writes:

> Thousand vicious years of enforced slavish yogic sleep
> in bestial bondage under the despotic ruthless alien yoke
> has transformed us into a toothless spineless indolent race,
> bowing race of labouring sloth and servile surrender. (18-21)

These lines remind me of Derozio's following lines, from his sonnet "To India—My Native Land", that bewail the misery of India:

> And groveling in the lowly dust art thou;
> Thy minstrel hath no wreath for thee
> Save the sad story of thy misery!   (6-8)

The cause of India's misery is, in unequivocal terms, ascribed, by both these poets, to foreign domination of India. While Derozio wants to unravel from past history how glorious India has been—"And bring from out the ages that have rolled / A few small fragments of those wrecks sublime, / Which human eyes may never behold;" Reddy does not rely on past glory, but wishes that under honest leader "with the spirit of sacrifice" India, once again, will emerge as a glorious nation and become the world leader. Such transformation has begun to appear like the first rays of the rising sun in accepting Indian Yoga world over.

His search for the antidote to "life's tedious journey full of wiles and guiles" is a smile that "dispels the clouds of heart / with an inborn shine", in "Smile, the Saviour" (14), and puts forth his premise of cheerfulness, the significance of smile in human life. Smile is the real saviour of a person, who is always bold. It is very useful and helpful. It is like an oasis in the dull and drab life of a person. It not only cheers up the drooping soul in adversity, but also nature's gift: "the shield guarding us from gloom till the end / To mankind Nature's precious gift a real godsend" (19-20). Thus, the poet values smile the most in human life. It helps him from slipping into melancholy and glumness.

His quintessence of smile in human life leads him to tender sound advice to people, in "Choose the Right Path" (16). It smacks a little of Robert Frost's poem, "The Road Not Taken". Like Frost, the protagonist of the poem also comes to a point, from where "I stare at the split / The path splits in two" and finds it difficult to make his choice: "Which path I choose is above my simple wit" (8). From this point, the persona looks at the two:

> The branching into two hostile ends I watch with a will—
> One seems smooth and safe, leads to majestic metro lights,
> The other a zigzag climbing tack up the winding craggy hill;
> One, a feast of festive lights teeming with tempting sights,
> The other, a hard and arduous climb through haunting nights
> Mind tempts me to sail through the warping windy way,
> Inner voice urges to climb higher above the clay;
> Search for Truth, an uphill task, leads to lasting bliss,
> We are not sheep to graze and relish ephemeral kiss. (17-25)

While Frost concludes, in his poem, that whatever he is, is because of the choice he had made; however, Reddy holds that truth is difficult to arrive at and one should follow the path of truth howsoever difficult it may be, because it leads to lasting beatitude. For a better comparison the two poems may be read side by side.

Truth, verily, difficult to arrive at, brings to mind the loss of loved one. At the loss of someone or something dear to human beings, they are lost in melancholy; brood too much about that person or thing and shed tears in his/her/its memory. The poem, "No More Tears" (20), embraces the theme of the loss of loved one and mourns the loss. In this poem, the persona, after having done a lot of brooding over the loss of his love, falls short of tears and avers: "No More tears are left in my heart proud / vacuum reigns with the exit of my love / On dull mechanical lines life does move" (12-14). He has earlier told his love that in his life there is "No more light or delight" (6). After the death of his love "light and delight" both have deserted him and he is leading a dull emotionless life. After the death of one of the two loving hearts, the life of the surviving one becomes dull and dreary and s/he continues to live in the memories of the departed.

In "Forget Me Not" (21), he feels that life has now become a burden for him: "For a bereaved man heavy is the load" (5). He feels that his end is also approaching but the children are young as yet and he has to look after them. In nostalgia, he remembers the last words of his love: "Look after the kids and see them fly / In joy I will see from above the sky" (11-12). He tries to keep his words given to his beloved. He is sure that his beloved still remembers him in her heavenly abode as she there "waits with loving eyes" (19).

In "Meaning of Love" (22-23), he tries to explain what love is and realizes that "The word love is a complex thing" (5); it is beyond definition and description. Certainly, it is "an amazing, dazzling expression" (10); and if someone tries to unravel its mystery many years of life will be lost "Still its total meaning we can't learn" (15). Therefore, it remains unexplained, unfathomable and mysterious. However, the persona/poet realizes: "It is pure and lucid for one who is pure at heart / It is shady or awry for one with veiled art" (29-30). Thus, the true meaning of love is understood only by the one who is true in his love. In the "Syntax of Love" (30), he says:

> Love is the key to soften the clouds
> and shower recharging smiles as rain
> to analyze the complex structure
> of the woven threads of subtle life, (1-4)

These lines clearly manifest the poet's idea of love that it is refreshing like rain and helpful to disentangle the complexities of life. Life is complex. Love helps to balm the kinks in life and gives "bliss", which is the true goal of life.

"Dumb Toys" (25) is Reddy's highly philosophical poem. A man is born with his mind like a clean slate. He knows nothing at that moment. When he comes face to face with the realities of life, he makes efforts to understand life and solve its problems. Life, here, on this earth, is difficult to live without "God-sent boat", which suggests life partner. With it, one braves the "world of whales and crocodiles". It symbolizes the dangers of life. In this wide and vast sea, he faces life "with the help of boat, my prop, my half". Once again, the idea moves round "my half" or my better half, a phrase for wife. Because a "virtuous woman is a crown to her husband" (Proverbs 12:4, *KJV*). Man alone is unable to withstand the winds of life, but he is supported by his wife/love, and with him/her s/he can even fight with the deadliest demons. However, when the same love/wife is snatched away by the cruel hands of Yama, he feels helpless: "One stormy night in the dark waves / the boat sank leaving me near the shore"—they had together lived life to their fulfillment that is why he is near the shore and not in the middle of the sea.

Two hearts come together by "a tide of chance or destiny" and the same fateful "chance or destiny" separates them: for, husband and wife, in rarest of the rare moments, die together. Thus, all human beings are "dumb toys" and the victims of "sealed fate"—preordained fate. It is the love between the husband and the wife that makes them brave the world. "Thy Echo" (36), another poem, does not allow him to forget his love/wife even after his death. He, asks, "How can I forget you?" he remembers the coconut plants planted by her behind their house makes him feel her "smiles in the shining orb of the moon" and the tender jasmine flowers, also planted by her, revitalize his "failing spirit". Though he wished to live together till the end, but she was "cruelly snatched away". He ever remembers her and can't forget her: "As long as this heart beats there is thy echo." She is unforgettable.

"Make This Life Real" (24) is, in fact, an attempt to remember the Supreme one: it is by keeping Him in one's mind one can make one's life real. It details how the protagonist has spent his hitherto-lived life, and, finally, he thinks that his present life should be spent by fixing his attention on the Almighty: "let my time rest on the One Supreme / and make this piece of life real, not a dream" to make it genuine, which is the goal of every human being as mystical philosophy teaches. The human beings, besides eating, drinking and merry-making, the Epicureanism precept, should also evolve spiritually by meditating on the Supreme, who has created the whole cosmos. It elevates ordinary human beings to a higher stage of beings.

As a social realist, the poet also contemplates the problem of water scarcity at his place. The protagonist avers: "Here in my land water is dearer than blood; / in this rainless land, haunted by draught, / water is a rarity, rain a rare spectacle;" ("Water is Dearer than Blood" 26), clearly shows how rare and important water is. Water is the greatest need of life, without which life is impossible: "Road to water leads to life, not to pools of blood, / road to life lies in peace and smiles, not in lies" (24-25). Here, "lies" suggest politicians' false election promises to solve the problem of water. Life, really, is difficult when there is shortage of water. He writes: "Village is hard-hit with lack of water, lack of order; / thrown in the tiger's grinding jaws of factions" (18-19). When people, instead of living as one, are divided due to "petty politics", the situation is very much akin to be "in the Tiger's jaws". This factionalism helps the politicians but harms the villages—common people. He also takes a dig, in this poem" at politicians: "deceptive clouds of election promises don't rain". Political promises remain unfulfilled as our politicians are never true to their words and never want to allay the miseries of the common masses. His anger is evinced in "bastards born of dirty elections and petty politics".

Reddy hails from a village. So, the memories of rural life constantly haunt his imagination in poems like "Sylvan Scene", "Riverside", and "Our Thirsty Land". In the "Sylvan Scene" (40-41), the poet/protagonist describes a stream flowing from the slopes of the nearby hills to the plains below. The poet compares the movement of the stream to free flight of the bird. On its way to plains, it fills all ponds and pits without any discrimination. Now it's movement is compared to the movement of a dancing girl. He calls the stream "a rare boon from bounteous Nature" and gives pleasure to the inhabitants of a colony of "a few cottages." Music of leaves and flowers alongside the crystal-clear water of the stream presents "Bewitching beauty, green and serene", which becomes "its majestic mark". The tall trees look like sentinels by the ponds and streams and simulate thick forests as if in heaven. Flowers blooming beside these sources of water are no less beautiful than the "rubies and sapphires"—indeed, priceless. In the breeze, the flowers dance, like the "tribal children", "to the melodic tunes of water that glides and races." Chirping birds, flapping their wings, seem as if they are applauding the dance and music. Moon also looks like enjoying "this ravishing bliss" from its home in the sky. The poet is so charmed of this beauty that he, like Wordsworth, sings in joy: "Long after rinsing the golden glory of the sylvan scene / its balmy beauty lives in mind with its emerald green" (27-28). Reddy's joy, in these lines, can be simply compared with Wordsworth's joy in "The Daffodils", expressed in these lines: "And then my heart with pleasure fills / And dances with the daffodils" (23-24).

In "Riverside" (42), the persona invites his companion, who may be his love, to go to the riverside, because it is flooded after decades, as now the area/region has very scanty rains: "For years and years hardly does it rain". Now, the bank of the river appears like a snake. They can't delay their movement; for, the river may dry soon. The protagonist is of the view that such a beautiful scene may not come again in their lifetime. It is getting dark: the sun is setting. The land is barren for want of sufficient water to grow crops, but the waters in the river now, enchant him: "Waters with mellowed music move and glide" without making much noise as it does when it flows down from the hills. As in Robert Browning's monologue, the persona, here, too, talks himself. His companion is made alive only in his words: "Let us walk and feel the kiss of the breeze / Moonlight hugs all the land very soon". For him living is an art:

> Ah. My love, the bank is bright with light
> It is cool and clear as a mother's heart
> No longer can we walk, it is night
> Duty calls us back as living is an art. (15-18)

These lines seem to bear the burden of Matthew Arnold's "Dover Beach" in mind.

"Our Thirsty Land" (43-44) describes the topography and surrounding vegetation that is surrounded by "crescent shaped range" of hills covered with forests that keep on changing moods: these are green only for some time, while most of the time they remain leafless; the larger part of the hills, too, is "bare and bald / full of rocks and rocks". The clouds do visit, but seldom rain; and, whenever they rain, the water flows down the hills. This water goes waste as there are no ponds or canals: thus, "draught—only record in our annals". The village women draw drinking water from far off places and to tide over the weariness, they keep singing while going and coming. Even the seeds sown with hope of rain fail to germinate in the absence of rain. The people of this region are "regular victims of heat and hot waves / and total aliens to foggy morns and cold winds" of "the northern slow-clad peaks". The poem ends with a prayer to Rain, so that they cultivate their land and do not die of starvation:

> Rain, rain, humbly we pray you not to go away
> Please do not wait to come another day.
> We cry and die for a drop of rain like chakora
> To feed our children; let not our prayers go in vain. (30-33)

This poem, in fact, presents a realistic picture of the suffering of the land and the people, who live there.

In "Today's Rural Life" (62), he writes about the political intrusion and pollution of the innocent life of rural people and their life by the rich and crafty polity. It is no longer a happy and contended life. The rhetorical questions, ending the poem, pin-point this loss of pure and innocent rural life: "Can we ever breathe the rich harvest breeze, / Can we ever see the good olden days with ease." The poems, "Green Canopy", "At the Field at Noon", "Watching the Field at Night", "Night Watch",

"Erstwhile Farmer", "Seeded Soil" and "Bankrupt Clouds" portray the sorrows of the farmers of the rural India, especially Andhra Pradesh.

"Look at the Stars" (45) is about the beauty of Nature. The persona looking at the stars, at night, feels very happy and is doubtful whether they really affect the lives of the people on the earth. He doubts about the astrological effect of stars on the lives of the natives of the earth, but they surely are wonderful like gems to look at. The following lines place him beside the poets of Nature like Wordsworth: "Indeed like white gems they sparkle in the blue sky / Life is futile if we fail to watch the wonder so high" (10-11). The poet believes that these stars guide humanity on the right path; in their absence, life will be lost. Wordsworth calls Nature best friend and JJ Rousseau, the best teacher. Similarly, Dr. Reddy blends both the ideas and opines:

> Live in Nature, live with Nature
> Move in nature, merge with nature
> Nature is our mother and teacher,
> Nurse, guide friend and preacher. ("Nature" 83)

Nature gives us the required fundamentals of subsistence without which man cannot survive. We should learn from nature to respect the dignity of others. In fact, in this poem, the poet wants people not to exploit nature for their personal benefit—we should not destroy our ecological balance. When man goes beyond the limits, he does so at his peril. To human excesses, Nature reacts in her own manner as is evident in floods, cloud-bursts and earthquakes. He writes: "If we flout and defy, she reacts in her ways / In the flood of her fury we end without a trace" (21-22). It's a warning to the ravenous man.

The poet, in "Aim High" (46), presents his philosophy of achieving goals without caring for what others say and think about them. He exhorts people to brave obstacles that beset their path to become a face in the crowd: "Mounting all hate and hurdles we should grow tall". People are often jealous of those who rise in their life by dint of their hard work. He advises that we should not care for the people's jealousy and torpor but attain goals with will power: "At our aiming high, let envy and ennui frown / with the power of will let us reach the crown" (13-14). His philosophy, in "Ultimate End" (47), is that men should not fall prey to the sensual pleasures of this life. It is the greed to amass wealth that makes people adapt to fair and foul means without caring for those who are honest and earn bread with their sweat. All these mundane meretricious things are transitory and vanish with time; if anything survives, it is "the truth of the ultimate end".

Death is sure to all. Therefore, men should live an upright life of toil and morality and not yield to the baneful sensual pleasures. "To Rest in Peace" (48) is about death. Human beings are mere "players in the masquerade" [indirectly recalls Shakespearean philosophy]. He holds that "Life is a race, rough and tough; let us move with grace / Let us dream and die, die and dream to rest in peace" (13-14). Life should be lived with moral elegance and achieve our ambitions in such a manner that we do not have to be penitent at last. In "Eden Garden" (49), the poet envisages that a park, where children free from the guile and vile of the grownups, is no less than the heavenly garden. It is here that "Children play with ball and bloom as flowers / clapping their hands at the sprinkling showers". With an allusion to the biblical myth of the original sin for which the first man and woman were expelled to live on earth, he says: "They are not the children of the fallen pair / They are the sparks of the One Eternal Sire" (19-20). He visualizes paradise in a park, where children, free from all human vices, play with absolute innocence and "pure minds". In "End of the Arch" (50), he philosophizes that only an age of peace can engender happy and long life and fear makes generations weak: "Look at the mocking lines on my ageing face - / a face book full of falls and failures they trace" (12-13).

The poem, "The Cold Foe" (51), points out that a purposeful life drives away all fears of life. Struggle, the essence of life, should continue till the end or death. Hope sustains life: "At the other end of the tunnel there is a ray". With one's courage, one can vanquish death. He says: "Let me be bold enough to chase away death in life, / beat and defeat the burning heat of the cold foe, / march ahead and walk with a laugh" (18-20). One should not fear death; instead, when it comes, one should hug it with a smile. In "A Heart Unbowed" (52), the poet is of the view that courage is the only antidote to the vices of fear and lust: "My spirit, reeling and bleeding, chases the dark cloud / of fear and lust, stands with a valiant heart unbowed" (13-14); his spirit remains unbent. The philosophy inherent, in "My Father's School Days" (56), is that olden days, despite lacking in modern amenities, were far better: the students learnt their lessons in the open and were taught, besides regular lessons, moral lessons: "The lines they learnt stayed alive till their end". The very title of the poem, "Flowers Shall Bloom" (65), is optimistic and seems to echo the Shelleyan optimistic philosophy of "If winter comes, can spring be far behind"—the philosophy of hope. His ideas find force in the native image of these lines: "Life is not an endless autumn, it has its spring / Flowers shall bloom and koels are sure to sing" (13-14). He says that "Hope" (84) sustains life. It subdues and subjugates the "wily art". One should never give up hope; because, "It is the straw that leads to the desperate man to the shore / and hope is the miracle key to open the victory's door" (13-14).

"The Middle-class Man" (74) is about the misery of middle class people. They are badly hurt and exploited by politicians and bureaucrats. His hatred for them comes out in these lines: "How long should I bend and bow / to these proud unscrupulous political thugs / and corrupt bulging bureaucratic bugs" (1-3). Here, the words "thugs" and "bugs" are potent enough to suggest how the politicians deceive and babus suck the common man's blood. Both are hand in glove in exploiting the common man. He warns them: "The day is not away, you have to pay the price" for their misdeeds. The common man is no less dangerous than tides: "I am a drop, I am the tide, turbulent and hungry, / riding on the crest of cries of wounded time" (25-26). He warns that like atom, he will explode and destroy the whole lot: "I, an atom, am sure to explode and blast this rot". He also exhorts his fellow-men to see through their tricks and evil designs that do not let the middle class man to progress, and adds that their (middle-class men's) honesty is the shield that'll protect them from "political thugs" and "bureaucratic bugs": "Time it is to open our eyes and cease to be fools, / Our conduct, clean and non-corrupt, is our shield" (42-43).

The poet is also critical of politicians, in "End the Dynastic Rule" (80), who have been ruling the people generations after generations. He wants to put an end to this dynastic rule: "Let the power-drunk dynasties pine and perish / Let the greedy dynastic rule die" (1-2); and, if such rulers/politicians refuse to be out, then "Chase the old worn out political weights", who are branded as "fatty hogs" and "lazy lumps and cancerous growths" in the body of society. Whatever change was professed by the champions of freedom has not been realized even after the loss of seven decades. So, he asks the voters to "Bring real change for the better, not for the worse, / to lead to an upright joy, not to the path of curse" (19-20). He thinks that our politicians have failed in their purpose, so they should be voted out of power and chance must be given to new minds, which think better and think clear than these "leeches sucking nation's wealth". This change should be for the betterment and happiness of all.

In conclusion, it can be safely said that, as is apparent from the foregone study of Reddy's poems, in this paper, from his last work, *Golden Veil*, that Reddy has emerged as a champion of the poor, a representative of rural India holding human ethics to his heart and a detractor of the present polity, lost in "vices, lies and crooked deeds" and rests his faith in Almighty, the creator of this universe, for protection of humanity from indescribable pandemonium, human misery and suffering. He envisages his original ideas about love for nature and hope. He believes in the collective power of the people and the democratic values of defeating the powerful politicians with their votes. He awaits a political avatar that has the strength to steer nation from the present chaos to world-leadership through honesty and hard work. Let's hope that his ideas come alive and death-knell is tolled for contemporary vices of greed, deception and exploitation. All human misery is banished and this earth becomes a heaven to live in.

Note

While writing this article, I have been benefitted by the following works and I believe the readers of this article are familiar with them.

Henry Louis Vivian Derozio. "To India—My Native Land."
Matthew Arnold. "Dover Beach."
P.B. Shelley. "Ode to the West Wind."
Robert Browning's *Dramatic Monologues*.
Robert Frost's poem, "The Road Not Taken."
W.B. Yeats. "The Second Coming."
William Shakespeare. As You Like It, 5.7.

Works Cited

Frost, Robert. "The Road Not Taken." *Selected Poems*. Edited with introduction by Ian Hamilton. 1973. Harmondsworth, England: Penguin books, 1975. Print.

Reddy, T.V. *Golden Veil*. New Delhi: Author's Press, 2016. Print. [All references to the text are from this edition.]

Shelley. "Poems". OUP, *The World's Classics*, 381.

The Bhagavad Gita. Chapter 4, slokas: 7-8. Gorakhpur, Gita Press. 1st ed.1943; 23rd ed.1978. Print.

The Holy Bible (King James Version), Old Testament. "Proverbs." XII. 4. New York, American Bible Society, 1971 edition, 597.

4 Speaking Through Images: A Critical Study of T.V. Reddy's Poetry

Abida Farooqui

T.V. Reddy's poetry collections *Melting Melodies* and *Pensive Memories* offer a garland of poems with a wide range of themes. They cut across the ordinary, the political, the historical, the contemporary, the spiritual and the metaphysical, the mythical and the philosophical. The most striking feature of his poems is the conveyance of sense through images.

The poems stand out for their musical quality. Most of the poems have an alliterative quality. The expression "wearied waters" of Kalyani Dam conveys the suffocation the unbounded water feels in the presence of the dam. The frenzied race of the water is arrested until it yawns out of ennui. The enchanting beauty of the Taj Mahal that is manifest at moonlight is described as "lunar light on lunatic love." The phrases "haunting hues" and "gorgeous garland" beautifully convey the charm and allure of the rainbow. So do the expressions "vale and dale, hill and rill" stand out for their musicality:

> All lust and carnal quest vanish,
> Fabulous memory of a pensive tale
> a marvel chiseled elegy in marble
> whose every stone echoes the epic of love. ("The Taj", *MM* 6)

Oxymoronic expressions lend a unique quality to the poems. The expression "vanquished victor" to refer to the setting sun is apt in suggesting that after having held sway over the sky, at its zenith, the sun has to set. The spiritual serenity of Dharmasala draws fluttered souls from various corners seeking solace from worldly worries and cares. It is a place where contradictions are reconciled. This reconciliation is conveyed through the bringing together of the "snow and the sun" and the "chill and cheerful." The water that is arrested by the dam reminds the poetic persona of a pregnant woman with "terrible beauty", the oxymoron at best conveys the opposed qualities of the water. So is the expression "wild beauty" to convey the poetic impression of Dharmasala:

> The place with the snow-clad peaks
> of Dhawaldhara kissed by morning rays
> looks like the peerless virgin beauty
> of the coy Indian maid in milk white saree
> that hides her heaving bosom
> after her entrancing bridal bath; (*MM*,3)

In "The Fair Sex Centre", the expression "mild malicious mutter" is both alliterative and oxymoronic. It aptly conveys the chatter of the women who like "buzzing butterflies" move in "frantic flutter." Rajiv Gandhi's dint of courage and leadership is brought out in the expression "steered the ship in strain and storm" in the poem "In Memoriam." "This Dull Evening" depicts the evening with a lot of alliterative expressions that convey the dullness of the evening: "weary way", "grisly, ghostly", "fuming fallow, furrowed fields" are cases in point.

"A Violent Winter" traces the chillness of the winter that is interrupted by the shy rays of the sun. "The winding worsted winter" has frozen the "dazzling delights." "Migrating Birds" looks at the trauma of migration in all its ugliness. The expressions "wings weak and weary," "hostile heat", "soiled sarees" and "raucous rays" bring out the emotional agony and turmoil associated with migration. They look back to their homeland and their past in a pensive way. The experience of migration has taken a toll on their movement that they are rendered immobile. The housewife's struggle in "This is the City" with the "sooty smoky hostile hearth" is a potent reminder of the perpetual agony her life is enmeshed in. Hostile hearth is also an oxymoron in that the hearth which is to provide sustenance to the household has turned hostile in suffocating the woman with its dense smoke:

> The dim light from the AC rooms
> winks at the ghost of kerosene lamp
> near the tearful eyes of the poor housewife
> struggling with her scanty breath
> at the sooty smoky hostile hearth. (PM, 28)

The cacophony of human lives is described in the poem 'Unpredictable Man' in alliterative phrases like "jaded jackals" and "filching foxes": 'None can predict or define / the odd unpredictable man / at once a man and a monster'(32).

"Ageing Smiles" talks on the acceptance of old age. A series of negative images like "blunted broomstick", "contorted contours," "grisly, grey hair" that indicate the barrenness of old age is followed by "patches of puffed up pride" indicating their pride in what they have been and their acceptance of what they are. Much of the poet's communication happens through images. "From Fallow Fields" lists a series of images all of which are unpleasant: apparitions, fleeting deceptive clouds, springing sweat, gaping hunger, listless eyes, blinking kerosene lamps and cold hearth that convey the poverty and squalor of the agricultural folk:

> Nakedness covers the thatched roofs
> Hugging raping rays and showers;
> chill to the meager marrow bone
> the hamlet beneath the tamarind tree
> with a few hutments shivers; (PM, 37)

The poet also engages in clichéd images while describing the virgin beauty of the coy Indian maid in milk white sari and the seductive beauty of a woman in "Sailing Saree" with her voluptuous snare and flirting fragrance. The use of contrasts serves to heighten the experience the poem is trying to evoke. "This is the City" is built up on such contrasts. – skyscrapers are set against slums, weird round of poverty against the tipsy steps of the club, rosy, chubby swollen faces against sickly sunken cheeks, fatty flesh global stomachs against fainting famished bellies, dim light of the AC rooms against the ghost of kerosene lamps.

Reddy infuses his poetry with themes ranging from the commonplace to the philosophical. "Dharmasala" that takes us to the haven of spiritual bliss, has a meditative quality. "The Fort" takes us on a historical journey of royal dynasties and bygone glory. The relics of the past speak volumes of the times in which they came into existence and the times they have gone through. The poem powerfully brings in the razing of the glorious past by the alien powers.

The theme of toiling recurs in the poetry of T.V. Reddy. He expresses solidarity with the suffering humanity. The toiling woman who breaks the rocks is mocked by Fortune while the affluent thrive on her toil: 'She lifts stones and bricks/ with eyes full of wicks, /builds for others mansions and forts/ to roll in foaming comforts;/All her sweat insures her a hut/ while her toil enthrones the lust.' (*MM*, 7). In 'The Tiller', the tiller is idealized for impregnating the earth with golden grain and for feeding mankind. In "Wrinkled Brows" he makes cause with the downtrodden with two disturbing poignant rhetorical questions that underline the bare reality that hunger cannot be assuaged and the lust for wealth cannot be mitigated. "The Orphan Lad" is a short poem on a boy who makes his living by begging alms in the railway compartments. The simile that compares him to an "unclaimed, disowned article/ floating on the slimy waters of Lethe" (*PM*, 15) is suggestive and powerful.

Reddy shifts from the commonplace to the metaphysical with a casual ease. "Can I Sing" raises philosophical issues in the form of a few rhetorical questions. The poet talks of the impossibility of singing, dancing, smiling, thinking, seeing and even peacefully dying when he is pegged down by inner and outer struggles.

The poem "Life" (*MM*) describes the varying shades of life through a series of diversified metaphors. It is "deep as the Pacific, frozen as the Arctic, terrible as the tidal wave of the Bay of Bengal, harrowing as birth-pangs, vague as blurred vision and keen as the gleam of an expiring candle." Life again becomes the topic in "Pensive Memories" where a sixty year old man looks back at the "weary, jaded journey" and laments the loss of his wife. "The Voyage of Life" also delineates ebb and flow of life with a series of alliterative expressions such as "eerie eclipses, evanescent events, somber situations, tedious troubles, turbulent tears." "A Bubble" exemplifies the evanescence of life and philosophizes on the unpleasant realities of existence.

"Ageing Smiles" is a philosophical reflection on ageing as a natural, unavoidable process which is described by the images of "blunted broomstick, mocking bristles, contorted contours,, grimacing lines of fate, wrinkled face, grisly grey hair" as they march with confidence indifferent to the inevitable end . "This Dull Evening" is an ensemble of images through which the poet suggests the movement from despair to hope. A series of negative images that convey the gloom, hopelessness and despondency- dull, eerie, dreary evening, sullen sultry shadow of the midsummer, apparition of the deceased sun, tottering and faltering herd, dusty road, trees like hapless bony skeletons, elusive sepulchral clouds, bare and bald rocky hills and feeble thatched huts - are followed by the waiting for Christ's resurrection with moist eyes alive with a flicker of hope. In a similar vein, "A Violent Winter" shifts the lens from a couple of negative images like "joys frozen, unbent heart and frozen face," to positive images of hope as the "shy sun melt(s) the thawed layers (with its) balmy touch. "A Task Uphill" is a stark reminder of the ultimate aim of human life which is the realization of God. An uphill task, as the poet calls it, is unattainable for the common man caught in the false glitter of ephemeral joys. "Maya" dwells on the Indian philosophical concept of reality and illusion. Life is described as an alluring snare which finally falls into dust. "Unpredictable Man" takes a look at the trajectory of human life that has taken such an ugly course that it has outgrown God. "Veil of Death" accepts the stark stony end of life with resignation. What separates life and death is a thin veil and hence it is nothing to be feared. "The Supreme Lord" is a poem on devotion to the Creator.

Love also forms the theme of some of the poems. In "The Village Girl", the sight of an innocent girl gracefully filling her pot with water creates ripples in the poet's mind. "Vernal Love" is a celebration of love, its alchemizing power making wonders on the poet. "Thy Loving Grace" also describes the transformative power of love. "Love" explicates the feelings of a lone bird as he grapples with the unexpected death of his beloved. "A Pair of Doves" also addresses the male dove's bereavement. "The Power of Love" celebrates the eternity of love. In "Waiting," the poet is craving for death to reunite with his beloved.

Reddy also enters quite audaciously into the zones of maladies suffered in social and political life. His poems indict the modern education system both in terms of its efficacy and the decadence that has set in. "University Wits" satirizes the erudition of University teachers who flaunt their intellect and create an aura of inaccessibility and the helplessness of the students who fail to get to them despite "bowing head(s), selling soul(s), bending spirit(s), mending sole(s) and climbing steep cliffs." The poem is in sharp contrast with "Omniscient Teacher" who is the "life-giving breath" and the "guiding light." "Seminar" is a cutting satire on the educational system where grand seminars are conducted on matters of large scale significance and the participants are like crows some of whom played merrily, others displayed with their plumage and others tried to establish their hegemony over the realm of knowledge, claiming that they are the only ones who know how to fly."An Interview" takes a dig at the nepotism and corruption inherent in the selection of candidates during an interview. In a comic vein, the poet feels as if he has entered the universal gas chamber where the interviewers were enthroned to grill the deserving candidates only to be shunned later on:

> As gales of regalia kissed his frame
> the sons of Shadwell reigned supreme
> wielding the sceptre of caste and sloth
> and shielding their brains from glory's path;
> Creative work was never a credit
> While garrulous tongue the only merit
> Show and shallowness filled the grace
> While true values fled in disgrace;   (MM, 25-26)

Reddy is incisively critical of politics. The poem "Thirst" is a metaphor for the unquenchable greed for power and acquisition. He indicts tooth and nail the "massive pillars shattering the fabric of the state." "Our Leader" is a comic satire on the course the life of a politician takes before and after his election – how he resorts to various isms to justify his deeds and how his henchmen take the law unto their hands. "Assembly of Quadrupeds" is a comic allegory on false promises delivered by politicians. A vegetarian tiger is voted to power and he promises a New Atlantis which is casteless, classless and creedless. "That Thing Money" is a scathing attack on the reigning values of the day where money is everything and where ends wink at the means. "Vision Four Two's" is his futuristic, dystopian vision of India where corruption, hypocrisy, parochialism, war, price hike and poverty will be rampant like never before.

With a characteristic deftness, he incorporates the ordinary into his poetic fabric. The sound of the roller or a pair of sparrows that make love inflames the poetic imagination. No one would have written a poem on a Bicycle or a Coconut Tree or even crows. "The Crow" is a very Indian poem in that from a casual description of the bird the poet moves onto the cultural specifics of India with the crow as "the special invitee to funeral morsel." So is "The Taj" that celebrates the legendary love as a "chiseled elegy in marble." In "The River," he describes the beauty, swiftness and melody of the river through an array of action verbs: hop, rush, chatter, ramble, tumble, rumble, leap, race, pass, slide, gaze, linger and groan. The catastrophe and havoc wreaked by Tsunami also becomes a topic of concern in "Tsunami." Alliterative expressions like "callous calamity", "ghastly guise", "fuming fury", "catastrophic havoc callous, cruel and complete", "bereaved souls, battered, bruised and beaten" enable the readers to visualize the calamity:

> Can hundreds of rescue ships, planes and trains
> Revive the lost melody in the benumbed brains
> Of the bereaved souls, battered, bruised and beaten?
> Can devastation be so sudden, so cruel, so cryptic,
> So abrupt, so terrifying and acidly apocalyptic?
> Indeed as ants to human feet or flies to wanton boys
> so we to Nature's fury leaving a trail of hushed noise.   (PM, 57)

He makes inroads into myth also in the poem "Sabari" which describes the story of Sabari who gave refuge to Ram and Laxman:

> The aged Sabari, dazed in joy and supernal ecstasy
> wasted not a moment, lit the pyre as in a fantasy
> and leapt into it chanting Rama's name filial
> as her divine form ascended to the world celestial. (*PM*, 54)

Reddy's poetic canvas is a vast one dealing with a wide variety of themes and a wide range of moods. At times he is cryptic, at times satiric, at other times dejected and pessimistic, at times very hopeful and optimistic. His is a discerning eye and he has a special way of blending the ordinary and the extraordinary.

Works Cited

Reddy, T. V. *Melting Melodies*. Madras: Poets Press India, 1994. Print.
--- --- ---. *Pensive Memories*. Madras: Poets Press India, 2005. Print.

----

5   Chronicles of Life and Times: Exploring T.V. Reddy's Poetry

C.A. Assif

"Poetry is a matter of life, not just a matter of Language"

- Lucille Clifton

Post-Ezekiel phase of Indian English poetry has opened up variegated vicissitudes of literary sensibility. Moving away from the canons, modern Indian English writers have carved a niche for themselves which is illustrative of the wide variety of themes and techniques they employed. T.V. Reddy, a typical poet of this period, has attempted to delineate both the rural and urban cultures as well as that of the culture of the self. He is the one writer who seems to possess a world view that literature is always local and particularized and interestingly, the more local it is the better aesthetically. The age of talking about the universal has gone by and the focus of the writer now should be on the particular which may lead to the general. Reddy's poetic explorations, for that matter, have attempted to imbibe this worldview in a more or less effective fashion. The fact that he has been trying to articulate the ingenuous in a foreign language doesn't deter him from putting this into paper. Language has been appropriated to the extent that it looks very much Indian in nature. Rather than merely writing under the overwhelming shadow of the so called Canonical writers, poets of this era have attempted to shirk off the unnecessary influence of earlier writers. As T.S. Eliot has put it elsewhere, every age requires its own language and sensibility. Writer, in Wole Soyinka's words, "is the visionary of his people. ... He anticipates, he warns." Elsewhere he says writers are nomads of imaginations and society is responsible for degradation. T.S. Eliot has also described poets as the purifiers of the dialect of the tribe. They are gifted beings with a keen sense of observation which makes even the ordinary look peculiar.

Reddy is a writer with a postmodern sensibility as he more often dwells in the realm of what we call everyday life. He has attempted to depict some of the perennial issues of the age and thereby tried to chronicle his life and times. Themes which may sound "unpoetic" to the conventional readers find ample space in his poetry. Their straddling between cultures has been a matter of discussion to the readers as well as to the interpreters of literatures. What is attempted in this essay is to explore the contours of poetic sensibility in his writings. The question of belonging to any traditions is a recurring theme in literature. How far this has been manifested in the writings of Reddy is another concern in the essay. He is a poet who has believed there is no such thing as mere form in poetry. Aesthetic worth of its form as well as that of particular matter it conveys is important.

The collection *When Grief Rains* contains poems of self as well as that of social issues. In most poems the focus is on the intimate experience of the poet. "Sweet Scar" is a short poem which refers to the experience of "aching Joys". The oxymoron in the title is suggestive of how even a painful experience turns into a joyous one. The speaker's assumption that "sweetness erupted when we peel / and vacillate in the blissful union" (*When Grief*...10) is proved otherwise here. Similar experience is narrated in the poem "Dreams". The poem communicates a terrible angst that has struck the narrator. Otherwise colorful dreams have "dried up". They are "like beads of tears/ on burning cheeks (12)". Even music becomes dreary and it ceases to have its proverbial soothing effect. Anguish is subtly expressed in the poem.

Poems of despair and desperation abound in this collection often reminding us of the famous words of the British Romantic poet Shelley that our sweetest songs are those that tell of saddest thoughts. Despair seeps through the poem "Life is a Desert" (14). The speaker is caught in a peculiar dilemma as he stands in the desert as a "marooned man/ amid a world of kith and kin/ All the way, chary and worldly-wise (14)". It is a situation which is really pathetic in the sense that he has a fear that he has been haunted by countless constellations of the forces of despair and hatred. Nowhere could he heave a sigh of relief. In moments of crisis a messiah used to come but here there is no hope. In an age of confusion and chaos, anarchy sets in and there is not much to dream of. He puts the matters rather bluntly:

> The dear are becoming dearer
> The nearer much averse to come nearer
> The deadly ulcer of penury consumes
> My fleshy body progressively ("When Grief Rains", 14)

He is unable to resist the envy and ennui of the society and he describes himself as "lone man in the barren land (14) and the last two lines are pointer to the height of despair he is in. "Life is an elusive endless desert/ Full of sands and storms, no oases (14)".

"To Love" is a short poem dealing with an age old theme. From time immemorial people have loved and jilted the love. But to the speaker of the poem "To love and yet to jilt the love/ is to squeeze the throat of a dove" (11). His concept of love is rather very traditional that it is the union of true minds.

This collection contains poems which express social concerns also bearing in mind that writers have larger social responsibility in talking about issues pertaining to the outside world as well. They are the unacknowledged legislators of the world, as Shelley puts it. "Civilization" is one such poem which as the title indicates expresses the very nature of the civilization itself. The poet doesn't have a very bright view of the present-day affairs and hence he focuses on the discontents of so called measure of human progress. What looms large is the sense of foreboding which defeats the very purpose of it. Where ever we go we could see the great disparity between the percept and practice. He says, "The shell of sophistication/ conceals its foul interior...." (23). what is seen is the return to the primitive in its crudest form. Change, as everyone knows, is ephemeral and skin deep and so it has the opposite effect. The speaker is overwhelmingly frank in expression as he says, "The age has specialized/ in each sucking other's blood" (23). It is a typical example of direct poetry.

"Futility" is an adjoining poem which can be read along with the poem mentioned above. The very theme is there in the title itself. The opening line is a pointer to the remaining, "The nothingness around me gapes and gasps/ It hardly breathes – a baneful breeze" (24). A desperate and desolate speaker who couldn't even smile as everywhere nothingness stares at him and futile is the only word that buzzes in his ears. Even towards the end of the tunnel he could see no hope. The poem ends, "Life recedes into the vast barren expansive" (24).

"When Grief Rains" (25) is a typical poem as it is emblematic of the peculiar predicament of the poet who is obsessed with the sense of grief. To quote the poem in its entirety would be of much relevance:

> When gales of sorrow
> Wreck my surging spirit
> Misery storms my being
> And grief rains incessantly
> I wish to drench myself
> Depart from these ills
> And enter the pores of earth
> With drops of rain that seep
> Still somewhere in me
> A dim desire creeps unawares
> To possess the instinctive mackintosh (25)

In poem after poem the key concern of T V Reddy seems to be the melancholic nature of human nature and the helplessness of mortals in the vast eternity of life. "The Dying Wick" is one such poem which metaphorically describes the loss of faith and its attendant problems. Terrible loneliness haunts the speaker of the poem and he feels like one who has been trapped in a blind alley which leads him nowhere.

> I do not know, to be true,
> Where this darkness leads to;
> It invades my desolate spirit
> And saps my sinking soul (27)

Yet another short poem of significance which can be read along with the earlier poem is "Thirsty Field" (28). In a poem containing fourteen lines, a kind of an irregular sonnet, he embarks upon the same theme of desolation. Here the thirst is not merely physical but spiritual also. Accompanied by deafening thunders and lightning "drops of rain traversed sky/ and touched the thirsty fields, / Hardly they entered the countless cracks, / the period proved abortive" (28).

Poets of yesteryears were adept at portraying the contrasting nature of human life. On the one hand they talked about the glory of mankind and the infinite capacity of human beings and on the other hand they also tried to delineate the image of man as a victim of destiny. We are at the mercy of greater forces and our little life is rounded with a sleep, as Shakespeare says. "Transience" is a poem which throws light upon the impermanence of human life. Juxtaposing the vastness of the land and the frailty of man the speaker says;

> There is nothing to gain in life
> or anything to lose in death ...
> ......Great deeds are writ in water
> All glories lead only to dust ("Transience", 29)

"The Mortal Frame" (67) has the same concern as that of the earlier poem. What looms large in the poem is the dark vision of life which doesn't offer any ray of hope. According to the poet the beads of sweat that drain over/ the gloomy brow of the tiller/ the pearls of tears that travel from/ the sunken eyes of the starving beggar" (30) and many other instances teach him one lesson. The lesson is that, "Life is a gruesome game full of stink and stench/ with neither sunshine nor raindrops/ to guide to the shore" (30). As is obvious from the title "Endless Night" also has the same thematic concern. Enveloping darkness never seems to fade as there is "immeasurable stretch of darkness" (31). Heart-rending scenes of misery and woe are there in the poem. With images of the "piercing cry of the child/ intensely struggling in vain/ to suck the bony breast / of a famished mother/ whose naked body is wrapped by / the sable shroud of endless night", the poet presents bizarre atmosphere indicative of the deprived state of the society. The poem has a very pessimistic ending. "The wretched moon dare not appear ever again;/ Are the stars just struck as sadist spectators?" (31)

Saga of the futility of life is continued to be narrated in poems like "Realization" (33) also. Life is described here as "a vague and obscure career" (33) and the persona in the poem resigns himself to his finale and waits for the inevitable moment (30). The following poem "In Memoriam" (34) is also one which pursues the same thematic thread as it also talks about the transience of human life. The narrator presents the picture of his son taking a clean slate and writing alphabets from A to Z and later rubbing them off. The boy can easily remember his father but he has a faint memory of his grandparents. The speaker is a philosopher in disguise here as he says,

> Our lives, when we depart
> are letters swept off the slate:
> Death in a sense is the only reality.
> And dust, the earth, the only eternity (34)

Same notes are struck in several other poems in this collection. Melancholy and despair are recurring motifs in poem after poem. "I see no other Way" is a direct poem which openly puts forth this view of life. He says, "I see no other way/ To solve the puzzle of life" (41). Though he has tried different permutations and combinations, no respite has been found. He becomes sentimental when he says, "I am quarantined against the iron clasp". The dark vision of life is evident as he concludes, "The exit of the grasping breath alone/ shall release me from the lingering pain" (41). Jarring relationship between the man and the self seems to be a prevalent thing here.

Poetry, to T.V. Reddy, is not merely a matter of tropes and metaphors but of life itself. Life here doesn't mean the physical or material aspects alone but something which is seen in its totality. The vision of life that embodies his poetry had many takers in history. When we look at the poetic oeuvre of many others, what we see is that they seem to envisage a clear cleavage between the physical and spiritual. But in Reddy's case there seems to be a unique blending of both aspects which to most are irreconcilable contradictions.

The Broken Rhythms is another major collection which was published in 1987. It contains poems which are of different nature ranging from the merely physical as well as that of the meditative ones. Poetry as vehicle of propaganda is evidently manifested in "Thousand Pillars" (1) and "Fortune Teller" (2). While the former is about the sculpture and the heartless hands that destroyed them, the latter is about a superstition amounting to social evil. Great artists under the patronage of great kings chiseled marvelous statues out of stone and fanatic invaders ruined the beauteous sculptures and turned them into pitiable wreckage.

No poet of this era can shirk off his responsibility of creating awareness to preserve the ecological balance and environmental issues. Reddy's poem "The Naked Tree" (4) shares these concerns as he portrays the dastardly acts of man's exploitation of nature. Unmindful of the consequences we tend to conquer everything that maintains the very balance of ecology. In order to satiate our greed we forget about the posterity and their needs.

"The Train" (6) and "Travel by Bus" (7) present before us the travails and blessings of rural life. Living in an urban society provides us with conveniences galore and at the same time it brings in hazards also. Many have seen train as a signal of the progress of man's civilization as it is indicative of the beauty of speed. But in Indian situation the journey by train is also not very happy as it is a suffocating experience with its heavy rush and related problems. For most of the people it has become part of our routine. The poet says,

> Men may come and men may go,
> Grey heads die and babes tumble
> But the train translates on parallel rails

As time sprints forever on invisible tracks ("The Train", BR 6)

Travelling by bus in the countryside is a risky affair on most of the Indian roads. "Much crowd and more cargo" (7) could be seen on board and they are a "barbarous blend". Much has not been changed even after many years of publishing this poem. Especially in suburban areas people have to sit "like frightened cats" in these.

T.V. Reddy has been often hailed as a poet whose main concern is rural life and its ethos and his farmer-centered poems are classic examples of this category. In a series of poems like "Farmer" (9), "Pensive Farmer" (10) and "The Village" (11), he lays bare his encounters with farming life and the difficulties faced by the agricultural laborers whose untold miseries and unmitigated sufferings have never been represented in literature in the proper sense. These "mud bound" poems do talk about the drought and the consequent issues. As farmer suicides are more in number due to their inability to make both ends meet, these interventions on the part of the writers will at least bring to light the sad plight of the underdogs in the society. The poem "Pensive Farmer" concludes like this: "the village is quite as the graveyard/ veil of darkness concealing its flaccid face" (10). Slices of life from the rural scene are presented in these poems succinctly.

Poems which deal with social issues are the favorites of T.V. Reddy as most of his poems have socially oriented themes. At one point he satirizes the peculiar practices in his society and at some other points he feels so sad about the plight of his country and people. Indeed much has been talked about the glorious tradition of "the sacred soil" of our country. A poem of the namesake, as has been wont, juxtaposes the magnificence of the past and the sordidness of the present. The poem has a candid opening:

> In this ancient land
> Of glorious cultures
> Omnivorous vultures
> Reign supreme ("The Sacred Soil", *BR*, 36)

Once it was a heaven of faiths and now it has been, "a cubicle of callous creeds/ blind, dark and dubious" (36). He laments that long ago Buddha's soul had escaped to foreign shores in dread. People of our country even resort to chasing Gandhiji's trembling ghost. Conflicting tendencies are at large here and corruption is at the core of the society. There has been no solace for the sufferings of common man and he has been left in the lurch as politicians thrive and prosper at the expense of common folk. There has been a wide gap between the precept and practice and expressions like "unity and diversity" remain only in letters. He doubts whether there will be any change for the good at all and the poem concludes with a faint ray of hope, "Still after scorching summer/ can rains evade for ever/ with elusive clouds?" It is a poem with overt political overtones where he criticizes the politicians and others for their shrugging off responsibilities and being corrupt to the core.

India in twentieth century is a land which has been spoiled by some of its people who tried to misuse the rich tradition and glory of its ancient culture. Basking in the shine of cultures they tried to mint money disguising as "sages" and "saints" with fake intentions. A typical Swamiji who exploited the sentiments of the really downtrodden rural folk has been portrayed powerfully by Reddy in the poem namely "Swamiji" (13). Exploiting the ignorance of the believer followers, "His fingers shone with rings of gold/ His wrist radiant with an imported watch; / They say His Holiness, feet, soft and gentle, / would never touch this mortal dust (13)". He travels in a Cadillac. Poet's criticism seems to be sharp when he says, "His savings swelled like elephantiasis" (13). Talking on Man, God and Soul, the poor became his easy victims. His spiritualism and simplicity were praised as he ate only apples, cashew and dried grapes. He drank pure milk and juice. God men in the country are at large and they move without any problem fleecing the very poor of the country.

Whereas most of his poems are materialistic in nature and theme, there are some which explore the uncharted realms of human experience which are shrouded in mystery. Poems like "My Soul's Plea" (24) and "I am in U" (25) are examples of this type where he unravels the obscure and the mysterious. Along these lines what interests us is a verse namely "A Poem" (39) which is distinctly different from the run of the mill poems on poetry as it opens up a different perspective on the quality of this art. What an ideal poem shouldn't be has been suggested at the beginning itself. It shouldn't be "a hammer of stammered words/ dry as hard nuts" (39). It shouldn't make the readers feel that it should be thrown into a dustbin. At least it should provide the reader with a "substance of pleasure/ in our scanty leisure (39)". He prescribes a qualification for a good poem as it should be pleasing and if it fails to delight it becomes a curse. After suggesting what a poem shouldn't be, he moves onto say that poetry has to be "a line that refreshes the mind/ an ennobling line serene/ a true taste of the Hippocrene". The last but one poem in this collection is a signature piece by T.V. Reddy.

To T.V. Reddy, to quote A.C. Bradley's expression, poetry is not for poetry's sake, but it is to reform and criticize life. Along with the famous British Marxist critic, Christopher Caudwell, he also seems to believe that art for art sake is an illusion and that art must be propaganda. Caudwell argued that, "Art is a social function" (29). Though mostly he tries to present a dark vision of life which is highly pessimistic in nature, this sense of desolation doesn't make him hate life. In some poems we could see rays of hope flickering. What makes his poems remarkably readable are their frankness of expression, sincerity of emotions and ease with which he handles them. Rather than going by the parameters of aesthetic conceptions of poetic endeavors, Reddy has tried to look at it as a criticism of life. He wanted writers to be sentinels of Democracy, culture and ethos. Terry Eagleton's observation, "To write the history of poetic forms is a way of writing the history of political cultures" (163), seems right in the case of T.V. Reddy when we look into the poetic forms that he has made use of in satirizing the political cultures of our own country. In a way his poetry can have the tag of being political as most of them address political issues and many of them have polemic content also. He, being a poet of ideas, has used poetic art as vehicle of thought which very well conveys the messages to the larger public if they are written without much obscurity and obliquity.

Abbreviation: BR = Broken Rhythms

Works Cited

Bradley, A.C. *Oxford Lectures on Poetry*. Kolkata, Radha Publishing House, 1985. Print.

Clifton, Lucille. http://www.azquotes.com/author/2992-Lucille_Clifton/

Caudwell, Christopher. *Studies in Dying Culture*. New Delhi, People's Publishing House, 1990.Print.

Eagleton, Terry. *How to Read a Poem*. London : Blackwell Publishing, 2014. Print.

Eliot, T.S. *Tradition and Individual Talent. English Critical Texts*, Ed. Enright, D.J. & Ernst De Chickera, OUP, 1962.Print.

Reddy, T.V. *When Grief Rains,* New Delhi: Samakaleen Prakashan, 1982. Print.

Reddy, T.V. *The Broken Rhythm,* Madras: Poet's Press, 1987. Print.

Soyinka, Wole. Web. http://www.azquotes.com/author/13902-Wole_Soyinka/

6 A Critical Exploration of the Pastoral Panorama of T.V. Reddy's Poetry

K. Padmaja

"As I was born and brought up in the midst of rural surroundings rich with nature's plenty I am inspired and influenced by nature. Belonging to a middleclass rural family, I have seen and experienced the agony and the anguish of the life of a poor farmer who has to depend for farm work on undependable workers who more often indulge in exploiting the situation as a result of which we the poor farmers are reduced to abject poverty and thrown into debt-trap... That is why life is a wonderful blend of moments of romantic imagination and hard realism. This is what I am as a writer and a social being." (Karmakar, 62)

These words of T.V Reddy, shared with an interviewer, present not just a holistic view of what his poetry is but project the recurrent motifs of his poetry. Nature, villages, people in villages; the agony at the loss of values of rural life and the melancholic pain that the author experiences at the change are the major themes of the selected volumes of poetry taken for study. An aerial survey of the Indian poetry in English shows us that not many of the major and well known Indian poets in English dealt with rural life at such great depths and insight. Words of K.V. Raghupathi endorse this observation when he says, "Writing about common scenes and people in countryside is a rare phenomenon in Indian English Poetry. Not many poets writing in English have depicted rural life in their poetry." Occasional poems like "Village Song" by Sarojini Naidu; "The Night of the Scorpion" by Nissim Ezkiel; and Kamala Das's "Grand Mother's House" take us to the world of villages. T.V. Reddy's love for eternalizing everything that belongs to village and nature is appreciated by K.V Raghupathi in terming him as rural poet in these lines. "The contemporary poets who have emerged after 1980s with their potential voice, I.K. Sharma, D.C. Chambial, P. Raja, P.C.K. Prem and T.V. Reddy have written several poems depicting rural life. Of these T.V. Reddy occupies a permanent place as a rural poet..."

With this introduction to the author that establishes him as a rural poet the article proceeds to elucidate and validate upon the aspects of his poetry that establish him so. A thorough reading of his poetry with a focus on his poems of nature and rural setting guides one to categorize them according to the major recurrent themes in these poems. His poems celebrate the beauty of nature and also mourn the loss of the pristine quality of nature because of the irresponsible and negligent acts of humanity. Similarly they depict the indigenous village life and the happiness it gives as well as the simultaneous erosion of rural life due to selfishness, cruelty and urbanization. Endorsing the view that women are the most important part of the Indian society especially that of the rural society, his poems extol the undying spirit of these women. The poems also express his concern for the difficult lives that these women lead and the exploitation they encounter. A farmer, a hunter, a toiling labourer, or even toddy tappers, the epitomes of the physical hard labour and sons of the soil, are eternalized in his creative works with an empathetic outlook that is a result of his very close association with the rural life. The following sections of the paper present his poems taken from *When Grief Rains* (1982), *The Broken Rhythms* (1987), *The Fleeting Bubbles* (1989), *Melting Melodies* (1994), *Pensive Memories* (2005), *Gliding Ripples* (2008) and *Echoes* (2012), along the major thematic concerns of his pastoral poems.

> I have tried to present multiple colours and shades of nature in my poems. I love nature and I like to paint nature in most of my poems. Whether we like it or not we have to live in nature and with nature. Therefore, it is our duty to preserve the purity of nature… Already we have done greater harm and it is time to protect nature so as to protect the human race. We are children of nature … In short; I have tried to present the real life of our villages.

As expressed by the poet himself in the above words, many of the poems unfold the sheer beauty of nature that he has observed not just around his village but also during his visits to America. These lines from "Nature's Play" (*Echoes* 5) are a befitting opening to present his love for the beauty of nature.

> My heart opens like a lotus
> blossoms like child's smile
> to see, hear, relish and feel
> Nature's countless miracles   (*Echoes*, 5)

The subsequent poems on nature that are discussed here exemplify the love that he has borne for nature. These poems on nature include loving depiction of the elements of nature like woods, lake, farm fields, skies, clouds, rains, rivers, seas, rainbows, flora and fauna too. The woods are described in their sight and sound and in consonance with the hills, streams, gorges unveiling an idyllic picture of "a paradise with such sylvan scene" (37). A similar description of a calm lake at night makes him feel that the still waters are "like face of a sleeping babe" (75). A recurring quality of his imagery is that he attributes human qualities to the aspects of nature. Thus it is the "breast of the rock" ("When Grief Rains", 37) and the bank of a lake becomes "… a girdle of gold around the waist of the bride" ("The Lake at Night", 38). The lake has become a beautiful bride while "the earthen bank" ("The Lake at Night", 38) is the arduous lover.

"Kalyani Dam"(*Melting Melodies*, 1) takes the poet's penchant for applying human attributes to nature far ahead when he views "the thorny waters" and "seminal cataract" as the male force that "rape the rocky bank" by " caressing the frigid stones" and "gushing into the rocky crevices"(*M.M*,1) wherein feminine qualities are attributed to rocks rather unusually. The poet makes an unexpected reversal of the employment of this image when he says that "wearied waters glide" like "a pregnant woman" (*M.M*, 1). The same 'water' which was presented as masculine force earlier is presented as a woman. He seems to dwell on the indistinguishable amalgamation of 'yin' and 'yang' or '*prakriti*' and '*purusha*' combined into one in all the aspects of nature. Carrying forward his favourite superimposing of human qualities on to elements of nature he calls the cloud "churlish" and the mists as "impish vapouring brethren" that form themselves into "pearls of piercing showers" filling the flora with "resurrecting manna" and finally decorating the skies with the ornament of "magical arch"(*M.M*, 38). The "intoxicating" and enchanting "primitive smell" (*Echoes*) of first rains and the desperate wait of the parched fields as well as that of humans and animals are presented in these lines.

> a drop of breathing rain may bring
> fresh lease of life to million sighs;
> parched tongues and sunken eyes

> for a shower look up the skies
> amid hungry yells and cattle bells (*Echoes*, 13)

His portrayal of the sea in "Watching the Sea" (Gliding Ripples 49) evokes the Arnoldian image of the beach at Dover, when the poet says,

> I stand on the soft sheet of sandy shore
> gazing at the vast blue expanse before;
> As I watch the roaring militant waves
> ...waves of thoughts tease and toss my mind, (*GR* 49)

The expansive Sea and its eternal nature are contrasted with the temporal and futile

> this march of ego and human pride
> with its hissing echo is a futile ride;...
> in the ebb and flow of tossing tides,(*GR*, 49)

Enjoying the beauty of nature and at the same immortalizing it in aesthetic terms, he introspects on the way nature is exploited and destroyed for the selfish human ends. In the poem "Thirsty Field" (28) the parched fields await the refreshing rain that arrives with "deafening thunders", "line of lightening" and then touch the "thirsty field" (28). Contrastively, as the innate course of nature is disturbed by the human greed, the rain failed and the field is like "a dissected corpse on the postmortem table" (28).

"The River" (*Melting Melodies*) speaks of its form, shape, flow, its topography, its destructive force, as well as of its ability of endowing the fields with fertility. The verdant beauty of nature presented in poetic terms is contrasted with the banes of human intervention. The river mourns,

> My full freedom has been curtailed;
> By tying my legs with dams wide and wild (*MM*, 40)

The sad state of holy Ganges in "her impure state" (*Pensive Memories*), the result of pollution in the name of religion and sacred rituals, is mourned in these words.

> The Ganges flows deep and dreary
> muddy and murky, miry and weary
> at the divine feet of her Lord Viswanath (*PM*, 3)

In fact the holy Ganges smiles "in the lushy lap of the snowy Himalayas" at Gangotri the place from where the river starts.

His pondering on man's intervention in the course of nature continues when he talks of "Wounded Sky Frowns" (42). Man with his unruly greed damages the nature and the nature reacts in quite unpredictable terms. The earth warns to the extent that the skies turn angry and refrain from rains. The angry restlessness of the fuming cloudy skies and the resultant cloud bursts are presented with remarkable choice of expressions like "seething lover", "borrowed from the blood bank", "perennial supplies from leeches" and "rains in drops of cold blood..." (When Grief Rains 42) foregrounding the sinister. The vagaries of nature, it's anger and destructive force are well presented in the poems like "Biting Breeze" (Echoes) and "A Violent Winter" (Echoes) where the poet shows the mortifying experience of "violent and gnawing" (*Pensive Memories*, 19) winter and the winter breeze that makes life unbearable,

> The unwanted non-stop
> wind service binds people
> to their warm bedrooms...
> in the hollows of books...

> Four doors down eagles wait
> with sharp eyes, claws and gait. (*Echoes*)

Having deliberated on his poetic engagement with the elements of nature, it is quite becoming to throw light on his depiction of the flora and the fauna that are the integral and inseparable part of nature. He immortalizes birds and their songs and the cultural associations with them. Sparrow is a recurrent motif in his poetry. Urbanization has made this grain feeding as well as home and farm dependent bird disappear. In this poem "The Sparrow" (When Grief Rains 15) it is presented as a symbol of growth of life and fertility.

> wove a nest
> with its beak
> to hatch the eggs (15)

And with the arrival of crow, which is nothing but the onset of urbanization that has destroyed everything that is natural, "the sky squawked in requiem". He uses sparrows as a symbol of love when he says,

> two twittering sparrows steeped in love
> vied with each in showering its essence
> their beaks became one at its peak;...
> Their unintelligible notes
> steeped in the balmy nectar of love
> touched our hearts ("A Pair of Sparrows", *MM* 22)

They are the symbols of pulsating assuring life that goes on the earth in these lines.

> To greet so many this time
> echoing with their rhyme
> this vast serene space
> myself I forget to trace...
> Their picking the grain
> relaxes the heavy brain ("Sparrows", *Echoes*)

"The Crow" which was shown as the invader of the lives of sparrows is presented as the friend of man. This poem is full of the Indian idiom representing the village life and culture. Thus the crow

> rouses the drowsy rural folk
> to go to the furrow with the yoke
> and the housewives to cleanse the house ("The Crow", *PM* 16)

The poet holds mirror to people's belief that "it is the special invitee to funeral morsel"(p.16) in these following lines.

> They say departed souls enter you to taste
> Gates of heaven are closed to those
> who refuse to feed the black bird ("The Crow", 16)

"Pigeon" is illustrated as symbol of joy and carefree life, flying "from tree to tree full of glee, ... with sportive spree" (*GR* 59). The love of life in humans is presented through "A Pair of Doves", Pensive Memories 41) which are seen as symbol of love. The following lines delineate the typical story of man seeking companion and building family.

> Both alternately fed their young ones
> by filling grains into their tiny beaks;

> The little ones clung to them ("A Pair of Doves", *PM* 41)

As wont with the world the young ones grew, and when one of the partners is sick and dies, "...Young ones flew; still he waited there" (41).

Flora, a part of the glorious nature, is commemorated in these poems. The poems "The Rose" (Gliding Ripples 41), "Blessings of Jasmine" (Fleeting Bubbles 38) and "Lotus" (Fleeting Bubbles 37) present the flowers in their glorious best both in their rapturously aesthetic beauty of appearance and sweet fragrance.

> Jasmine is soft, serene and pure...
> its soothing scent...
> to enchant any in joy or sorrow (*Fleeting Bubbles,* 38)

However the poet makes us feel that the glory that it enjoys in being the "pride...in worship or wedding as rose garland"(41) is transient as "All the petals, withered and trampled still, found their cemetery atop the dunghill" (41). He teaches the significance of life by saying that the flower "begets purity" and radiates "divine fragrance" in spite of its rising "from the mud" ("Lotus"/*Fleeting Bubbles,* 37).

The dwindling nature and the effect of human callousness towards nature resulting in the destruction of nature are presented through the poem "The Naked Tree" (4). He grieves and lashes at the humans who use unkind blows to "cut the hand that fed them" (4). He projects the same human indifference and selfishness towards the living things around in "Penance for Cow" (*When Grief Rains,* 16) when he says "you have sustained the life of the Lord, who does not care to redeem you". His poetic oeuvre on nature can be beautifully summed up with these lines from the poem "Nature's Play" (*Echoes*) where he captures the robust nature in its vitality with flowers, leaves, birds, animals, sea, rain, rainbows in their fragrances , colours and sounds.

> the invading flood of fragrance
> of jasmines, lilies and roses,
> lush leaves' gentle rustle,
> sylvan wood's soft whisper,
> koel's song and wind's stir,...
> the soothing melody of rain...
> a mystery we can never unravel (*Echoes*).

Village, of all the places, is the most revered and loved one for the poet. He, the one who saw the beauty of village life as a child, now sees the downfall of the innocent pure rural ways of life. He expresses helpless acceptance of the way of life in villages and employs a thorough critique. "My village" (Gliding Ripples 50) is a moving account of the loss of all those things in villages once that made the people live wisely and comfortably. They are now either transformed or mutated in such a way that the changed faces of villages reflect the greed of man. The constant juxtaposition presents a glaring contradiction of the once "pristine glory":

> canopied trees once sentinels strong
> are felled by pitiless souls doing wrong;
> Most of the huts and thatched cottages...
> now stand erect in concrete avatar
> Most men ...
> now move feebly like famished cattle (*GR* 50)

However the poem "The Village" is a scathing attack on all those evils that people reflect even while amidst pure innocent rural surroundings. The rural folk show their true colours in their curses of fellow humans:

> your bastard cock has spoiled
> flour designs of my house'
> curses she showing her loud fangs...
> A war of words, a shower of filth
> a cloud of stench from the puddle (*The Broken Rhythms* 11)

The people turn so bare and vile that their words are "deadlier than scorpion's sting" (11). He takes the reader to the dark side of village life and the poems dawn on us the realization that villages are not any more pure, uncorrupt, and innocent. The poem "Migrating Birds" (Pensive Memories 17) shows how villages are deserted in search of greener pastures. The distressed villagers, as farming fails them, lead difficult lives even for a morsel and they are like "Silent shadows with sunken eyes ...on their drooping heads and shoulders" (17). Hapless and fated to be so, the villagers brood over the old parents who stay back "with heavy hearts near empty hearths" (17) as they are "too old and weak to move from their huts" (17). These 'migrating birds' "look back in a pensive way" (17) as they are not at all happy at leaving the native village and the elders."A Forgotten Bird" (Gliding Ripples 23) is the story of many an individual leaving the nest of home, the village, due to various reasons. On return home to the village, which he has forgotten, he finds that the village too has for gotten him. In the mean while the village has transformed too:

> the living bird flew depressed
> in search of peaceful pastures.
> A few colourless summers later
> he returns to his native nest
> to relive his treasured memories...
> village wears a commercial look –...
> in intoxication lingers long,
> darkness dances in the graveyard (*GR* 23)

The poet's own words, about his picture of the village and its life, aptly sum up that "For the most part I tried to give a genuine picture of the village life and the depressing situation of the poor farmers"...

Women in village endure many hardships and the rural life is incomplete without the portrayal of woman who cooks at home, who rears children and toils equally in the fields. Though his women are "like expiring candles" they weave "desires in the plaits of their cobra-long hair" and they wait for their men with flickers in their eyes" (Fleeting Bubbles 1). The poet admirably contrasts their toilsome desperate lives with their dreams, desires and flickers of hope. He presents a similar portrait of women in the "The w" where he contrasts the dreary, lifeless unproductive landscape and environs with a housewife who eagerly awaits her spouse "with a wick in her eyes", again a typical Indian idiom, and also "with fond hopes of blank future; (*Fleeting Bubbles* 23). His "Village Girl" (*Melting Melodies*, 16) is the embodiment of rustic beauty who "keeping the pot at the waist's curve" balanced "her lonely way". Life is not fair to her as she toils in the fields care worn, while "the lustful eyes of the land-lord fell on her heaving bosom" (*Fleeting Bubbles*, 22). Unaware of the threat, she thinks of "her wailing child at home" and also "of blows on her back given last night by her drunken lord". But the toiling woman ensures that her sweat will save her child from threat. Though frail in body she has the will of rocks as "she quells the defiant stone, with the hammer in her bone; (*Melting Melodies*, 7). She is exploited by the rich and powerful and yet she forbears all "with eyes full of wicks".

The Pastoral Panorama of T. V. Reddy's Poetry

The poet is quite empathetic of the struggling farmer of the Indian village. He believes and loves his land, toils on it but of no avail. The weather and rains play truant and agriculture in such conditions does not pay him off well. But he persists on his labour lovingly and hopefully. The woes of the farmer in the face of such hostile conditions make him "drew his wearied feet to his field – a still-born child": (*Broken Rhythms*, 9). The farmer's "life became a fallow field, with full many a thorn and weed" .The poet presents the farmer in true picture, "With a loincloth around his waist, and a soiled towel," (*Pensive Memories*, 10). The wearied farmer "plods his way with his feet bare and sore". The desperate families dependent on farming, whose travails are not cared for and bothered by rulers, have "empty clay barrels, their only inheritance to store the grain" (Broken Rhythms 10). However the poet is saddened that the labour of the tiller is exploited by the rich and powerful for their selfish needs.

> Braving the meridian heat
> of the midsummer
> You reap the crop
> heap the harvest
> and feed the millions in cities (*MM*, 8)

P. Bayapa Reddy, a critic of Reddy's poetry, observes that, "The poet excels in depicting the plight of the vast majority of the village people and he presents rural scenes in simple and moving terms. It is in the presentation of rural scenes that he excels other poets in the same field, the veracity of which is testified by the moving lines of the poems such as "The Toiling Woman" and "The Tiller". The practical difficulties and the horrors of drought experienced by small and marginal farmers are painted in true colors by the poet."

Village is home for hard working innocent laborer: a farmer, a hunter or a toddy tapper. Their skill, hereditary mostly, gives them the prospect of food. The beauty of physical prowess of energy and strength that a tiller or a hunter or toddy tapper exhibits reflects the bond of land and man.

> Black as the trunk of a palm
> naked as a he-buffalo…
> walks robustly
> with bare feet –two hard bricks
> that crush the thorns (*MM*, 13).

The poet observes satirically that the hunter in the village,

> kills only to save his kin
> while his superiors and leaders
> relish slaughtering values
> on the infernal altar of greed (*MM*, 13)

Similarly tapping toddy is one of the common sights in villages. The poet admires the tapper for the skill and agility with which he balances himself almost in the air while harvesting the toddy. The physical labor involved in the act makes him to keep himself "hale and hardy with meat, mate and mug of toddy" (Gliding Ripples 45) the primary needs of life and thus get on with the laborious work without grumbling.

Primordial emotions, elements of nature, food generating farmer, the rustic laborers, hunters and all those people who are dependent on the mother earth and at the same time who enrich her with their activity are the choice of the poet in all these poems of rural setting and nature. T. Raghavan feels that Reddy reflects an "ability to give uninhibited expression to his experiences in rural India, revealing a voice that is both personal and universal distinguishes him from his fellow poets." Thus

T.V. Reddy is quite a versatile poet as the themes of all of his poems are quite varied. However the authentic persona of the poet is found in these poems of nature and rural setting. These poems depicting idyllic nature, the rustic people and villages as well as the lasting damage done to the nature by the humans and the loss of livelihoods in village due to urbanization present a sweeping panoramic view of the chosen aspects of nature and the rural life encompassing a huge canvass of poetry.

Abbreviations: MM: Melting Melodies
PM: Pensive Melodies
GR: Gliding Ripples.

Works Cited

Arnold, Matthew. "Dover Beach". *Fifteen Poets*, ELBS and Oxford at the Clarendon Press, 483.

Goutam Karmakar. "Goutam Karmakar Interviews T. Vasudeva Reddy". *Contemporary Literary Review India*, 4:1(February). Online http://literary journal.in/index.php/clri/article/view/228/299. Accessed on 20-07-2017

Raghavan, T. "The Spiritual Progress in the Poetry of T. Vasudeva Reddy". *Indian Poetry in English*, edited by Birendra Pandey, New Delhi : Atlantic Publisers, 2001, 114-121.Print.

Raghupathi, K.V. "A Critical Appraisal". *The Rural Muse: The Poetry of T. Vasudeva Reddy*. New Delhi, Authors Press, 2014. Print.

Reddy, Bayapa. "T.V. Reddy's *Melting Melodies*: An Analysis". *Writers Editors Critics* (WEC), Mar.2017, 109-111. Print.

Reddy, T.V. *When Grief Rains*. New Delhi, Samakaleen Prakashan, 1982. Print.

--- --- --- *Broken Rhythms*. Madras, Poets Press India, 1987. Print.

--- --- --- *Fleeting Bubbles*. Madras, Poets Press India, 1989. Print.

--- --- --- *Melting Melodies*. Madras, Poets Press India, 1994. Print.

--- --- --- *Pensive Memories*. Madras, Poets Press India, 2005. Print.

--- --- --- *Gliding Ripples*. USA: Baltimore, 2008. Print.

7 Rainbow or Mirage? Life Beyond and Behind *Golden Veil*

Santosh Ajit Singh

T.V. Reddy's poetic collection *Golden Veil* has seventy-five poems that beautifully capture the quintessential spirit of life. He has skillfully depicted life in all its various hues and myriad forms. The poet has dwelt upon emotions like happiness, sorrow, victory, defeat, hope, fear, patriotism, indignation and anger (to name a few) in order to pen down his musings on life. These entire poems blend together harmoniously to create a captivating smorgasbord that is in fact a microcosm of life. As we read every poem life is unraveled gradually- as if a veil is lifted enticingly stimulating the curiosity of the readers. Themes chosen for the poems cover a wide spectrum ranging from the commonplace and the mundane to the philosophical and the mystic.

The unique feature of the poetic collection is that there is no systematic pattern in which the poems appear. It is apparent that the poet has willfully chosen to compile these various poems together without making any attempt whatsoever to organize them under various sub-themes. Any attempt on the part of the readers to discern the underlying scheme that guides the sequence of the poems appears a challenge. But what emerges out of a careful reading of the poems is that they seem to celebrate life as a whole. In this creative piece of work, T.V. Reddy seems to be guided by the premise that the true essence of living does not lie in clearly well-defined polarities but a range of various shades of colours, which lend their charm to create a spectacular picture of the canvas of existence as a whole. I have chosen select poems from the collection that lend their own unique flavor to the collection making it a composite whole.

The first poem in the collection is titled, "In the Shell of Solitude". The opening line of the poem marches swiftly with an urgency suited to the context:

> Unused to hawkish hues of dash and drive (*GV*, 9)

The poet ascribes the attributes of "dash and drive" with negative qualities. It is not viewed in a positive manner by the poet. T.V. Reddy then states that he is -

> Forced to wear the veil of cool reserve (*GV*, 9)

This is an acceptance of his own shortcoming as he projects it. The poet concludes that

> Courage often makes a common man a legend (*GV*, 9)

The point that is being made here is that leading a happy life calls for many virtues– one needs to have the fortitude to handle the vagaries along the journey of life. The collective consciousness of our civilization believes that success comes to those who are willing to take challenges, and overcome their own weaknesses in order to reach greater heights. Hence the true essence of life is hidden behind the veil and one can understand the meaning only by mustering the strength to undertake the act of unveiling the true form of life.

As we move on through the poetic text, we encounter a pleasant theme for a poem - the smile. T.V. Reddy has chosen the cardinal element of happiness - the smile, which spreads cheer and joy in an "infectious" manner. This welcome expression on an individual's face has the magical powers to unlock many hearts instantaneously and creates a bond that transcends all linguistic definitions. The point to be noted here is that poet has made an effort to emerge out of the "shell of solitude" of the opening poem and boldly embrace the colours of the kaleidoscope of life. To the poet it is "Smile, the Saviour" (as the title of the poem goes) - a personification that has likened it to God. In this he has made it the panacea for all problems. He has heaped endless praises as if it is endowed with magical powers. Barring the regular metrical pattern employed by the poet in this poem, this work is virtually an ode to the smile. And the closing lines of the poem are a testimony to this.

> It is the shield guarding us from gloom till the end
> To mankind Nature's precious gift a real godsend (*GV*, 14)

T. V. Reddy is foregrounding the fact that notwithstanding the various obstacles that life presents, the smile is the boldest hue in the palette of life as it overshadows all these by offering the ever glimmering ray of hope that endows us with renewed energy to take on all these predicaments and emerge successful each time.

The next poem that I have chosen to critique is, "Tell Me What He Is!" It is a satire on today's politicians. The poet is unable to identify the identity of this being who seems to who have confounded everyone. The genius of the poet is that he does not mention who this person is. It is a guessing game that he is playing with the readers. The poet presents an exhaustive description of its activities and its traits revealing his keen sense of observation. In the title, T.V. Reddy asks "what" he is instead who he is - in doing so he seems to have made an inanimate object the subject of his poem. He has sketched the contours of this figure and left it to us to fill in the intricate details and christen it. The allusions throughout the poem are to the corrupt politicians that virtually sap the blood of the common people. The hypocrisy of this class of people is best captured in the lines,

> there is magic in his dearer khaddar he thinks,
> though beyond scented measure it stinks;

The exasperation of the poet emerges in the lines that come later-

> he winks at our basic needs with looks of stealth

and further on in the last lines of the poem, the poet continues-

> in the grin of the chin or in his casual ride
> there is the arrogant mark of bubbling pride;
> In every sense it makes us sick. Tell me what it is! (*GV*, 25)

How does this fit into the scheme of this research paper? The answer lies in coming to terms with the reality albeit grudgingly that we have to contend with all kinds of people who threaten to wipe us out but we must never give up but put up a stiff resistance as we are hidden behind the "golden veil."

The juxtaposition of the poems in the chronology of the collection lends variety to the work and the contrast that emerges by describing two divergent themes is the chief characteristic of the poetic work. Just as we are completely taken in by one insight into the mystery called life, the poet deliberately springs a surprise in the next poem. I believe that T. V. Reddy reinforces the fact that although he has managed to steal a peek behind the veil, what passes off as an image is in fact an apparition.

In the next poem, "Water is Dearer then Blood", the writer has taken a different trajectory by proclaiming that, water is far more precious than blood. The title is rather hard-hitting if I may say so, and sets our mind thinking making us wonder about the causes that may have prompted the poet to re-phrase an old adage. The content of the poem is an expression of the angst of the poet who inhabits a drought hit land. T. V. Reddy blames the unscrupulous leaders who have brought on this dismal state to the land due to their nefarious designs. As the poet articulates it,

> bastards born of dirty elections and petty politics,
> words and acts lead to clashes and spills pools of blood;

Against this grim backdrop, the poet strikes an optimistic note by stating that-

> Road to water leads to life, not to pools of blood,
> road to life lies in peace and smiles, not in lies (GV, 26)

Thus, this poem that has started on a rather disturbing note mellows down at the end to reveal an acceptable of life – that is patience, forgiveness, non-violence and large-heartedness that creates a happy life; not deception and avarice.

The poem, "Unmask Thy Veil" marls the nodal point of this creative work that encapsulates the suspense and enigma that is life. Although T.V. Reddy has tried to depict the various forms in which life manifests, somehow he seems to be unable to place his finger on the inner core of life. It always seems to elude him, hiding behind a veil that cannot ever be truly lifted. Hopefully we should look forward in this poem, to the poet's core idea that he has tried to develop in the various poems. When the poem opens, the poet is addressing his beloved and gently coercing her to reveal her true self that she has fiercely guarded from even her own family members. While doing so, the writer gradually moves on to a philosophical plane and begins to narrate how all humans are Janus-faced, excellently masking their true face and only revealing the face that is acceptable to the world. This only serves to complicate things, making it almost impossible to forge true and strong bonds with all fellow beings.

> Vicious is the veil, need of the hour is truth
> With will let us free our self from the veil
> and try to seek the Truth behind the veil
> Ultimate Truth lies beyond the golden veil (GV, 33)

As it is obvious from the above instance from the poem, repetitive use of the word "veil", is a poetic device meant to reinforce the falsehood that governs our life. We must never ever be misled because although the world does insist that, "Seeing is believing", we must shatter this notion because the true persona can never really be identified from the make-believe one. The poet is cautioning us about the inherent dangers involved in taking things at their face-value. We must overcome our naiveté and try to look beyond the simplistic, mesmeric notion of things. Only then we can decipher the actual meaning of existence.

The poem "Jai Jawan" echoes with patriotic fervor, and recalls a common slogan that mirrored the India of the post-independence times - "Jai Jawan, Jai Kisan". This work is a tribute to the exemplary services of the Armed Forces personnel of India who unhesitatingly and willingly lay down their lives for the security of the motherland. This poem has been written from the perspective of the lonely wife of the Jawan, who lives in the fond hope of her husband's visit who comes -

> Once a year or so he comes with year-long dreams
> on leave granted for a month or so with all the rights (GV, 57)

Following this, the poet describes the unbounded happiness that the wife experiences on her husband's visit. She is ecstatic but the "imagined risk" always looms large on her being. It is the proverbial Sword of Damocles that is perpetually threatening to wipe away her happiness in a single stroke. Her apprehensions are not unfounded and her worst fears come true when the call of duty beckons and he valiantly sacrifices his life at the altar of his motherland. The next few lines are pithy, devoid of any sentimentalism whatsoever. But the poet's craft is best revealed in this technique - one long stanza captures the various sequences of events that occur in quick succession. It is almost as if the reader is unable to keep pace with the fast-paced turn of events in the poem. The last lines of the poem

> The next day his body would fly from the border cold
> and reach this remote village in State honors bold (GV, 58)

The detached tone employed by the poet serves to accentuate the misery of the hapless family of the Jawan, although there is no mention of it. It is as if their existence is rendered insignificant due to the irreplaceable loss that they have suffered at the cruel hands of Fate. This sentiment of patriotism is yet another aspect of life that lies hidden behind the golden veil. The golden colour conveniently masks the unpleasant hues of life making it seem forever beautiful and desirable. The larger message being sent across is that human life is not one-dimensional being composed of only pleasant elements, but a composite multi-dimensional one that includes unhappy and unacceptable components as well.

Moving away from the rather somber note of the supreme sacrifice of a brave and selfless Indian soldier who lays down his life trying to safeguard his motherland the poet discusses the major component of the Indian population- the bourgeoisie in the poem, "The Middle-class Man". The striking feature of this piece is the poet's deliberate use of the small case for "class". This indicates that the "class" to which they belong, is rather insignificant. It is as if to say that he is caught in between two opposing forces- the title can almost be read as "The Middle Man", the "class" being lost in the domineering shadow of the rich, and the united strength of the poor. T. V. Reddy intends to shift the focus away from the socio-political issues and draws attention to the precarious condition of this major chunk of the world populace that is forever walking on a tight-rope. The characteristic feature of the poem is the use of undisguised and explicit words to express the angst of the poet. T. V. Reddy blames the

> .....proud unscrupulous political thugs
> and corrupt bulging bureaucratic bugs (GV, 74)
> for the irredeemable state of the middle-class.

The ironical condition of their life is best captured in the lines-

> the more we despise the more they suck,
> squeeze and suck and hoard stealthy wealth (GV, 74)

The repetitive use of the word "suck" evokes imagery of gory, creepy blood-sucking creatures. T .V. Reddy also makes an important observation in the line- 'Classes above and below reap all the fairer fruits' (GV, 74).

This makes us ponder on the actual situation of the seemingly "poor" class. Keeping in line with the theme of this research paper, it would not be wrong to say that we can say that "poor" is in fact a misnomer for this societal group that enjoys all the privileges but cleverly takes cover under the veil of poverty. The seemingly dark cloak of impoverishment is a convenient means to enjoy the luxuries of life. Consequently, the working class crumbles under the pressure and its "spirits are badly broken". Perhaps the saddest aspect of their life is that the other two groups of people display utter disregard for the plight of this part of society - it is apathy without any trace of sympathy leave alone empathy that never be expected from those who are complacently ensconced in their comfortable socio-economic zones. In the latter half of the poem we observe a perceptible turn-around in the attitude of the intelligentsia - self-pity makes way for a steely determination to put an end to the miserable state. There is a proclamation of the identity -

> I, an atom, am sure to explode and blast this rot
> Further on, the voice of the educated class here declares
> I shall tear the thwarting veil like a leopard (*GV*, 75)

signaling an announcement of the war that will be raged to restore their lost dignity or regain the place that is rightfully theirs.

In this poem T. V. Reddy has compelled us to re-orient our beliefs about the various social strata of society. We can no longer go by the dictum that the economically deprived class is n dire straits, because here, the poet has presented us with enough evidence to compel us to take a re-look at the manner in which we view the various socio-economic groups. The seemingly lowest rung of societal ladder does not altogether live in penury. The most affected is the middle-income group and there is a necessity to look beyond the obvious, behind the veil if we are to gain an authentic insight into life.

As we traverse the terrain of the world of T. V. Reddy's poems, we spot a gem - the poem titled "Ego". Marking a divergence from the earlier poems which are written in the form of a single stanza, in this particular piece, we encounter a different style in which the poem is organized. The stanzas are clearly demarcated as also the rhyming pattern. The first half of the poem has virtually created a cadence by the skilful use of vocabulary, the versification, as well as the rhyming words.

> At the heart of the willful word
> centre of the sizzling sword
> in the cells of the boiling blood
> drop of the tidal flood (*GV*,86)

Once the composition touches the crescendo, we gradually notice stability in the stream of thoughts. It is almost as if the poet is attempting to rationalize the barrage of ideas that had come gushing forth at the outset.

> Neck- deep in the Serbonian bog
> we sink in abyss like rocks and logs(*GV*, 86)

For a better understanding of the poet's ideas we need to understand the reason behind the poet's usage of the Serbonian bog. According to Wikipedia, "Serbonian Bog (Arabic: مستنقع سربون) (relates to Lake Serbonis (*Sirbonis* or *Serbon*) in Egypt, as described by Herodotus. Because sand blew onto it, the Serbonian Bog had a deceptive appearance of being solid land, but was a bog. The term is metaphorically applied to any situation in which one is entangled from which extrication is difficult." (https: //en.wikipedia. org/ wiki/ Serbonian_Bog/)

By making a mention of the bog, the poet implies that our ego is a quagmire that will pull us down into a disgraceful situation from which we can never escape. The tone borders on the didactic as if the poet is preaching an important lesson of life. The poet tries to make us see reason and make us conscious of the folly we are committing by surrendering to the unreasonable demands of our ego. He makes a plea for giving up this mindless, vain pursuit of power that has been ignited by the conceited ego. T. V. Reddy reminds us that by being egoistic we are missing out on the simple but precious joys of life and contentment will always elude us we continue on this path.

> Till we are freed from the iron grip of ego
> the veil that makes us wail and fight
> we stay in dark away from the strength of light.
> Peace and bliss of light till then we forego (*GV*, 86)

On a deeper critical note, perhaps the poem echoes the fictional work, *The Unbearable Lightness of Being* by Milan Kundera. Reiterating Kundera's preoccupation in the novel with living a life free of any kind of affiliation, T. V. Reddy also underlines his belief that a life free from any kind of emotional burdens is always ready to be liberated from the shackles of the mundane and poised for a higher sublime state of being.

The penultimate poem of the collection is called "Waiting for an Avatar". The word "Avatar" is rather out of place in the sense that it is not part of the English lexicon. Before we undertake a critical review of the poem, it becomes necessary to understand the etymology of the word and its connotation in the context of this research paper. As defined by Wikipedia, "An avatar (Sanskrit: अवतार, IAST: avatāra) is a concept in Hinduism and it means "descent", and refers to the appearance or incarnation of a deity on earth.[1][2] The term also generally refers to "alight, to make one's appearance" and is sometimes used to refer to any revered guru or human being."

In the light of the above definition of the word "Avatar", its relevance against the backdrop of the theme of this work of literary analysis needs to be described. The information provided in Wikipedia states that, "The concept of avatar within Hinduism is most often associated with Vishnu, the preserver or sustainer aspect of God within the Hindu Trinity or Trimurti of Brahma, Vishnu and Shiva. Vishnu's avatars descend to empower the good and fight evil, thereby restoring Dharma. An oft-quoted passage from the *Bhagavad Gita* describes the typical role of an avatar of Vishnu: 'Whenever righteousness wanes and unrighteousness increases I send myself forth. For the protection of the good and for the destruction of evil, and for the establishment of righteousness I come into being age after age.'(*Bhagavad Gita, 4.7&8)*.

By strategically positioning this creative piece of work as the almost final poem of the collection, T. V. Reddy has marked the culmination of the various ideas and emotions expressed in the 73 poems that precede this poem. After having experienced the trials and tribulations depicted in the poems, the poet has now arrived at the conclusion that it is only an incarnation of the Lord that can deliver us from these conflicts that have filled our life with strife and antagonism. The poem opens on a note of timelessness - the poet narrates the plight of the caged parrot. The fourth and fifth lines of the poem are

> It can't be held any longer as a poor captive
> Time is ripe, it knows the moment has come (*GV, 98*)

We are left guessing about the content of the poem although the title is self-explanatory. Following these lines the writer takes off on a different note by stating that

> For a full thousand years we were bonded slaves (*GV, 98*)

This line marks the turn of ideas from the earlier abstract or generalized one to the specific. We now begin to fathom the direction in which the poet is headed for. T.V. Reddy is referring to the momentous events of India's history- the colonial, despotic rule of the British and our eventual deliverance from their clutches, best captured in the line

> The veil of ancient innocence is torn to pieces (*GV, 98*)

There is something more to come as we read on - the poet's disillusionment at the dismal state of affairs of the nation today.

> Thousand vicious years of enforced slavish yogic sleep
> in bestial bondage under the despotic ruthless alien yoke
> has transformed us into a toothless spineless indolent race (*GV, 98*)

At this point in the poem the writer voices the central trope of the poem - the need of a Messiah to provide salvation to our beleaguered country. We are now poised at a critical cusp of time in which only divine intervention can light the path to a new beginning. The criticality of the situation is captured in the grim lines

> on this blood-soaking and sobbing oppressed earth
> no common mortal can save this stinking bleeding land(*GV*, 99)

The poet wishes for a "Ugra Narasimha" to destroy all evil and usher in an era of peace and brotherhood. As documented in Wikipedia, "Narasimha (Sanskrit:IAST: Narasiṃha, lit. man-lion), is one of many legendary avatars of the Hindu god Vishnu, one who incarnates in the form of part lion and part man to destroy an evil. Yet another description of this re-incarnation of Lord Vishnu states that, "Ugra Narasimha (i.e. Narasimha in its terrifying form). The protruding eyes and the facial expression are the basis for this name." (Hampi.in/lakshmi-narasimha-temple)

The poet is not merely satisfied with the presence of one Supreme Being but also looks forward to "righteous Rama" and "Almighty Krishna"

> to counter the countless terrors, scams and schemes (*GV*, 99)

The final poem of the "Golden Veil" is called "Eternal Ethics". It seems a natural extension of the previous poem, taking off from where the earlier work stops. Here, T. V. Reddy poses a rhetorical question-

> O Sanatana Dharma, why do you choose to be mute? (*GV*, 100)

The poem is almost like an invocation, calling upon them to perhaps wake up from the slumber that renders invisible to them, the atrocities committed by the mighty and powerful against the weak.

> Fanatic fools and ruthless terrorists butcher and loot
> Lives of the righteous roll in poignant multiple cry (100)

Following an emotive description of the misery, the poet states explicitly,

> *Gita* alone can save the world and the chaos uproot (*GV*, 100)

In this context we need to understand why the poet has quoted the specific instance of the *Bhagavad Gita*.

> "The *Bhagavad Gita* is an ancient Indian text that became an important work of Hindu tradition in terms of both literature and philosophy." The name *Bhagavad Gita* means "the song of the Lord". It is composed as a poem and it contains many key topics related to the Indian intellectual and spiritual tradition. Although it is normally edited as an independent text, the *Bhagavad Gita* became a section of a massive Indian epic named "The Mahabharata", the longest Indian epic. There is a part in the middle of this long text, consisting of 18 brief chapters and about 700 verses: this is the section known as the *Bhagavad Gita*. It is also referred to as the *Gita*, for short."

> "The *Gita* was written during a time of important social change in India, with kingdoms getting larger, increasing urbanization, more trade activity, and social conflict similar to what was happening when Jainism and Buddhism developed. This ancient Indian text is about the search for serenity, calmness, and permanence in a world of rapid change and how to integrate spiritual values into ordinary life." (www.ancient.eu/Bhagavad_Gita)

T. V. Reddy's fervent plea for a God incarnate to save the world from slipping further into despondency recalls W.B. Yeats' poem, "The Second Coming". As Yeats described in his work,

> Turning and turning in the widening gyre
> The falcon cannot hear the falconer;
> Things fall apart; the centre cannot hold;

> Mere anarchy is loosed upon the world,
> The blood-dimmed tide is loosed, and everywhere
> The ceremony of innocence is drowned;
> The best lack all conviction, while the worst
> Are full of passionate intensity
> Surely some revelation is at hand;
> Surely the Second Coming is at hand (Yeats, "The Second Coming")

By echoing Yeats' concerns in his own poetry, T.V. Reddy has once again reiterated the fact that all progress is null and void. Yeats voiced his extreme unhappiness with this increasingly materialistic world governed by recrimination in the 20th century, and a hundred years later unfortunately things remain the same. A poet of the 21st century is making a fervent plea to the Creator to protect his most wonderful creation- the world from being destroyed by mindless forces. T. V. Reddy strongly believes that it is only "eternal ethics" that have withstood the onslaught of the ravages of time and these can be enforced only by the Almighty. It is only this Supreme Force that can once again restore the Paradise that the world was once.

In this critical work, I have undertaken an analysis of T.V. Reddy's select poems from his work, *Golden Veil*. Every poem, that I have reviewed, captured different facets of life. Life is a relentless pursuit of the eternal Truth that is the driving force behind all existence. Through the means of the poem, T. V. Reddy makes a strong case for re-working our rather simplistic notion of life. He is awakening us to the complexities that life is replete with but which we willfully choose to ignore or perhaps acknowledge grudgingly.

It wouldn't be incorrect to state that the poet has posited a larger philosophical debate about what life is. Numerous thinkers and renowned philosophers have propounded endless theories about life, but at the end of it all we have come to realize that a comprehensive doctrine has always evaded us and will continue to do so for eternity. We will always keep grappling with this question. The hidden truths that are cloaked in the "golden veil" of existence will always remain baffling and keep all beings engaged forever.

The ideas that I have deliberated upon in the course of this research paper are in sync with the poet T. V Reddy's belief's and ideology: "Moreover, poetry should be written in such a way that it should disturb our minds, it should unsettle whatever is there in our minds and unless poetry is a thought provoking one, we cannot say that it is a poem. Mere description can never be a poem at all. There are some certain old and worn out ideas in our minds. By reading a poem, those ideas should be unsettled, they should be disturbed. If the lines do not appeal to our hearts, it is not a poem" (www.boloji.com).

Note: Abbreviation: GV= Golden Veil

Works Cited

Avatar: https://en.wikipedia.org/wiki/Avatar
Bhagavad Gita - Ancient History Encyclopedia
    www.ancient.eu/Bhagavad_Gita/
"In Conversation with Indian Poet T.V Reddy" by Santanu Halder -
    Boloji.comwww.boloji.com/index.cfm?md=Content&sd=Articles&ArticleID=14049.
Lakshmi Narasimha - Hampi. /hampi.in/lakshmi-narasimha-temple/
    www.goroadtrip.com/explore/india/karnataka/hampi/.../ugra-narasimha-temple-2414/
Narasimha - Wikipedia. https://en.wikipedia.org/wiki/Naras.

Reddy, T.V. *Golden Veil*. New Delhi, Authors Press, 2016. Print.
Serbonian Bog. Wikipedia. https://en.wikipedia.org/wiki/Serbonian_Bog
Yeats, WB. https://www.poetryfoundation.org/poems/43290/the-second-coming./

8 Exploring the "Ultimate Truth": A Study of *Golden Veil* by T.V. Reddy

Vijaya Babu, Koganti

The collection of poems *Golden Veil* (2016) by T.V. Reddy, who stands as a significant writer beside Shiv K. Kumar, offers a kaleidoscopic view of the colourful feelings and emotions of his heart as a sensitive poet and as a keen observer of the world. A close examiner of nature and human nature, T.V. Reddy's oeuvre covers several aspects of human life against the backgrounds of 'being' and 'having'. We find a mood of celebration and dejection, anger and pain, and also a spirit of protest and displeasure. With inspiration from the Romantic and the Victorian poets and Indian poets like Toru Dutt, Sarojini Naidu, Sri Aurobindo and Tagore, Reddy, one of the talented and gifted poets of Asia, talks about the beautiful villages in serene settings with its poor peasants and also the cities with its mechanized and vainglorious people and their selfish attitudes. He lashes at the greedy and corrupt human behaviour and his poetry is fertile with aspects of naturalism, realism, irony and humour. It never "bites" violently but offers a vision to open our eyes to the gross realities around us. With his belief in *sanatana dharma,* he believes that "a good piece of literature, both directly and indirectly, shows the right path of life and aims at correction and tries to improve the moral standards of the society" (Interview, *CLRI* 2017:63).

As the poet expresses, 'the Ultimate Truth' lies 'beyond the golden veil' (2016:33 *Golden* Veil) and we need to lift it to seek it. Human life after industrialization turned mechanical and with the onslaught of 'globalization', man was dominated and molded by 'consumerism' and its evil effects. The innate innocence that used to bind man with nature is lost and man has become an 'object' and ceased to be a 'being'. This created a big void and man, in his quest for a luxurious living started erasing the divine footprints of nature and thus lost his identity as 'man'. This chasm pushed him away from his fellow beings making him an 'alien', an alien who is interested in amassing wealth, comforts and bodily pleasures foregoing the primordial feelings and emotions, like sympathy, sensitivity, sensibility and empathy and to put in a nutshell –the essential human nature itself. A thick veil of ignorance covered him forcing him to ignore his primeval responsibility towards nature and fellow human beings. The poet says:

> Indeed our self is hidden by an ignorant veil
> It is not easy to tear it and get the release;
> Dark and dubious is the veil, the foe of fulgent light
> Its scope is narrow; it blurs the real vision (*GV*, 33)

Only a poet can perceive such a transparent and sensitive veil covering the selfish human facade. Great poets have expressed their pleasure or displeasure, angst or anger and tried to mend the ways of the world. As a poet from a rural and agrarian background and with native innocence and strong belief in ethical values, Reddy observes every aspect of life closely and presents his poems with two essential gestures – the creative and the social. To put in his own words,

> As I was born and brought up in the midst of rural surroundings rich with nature's plenty I am inspired and influenced by nature. Belonging to a middle class rural family, I have seen and experienced the agony and the anguish of the life of a poor farmer who has to depend for farm work on undependable workers who more often indulge in exploiting the situation as a result of which we the poor farmers are reduced to abject poverty and thrown into debt-trap. This is the reality whether one accepts or not. That is why life is a wonderful blend of moments of romantic imagination and hard realism. This is what I am as a writer and a social being. (*CLRI*, Interview 2017)

He expresses his fondness for nature and human bonding and at the same time shows displeasure with the realistic image of the present day society. He believes strongly in the commitment of a true poet. As observed by Raghavan, this "ability to give uninhibited expression to his experiences in rural India, revealing a voice that is both personal and universal, distinguishes him from his fellow poets"(2001:39).

The poet touches upon several aspects of life starting from childhood. He satirically throws light on the joys of school days with 'less luggage and more knowledge' and with 'evenings rolled in games' as against the present day trend of 'more luggage and less creativity'. He fervently recalls how they used to combine the seasons of nature with their school calendar. He says:

> Those days blossomed with flowers of innocence
> The sky of our life was blue without a cloud…
> Walking and playing we reached school and our classroom
> Days were sweet as koel's song; faces were roses in bloom (*GV*, 72)

As a responsible member of society and especially as a member from the farmers' clan, the poet represents the pathetic plight of the farmers in villages during rainless days with all angst and pain.

> Sight of rainfall is a rare event of joy
> More often clouds visit, but they refuse to rain
> Rain for days in torrents is a dream in pensive pain
> Rarely does it rain (*GV*, 43)

The poet presents the pain of people in procuring water. He examines the apathetic conditions:

> No sincere scheme, no clean framework to develop
> We continue to be drought and hunger-hit;
> People at the top and bottom reap all fruits,
>   those in the middle bear all the breaking weight (*GV*,43)

Continuing the same strain, he mimics the nursery rhyme to heighten the effect:

> Rain, rain, humbly we pray you not to go away
> Please do not wait to come another day
> (*GV*, "Our Thirsty Land", 43-44)

As water is one of the most important elements for survival, Reddy talks about it in many of his poems like "Water is Dearer than Blood" (26). In "Bankrupt Clouds" (*GV*, 79) he says:

> "Yes, here water is dearer than this poor blood
> Who cares for blood, in street brawls it flows in a flood"0….
> No water to drink or irrigate the cheerless fields
> No water to wash our narrowed murky minds
> No water to fill our eyes and hearts with joys

> No water to helpless blades of grass to dance;
> Water struggles to emerge and deep it goes back
> in deeper dread of people who morals lack;
> Villages that waded in water buy bottled water
> Day is not far off to watch thirsty water wars (GV, 79)

Every creative work of art is shaped by the race, milieu and the moment of creation. As his lineage is from the family of farmers, Reddy does not forget to represent the hard conditions of squalor and the broken heart of the poor farmer in "Today's Rural Life" (62).

> Here farmers look at the skies
> Their bowed heads heave endless sighs
> Our fields how can we cultivate?
> Heat and hunger our hearts can't calibrate
> When can we see our fields green? (GV, 62)

He also whips at the cunning and opportunistic politicians with all his anger and angst.

> Streams and canals where we learned to swim
> have lost their address, now they don't exist;
> Both sides are annexed; picture is dim;
> Big landlords, political wigs, whips and thugs
> and reserved persons none can resist (GV, 62)

The poet portrays how the farmers sell their cattle to abattoirs and struggle to eke out a living as "the power mongers" have "their vision on vote harvest." This anguish appears in some other poems too like, "Erstwhile Farmer" (76-77), "Seeded Soil" (78), and "Listen to Our Song" (92), which show the dedication and social commitment of the poet. The poet talks about all the peasants who belong to various professions like 'weavers, fishermen, farmers, potters and blacksmiths'. He ends this poem on a sarcastic note expressing his pain:

> The day we got our freedom from alien yoke
> we lost liberty crushed under the corrupt yoke (GV,92)

The poet's social commitment does not stop with the delineation of the troubles of the farmers and peasants. He makes fun of the technological development which expands "the territory of hell" (11) and which fails to connect us with 'Divinity'. In "Tell Me What He Is" (25), he sarcastically draws the pictures of "the ladies and gentle men" of the modern society. He criticizes the tailor-made generation with its craving for "branded living" and artificial life. The pompous and audacious factionists, real-estate brokers, contractors and leaders "born of dirty elections and petty politics" (26) are lashed out. He says:

> A victim of insatiable thirst for power and wealth
> he winks at our basic needs with looks of stealth;
> in the tick of his watch, in the click of his wrist,
> in the jerk of his neck or waist or lip's twist,
> in the grin of the chin or in his casual ride
> there is the arrogant mark of bubbling pride;
> In every sense it makes us sick. Tell me what he is! (GV, 25)

In poems like "Ultimate End" (47) and "End the Dynastic Rule" (80), the poet's pen turns into a whip and his anger is felt.

> Chase the old and worn out political weights

> These fatty hogs, shameless old political hags,
> lazy lumps and cancerous growths, burden to the land,
> always stoop to wag in political rags and tags,
> cling to power like leeches sucking nation's wealth;"
> ...
> "Bring real change for the better, not for the worse,
> to lead to an upright joy, not to the path of curse(*GV*, 80)

T.V. Reddy never forgets his creative gesture as an artist. He speaks about his personal loneliness, aspects of love and affection, and mostly about his love towards nature. "In the Shell of Solitude"(9), "Forget Me Not" (21), "Meaning of Love" (22-23), "Pyres and Fires" (27), "Syntax of Love" (30-31) etc deal with his solitude and gloom.

'Satire' helps the poet reflect the ways of the world and mend them. T.V Reddy chooses satire and sarcasm to project several follies of the society. In the poem "Birthday Function" (53) he portrays the artificial glitter and pomp displayed by all "blank heads" and mindless "nodding faces" in the "grand decorated hall in the luxury three-star hotel". The poem creates a sarcastic smile on the face of the reader. Similarly the poems "Unsolved Mystery" (11), "Need of the Hour" (12), "Tell Me What He Is" (25), "Water Is Dearer than Blood" (26), "Ultimate End" (47), "End the Dynastic Rule" (80) too expose the poet's keen observation of society and its faults. In addition to these, Reddy's observatory skills are reflected in several other poems of this collection. "Need of the Hour" exposes the rotten reality of current day affairs. The poet observes:

> Here one who lives on honest means is a born fool;
> Only those who hate and cheat, garb and rob rule,
> robber kings reign in royal robes and crazy crowns,
> while pseudo-scholars shine in convocation gowns,
> powers at the centre thrive in shearing and sharing;
> While the righteous have lost confidence and courage
> anarchic forces are freely let loose with riotous rage
> by power-hungry political parties, rotten to the core,... (*GV*, 64)

As expressed by him his satire is never 'violent'.

Satire, irony and satiric humour are there in my writing, but not violence. Virulent and violent satire may be there, but there is no place for violence. When there are ills and evils at a large scale in the society, first they should be exposed and then corrective or remedial measures should be taken. Satire is the age-old intelligent poetic device or mechanism, which comes to the rescue of the poet or writer in exposing the unethical practices (*CLRI*, 2017). Despite despair and dejection, the poet keeps his faith and is optimistic. In the poem "Flowers Shall Bloom" (65) he ushers in a new spirit of life:

> Life is not an endless autumn, it has its spring
> Flowers shall bloom and koels are sure to sing (*GV*, 65)

As a follower of the Romantics, the poet loves and worships nature. This son of the soil, as a poet too asks us to protect nature as Nature protects us in turn. His love for nature and conviction reflect strongly in his words:

> I have tried to present multiple colors and shades of nature in my poems. I love nature and I like to paint nature in most of my poems. Whether we like it or not we have to live in nature and with nature. Therefore, it is our duty to preserve the purity of nature. By harming nature, we would be harming ourselves. Already we have done greater harm and it is time to protect nature so as to protect the human race. We are

children of nature and nature is our mother, guide and philosopher. In short, I have tried to present the real life of our villages in my writing. (*CLRI*, Interview 2017)

While revealing one of the ultimate truths, the poet says,

> Nature gives us birth, our birth and berth
> We need to be grateful till our last breath
> Nature's lesson is deep, long and brief
> We live to learn, take from Nature a leaf.
> If we flout and defy, she reacts in her ways
> In the flood of her fury we end without a trace. (*GV*, 83)

The mark of the Romantic poets is obvious and the poet excels in describing aspects related to nature. "A Bird in the Cage"(19), "Alone as a Bird"(39),"Sylvan Scene"(40),"Riverside"(42), "Look at the Stars"(45), "Green Canopy"(66), "Night Watch"(70-71) and some other poems bring out the mastery of his poetic craft. He believes that nature is "our mother and teacher, nurse, guide, friend and preacher" (83). In the manner of Wordsworth he says:

> As I walk on the lonely path for quiet relief and rest
> alone as a wearied bird flying back to its wonted nest
> my feet refuse to move from this yellow patch of land
> as the golden beauty casts its spell with a magic wand (*GV*, 39)

As an elderly observer he offers some truths, which guide us on a positive and a progressive path. For a bright future, he suggests to protect the ethics of life. He focuses on various aspects of modern life and despairs how values are being lost. He asks us to shed our ego.

> Till we are freed from the iron grip of ego
> the veil that makes us wail and fight
> we stay in dark away from the strength of light
> Peace and bliss of light till when we forego (*GV*, 86)

He observes that as parents, we should check the corrupt behavior of our children ("Old Napkins", 10), we should watch the "mischief making ways" of our mind (Choose the Right Path, 16), we should aim high (Aim High, 46), we should "move with grace" as "life is a race, rough and tough" (To Rest in Peace, 48), we should "learn and receive the good from all" ("Learning is Life", 81) and that we should cultivate hope as it "is the miracle key to open the victory's door" ("Hope", 84).

What is the 'Ultimate Truth' the poet wants to unveil? He wants us to realize the loss man has created on the earth. He asks us to identify the loss of relationships between man and nature, man and man and man and society. He asks us to prevent the hooliganism created by the power mongers in society. He urges us to protect nature and ethics required for a righteous living. He reiterates:

Right from the beginning I view from spiritual angle and now after my retirement I devote most of my time in reading the *Bhagavad Gita*, some of the *Upanishads* and Sri Aurobindo's spiritual poetry. In fact, I am not a metaphysical poet in the conventional sense. But eternal truths are there in our scriptures and *the Gita* is the best source to lead us to spiritual light. Our *Sanatana Dharma* is the most ancient way of moral life, most comprehensive and synthetic, integral and inclusive, with compassion and catholicity of outlook. Constant reading of *the Gita* has its undeniable impact on the mind. With all his faith in the *Sanatana Dharma* he says in "Eternal Ethics" (100)

> In vices, lies and crooked deeds, biped beasts are bold
> This dark face neither sword nor nuclear arsenal can slay;

O Lord, with thy trident protect us from chaos untold
Universe exists on Thy sole strength, order and fair play.
Thou art the glory of the Lord that holds the universe
Without thy base and breath world would be a curse (*GV*, 100)

Works Cited

Chambial, DC. "The Poetry of T.V. Reddy: A Saga of Human Grief", *The Post Colonial Space: Writing the Self and the Nation*. Ed. Nandini Sahu, New Delhi, Atlantic Publishers, 2007, 34-50.

"Interview (2017) by Goutam Karmakar". *Contemporary Literary Review India*. Vol.4, No.1, Feb 2017. ISSN 2250 - 3366; ISSN 2394 - 6075. Print.

Raghavan, T. "The Spiritual Progress in the Poetry of T.Vasudeva Reddy". *Poetcrit,* July 2001, 39-45. Print.

Reddy, T. V. *Golden Veil: A Collection of Poems*. New Delhi, Authors Press, 2016. Print.

....

9 Poetry as Social Commentary: A Thematic Study of T.V. Reddy's *Quest for Peace*

Arabati Pradeep Kumar

A poet is an ardent observer of the occurrences of the society. He reflects all his insightful observations in his poetry. His response mirrored in his poetry can illuminate many people across the globe. He tries to bring social awareness to his readers. A genuine poet always raises his critical voice against all the evils of the society. A poet having societal awareness can reform the society by driving away all the social evils. Most of the Indian English poets have drawn international attention and received accolades and awards at international level. Among the recent Indian English poets who have made a significant contribution to the development of Indian English poetry is T. Vasudeva Reddy. He is indubitably a potential signature in the area of contemporary Indian English poetry.

T.Vasudeva Reddy started writing poetry in the eighties after the Emergency period. He has succeeded in establishing his own identity as a poet among the other Indian English poets. His poems depict the inner essence of life. He has written his poems with sharp insightfulness, psychological insight, innate straightforwardness, and more prominently a flicker of Indian sensibility. Beyond any doubt, he is a humanist to the core. Using literary terms like satire and irony, he, as a social commentator, describes the loss of moral, cultural, and ethical values in the society. Being a true Indian nationalist, his poetry analyses the importance of harmony and national integrity.

India is a country where many people are living in miserable poverty. Besides, they are also facing many other problems namely corruption, nepotism, red-tapism, communal violence, terrorism, population, unemployment, bribery, political social, and economic disparity; rape, child abuse, dowry, exploitation of women, the victory of vice over virtue, smuggling, violation of code of conduct, and black marketing are omnipresent in our present society. A poet, having observed all these social evils, tries to portray them in strongly critical terms using satire or irony in his poetry so as to awaken the consciousness of the society. H.S. Bhatia aptly states that "Social consciousness is virtually a study of man in his social milieu, as a dynamic creature, sometimes alive and active, sometimes passive and tolerant, but sometimes volatile and aggressive and sometimes pursued and persecuted" (Bhatia 71).

The reader should be able to differentiate between 'criticism' and 'creative writing'. Criticism requires patience, intellectual effort, and analytical power. Creative writing is the outcome of originality of mind, universal approach and an intrinsic fire of genius. Being a genius, T.V. Reddy is simultaneously a creative writer and a critic. He is a wonderful poet, novelist and a critic of the highest order. What is more arresting about his poetry is the natural flow of the poetic lines along with the extraordinary felicity of expression. He reminds us of Sarojini Naidu's poetry as far as the melody and music of his poetic lines are concerned. The reader finds the harmonious blend of sense and sound in his poetry. The themes in his poems are degradation of moral and ethical values and dehumanization of relations which may lead the ultra-modern man to material prosperity, but eventually, he dies spiritually under the influence of westernization.

T.V. Reddy's *Quest for Peace - A Minor Social Epic (2013)* is a long poem consisting of seven sections or cantos with a total length of 1665 lines. It is chiefly known as a social satire. The theme of this long narrative poem is also not different from his previous collections, in which he intensely depicted the proliferating corruption and deterioration of moral and ethical values in the present society. The poet has elucidated his outline of writing this poem in his preface. It is divided into seven sections in consistent progression. After reading the poems, the reader understands the fact that there are no such clear-cut divisions between the sections, nor is there any progression established in its sequences. It is neither an essay nor a story. The same idea of dishonesty, corruption, and selfishness playing their roles predominantly in Indian society, particularly among the politicians, reappear in his poetical lines.

The subtitle of the poem is *A Minor Social Epic.* The reader gets befuddled regarding the subtitle. Genuine epics are things of the past. There are many literary epics, and a few are known as minor epics. But the critical reader finds that there is no hero, no story, and no progression of events in *Quest for Peace.* Surprisingly, the poet himself is the hero and the witness simultaneously in the poem. It may be justified in the sense that the long poem is a description of the struggle between moral and corrupt forces which has now assumed epic dimensions and the aim of the poem is to establish morality which alone ensures peace. Whatever it may be, the credit goes to the poet for writing such a lengthy poem articulating his ideas in a logical manner throughout his long poem. It describes chiefly the malevolent and corrupt aspects of the ultra-modern society.

As a poet fulfilling his social responsibility, he analyses how the life in a city is making the dwellers of it very deplorable and horrible. He states that the modern city has become a reckless and sinful city. The people are unable to lead a healthy and peaceful life. There is ubiquitous environmental pollution because of countless industries and vehicles in the cities. There is no proper administrative mechanism to curb this menace. The hazardous pollution coupled with deforestation is resulting in the depletion of ozone layer. This means that the ultraviolet rays directly fall on the people. They are prone to be affected by skin cancer, allergies, lung cancer, asthma, sinusitis, and various other pulmonary problems along with serious destruction to flora and fauna. The poet aptly states that any city-dweller cannot escape from the dust particles and sooty smoke. All kinds of vehicles keep buzzing in the city till late night. Further, there is no proper pollution-check by the transport authorities. One can understand very easily by staying at any cross roads or junctions of any city that it is becoming highly deoxygenated because of toxic pollutants in the environment. All this is resulting in the ecological imbalance. The poet, as a social scientist, depicts a very sorrowful sight of city life. Due to abnormal climatic changes in the atmosphere; the people are losing their valuable immunity power. Exploiting this grave situation, the medical doctors are treating the patients immorally and unethically. There is an unprecedented increase in the number of hospitals in the cities. The doctors have become greedy and money-minting machines.

> Need garlic pearls of morals, more moral pills,
> But never a huge laundry list of medical bills,
> And words of gratitude, small ethical capsules
> To commence in daily doses with rigid rules
> And save ourselves ...   (*QP* 15, 195-199)

Besides, the poet writes about the stark realities of a city. He says that the city has turned out to be an appropriate place for hoarders, brokers, smugglers, gangsters, greedy realtors, political jugglers, and the successful money multipliers who habitually crucify the morals. Sometimes, it appears for a morally-bound citizen that the words like morality, ethics, honesty, solidarity, and integrity have become obsolete in the contemporary society. The real estate business in metropolitan cities is at its worst. The realtors using the hooligans are occupying the land of the innocent people illegally and building apartments and villas in that place. If need be, they grease the palm of officers of the Land Registration Office of the locality to get their illegal work done. They sell these constructions to the rich people for an extortionate price. There are big land mafias in the cities. It is not to be forgotten that the politicians have a lion's share in these dealings. The city also has become

> a place of greedy realtors and dearer sites,
> murky layouts, block outs and tourist sites,
> gangsters, hired killers, parasites, thugs and pubs,
> licensed bars, drunk-driven cars and clubs,
> where a trivial incident tilts paradigmatic axis
> and aggravates the metropolitan abscess(*QP*, 108-113)

In the name of caste and religion, the politicians in league with a few communal thugs are transforming our sacred motherland into a veritable hell. There are unprecedented religious conversions in the society. This, in turn, is resulting in the volcanic eruption of extremism and terrorism. This has become a serious global problem today. Though ours is the largest democracy, the fruits of it are not reaching all the people of the country. The politicians applying the communal colour to their politics are taking undue advantage of extremism and terrorism by becoming friendly with extremists and terrorists. It is nothing but divisive politics. The terrorists even attacked our parliament a few years ago. In other terrorist attacks in our country at different places, the terrorists took the lives of many innocent people. Here, a common man is worried about his security. What are the seasoned politicians doing for the country? It is not to be forgotten that they are elected by the votes of these people. They are people's representatives. The politicians with their ulterior motives are also adopting 'divide and rule', which was once used by the British rulers. The poet appropriately states that our democracy is:

> stinking democracy filled with false visions
> crushed under fish-catching reservations,
> monstrous increase of contagious corruption
> and bribery's ugly face of volcanic eruption,
> mindless terrorism spilling pools of blood (*QP*, 65-69)

The poet, who was a great teacher, rightly remarks that our education system is fraught with many defects. The managements of the schools and colleges are only worried about money-making. Greasing the palm of the politicians in power or bureaucrats enjoying the highest government positions in the education sector, they have made the entire education system purely a commercial business. In fact, there is no importance to the true talent of the poor and deserving people in our country. They collect exorbitant fees from the parents, which a common man cannot afford. On the top of it, the managements are least bothered about the facilities to be provided for the students. Even there is no exception for professional education in our country. The rich managements get approvals from the highest authorities by greasing their palms. The entire education system has been diluted. Till twelfth standard, the teachers of the schools and colleges, as instructed by the managements, are only bothered about a very good percentage of marks to be secured by their students. But they never teach them the importance of practical learning. They never use the interactive teaching methodology in the classrooms. Thus, the teachers do not teach the value of independent thinking skills, critical thinking skills, decision-making skills and soft skills. This serious deficiency gives a death blow to the students when they choose to study any professional course of study. The poet observes that

> Nowadays everything even education,
> is a profitable marketable commodity,
> it is simply an open monetary transaction

converting the youth to ethical frigidity;
corporate schools expand their greedy wings,
convert admissions into financial springs,
fleecing sheep and fees is their only aim,
they mint money and marks at any time;
they nip in bud children's creative urge,
for play and joy sing a dragon's dirge,
transform institutes to grim grinding mills
multiplying wily monstrous boarding bills. (*QP*, 587-598)

The college teachers, especially in government sector, always think in terms of their emoluments, increments, and arrears. Surprisingly, these teachers are least bothered about the needs and career of their students. The same is the case with medical doctors working in government hospitals. For them, it is only a side business. Many government doctors run their own private hospitals with all advanced facilities. The ministers of health in the state and the centre do not provide basic amenities for the patients in the government hospitals. The poor people who cannot afford the private hospitals are destined to face the tragic consequences. If the poor patients visit the private hospitals in the times of emergency, the doctors squeeze the blood of them. Even if the poor people cry for justice, their cry will prove to be a cry in the wilderness. The poet very befittingly writes:

Mushroom schools as money-minting factories
robbing parents and sucking bread winners,
confused victims their aggrieved votaries,
college teachers always counting arrears
unmindful of students' needs and careers,
public hospitals without doctors or drugs,
Offices full of bribe-breathing bloody bugs
Who attend only when we grease their palms (*QP*, 149- 157)

The poet further expresses from the view point of noble and clean souls that

Future is sorely bleak to the cleaner souls,
for every scheme is sour full of black holes;
the present context doesn't need any text,
it knows how to capitalize any tiny pretext (*QP*, 207-210)

The poet is clairvoyant mentioning that the future belongs to the miscreants like criminals, communal thugs, hooligans, exploiters and unscrupulous actors,

who sailing with profit are for all waters,
to crafty men and greedy foul players,
to men with explosive power and slayers,
to hired thugs, swindlers and grabbers,
to divisive forces and political robbers
who take to vicious and devious ways (*QP*, 224-229)

Commenting on the contemporary politics, he is forthright in saying that backbiting is a common practice in politics. It is as common as village cock fighting which grows with renewed betting and crowing. It is a common sight in villages. It is just like our pseudo political leaders' dieting which is publicized in the print and electronic media. Regarding the filthy politics of our country, the poet makes a few serious derogatory remarks:

> Politics is the chosen game of clever guys
> who perfect negative arts and polished lies
> and the crowning act and art of swallowing
> thousands of crores released for nation-building;
> the rich and corrupt, strangers to morals,
> shine in modern politics with loud laurels (QP, 249-254)

Politics is very much responsible in the ultra-modern times for its nefarious and crooked role in bringing down the standard of the people's lives. As the maladies like red-tape, nepotism, selfishness, and corruption are ruling this part of the world, we are unable to ensure the progress of our country anymore. Hence, we are still treated as a 'developing country'. If our political system continues to be deprived of conviction and prudence, our country cannot produce the statesmen and will be a developing country even after hundred years from now. What about Twenty-Twenty vision of our country when the politicians are applying the formula of fifty-fifty share of benefit in any deal? These deals are made surreptitiously.

> We can't go to the problem's root
> with their much hyped murky facial formula
> of the trumpeted Vision Twenty Twenty
> a means to cement their power amid gala
> a mask for the longer dear deal Fifty-fifty (QP, 274-278)

The poet becomes a philosopher and remarks that

> We believe in our age-old doctrine of Fate
> and karma which indeed is great at any rate;
> the poorest old fall like leaves with sunstroke
> while the leaders at the top with 'son-stroke';
> once emperors built monuments for their wives,
> now sons build empires on their fathers' lives
> using and abusing to the extreme the high position (QP, 349-355)

The other nations are developing in all spheres. But our political leaders make vote bank politics to ensure their political power. They make tall promises as a part of their election campaigning which will never be kept. They use 'caste-based reservation to their advantage. They play different political games to get extra mileage out of it. The budget allocated for the development of our country in all spheres will be misappropriated. This will weaken our economy and a result of which there will be an unusual rise in the prices of essential commodities. With this crippled economy, the poor people bear the brunt. The callous politicians are not at all bothered about it. The sole objective of the politicians of today is to emerge victorious in the elections by hook or by crook.

> While other nations march in leaps to big evolution
> our democratic leaders to insure their voted power
> revolve round the axle of worn-out static reservation
> through endless populist schemes at every hour;
> constant play of this deceptive political game
> has rendered our brittle economy horribly tame
> and a lion's share of our budget is lost as a whole
> mysteriously without a trace in the black hole. (QP, 363-370)

The poet gives a very good example of government's maladministration. The government imposes the prohibition of the use of liquor or wine. And, it does not last for longer period. They lift the prohibition within a short span of time. The people living on daily wages become addicted to it, and their family will be on the roads for their livelihood.

> Governments lift the closed curtains of prohibition
> and open the doors of liquor sale with ambition
> and let the people drink and drink and drown
> till they burn whatever they earn as a clown (QP, 377-380)

It is a common practice in India that all parties shower boons for the people during their election campaigning. They make these false promises to win in the elections. After they win the election, they will reappear only after four years in their respective constituencies to attract the voters again with their false promises. The poet seems to suggest that the voters should not be deceived by the false promises made by the selfish politicians. There should be a social awakening in our country so as to taste the sweet fruits of our true democracy. The poet also states that there should be a fairer voting process without any election rigging.

> now comes the leader of the Grow More Green,
> after being elected, for four years he is unseen
> in the vast aerial space of his limping constituency
> where he continuously wins with foul currency (QP, 694-697)

As far as income tax is concerned, the rich people have their own plans to avoid paying it. The motto of all political leaders is to enjoy all the possible bank loans. But they never pay back to the banks. It is quite sad that our activists of human rights protest against the functioning of the government as and when the extremists or acid killers are shot dead. But the eyes of the same activists of human rights become blind, and their voices become dumb when the innocent citizens and duty-minded police personnel are killed by terrorists. It is quite flabbergasting that if the terrorists, who kill the innocent people mercilessly, are arrested and sentenced to death by Supreme Court, the politicians show undue and undesirable sympathy on them. These politicians visit the President of India to request him to show clemency on these cold-blooded murderers. It is indeed a political game played by the vicious circle of politicians of the country. It is more disheartening and exasperating that they try to win the votes of minorities during elections. They play communal politics and divide the people on the basis of religion:

> Our human rights leaders protest very hot
> when extremists and acid killers are shot;
> but when citizens and police persons are killed
> or with acid bottles college girls are killed
> their eyes become blind and their voices dumb,
> their human hearts turn blind and minds numb (QP, 449-454)

The poet is forthrightly critical regarding the functioning of electronic and print media in our nation. They always try to be on the side of the ruling party. They forget about the journalistic ethics and social responsibility of the media. In fact, the media is supposed to play a pivotal role in reforming the society. They do not hesitate to tarnish the image of honest and ethical political leaders. While dancing to the tunes of the leaders in power, they try their best to mislead the society:

> Our sipping sails with the skipping of stinking pages
> stuffed with misleading news and false images;
> gone are the glorious days of media ethics,
> now it stinks with foul pranks, pricks and tricks (QP, 501-504)

The poet tries to mention that money is playing a spoil sport in the society:

> Everything is determined in economic terms
> from pins, pens, books, brides and brooms
> to foods, goods, brushes and bridegrooms (*QP*, 601-603)

It is a well-known fact that there is no permanent friend and permanent enemy in politics. The politicians change their chameleon colours to be suitable to any situation. The present politicians are only bothered about the end, but not the means:

> In politics revenge and compromise coexist
> like pride and poverty in a well-knit twist;
> it knows only the result-oriented experiment,
> all the supporters are given a liberal increment (*QP*, 639-642)

The poet describes the realistic scenario in our nation's capital. Here, women cannot travel safely. The girl or woman is becoming an easy target for the uncivilized and lecherous men. It is to not be forgotten that there is 'Nirbhaya Act' exclusively meant for these sexual offences. But it is not able to provide any safety to the women and girls, as it is not at all implemented effectively. It is truly a sorry state of affairs in our democratic country:

> even in our nation's capital woman can't walk
> or travel alone even at noon safe without fear;
> it is now a hot topic and food for global talk
> and a member of the opposite sex, old or a child,
> falls a prey to the beast in man savage and wild (*QP*, 1704-709)

The poet rightly remarks about the existence of the VIP culture in temples as witnessed in the well-known shrine of Tirumala and Tirupati. Many rich and poor devotees visit Sri Venkateswara's and Sri Padmavati Devi's temples. The *darshan* takes ten to twenty hours for ordinary people. But quicker *darshan* is provided to the wealthy people. All people should understand that there is no VIP or an ordinary devotee to Gods. All are equal to Him or Her. Truly money plays a big role here. Our life on the earth is unpredictable and ephemeral. One must understand the naked reality is that we do not bring into the world at the time of our birth, and we do not take anything with us when we die. The birth as a human being is the most sacred one, and we should lead a morally righteous and spiritual life till the last breath of our life. One of the greatest spiritual places is temple. Even if we politicize the spiritualism, there is no meaning to human birth:

> If one goes to Tirupati to visit the famed Temple
> one has to stand and wait in the endless queue
> for ten or twenty hours till feet fail and tremble;
> quicker darshan is only for the chosen wealthy few,
> Darshan of different dimensions has varied price tags,
> the more you pay the sooner you visit and finish
> and come out of the temple with a higher polish,
> counted currency is poured into sacks and jute bags
> money plays a big role before Lord Venkateswara,
> money is the big player here on the sacred Hills (*QP*, 782-791)

The priests of the temple serve the VIPs more than the other devotees. The officers holding the high offices feel taller than the Lord Sri Venkateswara. As the poet himself has a personal attachment with

Tirumala and Tirupati, he writes about the VIP culture which has crept even into the world of spiritualism.

> priests compete in serving VIPs than the Lord,
> higher officers feel taller than the supreme Lord
> they feel stronger in temple jungle than the leopard,
> they feel blessed in the service of the VIPS;
> how can the media lag behind in this game? (*QP*, 797-801)

The poet mentions how the global threat of terrorism is spreading to nook and corner of the world like a wild fire. The terrorism has become the biggest obstacle for maintenance of global peace. One must say that there appears to be no place which provides total security to the people. Islamic terrorism in the form of jihad created havoc in the most developed country like the United States of America. As everyone is aware that Osama Bin Laden was the mastermind behind the terrorist activities in the USA, Christopher M. Blanchard analyses that Osama Bin Laden's beliefs are understood to have been formulated by his exposure to the teachings of conservative Islamist scholars in Saudi Arabia, as well as his work with Arab militants in Afghanistan who provided the theological and ideological framework for his belief in the desirability of puritanical Islamic reform in Muslim societies and the necessity of armed resistance in the face of the perceived aggression - a concept Al-Qaeda has since associated with a communally-binding Islamic principle known as 'defensive jihad'.(Blanchard 13)

As per the instructions of Laden, the terrorists of Al-Qaeda, a militant Sunni Islamist organization, attacked the twin towers in New York City on September 11, 2001. In this brutal 9/11 attack, many innocent people were killed and injured. Besides, the terrorists wanted to attack Pentagon, the hub of American security and all kinds of ammunition, the White House and Pittsburg. The terrorists made suicide attacks on the USA the strongest nation in the world which provides airtight security for its people. Astonishingly, this country allocates a lot of money for the security of the country and proclaims its supremacy across the globe.

When the terrorists could target and destroy this highly developed nation, the supreme power in the entire world, it is unimaginable to think of the security of the developing and underdeveloped nations. The terrorism is the biggest global menace today. How can we think in terms of global peace when we find ourselves in the quagmire of Islamic extremism and terrorism? All the veto nations of the United Nations Organization and members of Security Council have to think of it very seriously to curb terrorism and ensure the global peace. There should not be any divergent opinion in fighting against terrorism and also those that harbor terrorists. Otherwise, a day is not far away when the terrorists would attack any nation with nuclear weapons. If that happens, there will be a third world war, and nothing will be more cataclysmic than that of this heinous act.

> Already walls of New York face the blasting wreck
> when Twin Towers fell to terrorists without a check;
> imperial World Trade Centre suddenly crashes
> reduced to sky-high flames and chilling ashes
> to become a mourning center of the terrorist act
> and Pentagon too shivers under Terrorist pact;
> when the land of peace, power, joy and wealth
> loses peace with bold terrorist attacks of stealth
> how can smaller nations stay and feel secure
> when sons of Satan strike with hands impure? (*QP*, 904-913)

The poet is very keen about another serious social malady called corruption. It is the most significant contributing factor which is impeding the growth of our nation. Hari Sadhan Das remarks that "corruption pervades everywhere such as social, legal, political and even in religious field." (Das 1)The poet is of the view that India is a very suitable country for corruption which has corroded our society. There is not a single government office which is free from corrupt practices. The land suffers from the bane of corruption which is rampant from top to bottom and it is practiced from central cabinet minister to the fourth class employee of any department. It is truly suppressing and demoralizing the honest and talented people of India. It has an incurable cancerous effect on the society. The poet befittingly remarks that India has grown to be the world topper in corruption. Our well-experienced political leaders and bureaucrats are not sparing a serious thought to curb this problem. Our political leaders themselves are highly corrupt people. They have earned huge amount of public money, and they also do not pay income tax. They cleverly deposit this corrupt money in Swiss bank.

> For corruption most fertile is Indian soil,
> the weed has full growth without any toil;
> our 'bribescape' is as vast as the skyscape,
> there is no escape route in this landscape;
> this holy land dons the avatar of corruption
> and shines as world topper sans correction;
> Our leader knows there is no magic wand
> to cure or end this cancer with a single hand (*QP*, 970-977)

Those who are in political power become money-minting machines illegally. In fact, the middle-class people are bearing the brunt. They are leading a very poor life as a tenant in a rented room with his old parents. The monthly rent and the fee structure of their school-going children are highly exorbitant, which a common man is unable to afford. The wife of a middle-class man living in the metropolitan city thinks in terms of her status. Her feet are never found on the earth. She always tries to compare herself with the rich people.

> At the other end, the metro middle class man
> in a single bedroom apartment with no fan
> with his old and ever grumbling parents
> lives hard struggling to pay monthly rents
> and to equip his two school-going children
> with sky-high fees and loads of books barren
> and a competitive wife with plans too high
> with her feet never on earth but in the sky (*QP*, 1006-1013)

To conclude, T. Vasudeva Reddy's *Quest for Peace - A Minor Social Epic* remains distinctive in Indo-English Poetry. Chiefly, it is a social satire and, at the same time, there are lyrical passages of exceptional quality. It is to be noted that the theme of this poem is not different from his previous collections. This research article critically analyses the social problems such as terrorism, corruption, environmental pollution, our defective education system, filthy politics, unethical print and electronic media, our unethical medical profession, VIP culture in temples, and degeneration of ethical moral values in the society. In the firmament of Indian English Poetry, the bright star called T.V. Reddy shines everlastingly with his glittering brilliance, keen insight, word music and profundity of thought. He champions the cause of the suffering people by exposing social evils through this wonderful poem.

Works Cited

Bevy, Lawrence. *Ed. Al-Qaeda: An Organization to be Reckoned with*. New York: Nova Science Publishers, 2006, 13. Print.

Bhatia, H.S. *Social Reality in Indian English Poetry*. Delhi: Oriox Publications, 1994.71.Print.

Blanchard, Christopher. M. "Al Qaeda: Statements and Evolving Ideology". Dian Publishing, 2010. https://play.google.com/store/books/details/Christopher_M_Blanchard_Al_Qaeda?id.../

Das, Hari Sadhan. "Poetry As A Social Commentary: A Selective Study of Keki N. Daruwalla's Poetry." *Research Front: An International Peer-Reviewed Multidisciplinary Research Journal*. Vol. 5, No. 1, Jan - March, 2017, 1.Print.

Reddy, T. V. *Quest for Peace: A Minor Social Epic*. New Delhi: Authors Press, 2013. Print.

(Note: All references from *Quest for Peace: A Minor Social Epic* are mentioned as 'QP' with the number(s) of poetic lines in brackets throughout the research article.)

---

10 Portrayal of Nature in T.V. Reddy's *Melting Melodies*

Palakurthy Dinakar

Indian English poetry has emerged as a divergent and promising genre, which can be considered praiseworthy in contemporary Indian English literature. It experienced different movements and styles ranging from 'fixed form' to 'free verse'. It has limitless choices in form, meter, prosody and subject areas. "The contemporary poetry can give us a feeling of excitement and a sense of fulfillment different from any sentiment aroused even by very much greater poetry of a past age" (Eliot 186). It experienced a sea change before and after India's independence. Pre-independence poetry was the embodiment of mythology, legends, patriotism and divine love. But post-independence poetry is remarkable for innovative themes, forms, techniques and attitudes. The contemporary poetry is well marked in its originality and experimentation in word-craft. It tries to represent social, cultural and rural life of India from its beginning. It deals with concrete themes and continues its quest for originality, individuality and the poets keep themselves away from the influence of the Western poets; moreover their poetry is fresh, sensible with the vital experience.

T. Vasudeva Reddy has an intensity of thought, strength of feeling, clarity in expression, freshness of words and sensibility in his poetry. He has evolved a distinct idiom to express his voice. He is rooted with a sense of sympathy, love for nature and spiritual sensibility which is marked in his poetry. He covers a wide range of themes like love, poverty, politics, money, academics, life, philosophical issues and nature in the present anthology of poems entitled *Melting Melodies*. The article tries to focus on the nature which was nurtured by T.V. Reddy in poems like "The Kalyani Dam", "Dharmasala", "The Fort", "A Pair of Sparrows", "Coconut Tree", "The Cloud", "The River", "Rainbow", "On the Sacred Hills" and "The Supreme Lord".

The first poem of the anthology "The Kalyani Dam" is full of illustrations about the scenic beauty of the dam, which was constructed across the Kalyani river near Tirupathi, the temple town in Chittoor district of Andhra Pradesh. The poet describes that the river was stopped like a defeated champion and the sun set is picturesquely described as the sun sets near the golden edge of the western pagoda near the famous temple with the tall tower with several levels. There was green foliage with teak trees, tamarind trunks on the banks of the river:

> Near the golden rim
> Of the Western pagodas
> The vanquished victor sets.
> Veiled by green foliage
> Teak trees and tamarind trunks ("The Kalyani Dam", 1)

The river water flows with a roar and tries to assault the rocky bank as if the river tries to rape and caress the bank. Sometimes the water tries to touch gently the frigid rocks but there is no response from the dam. The freedom of the river is curtailed by the rocky bank that has no feelings at all. T.V. Reddy employs the technique of personification in the poem and the situation may be compared to the human relationship of men and women. Women have no freedom in this men-centric world which is always curtailed by men.

> The thorny waters roar
> And rape the rocky bank;
> Fiercely caressing
> The frigid stones
> Seminal cataract gushes
> Into rocky crevices
> Of craggy cliffs ("The Kalyani Dam", 1)

The poem further describes the pitiful condition of the river and its frenzied race which is stopped by the dam. The poet's art of presenting the nature is beautifully displayed and it reaches its high watermark in the lines, 'the two hills, whose stony nipples invite the starry clouds'. Because of the hard nature of the dam the crystal water becomes still, dull and lifeless. The poet illustrates the majesty of the river aptly comparing it with that of a pregnant woman:

> The frenzied race
> Is arrested by the dam
> That bridges the two hills
> Whose stony nipples
> Invite the starry clouds;
> Crystal waters become still
> Yawning its deep dark womb
> Like a pregnant woman
> With terrible beauty
> The wearied waters glide ("The Kalyani Dam", 1)

The next poem *Dharmasala* is a picturesque narration of the beauty of the Himalayas, where the soothing breeze brings peace and bliss to the visitors. The gentle winds greet the visitors with a kiss and provide immense pleasure to them. These soothing waves of breeze chase away fatigue and fretful thoughts out of the region and they become alien elements in that pleasant atmosphere. The tiredness and worries will run away from the area to the distant plains:

> Thy soothing waves of breeze
> Harbingers of peace and bliss
> Greet the visitors with a kiss
> Fatigue and fretful thoughts,
> Alien elements here,
> Flee to the peevish plains ("Dharmasala", 2)

T. V. Reddy explains the beauty of the Himalayas where the sun and the snow provide cheerful smiles to its guests. The Himalayas have perennial crystal flow of water which murmurs with the nature with 'an amber-tinted aura' and becomes the center of attraction to the visitors. The mountain ranges are covered with tall pine trees which provide shelter to the tired mountaineers and fill their hearts with beauty and enchantment.

> Snow and the sun alike sprinkle
> Cozily chill and cheerful smiles
> With an amber-tinted aura
> The murmuring streams

> With perennial crystal flow
> Throb the heart and arrest is beat
> The range of high mountains
> With battalions of tall pines,
> Wearied mountaineers
> Resting while scaling the heights,
> Pours its beauty into the pores of hearts ("Dharmasala", 2)

The Himalayas arrest the sight of its visitors and their breath seems to be stopped for a moment by its magnificent beauty. One's soul will hop and gallop on the green cascade of the fields which takes everyone into transcendence and it seems even frogs can meditate in that quiet and tranquil place. Particularly the night time is excellent for its deep, undisturbed and serene environment:

> The steep and deep valleys all around
> Seize the breath and make it free
> To gallop on the green carpet
> And hop in joy on the ascending
> Green cascade of tea and corn fields
> The place is quiet, leaves are still
> Even frogs seem to be in meditation
> Night deep and still and undisturbed
> Save the melody of the dancing rills ("Dharmasala", 2)

The beauty of the Himalayas, covered with snow, is beyond the range of words to describe and it is at once marvelous and majestic with its silver shine. The ranges of mountains turn into golden color when they are kissed by the rays of the sun. The poet compares the mountains to the shy Indian maid in milk white sari. She is portrayed as a virgin with incomparable beauty in the role of a bride in milk white sari that hides her heaving bosom after her entrancing bridal bath:

> There is majesty in its wild beauty
> The place with the snow-clad peaks
> Of Dhawaldhara kissed by morning rays
> Looks like the peerless virgin beauty
> Of the coy Indian maid in milk white saree
> That hides her heaving bosom
> After her entrancing bridal bath ("Dharmasala", 3)

The poet compares and contrasts the littleness of man and the abundance of nature in the following lines. There is a comparison between dusty pins and might pines. He strongly believes that place of the Himalayas is the suitable and tranquil place for lofty thoughts. The place is considered as *thapovan*, a place of meditation on the earth for sages. The peaks with full of snow inspire the human souls towards divinity. The creativity of the human beings can be enriched with its beauty. It is the abode of eternal truth and gateway to eternity. The poem is a masterpiece in presenting the littleness and the transience of human life and the omnipotence as well as the divinity of nature:

> Of our littleness and nature's abundance
> Dusty pins before might pines.
> A tranquil place for logy thoughts
> An unearthly spot on the heights of earth
> A *thapovan* for sages to meditate
> The snowy peaks make the soul sublime

> Torrential rains enrich the creative springs
> True to the name you preach
> The shining value of eternal truth
> And host the wearied pilgrims
> In their march to the celestial summit
> In the diverse ways to reach the goal eternal ("Dharmasala", 3)

The poem 'The Fort' refers to the famous ancient Chandragiri Fort near the temple town of Tirupati in Chittoor district of Andhra Pradesh. While the Royal Palace was built in 1000 A.D., the Fort was constructed by Vijayanagar Kings in 15th and 16th centuries. Chandragiri was the last Capital of the great Vijayanagar Empire after the fall of Vijayanagar i.e. Hampi. The poet explains that nature is permanent when compared to human beings. The great dynasties were submerged in the history but nature is everlasting. The Royal dynasties became invisible in dust but the sweet crystal pearls of the royal tank move perennially down the rocky hills and dance like princesses on the lotus leaves to the unheard and fragrant songs of the matchless petals of beautiful lotus:

> The barren stretch of invisible cemetery
> Of the Royal dynasties in dust
> While the sweet crystal pearls
> Of the royal tank down the rocky hill
> Dance like princesses on the lotus leaves
> To the unheard fragrant ditties
> Of the peerless petals of beauteous lotus ("The Fort", 5)

T. V. Reddy explains every scene with right image dressed in appropriate words which succeed in beautifully creating the circumstances and portraying the situation. In the present context his words describe the pleasant atmosphere delightful to lovers in the following lines of "A Pair of Sparrows". The pair of sparrows on the green and shady bough represents the lovers under the cool shade of a guava tree. The touch of the hand of the lady love is as gentle as the caressing breeze:

> Under the cool shade of the guava tree
> The touch of my love's hand was soft
> Gentler than the caressing breeze
> On the green and shady bough
> Two twittering sparrows steeped in love ("A Pair of Sparrows", 22)

"The Coconut Tree" symbolizes the absolute selflessness. It stands like a giant with its many firmly planted roots in the sandy soil. It is a symbol of self-respect, ready to disobey the authority like the Olympic Powers with its fiber-firm fatty base.

> With its legion knotted roots
> Firmly planted in the sandy soil
> Like an angler's fishing net
> The coconut tree stands like a giant
> That stoutly defies the Olympic Powers;
> With its fiber-firm and fatty base ("The Coconut Tree", 37)

The poet symbolizes the coconut tree for its individuality and firmness. It never surrenders to the troubles and tribulations created by the wind and the flood. It fights with oddities till it breathes with its firmly matted roots. When it loses its power it falls like a lone hero but never surrenders to its enemies. T. V. Reddy personifies the coconut tree as a great Indian hero who shines wherever he is –

as a farmer in the field or as a soldier at the border. They never give up their duty for their individual interest but sacrifice their lives for the sake of the nation.

> Like an undaunted sentinel on guard
> It defies the force of wind and flood,
> Till it breathes with its matted roots
> It fights and falls like a lone hero ("The Coconut Tree", 37)

The poet exemplifies the many benefits of the coconut tree in the poem. The coconut tree is useful when it is alive and it is also useful even after its death. Every part of the tree is useful to the human beings. It is useful to the prince and the pauper. It soothes the aching bodies and craving souls alike. Human beings, birds and animals can enjoy its presence. People of all categories, from poet to the lover, from the educated to the uneducated, from the civilized to the uncivilized, from the sick to the healthy, invariably appreciate its greatness as well as its utility. Its kernel pleases both the cook and the eater. It helps the poor for the hut and prince for his mattresses:

> Aching bodies crave to lie in its shade
> Its fanning leaves, a lushy green canopy,
> Kiss the lucid starry sky, cheer the sphere
> And bless the weary animate world
> With cool shade and balmy breeze;
> It throbs the poet and thrills the lover
> It gives succor to the sick and the thirsty
> While its kernel pleases the cook and the palate;
> While the dry leaves help the poor man's hut
> Its coir adorns the royal chamber ("The Coconut Tree", 37)

Apart from the above the coconut is useful on many occasions. The temple bell never rings without its help. From the wedding bells to the death knell it is inevitable to use it. It lights the eye and delights the heart with its magnificent presence:

> Without its aid and selfless help
> Neither the temple bells ring
> Nor the wedding bells nor the knell;
> It lights the eye and delights the heart ("The Coconut Tree", 37)

The poem "The Cloud" presents the aspirations and expectations of the people at the very sight of the cloud and at the same time the poet tries to describe the deceiving nature of the cloud. The poet portrays boorish, uncanny and uncivilized nature of the cloud, which starts its journey from the East by creating a lot of hopes to the people but flies very fast as if there is a feigned feast waiting for it. It starts its journey with its dark wings in the strange weather and moves very fast from the sight of the starved animate things and parched lands as if it were very busy. It leaves the place quickly on the flood of foaming fleece by charging too much from the needy. It has to rip and peel its airy skin to bring back the moisture that has disappeared for many days. It appears to be manna, the Biblical food that God provided for the people of Israel during their forty years in the desert. It is like an unexpected and welcoming gift for the needy.

> Yonder the churlish cloud at the east
> Flies fast as if for the feigned feast
> With his impish vapoury brethren
> With his dark wings on eerie weather
> At the sight of the starved and parched

Portrayal of Nature in T.V. Reddy's Melting Melodies

> Or flees on the flood of foaming fleece
> Rich with pearls of piercing showers
> That rips and peels its airy skin
> But fill with resurrecting manna ("The Cloud", 38)

The Cloud with its aerial thunderous roar and cosmic brightness soothes the world with its magnificent rain and pleases everyone with its colourful rainbow. But the poet does not like the crooked nature of the cloud because it deceives innocent farmers who wait for days together and look always at the sky for its arrival for their survival. The cloud complains against the parched furrowed fields and threatens the starved animals without giving away the needed drops of water:

> With its aerial thunderous roar
> And blinding cosmic brilliance
> And soothes the world with its magic arch;
> It deludes the humble peasant
> Whose eyes are glued to the stars for survival?
> And whines at the parched furrowed field
> And frightens the famished cattle ("The Cloud", 38)

Dr. Reddy in this wonderful poem *The Cloud* appears at once as a romantic and realist and this poem compels comparison with Shelley's popular poem 'The Cloud' which is purely a romantic poem. In this poem Dr. Reddy criticizes the behaviour of the cloud that it has no sympathy or pity for the people who fight at the taps for water with their vessels. It is described as a grey chameleon that moves slowly at the meridian hour. It changes its shape very often and appears in different shapes like an elephant, a lion, a serpent, a lying leader, a beheaded hero or a ghost, the map of a country or a continent without being of any use to the people:

> Has no sympathy or pith of pit
> For throws of vessels near the tap
> That clink, clank and clash
> At the hungry roasting meridian hour;
> It moves like a grey chameleon
> Incarnating many a livid and living role
> An elephant, a lion, a serpent
> A lying leader, a beheaded hero or a ghost
> Or the map of a country or a continent ("The Cloud", 38)

The poet at last shows some sympathy for the cloud and expresses his support to it and consider it as our friend amid many differences. The cloud is considered as a friendly messenger from the kingdom of the sky that dispels gloom and depression from our minds with its soothing showers of life-giving rain. It can be treated as the surging spring of life and all the animate world depends for its existence on the cloud:

> Amid the sea of apathy it is our friend
> A friendly messenger of the airy realm
> Sailing over hills to distant shores
> Conveying tender thoughts of weal and owe
> To the members of melancholy heart;
> With the capricious clouded grace it rains
> And dispels the clouds of ills and pains;
> On earth it is the surging spring of life,

> On it depends existence or extinction of life ("The Cloud", 38)

Another poem "The River" is about the river that is sometimes considered as a friend and sometimes as a foe. The poem is expressed in first person narration and it describes about itself in every line of the poem. The river has been flowing on the earth from the time immemorial. It considers the nature as its true, noble and bosom friend. It considers that service to mankind is its only duty on the earth:

> I am as old as the lofty ageless nature
> She is my only friend of noble stature
> Service to mankind is my only duty
> Which for ages enshrines divine beauty. ("The River", 39)

The poem can be treated as 'a song of the river' which flows from the top of the hill and rush through the bush and briar with great skill. On its way it fills every pit and pond to the level of its brim with its sweet and fertile water. The poet has used his creative talent in using rhyming words and in well maintaining rhythm in describing the running flow of the water in the river. The rhyming words in pairs like hill-skill, fill-still, tracks-cracks, hurry-bury, valley-sally are perfectly used by Reddy. The alliteration is used with extraordinary power by the poet in the lines like 'I swiftly tumble into turning tracks' and in this respect he comes closer to Tennyson:

> I hop down from the top of the hill
> And rush through bush and briar with skill
> Pit and pond to the brim I fill
> Water on my bosom is sweet and still.
> I chatter and ramble through pebbles
> I swiftly tumble into turning tracks
> Rumble and leap into rocky cracks ("The River", 39)

The river and its water give life to many living beings, but sometimes take away life from them. It gives charming sight to the people but when it is enraged, it swallows many villages and fields and thus it wants to teach a lesson to humanity. People of all ages, all castes, all ranks and all trades enjoy the company of the river. They include lovers and poets, whose minds are filled with creative powers with the presence of the river.

> When enraged many a village I swallow
> Submerging fields pregnant or fallow
> When people grow vile and vicious
> Through floods I teach a lesson specious.
> Joyous lovers wanted on my sandy banks
> Rest on grassy beds men of all ranks
> Poets muse on my lap in solitary hours
> I fill their minds with creative powers ("The River", 39)

The river wanted to move freely on the earth meeting rocks and pebbles, plants and trees, birds and animals, hills and plains, pit and pond, tracks and cracks, town and village, grassy beds and sandy rocks, farms and fields. But its blissful journey was forcibly stopped by crooked human beings by building wide and wild dams. The poet expresses empathetically the feelings of the river that science has grown, but on the contrary the river as well as nature has to groan:

> Science has grown and grown and grown
> I have to groan and groan and groan

> My full freedom has been curtailed
> By tying my legs with dams wide and wild ("The River", 39)

The Rainbow is an outstanding example of the description of nature by T.V. Reddy. It is described as mystic and appears in the sky as a sign of joy and peace after the dreaded dance of storm. Everyone considers that it is their own, but it is out of everybody's reach. It is as beautiful as the bright bangles of the bride and bewitching as the beautiful garland of haunting hues. The description reminds us of Sarojini Naidu's poem "Bangle Sellers"; let us feel the beauty of Reddy's lines:

> The mystic rainbow dawns in the sky
> the sober soothing sign of pallid calm
> after the densely dreaded dance of storm,
> the thrilling celestial arch so nigh and high;
> .... the enchanting colours of the aerial pride
> vie with the bright bangles of the bride.
> The gorgeous garland of haunting hues
> Shining with prismatic virtues of dews ("The Rainbow", 41)

"On the Sacred Hills" is another wonderful poem depicting the nature in which the poet advises the readers to take rest on the lap of nature without having any kind of fear, tear and care. The poet strongly believes that the nature and its music soothes the troubled mind, contributes to the inner harmony of human beings and reduces the negative effect of tensions, troubles and tribulations:

> In the sacred shrine on the hills
> Abound by the shrill sounds of the rills
> Whose music moulds the inner harmony
> Beneath the canopy of trees and flowers
> You rest on the lap of nature's beauty
> Oblivious of our fears, tears and cares ("On the Sacred Hills", 43)

T. V. Reddy's poetry operates at a higher level and succeeds in giving the real feel of the beauty of nature. Every line of his poetry is embedded in nature and reverberates with its natural intonation. His language is extraordinary with all its natural rhyme and rhythm. It acts like a catalyst for ideas that provide a serene atmosphere in the minds of the readers. He has empathy and sympathy, compassion and consideration towards nature which spreads across his poetry as an integral ingredient. He is a successful poet in arousing the curiosity of the readers towards the pastoral life of India in presenting which his expression as well as the right usage of proper words is highly commendable. In the presentation of the pastoral life as well as nature there is hardly any poet in Indian English who can be compared to T.V. Reddy.

Works Cited

Eliot, T.S. *Haydn and the Valve Trumpet*. Ed. Craig Raine. U.K: Pan Macmillan, 1990. Print.
Reddy, T.V. *Melting Melodies*. Madras: Poets Press India, 1994. Print.

11 Poet as Man Speaking to Men: An Appreciation of T. V. Reddy's *Melting Melodies*

S. Karthik Kumar

"Poetry" has been defined in many ways by many poets and critics. While Wordsworth calls it a "spontaneous overflow of powerful feelings," Arnold describes it as a "criticism of life." In the opinion of Coleridge "The poet, described in ideal perfection, brings the whole soul of man into activity." According to Frost, "writing a poem is discovery." Shelley claims that "poets are the unacknowledged legislators of the world." A poet is "a man is speaking to men" according to Wordsworth. There may be many more definitions of poet and poetry.

Whatever may be the definition of poetry or the emphasis on the function of the "poet", the undeniable and the inextricable implication that lies at the bottom of the word is that the poet is one among the people whom he represents. He is, in other words, the spokesperson "of the people, for the people and by the people." He is noticeable or recognized because, he sees the unseen, notices the unnoticed, and observes what is ignored by others. Thus, the poet brings out the unfamiliar from the familiar. T. V. Reddy is essentially a poet of the people. To use the words of Wordsworth, he is essentially a "man speaking to man." His poetic sensibility is so keen that anything he comes across in everyday life becomes a source of his poetry. The ordinary becomes extraordinary in his hand. Even the most familiar sight or a most common incident is magically transformed into poetry by him. He is endowed with such a poetic deftness that never makes the reader feel estranged from him. Rather he takes the reader along with him to the heights to which he soars.

Melting Melodies is a poetic collection of T. V. Reddy which was published in 1994. The poems are so varied in subject matter and tone. But what runs through all the poems in common is his unconditional love for interest in life and things around him. Brevity is the soul of his poetic genius. As a seasoned poet, he is able to suggest a lot with a few apt words and phrases. Words often take unusual combinations in his poetry that infallibly arrest the attention of the reader.

"Kalyani Dam" is the opening poem of the anthology *Melting Melodies*. The poem creates with simple words a vivid and lasting picture of the waters arrested the dam. The poem "Dharmasala" makes one feel the "peace and bliss" of the place described in the poem. The poet is able to transmit to his reader the feeling he gained during his visit to the holy place. As one reads the poem, his/her fatigue and fretful feelings become alien and flee to the peevish plains of ordinary mundane life. As we read the poem, we are taken to the height of life's philosophy that we tend to leave the petty thoughts. The mountaineers who are said to trek through the mountains feel wearied and take rest while scaling the heights. But the reader of the poem who is made to climb the huge mountain of life never feels tired because of the helping hand extended by the poet. The poem symbolically suggests that peace and bliss are heavenly feelings that one can get only when he rises above the everyday affairs of life. The poet captures the bliss of the place in the following lines:

> The place is quiet, leaves are still
> even frogs seem to be in meditation (*Melting Melodies*, 2)

The poet sees Godliness in every inch of the place as the spot is known for unpolluted beauty of nature. The serene atmosphere makes one feel the sublime within and makes him march to "the celestial summit and goal eternal."

Another interesting poem in the anthology is "The Fort" which is actually about the historical site Chandragiri Fort near Tirupati, Andhra Pradesh. The poem opens with a paradox:

> It stands defenseless (*MM*, 4)

It is the fort that defends the people inside, but the fort itself is said to stand defenseless. Thus the poet creates the condition of abandonment and destitution in which the fort remains. Further he elaborates the image he has created in the first line of the poem. He says

> Bare and bruised and deserted
> A skeleton of a maimed and mangled soldier (*MM*, 4)

The poem is replete with words and phrases associated with soldiers and battles and thus it creates a perfect picture of the bygone days of monarchical rule. "The Fort" reminds one of the poems by Derek Walcott "Ruins of a Great House," in which the ruined house reminds the poet of his ancestral past which was ruined by the colonization of Europe. "The Fort" is also a poem that reminds one of the historical past of India when it was ruled by kings.

Another poem that evokes the memory of the past is "The Taj." The poet sings of the four towers that stand majestically as the four sentinels "spreading lunar light on lunatic love." The beauty of the Taj is not just its architecture; rather it lies in the love that led to its birth. The poet sings: "you enshrine the boundless love in your solid stones." The poem ends with a beautiful note of admiration of both the Taj and love behind it:

> a marvel chiseled in marble
> whose every stone echoes the epic of love (*MM*, 6)

"The Toiling Woman" is a simple poem about a familiar sight of a woman labourer breaking rocks. The poem clearly brings out the resoluteness of the toiling woman. Though she is thin and weak, her heart is as resolute as a teak. The poet finds the hammer in her bone.

> She quells the defiant stone
> With the hammer in her bone (*MM*, 7)

It is not enough that one is equipped with the instrument unless he or she has the courage or determination within to accomplish the task. Even the instruments are helpless. So it is not the hammer that breaks the stone but it is the resolute heart of the woman that wants to ensure a safe and comfortable life for the child at home. The poet finds an occasion to expose the social inequalities. He says:

> she lifts stones and bricks
> with eyes full of wicks
> builds for other mansions and forts
> to roll in foaming comforts (*MM*, 7)

It is the toil of a woman laborer that paves way for the comfort of many others. She is made to toil for other's comforts. She sweats for the construction of a mansion but her lot permits her to live only in a hut:

> all her sweat ensures her a hut

> while her toil enthrones the lust (*MM*,7)

T. V. Reddy's social criticism continues in "The Tiller." The poem begins with a question:

> Is there a scarcely a heart
> that sighs for your sweat
> and feels for your toil? (*MM*, 8)

The poet glorifies the nobility of the tiller's profession in the following lines:

> You reap the crop
> Heap the harvest
> And feed the millions in cities
> In a. c. rooms in skyscrapers (*MM*, 8)

The poet's heart goes out for the poor destiny of the tiller when he sings, "Your roots are firm in an uprooted land." The paradox in the above line portrays the pathetic condition of the farmer in India. It is the farmer who feeds the entire society. But he dies of starvation unable to feed himself. Thus his "roots are firm in an uprooted land." It is an eternal truth that unless the farmers in the society are happy, the rest in the society cannot be happy. The ancient Tamil poet Sage Thiruvalluvar says that "the world revolves around not the sun but the farmer" and "the farmers are the linch-pin of the world". But unfortunately in today's world, the farmer is crushed under the giant wheels of industrialization and globalization. His prospects are very dim and that is why the poem ends with a pessimistic note:

> your cankered heart
> breeds dreams dry and hot
> that bridge the soil and the sky (*MM*, 8)

The poet lashes his whip against the social evil of corruption in "Thirst." The poem is about the social inequalities. While a small section of the society enjoys the maximum wealth of the country, the vast majority of the people remain in eternal poverty. The title of the poem is symbolic. It means more than one thirst: thirst for power, thirst for money, thirst for sex, etc. While the poor people are unable to get even a pot of muddy water to quench their thirst, the poets says, the corrupt politicians are not satisfied with even barrels of liquor.

> thirst has parched the tongue
> transformed the throat
> into a radiating desert
> skeletons pace the mirage
> for a pot of muddy water
> and fade away into shadows
> while
> barrels of liquor
> fail to quench the thirst
> of our pot-bellied leaders (*MM*,9)

The tone of indignation continues in "Chariot of Jagannath." The corrupt leader is satirized in the following lines:

> At last I faced in awe and owe
> the defaced face of the elected leader
> whose capacious stomach
> another sub-continent

had grown fat with rice and lies
his balloon mouth showered
smiles and miles of promises; (*MM*,10)

"Defaced face", "capacious stomach", "balloon mouth" and "miles of promises" are unique phrases that appear in the poem to drive home the ideas of corruption and hypocrisy associated with politics and politicians. In another poem entitled "Our Leader" the criticism of the political leader becomes harsher.

before he got elected
he was everything else
except a nationalist (*MM*, 10)

He comes down upon the practices of the leader:

as his health, a curse to the land,
grew by arithmetic progression
his wealth vying with his vices
swelled by geometric progression:
....
his ideal has been to bury
the nation's ideals
which he gave up ages ago
....
makes promises only to break (*MM*, 11)

The poem "Bird Hunter" is apparently about a hunter of birds in the forest. But the poem contains subtle criticism of the greedy leaders. The hunter hunts, the poet describes, only to feed and support his children. But he has to be contrasted with the "hunters of money and power" in the society. The poet says:

he kills only to save his kin
while his superiors and leaders
relish slaughtering values
on the infernal altar of greed (*MM*, 13)

The poet has not spared the other social evils too. For example in "University Units," he criticizes how educational institutions, especially the universities, have ceased to be centers of learning and how the scholars in the university departments treat their students with indifference. The duty of a scholarly teacher is to share his scholarship with his posterity -- the students. True scholarship makes one humble and simple: But the present day university scholars are notorious for their indifference. This is condemned by the poet. The poem is in the first person point of view and the persona in the poem is an aspiring research scholar:

Poor I uneasily went and went
round the so-called learned and stout
like a satellite around a planet
till my shoes wore out
for the so-called guidance (*MM*, 23)

The poem continues:

they always seemed to be busy and ideal
but indulged in gossip idle

> killing the radiant self-respect
> on the altar of dubious quest
> to gratify the ego of the eccentrics
> that delight in practicing tricks (*MM*, 23)

The indifferent nature of the so-called "university wits" is brought out vividly in following lines where the poet describes the atmosphere of their cubicles:

> the room was as cold as corpse
> full of volumes, bound and buried:
> his eyes winked through the spectacles
> but feigned to go through lines-
> live electric wires to such lives   (*MM*, 23)

In the same vein the poet comes down upon the interviews where the unqualified is preferred to the qualified one. The poem entitled "An Interview" exposes how fair selection is not done in the interviews for employment and promotion. In the poem, the poet becomes a mouthpiece of the innumerable people who have experienced the unfortunate rejection in the interview despite their qualifications; when describing the interview hall, the poet describes:

> where hours burnt like camphor
> on the Royal altar of Alma Mater
> emitting pungent fumes of sulphur (*MM*,25)

The poet gives expression to the feelings that many have in their mind:

> creative work was never a credit
> while the garrulous tongue the only merit
> show and shallowness filled the grace
> while true values fled in disgrace:
> as a rule the wise were overthrown
> while the wiseacre adored the throne (*MM*,26)

The frustration finds the finest expression in the following lines:

> on crows and cranes the mantle fell
> while the swans flew from the hell (*MM*,26)

The poet's critical scanner has not failed to note the increasing materialistic tendency of the modern world. The poet as a true humanist -- a man speaking to men -- laments the fact that money decides everything in the world. He calls money a "thing." In the poem entitled "That Thing Money," the poet describes the role of money in the modern world in a critical vein:

> without that thing money
> you are nothing in this sphere,
> ....
> it is how much you have it
> that matters most
> the end winks at the means(*MM*,33)

In "On the Sacred Hills," the poet comes down upon the materialistic practices of the modern days. Even in places which are said to be holy, materialistic tendencies play a dominant role. Without referring to any particular place of worship, the poet expresses his displeasure for the commercial activities taking place in the name of devotion or bhakti:

Poet as Man Speaking to Men

> I climb, strive and crave for thy grace
> in this life's tedious aching race
> to shield me from sly and vile disgrace
> till my certain grave I embrace;
> While we struggle for rags and remnants
> you roll in gold and gloat in diamonds
> and sit in solitude on the heights of wealth
> and pamper the vultures and black marketeers
> who bribe you with bundles got in stealth
> to transform their dark devilish deeds; (*MM*,43)

Poetry celebrating the finer aspects of life are not absent in the volume. There are fine poems on love replete with graceful flashes of poetic expression. For example in "Two Plus Two is Two," the poet celebrates true love. The exchange of emotions between the lovers is beautifully expressed in the following lines.

> our eyes meet -
> a mute discourse,
> Two plus two is two (*MM*, 21)

In "A Pair of Sparrows," the poet describes the romance of a pair of sparrows:

> on the green and shady bough
> two twittering sparrows steeped in love
> vied with each in showering its essence
> their beaks become one at its peak (*MM*,22)

In "Vernal Love," the poet as a typical romantic poet indulges in the description of this beautiful lady love. He asks her:

> Shall I find my life's bliss
> in the transporting kiss
> of your bushing cheeks
> whose crimson colour
> shames the petals of hibiscus (*MM*,31)

A poet is also a philosopher for he looks at the world through his soul. He is not merely concerned with the immediate and the present; on the other hand he is visionary and universal. T.V. Reddy's philosophical mind is revealed in several instances. In a poem entitled "A Bubble," he is totally philosophical. He conducts a philosophical inquiry into the transient nature of life. He asks:

> who is to whom in this world?
> all the familial bonds
> familial ties and chains
> dilute and disappear (*MM*,34)

The poet reminds one of the immortal lines of Thomas Gray who says: "The paths of glory lead but to the grave." Everything in and about life is temporary and we all wait for the "inevitable hour." Without realizing this fact, people make a lot of fuss during their lives. The poet refers to it in the following lines:

> in this interim period
> in the fog we croak like frogs

> we are swayed by the tides
> of love and hate, warmth and sloth
> and drowned by tidal waves of lust (*MM*, 34)

The collection of poems *Melting Melodies* is a significant contribution to the corpus of Indian English Poetry. It contains poetry that deals with varied aspects of life ranging from love to politics. To go through the poems in the volume is to take a close look at the society in which live. The poems are simple and straightforward. With unadorned images, T. V. Reddy creates a poetic world which is worth visiting for everyone.

Abbreviation: M.M: Melting Melodies

Works Cited

Arnold, Matthew. "The Study of Poetry", *English Critical Texts*. Ed. D.J.Enright & Ernst De Chickera, London, OUP, 1962, 261.Print.

Coleridge, S.T. "*Biographia Literaria*, Chapter xiv", *English Critical Texts*. Ed. D.J.Enright & Ernst De Chickera, London, OUP, 1962.196.

Reddy, T.V. *Melting Melodies*. Madras: Poets Press India, 1994. Print.

Shelley, P.B. "A Defence of Poetry", *English Critical Texts*. Ed. D.J.Enright & Ernst De Chickera, London, OUP, 1962, 255.

Thiruvalluvar. *Thirukkural*. https://www.goodreads.com/.../9862398-holy-kural---thirukkural-in-tamil-with-englis./

Wordswth, William. *Preface to Lyrical Ballads*. *English Critical Texts*. Ed. D.J.Enright & Ernst De Chickera, London, OUP, 1962. 165. Print.

12   T.V. Reddy: A Study of his Poem "Life is a Desert"

DC Chambial

A poet loses himself in the flux of his imagination mingled with his thought when he voyages through the unfathomed sea of his imagination in a bid to create something new. He experiences the pangs of this creative flux and gives to the world something hitherto unknown. Society exists and thrives on human relations and emotions. Emotions of love, sympathy and empathy bring the individuals together for harmonious living and those of hatred, envy, ennui, and jealousy distance individuals. Money comes at the root of all these. Those who are rich and have plenty of money attract more and more persons towards them, but those who are poor and find it hard to make both ends meet have no friends or relations. People are drawn towards the rich and always remain in their company, but when money or wealth is gone, the same persons turn their backs towards him/her and desert.

This is the way of the world. In this paper, I endeavor to make an in-depth textual study of Reddy's poem "Life is a Desert", the sixth poem of his first book, *When Grief Rains*. In this poem the poet also shows unto humanity how poor people are despised and forsaken even by their close relatives.

This book was published in 1982 as first book of his poems. While going through his poetry, I was struck by the thoughts contained in this poem; by then, he was about thirty-nine years old. Life seems to have taught him so many lessons coupled with his struggle to express and establish himself in his academic as well as social life. The bitter pinches, he had borne in his life till that date, make him look at life in despair and calls life as "a desert". Let us study it, word by word and line by line to reach at the core of his thought that makes him pensive.

The poem has 18 lines, which, on the basis of punctuation, can easily be broken up into four quatrains and one concluding couplet. The first quatrain introduces him to the readers about his whereabouts:

> I stand in the desert,
> A marooned man
> Amid a world of Kith and Kin,
> All wary, chary and worldly wise (*When Grief Rains*, 14)

The very first line makes it clear for the reader that the protagonist is alone in a desert. There is none to accompany him and he feels lonely. He considers himself "A marooned man". As the key word of the firs line is "desert", a noun, which itself hints at the isolation of the protagonist as he has none to look toward who could lend him a helping hand; the key word of the second line is "marooned", an adjective, which reveals him as cut off or left behind. The verb, "maroon" means to leave someone stranded or isolated with little hope of rescue; and also to leave someone stranded on a desert island without resources of sustenance. The reader wants to know about the "desert" where he is left alone and who are the people who have left him "marooned". He does not leave the reader to conjecture for himself, but the protagonist of the poem comes to his help in the third and fourth lines. His desert lies "Amid a world of Kith and Kin". The phrase "Kith and Kin" needs our attention in this line. It reveals that he is not deserted on any piece of a resourceless land but very much in the midst of close relatives. The capital "K" of "Kith and Kin" suggests the close relations. They are close only to say and for the world to see, but their behavior towards the protagonist is completely alienated and they do not look at him as one among them, but as a stranger. These relatives are "All wary, chary and worldly wise." In this line, the words "wary", "chary", and "worldly wise" demand readers' and critics' attention. These are adjectives and reveal the qualities of his "Kith and Kin". The first word, "wary", suggests keen caution and watchful prudence; hence, his relations are very cautious in not helping him. The second word, "chary", again hints at their cautious behavior that has become their attribute towards the protagonist. The third, "worldly-wise", means experienced in and wise to the ways of the world or sophisticated: they know that the protagonist is of no use for them. Therefore, they do not want to help the protagonist; for them, he is a worthless fellow and they do not want to waste their time and money on him. They seem to have turned emotionless or apathetic towards him. Under such environs of society, especially his relatives, who are supposed to help their relations in distress, the protagonist feels doomed and helpless in his present position that is no less than of a man left alone in a desolate desert without any source of sustenance.

> The second quatrain reveals:
> The dear are becoming dearer,
> The nearer much averse to come near
> The deadly ulcer of penury consumes
> My fleshy body progressively (*When Grief Rains*, 14)

In this stanza the protagonist tells about the effect of poverty in life. Here, he relies on the phrase "nears and dears" which suggests close relations. In human society, people most often bank upon their close relations and feel proud of them. However, in these lines the behavior of such relations is opposed to the very meaning of the phrase. The protagonist tells about his close relations: "The dear are becoming dearer". The poet/protagonist plays on pun here. The word, "dearer", is not the comparative of the adjective "dear" which means loved one, or in a close or intimate contact or having strong feelings of love or affection, but it means having high value or beyond his/one's reach. They don't let him come close to them. Though, in normal behavior pattern, dear is one with whom the other stays in close contact: often remains together. But, here they do not permit the protagonist to come near them or to be in their proximity. Thus, they have become "dearer" for him. The second line of this stanza: "The nearer much averse to come near", again emphasizes what the poet/protagonist has already said in the first line: they, in other words detest the protagonist. The reason for this becomes clear in the third line: "The deadly ulcer of penury consumes / My fleshy body progressively." The key word, in these two lines, is "penury". It means a state of pennilessness. A condition when a person has no money even to meet the bare minimums of his living: food, clothes and shelter. It is a condition of utter wretchedness. The poet/protagonist terms his poverty as an "ulcer", a disease of suppuration that leads to localized death of the living cells. He compares his misery to this disease: as this disease kills living cells, similarly, his poverty is killing his body and he finds it very, very hard to survive. Thus, his impoverishment is the sole cause behind the aversion of his nears and dears towards him and leaves him high and dry in a proverbial desert. This leads to the third stanza.

In this stanza or quatrain, he affirms:

> How long shall I resist the jealousy?
> Envy and ennui of the society?
> Leeches have sucked my blood
> And asses kick me with hind-legs (*When Grief Rains*, 14)

This stanza is about the protagonist's abject helplessness. His poverty has not only estranged him from his "Kith and Kin" and "nears and dears", but has also made him the object of social "jealousy, envy and ennui"—the butt of social ridicule due to social distrust, spite and tedium—that he can't withstand any more. He asks himself: "How long shall I resist the jealousy / Envy and ennui of the society?" He, with the help of two images of leeches and asses, expresses his present situation. He has grown very weak because "Leeches have sucked my [his] blood". When there is no blood left in the body, the person is at the verge of imminent death. His condition is no better than this. At the same time, his drudgery is increased because "asses kick me [him] with hind-legs." There is no end to his troubles: he is literally bombarded with misfortunes. He is already weak and at the top of it "asses kick" him. The poet has used two words from the domain of animal kingdom, "Leeches" and "asses" that emphatically portray his wretchedness and problems resulting from his destitution. "Leeches" and "asses" stand, here, for his relatives in the society who are single-mindedly bent upon decimating him. So, how can poet/protagonist hope for any balm in life in such a society? All this makes him abjectly hopeless, as becomes apparent in the fourth stanza.

In this quatrain, the poet/protagonist says:

> Even mules mock at my sore feet.
> I am a lone man in the barren land.
> Dissembling mirage tantalizes me,
> A thirsty man with a parched tongue (14)

In the first line of this quatrain, the protagonist tells the readers that his condition is so miserable that even mules, the beasts of burden, who are supposed to be without any intelligence, laugh at his hardships—"sore feet". Here these animals consider themselves fortunate than the protagonist for, their feet do not bleed. Under the present situation, he has become the butt of social derision. Therefore, he avers: "I am a lone man in the barren land"—this line, again, closely knits the quatrain with the previous ones: he is "lone" and in the "barren land", which reminds the readers that he, all alone stands in the desert (1st line). Once again the poet heightens the situation by narrating his solitude and that too in a "barren land", a desert.

Well off people, his relatives—"Kith and Kin" and "near and dear"—in the society serve as a mirage to him. Now his imagination rambles to the domain of physics and picks up the word "mirage". The phenomenon of mirage is also associated with desert: in desert areas, due to high temperatures, the layers of air touching the ground get heated up and become thinner; while the upper layers of air remain thicker as compared to the lower airs. Due to difference in the density of the two layers, a ray of light travelling from one layer to the other gets deviated, and as a result of this phenomenon, a solitary traveller in desert sees the inverted images of date palms or other trees as if they are on the bank of a lake or any other source of water. The man, who sees it, thinks that he is near the source of water and he starts moving towards it to quench his thirst. The farther he goes, the farther moves the image of this delusion. He tires himself in this pursuit but never comes close to any source of water. In fact, it is an optical illusion in which atmospheric refraction by a layer of hot air distorts or inverts reflections of distant objects and the poor man falls prey to it. As the illusion remains an illusion and never becomes a reality, similarly, the protagonist's imagination of getting respite from the rich in the society or his relatives also never matures and his hours change into days, days into months, so on and so forth. The word "tantalize" has been very aptly chosen to depict his present desperation. This word, "tantalize", as a verb collocates with words tease, incite, excite, tempt, torture, and torment. So in his present situation, he experiences all these and feels overwhelmingly tormented in his mind. There is no hope of any redemption for him, so he comes to the factual realization in the concluding couplet:

> Life is an elusive endless desert,
> Full of sands and storms, no oases (14)

Like an adept advocate, the poet puts his arguments logically and builds up his argument about his conception of life as "an elusive endless desert". He has used two adjectives, "elusive" and "endless" and one noun, "desert" to illustrate his hypothesis of life. A life of penury is never-ending torment and, at the same time, vague and obscure, one can never hope to rise above it. Besides, it is "Full of sands and storms"—there is nothing amenable to make life enjoyable. The last two words "no oases" conclude the poem. In desert oasis is a place that has greenery due to vegetation and vegetation results from the availability of water. However, the life of a poor man is very much like the one left all alone in a desert; it is only miserable and one can only hope but no actualization of that hope ever takes place.

In this poem the poet has very skillfully put forth his arguments to prove his hypothesis like a scientist. All lines in each quatrain and the concluding couplet emerge from the previous one/s and are not only logical but also organic in structure. The poet, though, has used iambic pentameter but does not delve on rhymes. He has very successfully employed alliteration (assonance and consonance), for example look only at the concluding couplet for sample, in his, almost, all lines and that makes the poem a sweet lyric singing the tale of a troubled heart left lonely in the destitute desert and successfully proves that no one helps a poor man and his wretchedness never comes to end.

Note:
All references to this poem are from this book: page number after the title and line numbers after the verse lines.

Works Cited

Reddy, T.V. *When Grief Rains*. New Delhi: Samkaleen Prakashan, 1982. Print.

13   A Critical Study of T.V. Reddy's *Thousand Haiku Pearls*

G. Srilatha

T.V Reddy has contributed immensely to Indian Writings in English through his poetry and criticism. His recent collection *Thousand Haiku Pearls* published in 2016 is written in the form of Haiku verse. The poet focuses on the varied aspects of modern life with special reference to education, politics, and society. The poet criticizes the present social condition as chaotic due to never ending crime rates. To mention, the city which was once upon a time called as pink city now has turned to be violent and chaotic. The poet laments on the past glory of the city and the need to revive new life.

The poet draws our attention towards the younger generation who are not only young in body and mind but also energetic and highly spirited. They should be given the right education and right direction for life. By educating the younger generation our future would be peaceful and harmonious. But the present education system is deteriorating. Education has become a business. The entire system should be considered for reform. Unless the younger generations are educated in the right manner we cannot have a better society. The existing system is in the form of an industry with more number of corporate colleges growing everywhere. The focus of education has shifted from holistic education to materialistic life:

> Corporate colleges in fact
> Are big fleecing mills with hard tact
> Soulless minting magnates (*Thousand Haiku Pearls*, 10)

The poet illustrates the plight of the modern man. The poet draws parallel reference to the seasonal changes in nature and the struggles of human life. Each and every season has significant feature that reflects hope for life. Spring season is a season of hope and spreads fragrance symbolizing life. Similarly, the aura and the beauty of summer season are narrated in an eloquent manner by the poet. Summer restricts birds to fly and men also restrict themselves to the indoors. The hottest season spreads its burning feet everywhere. Yet, the full blown flowers leave a beautiful sight for the people. The summer night too is beautiful as the moon rises from the sea bath. The music that comes through the summer night adds more solace to the heart.

The poet criticizes the existing political scenario is the society. The politicians are neither bothered about the safety of the people nor the plight of the farmer's. They are blind and deaf to the cries of the farmers. The village or the city which was peaceful has turned to be a centre for political games and crimes. Except during elections the politicians hardly appear before the people. Election time is the time when money and liquor flow like flood to lure the voters. The victory of the winning party on false notions is the norm of the day. The plight of the politicians is succinctly presented by the poet:

> We want your ballots
> You are sure to get bullets

> From our bullet-proof cars
>
> To ensure their political power
> They stoop to touch your bleeding feet
> And all false promises shower.
>
> He gave a loud talk against dowry
> The place resounded with full applause,
> He got ten million, his son's dowry. (*THP* 20)

The poet laments at the games played by the politicians. To thrive in politics, politicians please the common man by supplying free gas and gifts. The poet focuses on the physicians also. Doctors who are supposed to save the people are in fact educated by spending a lot of money. Therefore, their stethoscope is the only source of economic growth; hence they turn to love "ill-gotten wealth." They are not seeing the society in the right way. The schools are spreading like mushrooms and the entire system of education is a faded one with low-paid teachers and spoon-fed creatures. The children who are educated in this system later become engineers and construct tall buildings only to collapse in no time. The poet ponders on the art of life:

> The greatest art
> On this vast museum of earth
> Is the art of life.
>
> The brightest light
> Under the light-giving sun
> Is the light of the eyes.
>
> The happiest thought
> Is the simple artless thought
> Of being pure and clean   (23)

Over the years human being has shown advancement and proved his talent in every march. Ironically, the advancement is a vague one. The society is corrupt. Politics depends on the donations and the fate of political leaders. The streets are not safe due to rape and robbery. Pubs and liquor-lovers are growing more in number. All saints day which should be bright ironically is bright with rape and murder.

Urbanization has left India to lose the beauty and glory of agriculture. The harvest festival that has been celebrated from times immemorial loses its sheen. During the harvest festival the flowers in various colors add beauty and glory to the nature. Butterflies suck honey from the flowers and there is music all around. Such a beauty is curtailed and is not visible because the buildings are growing tall like skyscrapers. Summer heat is an unbearable one but the peasants toil in the noon for cultivation. Mid day summer with scorching rays kills the sparrows. Many birds die due to the heat and fall like dry leaves:

> Mid-summer
> Roads and heads radiate heat
> Wings fail to beat   (12)

The hot sun may also kill the sparrows and in the scorching summer they may fall like the falling leaves.

But with the arrival of the Autumn season situation changes and in some parts of the world leaves change their colours and the entire land with trees and plants presents an enchanting sight with glorious colours. The poet captures the beauty of the autumn which is described in varied ways:

>Fall leaves
>appear unusually brighter
>The old think better (28)

>Autumn arrives
>Leaves decay to spring again
>With life, a fresh gain (34)

The poet refers to autumn season to mention how the falling leaves fall like dead arrows. Autumn season is a season that changes the color of the leaves. The poet views autumn as a season of hope, maturity and ripeness. The season bears a huge load of fruits. The beauty of the autumn season is enriching as roses blossom and it brings fresh life. Nature is beautiful, plenty and abundant. The poet enjoys the nature, especially the spring season when bees gather and birds flutter. Nature is plenty; bees suck the honey from the sweet essence of flowers. The parrots perch on boughs that add to beauty.

Ugadi festival marks the beginning of the Telugu New Year. The festival is celebrated with a mixture of neem, mango, and jiggery, a mixed taste indicating life as a mixture of joy, miseries and bitterness. Other festivals too follow with rituals. On the Diwali day sacred hymns are sung and on the sacred Sivaratri the whole night echoes with prayers for the God. Festival season delights each and every one:

>Spring showers---
>Sunny fields full of flowers;
>Leaves dance in joy.

>Morning breeze
>Old man walks on the beach,
>Gets a fresh lease (44)

The poet criticizes the degrading trend of awards given to worthless books. According to him, today writers who write trash get prizes. He says one need not have a stylish haircut or go to a beauty parlor to get fame because mass image has become an art. Similarly, if a writer writes ill about his land then he or she is sure to get a Booker or looker prize. Such an award winning book would be full of trash and lies. Even if a poet writes ill of God then he is sure to get Commonwealth award.

The poet laments the system of education and the changing trend of the teachers. According to him once upon a time teachers were dedicated and they were thinking of the student's progress but now they are worried about the scales and arrears. Thus materialistic pleasures have occupied the topmost position in every field. Earlier teachers used to refer to reference books; now they spend time in lazy looks. Time is a never ending factor; so days and months pass on and age advances leaving us with neither progress nor any achievements. Towards the end of our life if we look at the past, it appears as though the entire life has been wasted.

Summer heat leaves urban life at a halt where withering leaves are seen. The bore-well too fails and not a drop of water is to be found. The summer heat leads to the collapse of birds. With the coming of the autumn season the trees tend to become naked and we can find enlarged mushrooms. The beauty of all seasons is illustrated by the poet. The autumn season is beautiful at night with the moon and the moonlight falling on jasmine flowers. The beauty of the night in the words of the poet goes as -

> Dark damsel of night
> Dances in trance in star-studded blue sari
> Wrought with golden lace bright.
>
> With lightning in the eyes
> Spewing thunders from the mouth
> Stormy night shines.
>
> Pregnant night
> Bearing the weight of the universe
> Delivers sunlight   (51)

The morning sun rise is a symbol of life. The boy who delivers the newspaper is of a tender age when the boy is supposed to play, but poverty draws him to work. The poet is philosophical in stating that our life is short and brittle like an earthen pot. Man should live life thoroughly. Therefore we should live to the fullest. He compares human life to a candle that is exposed to the wind. Our mind is never calm; it oscillates between ebb and flow and loses balance like a leaf in the wind. Chaos rules the mind due to the imbalance. Therefore, control of the mind is the need of the hour. The poet ridicules the human life that

> For a morsel of food
> We withstand blows too rude -
> A cruel game   (53)
>
> To breathe liberty
> This slavish life struggles and bleeds,
> Blood flows and leads.   (54)

The poet is concerned about the community of farmers. The farmers go to the village head and the politicians to resolve their problems. But their issues are not solved; the only place for relief for these farmers is the tea shop where they enjoy the morning breeze. The Irani tea definitely refreshes the parched tongue and gives a fresh lease of life. The coffee house too is full of politicians and leaders. Many political matters are resolved at the coffee houses. Law and order too is in the hands of the lawyers who often reduce the High Court to a baseball court. What happens to justice? Does justice prevail at all? For over years India is a place for factions resulting in a pool of blood of the millions who are killed. The plight of the beggars leaves us sad as they sleep on the pavement. They depend on the leftovers thrown in the street. They along with animals fight for the leftover food. Thus the poet makes a bird's view on the varied aspects of human life in India:

> Incredible India!
> Amazing spectrum of scams and scandals -
> Ruled by mafia   (56)
> Mushrooms bloom
> After the thunderous rainy night
> Greeting day light   (57)

Life is a struggle. Calm and peace is unknown. The new age leaders are corrupt. The present age is an age of depravity where life is impure with scams in flood. Life is a network of duties constantly striving for success. All our efforts may not succeed just like the waves that may not touch the shore. When we look at the nature everything appears beautiful; the sound of the waterfall from the hill is a clear musical call, at night under the moon light the jasmines smile and the twinkling stars add beauty.

The poet views life as a goal. Everything in this universe is destined to reach the goal. The sage goes to the jungle in search of peace. The plant has a purpose of life to see the bud blossom. So, one should have a purposeful goal to reach the target and thereby make the life meaningful:

> Let us be conscious
> of the One Divine in us, the most precious,
> to spread the Kingdom of God
>
> A state forlorn
> Or intense heartache forces its way--
> A poem is born. (66)

Over the years man has progressed extensively. The urbanization has caused a great damage to the nature by the continuous process of cutting the trees. When the trees are cut the fruits are not born. Let us be grateful to the earth as we depend on the air, food and water. Rain is nature's boon that sustains life. Let us be true to our self and let us be close to nature. Let us concentrate on the good and aim higher. As life is an adventure the poet urges us to struggle. It is better to set right our home rather than going to moon and mars and waging wars.

> Simple folk don't need
> huge guns to settle their old scores;
> They are free from greed.
>
> Ignorance is Paradise,
> But we can't live in dark for long;
> Better to see sunrise.
>
> Philosopher has no fears;
> Seeing people's hungry cries and tears
> He remains a stoic. (76)

The poet makes a philosophical study and ponders over the issue of life and death. The journey of life is too long. The more we travel the longer the distance. As our journey ends in grave let us be brave. Our mind is overtaxed and preoccupied with many things. Let us be fearless and draw inspiration from nature.

Spring season is a season of hope. The new buds and showers are cheerful and delight us. Nature appears peaceful as plants and flowers bloom and smile. The spring season adds beauty and glory to life. The cool breeze and the flowers are a symbol of hope. Summer season is scorching with blazing sunlight, yet it is a source of renewal for life. Birds and cattle die as fallen leaves on the ground due to the heat. Summer season decides the future to bloom or to perish. Autumn has its glow and the falling leaves leave a message. Autumn is mellow and all trees are nature's dress. Neither flowers nor bees are found during the season. The winter dawn is beautiful with dew drops on the lawn. The sky appears beautiful with the formation of rainbow. The poet laments the generation gap between the young. They are standing on the corrupt sands and looking at the sky. Every moment is fraught with uncertainty.

> Courage is power,
> Potent medicine to cure any crisis -
> Need of the hard hour. (83)

> No shade of courage
> While there is the cloud of fear;
> Proven fact of any age
>
> Hunger leads to anger;
> To nip uprisings, banish hunger -
> Path to progress   (84)

The poet evokes eco-consciousness and appeals to protect the nature. Water is a source of life. Trees perish if water is reduced in the ground. Due to lack of ground water the wells have become dry. Lack of water leads to water wars. Nature is our mother so let us protect it. Lack of rain water makes the land a desert. The only remedy for the solution is to store water. The felling of the trees and the greed for materialistic needs should be checked. Loss of vegetation results in dry land and to human migration. Various problems add to the water scarcity and with that the agriculture gets disrupted and the dry land is multiplied. We should live in harmony with nature without causing any harm to it. We should live as the children of nature. If we tread on the right path, the seed that was sown yesterday blossoms today or tomorrow. Trees are our sages as they donate all their organs and fruits to us.

> Econometrics -
> All life here on earth is a big trade,
> Search elsewhere for shade.
>
> Here, life is a game,
> Endless search for pleasure the other name;
> Cycle repeats.   (90)

The loss of humanity is a painful task. Every year it is packed with war and fear none wins only blood gains. No land is free from violence. Human has progressed from making atom bomb to human bomb. The end result is mass grave.

> Outbreak of slaughter
> Blood is cheaper than water;
> Blood-thirsty vampires (93)
>
> On blood devils feast
> Let us not go down to the level of beast;
> Animals feel shy.   (93)

The poet views varied aspects of life. Life is like a journey and we all sail to reach the shore. The poet's approach is optimistic. He says that life is not a cave but a tunnel with light on the other end. Life is interesting and there is fun:

> Life is a voyage
> Even in storm let us sail
> Or we shall fail.
>
> Life is a tidal wave
> A roaring challenge to the brave
> Risk is the spice of life.
>
> Life is a battle
> for those who think and struggle;

> For others, a rattle (96)

The beauty of life as well as the positive approach towards life is very obvious. The flowers bloom and life is positive. The poet experiences the old age and he compares the scope of life to a missile and that life is massive like a banyan tree. The everlasting relationship is the unification of the hearts to become one. Man should know the merits of the spiritual life and lead a spiritual life. The greatness of man is the spiritual power. Only when people are educated spiritually there will be real advancement. The violence and the horror will be reduced. The need of the hour is peace. Let us not think of crime. It is peace that matters.

> I need no Paradise;
> Let us transform our home into a heaven
> And spring a surprise.
>
> Not fair to enter a deal,
> Wealth is not the be-all and end-all;
> Before sages let us kneel
>
> It won't last,
> This purchased peace burns fast;
> And melts as a candle (108)

The state of the modern life is devastating. Reddy says urban children live on instant artificial energies in the midst of stress and as such they become victims of all sorts of energies. Our travel is mostly fruitless. The world is like a trade centre. Envy and anger mislead our mind. Right values should begin at home. Youth at present are violent and it is on account of the negative influence of TV and cinema which promote the vicious play. The present modern education focuses on market values and has lost moral values:

> Studies of humanities
> Suffer unpardonable neglect, face exile;
> Morals, buried in grand style (116)

The poet focuses on justice and equality. Inequality is nature's mark. No two minds are equal. Our minds should be healthy to reap fruits. When the minds are rotten it is foolish to expect any fair fruit. We need healthy minds. Religion is the right path for all to reach the divine goal. Earthly glories go away with all the glow and glitter and man's power is only a fleeting bubble. Modern civilization centres round pleasure and enjoyment. In the present day money rules and we dance to the tunes of wealth. Castes and creeds are man-made walls and so let us demolish them and uproot the weeds. Let us fight for our natural right. Life is a struggle. To reach the goal let us go by any route; what we need is tact. The need of the hour is to straighten the curves of destiny and great is the will power.

> Dharma is eternal,
> Living beings now or later perish;
> Moral values cherish.
>
> Truths don't change
> We may drink water in a mirage;
> Fools we can't enlighten.
>
> Wedded couple
> To rest on the rock bed of love and trust;
> Truth is a must. (122)

Let us all strive for peace. War is death and mutual wreck. Better to banish pride. No use in feeling proud. Let us open our mind's gate so that noble thoughts flow. This is a cold blooded game. Life needs a balance. Let us not casually laugh and lament; it may be fair or foul. The order of the day is violence. Let us be optimistic and wait for tomorrow and let us march with peace as torch. Our goal is set; so let us travel beyond sunset and not rest.

The poet compares our brief life to autumnal leaves. We should have a vision and our life's mission should not be worldly ambition. God is supreme and is present everywhere. He is present in infinite ways and forms and shows his power. Although we have many religions the One Supreme is in all and so why should we have these fanatic faiths and castes? True knowledge is one that leads us beyond the desires. It lights inner fires. We should care for the moral code. Life is a bubble on earth. The eternal knows no death. Without the trace of the supreme power and his grace nothing exists. So let us become the tools of God to do his work.

>Aspire for lasting glow;
>For material gains don't stoop low—
>Fading bubbles
>
>Life on earth is an iron gate;
>Beyond the dark iron gate and the golden gate
>Shines the true Light of lights   (129)

The poet says that life is precious so we need to have faith in God and experience His grace. If we ignore the Lord then life turns to be a useless page. Confession to God is the right way. Let us also thank our mother nature the only ruling God. Devotion is the only way to success and peace. God is present everywhere and so let us seek with one mind and one heart. Surrender to God is the only way to survival. We should cherish moral values and noble thoughts or else we shall soon perish. Meditation is the path to peace. We should know our self. Let us kill all sensual desires. Let our mind rest only on God and sing the glory of God:

>Supreme is the Lord;
>The day His glory is not sung
>Is a curse to the tongue
>
>Lord leaves us free
>We are free to shine or burn in furnace
>He is the pure Witness.
>
>Lord shines in act and art,
>Resides hidden in the cave of the heart;
>Being and Non-Being is He.   (131)

The only solution for this chaos is to acquire higher knowledge. The chanting of *Ohm* spreads vibrations and mind becomes calm. Let us be one-minded. Lord is one and only one. There is no bar for the devotees. The Infinite light has neither form nor name. We are impure with this sinful load.

Thus the poet is able to project both the society and nature in all his haiku and indeed it speaks of the poetic achievement of Reddy to write 1008 haiku of exceptional range, rhythm and vision. Through these micro-poems he makes an earnest endeavor to bring some healthy change in politics, education and religion. Politics is corrupt and the crime rate never comes to an end. Hence the present situation demands peace at any cost. In the name of democracy it is anti-democracy that is practiced. The poet emphasizes on the various sectors in the society which have become corrupt and lost moral values. Right education in the right spirit is the need of the hour. The poet suggests strengthening of our spiritual life. Human life is a mixture of joys and miseries. There cannot be peace as long as there is inhumanity. The references from nature are illustrated only to educate man to learn to be calm. What matters is ethics; ultimately what we need is inner calm.

Note:
Abbreviation: THK= Thousand Haiku Pearls

Works Cited

Reddy, T.V. *Thousand Haiku Pearls*. New Delhi: Authors Press, 2016. Print.

----

14 A Collage of Random Images: The Abysmal, the Angst and the Social Responsibility in T.V. Reddy's Poems

Anju S Nair

The poet is verily a creator, Brahma. He creates both from his personal experience and his imagination. He has the ability to put across his emotions and feelings in a very appealing way. He has the capacity of envisioning and the skill of communication. Poetic skill is a spark, holding in mind a flash of light which leads to an insight and revelation. (Rao, 170)

T Vasudeva Reddy occupies a significant place among the modern Indian poets writing in English. He is also a renowned novelist and critic. He is a formidable poet who astounds his readers by the simplicity and the intensity of his poems. His language is lucid and influential which effectively brings forth the philosophical approach of the poet on the mentioned themes. The titles of the poems are queer, catchy and self-explanatory. He focuses on the present problems faced by humans in the world –hardships, struggle, sorrows, aspirations, dreams and wishes of humanity in general. Thematically he shares the elements which are very similar to realists, naturalists and existentialists. The select poems are from his work *Fleeting Bubbles*, a collection which assimilates the head and the heart, the power of reasoning and the art of feeling.

The poet deliberates on each tiny particle of emotional upsurge. To him, poetry is seen as a different, more concentrated, economical, precise kind of communication about a person's felt and realized experience of life. The words may, therefore mean an attempt to re-present life so as to transform life. The poet, then, has in the first place to select an excellent action; and what actions are the most excellent? Those certainly, which most powerfully appeal to the great primary human affections: to those elementary feelings which subsist permanently in the race, and which are independent of time." (Seturaman & Ramaswami 3)

The poem 'My Soul in Exile' opens with an appeal to his love not to abandon him. Without his love he feels he will lose his identity in this world which he calls a prison. He wonders how long he has to hide this feeling, which is like a poison in his throat. When the soul is in exile it is impossible for the poet to produce melodies. The poet makes an appeal when his mental and physical activities are arrested. At an instance, when he is almost unable to express himself with his communicative ability and feels almost paralyzed, he earnestly appeals to his love not to leave him.

> Don't quit, my love
> Without you
> why should I live
> why should I be here
> and lose my identity
> in this prison of a world?
> ("My Soul in Exile", *Fleeting Bubbles* 19)

These lines express the mesmerized feelings of the poet and it seems they are plucked away all on a sudden. Many a time, it appears as though the poet gives expression to deeper experiences that words fail to convey. The poem is filled with emotions that penetrate the minds of the readers. Such a painful situation that creates turmoil within the poet is explicated in the verses.

The poem is also a reflection of the miserable existence of man who is gifted with the sixth sense. Man without company is as lonely as an island. Man may have been endowed with material and intellectual gifts which would all become insignificant when he is left alone. Life is worth living only when there is a responsibility. A man loses his senses when he is caught in a state of forlornness. The isolated, secluded and pitiable condition of man who yearns for solace depicts the state of helplessness.

T V Reddy is wholly realistic in his observation. Nothing appears irrelevant for the poet and this is the poet's strength. According to him, "Life is a continuous process, but every writer belongs to a place and lives in a period. The surroundings and situations have their inevitable impact on his mind and heart. After all, we are all human beings living in a society. I am a writer with social consciousness. That is the fact about me." He conveys his concerns through various images drawn from everyday experiences. His poems are spontaneous and natural outlets of his emotions. He highlights the ever-increasing gap between the rich and the poor, and instructs society to be compassionate and responsible by presenting contrasting images.

A familiar sight in any part of the world is the deplorable condition of the section of the human race whose means of survival depends on the large-heartedness of the fellow human beings. In the poem 'Old Woman' the poet paints a picture of a woman who earns her livelihood by sitting near the temple gate. She survives on the alms given by the visitors to the temple. The following lines give a picture of her abysmal situation.

> Her hair as gloomily grey as clusters of snakes,
> Unkempt, uncombed and untouched by oil ("An Old Woman", 21)

The repulsive condition of the woman is brought out through the verbal encapsulations made explicit throughout the poem. The despicable appearance conveys her misery. Her withered frame was too heavy for her legs that she required a 'third leg' as a support for her bodily movements. Her diseased skin was wrinkled and repulsive. The whole frame was a hideous sight. The ugly disposition of the beggar woman mirrors the degenerating state of the destitute. Her happiness comes in the form of a smile on her face as she feels the coins in her begging bowl. She belonged to the lot of people who are satisfied with what they were blessed with for the day, that which will satiate the pangs of hunger. She was satisfied and contented with whatever she earned for her living. She wasn't interested in her neighbour's collection. She implored to the Almighty to relieve her off her earthly turmoil. The poet then makes a comparison between the plight of the creator, the all powerful who the poet says is 'imprisoned' in the temple and the lonely woman, a part of His creation who is a victim, to the hardships and sufferings of life. The presence of the old woman is horrendous and she is seen by others as a symbol of ill omen. She had shut her eyes and ears to the contemptible attitude of mankind towards her. The concluding lines of the poem seem to be the most heart-shattering.

> She sat on the hard but hospitable stone for decades;
> A statue of tolerance fed on harsh ignominy
> A haunting figure with soul wrung in agony ("Old Woman", 21)

Her sight leaves a haunting memory and it will linger long while she continues to live in agony.

In a conversation with Santanu Haldar, T V Reddy says, "...poetry should be written in such a way that it should disturb our minds, it should unsettle whatever is there in our minds and unless poetry is a thought provoking one, we cannot say that it is a poem. Mere description can never be a poem at all. There are some certain old and worn out ideas in our minds. By reading a poem, those ideas should be unsettled, they should be disturbed. If the lines do not appeal to our hearts, it is not a poem."

T.V. Reddy's poetry shows his deep interest in ordinary people. His poems present the challenges of life that teach us how to live and how to find the meaning of life amidst frets and fevers. The multifarious lyrics he weaves into his versification relate to the poet's day-to-day experiences and the meaning he derives from them. He communicates each experience with a sense of social obligation and responsibility. "The poet who would really fix the public attention must leave the exhausted past, and draw his subjects from matters of present import, and therefore both of interest and novelty." (Seturaman & Ramaswami 3) The poem 'Women of the Village' is a verbal representation of a familiar picture of an Indian village which is under the grip of a scorching summer. The only sigh of relief is the Peepal tree beneath which the pond is losing its sustenance. The hamlet is dry and arid. The women who are the major workforce in all Indian households are familiar with the condition. They have little strength left to fill their empty earthen pots. Metaphorically, the women are like the cattle in a desert fetching water that is left for their sustenance.

> The clear water moves
> In concentric circles
> Like their day dreams ("Women of the Village", 1)

After a hard day's labor they trek homeward with pitchers and wait for their men to return home from work. The poem has an interlocking of multiple issues. The picture of the village, the women carrying the pitchers have been immortalized in paintings- on canvas, on fabric, on walls – sculptured in wood and stone and woven on fabric. From time immemorial the picture of women carrying pots has been synonymous with the rural scenario. The image brings forth myriad meanings – the scarcity of water, the tough conditions of life of women and above all the lives of women who have been /are symbols of hard labor. They not only bring forth the hardships of their cattle-like existence (with a feminist orientation) but also strive hard to deal with all conditions to give support and relief for others. The image also furnishes enough information about what is required. The poet records the state of life and the underdeveloped way of living or existing. When the whole world is marching towards development there exists a raw and an obnoxious reality in the villages where the people face hardships in life and struggle for livelihood.

'The Corn Reaper' is another truthful portrait of the woman who toils for her livelihood and for her family. Like Wordsworth's The Solitary Reaper, she is working hard in the fields.

> Under the scorching sun
> In the ripened paddy field
> She reaped the fallen crop
> With the multi-toothed sickle,
> Sweat flowed drop by drop
> From her care-worn brow; ("The Corn Reaper", 22)

She is unmindful of who is watching her – her landlord's eyes scrutinizes her being but her mind is preoccupied with thoughts of her wailing child at home and also of the heavy blows which would rein on her when her drunken husband returns home. It had become a ritual for him to beat her every day. The poem brings to mind the lines from Wordsworth's Poem 'The Solitary Reaper':

> Behold her, single in the field,
> Yon solitary Highland Lass!
> Reaping and singing by herself;
> Stop here, or gently pass!

Alone she cuts and binds the grain

The poem "The Housewife" opens with lines that provide a glimpse of the evening scene in the valley.

> The sullen sun descends
> Behind the western hills
> Turning the land lurid and sultry ("The Housewife", 23)

The sun had set leaving the land arid and lifeless. The dusk has sneaked in and the brightness fades giving way to the haunting darkness. It looked as though the darkness had been eagerly waiting to set in on the valley. The noisy cows could be seen moving away to their resting place in the dried boughs of the large Peepal tree which dominates the valley. The village seemed lifeless with the thatched huts and walls of mud. The empty clay barrels speak for themselves about the poverty of the villagers. The empty vessels seem to smile at the housewife who expectantly searches for some contents within them. She hesitates to kindle the hearth as there is nothing. She has to satisfy the hunger with hopes of a blank future. The lamp of life and hope is burned with a twig as she waits for her partner to returns from the furrowed fields. He tries to make a point that human pain and suffering spans over space and time.

These poems bring out the state and condition of women and issues related to women. The poet shows the dominant patriarchal structure which pushes women to a secondary position. The poems bring several inter-texts and put them into a collage of random images which validate the trauma of human experience.

"The poet who would really fix the public attention must leave the exhausted past, and draw his subjects from matters of present import, and therefore both of interest and novelty". (Seturaman &Ramaswami 3).The retirement of a teacher who is the dispeller of darkness and who illumines the minds of multitudes in society for their bright future is the theme of the poem, "The Teacher".

> At last the gloomy day has come
> After decades of devoted duty
> The mind that struggled to transmit light to dark cavities
> Is now destined to quiet decay; ("The Teacher", 24)

The departure of the teacher leaves a vacuum and the place becomes devoid of the voice that had vibrated the walls and penetrated the ears of students. All the activities of the teacher had become a thing of the past. The echo continues to haunt the mind. The role of a teacher is brilliantly sketched by the poet through various comparisons. Just as a painter paints his masterpiece or a sculptor carves his statue, they are full of life though they are dumb and deaf. But a teacher breathes life into living beings and moulds their minds. The teacher breathes life into existence. For ages the teacher has been a candle that burns and spreads light. Just as the candle which sacrifices itself to give light is forgotten, the teacher who spreads light is also forgotten by others.

The poet is delicate and gentle in his approach and displays a very fine aesthetic sense in the poems related to nature and creation. The poem 'Blessings of Jasmine' offers a unique spectacle of grandeur and beauty that are both enthralling and endearing at the same time.

> The jasmine flower
> With its growth of pretty dower
> Spreading her flood of fragrance
> Is a divine blessing to mankind; ("Blessings of Jasmine", 38)

The jasmine flower spreads her fragrance which is a divine blessing for mankind. Its scent has the divine power to enchant anybody in joy and sorrow. The jasmine replenishes charms and enthralls people on any memorable occasion. The lingering charm of its fragrance engulfs the air purifying the senses with its aroma. Jasmine offers a 'wondrous balm' or cure for all moods. The poet brings forth the exuberance of nature which through its myriad ways enhances the mood of man relieving him from the pains of material existence.

Regarding the subjects of his poems, the poet says, "While some poems reflect rural landscape, a few present the stark reality of the present-day social life and atmosphere; some are purely romantic in their theme and treatment, while a few are on the spiritual aspect." The poem "The Supreme Being" is a verse in veneration of the incredible work of the Creator. The astounding perfection of the infinitesimal creations leaves man awestruck and makes him speculate on the infallibility of the handiwork of the Supreme. Every aspect of creation reverberates with the power of His creative genius. The 'smile' on the blooming petal of a flower which heralds the onset of spring expresses the intense mechanism of creation. The songs of the birds, the flutter of their wings, the roaring billows, the movements of the tiniest of beings and the 'terrible' beauty of the snake stand for the marvelous meaning of the existence. The unseen but formidable and inscrutable forces in nature abound with the spell of mystery that is yet to be unraveled. All this abounds with the grace of the Supreme Being as one wonders at the concealed dexterity. The concluding lines wrap up the sheer magic of creation.

> In the midst of deep mystery around me
> I feel the grace of the Supreme Being ("The Supreme Being", 39)

What strikes the reader immediately is the extraordinary peculiarity with which the world of nature is observed in all its various characteristics. The poet admits that, he "was so much influenced by the British Romantic poets. Right from the good olden days, even when I was a student, I was fond of Romantic Poetry - the poetry of Wordsworth, Shelley and Keats. Naturally it had made a deep impression on me. Moreover, I was born and brought up in a village - the village which was surrounded on all sides by the beauty of Nature. So the influence of my surroundings was there deeply on me. That is why I was very much impressed and began drawing so much of pleasure in describing the objects of Nature which I saw".

The poetry of T V Reddy is the creation of a poet who is restless soul. To read his poems in a sensitive way involves the experience of the feeling of angst generated by the degradation of mankind in our time. The world today is facing several threats, the most prominent being the threat of pollution- which in its variant forms is choking the life out of people, the living beings and planet earth. All the Indian cities are choked to death every day. In the midst of this the poet earnestly wishes that his eyelids remain shut or sealed so as to prevent any alien force from entering it and polluting it. He does not want his eyes to be invaded by the 'distracting' dust from the traffic-jammed roads. In the poem 'Let the Eyes Be Shut' the poet wants his eyes to remain shut lest they be distracted from pleasant 'illusions by elusive delusions'. The thoughts of the poet that reverberate in the lines of the poem are the thoughts of millions of people in Indian cities who want to breath fresh air and live a life devoid of pollution, the despairing dehumanizing influences, of the so called civilized existence, its socio-economic realities as recorded by the poet.

Reddy says, "My life, life of every person, life in general, human or non-human, needs peace. Since time immemorial, man's life has been longing for peace, domestic peace, social peace and peace for the mind and spirit. Without peace, there is no happiness; without these two, realization is not possible." The poem 'In Tense Flight' shows Man as an escapist. Looking at the worsening state of affairs of the world man tries to extricate himself from the situation. The mind at times forces him to take decisions that he would find himself difficult to extricate himself. Caught in a complexity of life, man tries to flee, thinking that loneliness may be the remedy or cure from that state of turmoil. But in doing so he realizes that it is only physically distancing himself from the problem. His mind is in turmoil. He realizes that life is a struggle and a quest for peace. The lines 'could I run from myself' bring forth the truth of the situation. It is 'absolute reality'. Man is caught in a quagmire as his own dark shadow chases and engulfs him. He is made a captive of what he is. Life is an undefined entity a person often tries hard to understand. In the poetry of T V Reddy the fragments of inter-texts keep recurring in an attempt to observe and analyze the present existential situation. Ina world of falling order, the poet tries to find meaning.

The poet states, "I want to be faithful in what I express. I am not cynical; I am speaking the naked truth. What I have seen all these years, I have expressed in some of my poems. When I write on certain truths that are inevitable components of life, how can I be cynical? I accept life as it is, conscious of its dark clouds and lights. As humble men with our limits, we sometimes feel depressed, but the next minute we reconcile ourselves to the situation accepting our lot and reposing our faith in the Supreme Lord." T. V. Reddy's poetry emphasizes on the experience of the senses and its narrative organization and presents the self-revealing emotion through expressionistic images. His poetry sets a new direction, a deeper vision of the ordinary reality. There is a great deal in the writings of his poetry which must be conscious and deliberate. According to Seturaman and Ramaswami , "this is the reason why such poems strike us as creations, not just manufactures, and have the magical effect which mere decoration cannot produce.... It means itself. (151)

Works Cited

Halder, Santanu. "In Conversation with famous Indian Poet Vasudeva Reddy by Santanu Halder". *Meri News .com*, 28 Feb. 2013.Web.

King, Bruce. *Modern Indian Poetry in English*. New Delhi: Oxford University Press, 1987. Print.

Rama Rao, V.V.B. *Sensitivity and Cultural Multiplicity in Recent Indian English Poetry*. Jaipur:Aadi Publications, 2014. Print.

Ramaswami, S and Seturaman, V.S. Ed. *The English Critical Tradition – An Anthology of English Literary Criticism*, Vol.2. New Delhi : Trinity Press, 2014. Print.

Reddy, T. V. *The Fleeting Bubbles*. Madras: Poets Press India, 1989. Print.

15. Rapturous Notes of Melancholy in T. V. Reddy's *When Grief Rains*

S. Malathy

Shelley in his poem, "Ode to a Skylark" calls the skylark, the "blithe spirit" as "pain and languor never came near" the bird. But the mortals, though they long for ethereal beauty, cannot reach it. As Shelley aptly admonishes, "our sweetest songs are those that tell of saddest thoughts". Like Keats' Nightingale, where Keats yearns to "leave the world unseen" and to do away "with weariness, the fever and fret of human life", Shelley also mourns in his "Ode to the West Wind" saying "I fall upon the thorns of life! I bleed" – Yet this is the reality that everyone has to acknowledge. Through their poetry they derive an understanding of the relationship between joy and sorrow, experience and knowledge and they enlighten their readers.

T. Vasudeva Reddy, a renowned poet of International repute, is an Indian poet writing in English. Through his poetry he brings out his agony and anguish at the sight of suffering around him. The inertia of humanity, their poverty and pain makes the poet feel heavy at heart - he gets obfuscate and finds it difficult to come out of it. He finally becomes a 'shattered man'. This psychological distress makes his poetry more expressive and stronger and it has become a 'saga of deep-felt suffering'. The poet occupies a significant place among the Indian Writers as his poetry unveils the inner essence of man.

When Grief Rains is a collection of poems by T.V. Reddy that spins the warp and woof of human dilemma and complexity. It gives not only an account of grief experienced by the poet but also the pain of the people around him. His poetry deals with rural and social themes. It clearly delineates the village life – the life of the depressed farmers who struggle but fail to make both ends meet. As the poet marks in an interview, "I have seen and experienced the agony and anguish of the life of a poor farmer who has to depend for farm work on undependable workers who more often indulge in exploiting the situation as a result of which we the poor farmers are reduced to abject poverty and thrown into debt-trap".

His poetry is a vivid presentation of the degeneration in all walks of life and it throws light on human exploitation. It also laments on the loss of values in life. The poet advocates the importance of values. While responding to Goutam Karmakar in an interview, he states, "without human values life becomes a curse and it is of no use". In his poetry, he exposes the all pervasive evil of corruption that has crept into every field of human life. His poetry focuses on the eternal issues like death, poverty, pain and cultural decadence that cause distress and despair to humanity.

While referring to a pensive memory in his poem "Sweet Scar", he says:

> the pensive memory of the sear
> on the wounded heart
> is tastier ..... ("Sweet Scar", 10)

Here the reader is reminded of Shelley's words.

The poet muses in perfect tone on the affliction of people in general, as it settled heavily in his heart. He declares in his poetry that life has become human grieving for eternity. His powerful, emotive language touches the very inmost nerve of his reader's heart. This destitute state of mind is clearly expressed in his poem "Dreams", where the poet throws light on the human longing for the 'ethereal', their unfulfilled dreams and how it gets "shattered and buried". He mourns over his bruised heart:

> ....my bruised heart
> is now muffled ("Dreams", 12)

And then he laments over his songs coming out in:

> a form of dirge
> Quietly echoing in the tomb
> of my anointed heart
> layered on buried dreams ("Dreams", 12)

His poetry is an outburst of his righteous indignation. The poet intends to satirize the social evils such as hypocrisy and corruption. David Kerr in his Foreword to "Melting Melodies" observes, "His poetry is an outburst of emotion and it succeeds in creating the basic human feelings." "When Grief Rains" is a work of art that gives an insight into contemporary Indian village life and the depressing, unhealthy situations experienced by the poor farmers. As the poet acknowledges in his interview, "I want to hold a mirror to the reality of social life", his poetry is indeed a reflection of real life situations.

Nissim Ezekiel in his collection of poems *A Time to Change* expresses his anger at the appalling poverty of the child-like masses in the dehumanized metropolitan city:

> Barbaric city with slums
> Deprived of season
> ......
> A million purgatorial lanes
> Child-like masses, many tongued
> Whose wages are in words and crumbs ("A Morning Walk")

Like Nissim Ezekiel, Vasudeva Reddy also connotes his anger, which is righteous in nature and corrective in purpose. His poem "At the Cross-Road" delineates the plight of the modern man who gets "..... stranded at the cross-road with his lungs "punctured with splinters" and who pulled his way through the crowd with his "sore feet" pricked by "gravel". He finds himself "cornered", becomes puzzled and remains in a dilemma. He makes a strenuous effort to get rid of the present plight:

> A world of memories and bruises –
> Raw and fresh as reechy cabbages,
> Swarming recollections and jammed traffic ("At the Cross-Road", 20)

In a subtle manner, he presents modern man's dilemma and explores the complex realm of the human mind. His poetry achieves its excellence by evoking a keen sense of regret, through the conflict between tradition and modernism, the city and the village. T.V. Reddy, one of the true representative poets on human values, advises the modern man to have 'Patience' in his poem "Patience" and directs him to "be firm and tolerant" as the "temple tower" that stands up to the "stormy winds". He admires those towers that "shelter the poor with open gates" and the tower emerges "unbeaten like a potent warrior". The elegant temple tower is standing as "a monument of patience" facing the onslaughts of time and preaching values to humanity. The poet gives a timely warning by stating that 'patience' has become "a patented prescription" to cure the ills of mankind:

> Be patient or become a patient
> Make an ashram or an asylum.
> The prescription has been patented ("Patience", 21)

The poet gets disenchanted with his social existence as man has become the captive of the monstrous python of greed, deceit and lust. The poet laments that the world will be engulfed one day on account of man's return to his primitive nature. The poem "Civilization" of Reddy is an observation on the degeneration of humanity and the loss of human values. With "the shell of sophistication" the civilized man who conceals his "foul interior" stinks worse than "an addled egg," as he has learnt to suck other's blood. He has had already started swiftly tolling the knell, laments the poet. With the "speed of a snail" civilization has grown with prickly thorns boring venomous snakes. The image of snakes and their venom is aptly mentioned by the poet to state that the nutritious values of human life have already got poisoned and the life morally has come to its fag end!

Life in a dehumanized, degenerated, uncivilized society becomes void. Under these circumstances the poet portrays in his poem "Life is a Desert" that

> Life is an elusive endless desert
> Full of sands and storms, no oases ("Life is a Desert", 14)

The entire physical environment in itself will become a crucial factor when man stands alone in a world of unhappiness. He gets tormented with the sight of mirage and stays with a parched tongue:

> I am a lone man in the barren land
> Dissembling mirage tantalizes me,
> A thirsty man with a parched tongue ("Life is a Desert", 14)

With a feeling of listlessness and dissatisfaction he feels that he is being marooned amidst his "wary chary and worldly wise" kith and kin. As the age has specialized in each sucking other's blood, man feels defeated and struggles to resist the jealousy, envy and ennui of the society. "Life recedes into the vast barren expanse" like the "wisps of receding cigarette smoke", in vain observes T.V. Reddy in his poem "Futility." With his beautiful simile the poet elucidates the point of 'Nothingness of life'.

P. Lal in his poem "Calcutta" expresses his anger at the appalling poverty, disease and apathy of the people. Dehumanization is focused by P. Lal with his sincere prayer for humanity:

> Pray they walk straight
> …. In the valley of our sorrow

Like P. Lal, T.V. Reddy also gets disenchanted with man's hushed speech. Man has withdrawn himself into a world of negative thinking and has entered into the "pervading futility and sterility." Even his attempt to "smile becomes abortive" as he feels so forlorn, and he finds it difficult even to recover his confidence. Being left in the "farthest edge of futility" he feels lost. "Futility" is a subtle work of poetic art that describes the baneful condition of life. It explores the unavoidable continuity of pain and exploitation and ends with subtle irony. It is one of the thought provoking and enlightening poetic creations of the writer.

The author has a remarkable skill to capture life and portray them in moving words. His effort in creating life-like pictures hangs around the reader's mind. His melodies that reverberate in the depth of silence whirl in our minds. The poet in his poem "When Grief Rains" brings to focus his "dim desire" that "creeps unaware". Being a literary genius he feels that it is his mission to present the contemporary Indian society as it exists, with its suffering crowd and their listlessness. The author excels in depicting the plight of man in a direct, emphatic way. He longs to "enter the pores of the earth" from this destructive, deadly world of sorrow as the "gales of sorrow" wrecks his "surging spirit".

The writer uses different images to paint his experiences. His keen insight and observation on life and nature is noteworthy. Nothing escapes his notice, not even the 'dying wick'. Left in utter darkness he feels miserable as it invades his "desolate spirit and saps his sinking soul". The minute power of his observation is quite obvious when he paints the wick that "withers with the last flicker". In his poem "The Dying Wick" the author re-creates the rural ethos with appalling poverty. He sketches the repulsive, dreadful conditions of their life and their helplessness:

> ...... the nibbling rat
> On the thatched roof
> ....
> and the egoistic thunder
> that awakens the child
> from the cradle in fright ("The Dying Wick", 27)

T.V. Reddy in his interview opines "as humble men with our limits, we sometimes feel depressed, but the next minute we reconcile ourselves to the situation accepting our lot and reposing our faith in Supreme Lord."

The poet being the true son of this sacred India draws the graphic picture of the rural landscape depicting the lives of the farmers, the snake charmers, the cow, the sparrow, thirsty fields etc. His poem "Thirsty Field" is an example of poet's task and gift. With its lucid, simple words and well expressed thoughts the poem becomes malleable. As K.R .Srinivasa Iyengar in his letter to T.V. Reddy comments, "the poet has a keen eye to mark the exceptional whether in life or nature." The poet presents in detail not only the modern world but also the nature. His description varies from the boundless sky to earth. He ponders over the lack of water, 'the thirsty field' and on the destruction that follows. With his fine imagery the poet precisely denotes the sad state of the "sun-burnt crop" as an irredeemable loss to the humanity. He explains this gruesome scene with his remarkable irony:

> the sun-burnt crop looked
> like a dissected corpse
> on the post-mortem table ("Thirsty Field", 28)

"Thirsty Field" powerfully presents the grim, repulsive state of the thirsty land and the practical difficulties and the horrors of drought experienced by the "thirsty farmers".
The poet has keen observant eyes for details. To elucidate the contemptible state of the thirsty field and its dryness the poet sketches a visual description. The imagery used by the poet creates a lyrical emotion in our minds:

> Hardly had they entered
> the countless cracks
> the period proved abortive ("Thirsty Fields", 28)

His poetry enriched with lyrical qualities fills us with a sense of exhilaration. It presents varied themes that elevate the soul to a higher consciousness. The literary genius Reddy talks about the precarious state of life in his poem "Transience". The poem is a discussion on the mortals who take up a long and tedious journey and how they succumb to the inevitable decay. These impermanent, wavering lots crave for "solace in the dark cradle". To indicate the inconsistency of life he attempts to portray the struggles of man who has no voice to claim even a mere six by two feet of land as his own, when the end seizes him.

The poet strongly makes his point that there is no discrimination between the triumphant and sloth. Beauty (being ephemeral) and beggary as they all merge in clay. Man fails miserably as there is "nothing to gain in life" or to "lose in death" and all glories lead only to dust. His realization shows the insignificance as well as the pettiness of life.

The poem "Realization" is again a powerful expression on labiality. Though beauty is ephemeral and evanescent that reminds us of death, man goes after it. Man, who fails to realize the significance of time goes after worldly pleasures and soon gets frustrated. Then he wakes up to find that he is left out in "a wasteland, a dreamy desert". The desolate man now waits for his "inevitable moment" of death – his final end, his final realization. The author describes the negative aspects of rural life in a realistic and appealing manner. He laments on the futility of life and the unavoidable, inevitable continuity of pain that human beings undergo.

His poetry is an expression of his experiences and as such it is characterized by truth and honesty. Reading Reddy's poetry is a delightful experience of exhilaration for the readers to enjoy as the poet excels in his art of highlighting even tiny moments and specks of life. His poetic presentation sustains the interest of his readers. Dr. Reddy who is a literary genius gives perfection to his poetry with apt imagery, profound thought and subtle expression that polish even the hardest things until they gleam and until they become part of the reader's psyche, thus enlightening them. Ezekiel observes that Dr. Reddy the poet "like a gifted sculptor, chisels his poems with the deftness of a master craftsman". His poetry throws light on varied themes and faithfully presents the inner truth with proper expression and simple diction. It is an outburst of powerful emotions that casts its spell on our minds and thoughts, and makes us ponder over the truth of life. His art of chiseling of lines makes his poetry unique and what is remarkable with his poetry is nowhere do we find an unnecessary word and every word has its proper place in the poem.

Krishna Srinivas, in his Editor's note to *The Broken Rhythms* calls Reddy, "a morning star in the firmament of Indo-Anglican poetry." Reddy presents the rural atmosphere with its flora and fauna. He explores the mysteries of life and nature. He sings of pain and pleasure and clearly maps the world of shadows found in our lives. Well tuned with words and thoughts, his poems reverberate in total silence and keep echoing in our minds just as Wordsworth's poem "The Solitary Reaper" with its romantic aura stays in our mind. This ingenious quality of the poet Reddy spells out the unique beauty and intrinsic charm of his poetry.

Reddy's craftsmanship in painting life's experiences and vicissitudes and presenting life as human's earnest grieving for eternity, with varied images is remarkable. Georges Friedenkraft considers his poetry "richly lyrical and imagist". Reddy is a poet endearing with simplicity as well as directness of expression and plain-speaking as his poetry illumines our minds with clarity of thought and directs our gaze towards things of permanence. *When Grief Rains* is a volume of poetry that adds to the verity and versatility of the poet's art. His poetry stands the test of time as his poems bear a strong testimony to their intrinsic charm and pleasing melody and it remains inimitable. Being an eminent poet with human values his poetry echoes not only the voice of the oppressed people but the eternal values of life.

Works Cited

Chaucer, Geofftrey. *Prologue to the Canterbury Tales,* from *Ideas and Forms in English & American Literature, Vol I. Poetry,* Ed. by Homer A. Watt & James B. Munn. New York :Scott Foreman & Co., 1925, 2nd ed.1932. Print.

Ezekiel, Nissim. "Foreword to *Pensive Memories* by T.V. Reddy", Chennai: Poets Press. Print.

Friedenkraft, Georges C. Foreword to *Fleeting Bubbles* by T.V. Reddy, Madras: Poets Press, 1989.

Goutam Karmakar. (2017) "Goutam Karmakar Interviews T. Vasudeva Reddy". *Contemporary Literary Review India,* 4:1(February). Online http://literary journal.in/index.php/clri/article/view/228/299. Accessed on 20-07-2017

Keats, "Ode to A Nightingale", Keats : Poetical Works, ed. H.W.Garrod, London: OUP, 1970.2 07-208.

Raghhavan.(2001)."The Spiritual Progress in the Poetry of T. Vasudeva Reddy", *Indian Poetry in English*, edited by Birendra Pandey (New Delhi: Atlantic Publishers, 2001) 114-121.Print.

Raghupathi, K.V. *The Rural Muse: The Poetry of T. Vasudeva Reddy*, New Delhi, Authors Press, 2014.Print.

Reddy, Bayapa. "T.V. Reddy's *Melting Melodies*: An Analysis." *Writers Editors Critics* (WEC), Mar.2017, 109-111. Print.

Reddy, T. V. *When Grief Rains*. New Delhi: Samakaleen Prakashan, 1982.Print.

Shelley, P.B. Poems. "To A Skylark" & "Ode to the West Wind". *Shelley Poems*. OUP, *The World's Classics*.

Srinivas, Krishna. "Editor's Note, *Broken Rhythms* by T.V. Reddy". Madras: Poets Press, 1987.Print.

Wordsworth, William. "Solitary Reaper" from *Ideas and Forms in English & American Literature, Vol I. Poetry,* Ed. Homer A. Watt & James B. Munn. New York : Scott, Foreman & Co., 1925, 2nd ed. 1932, 460. Print.

16

T.V. Reddy's *Gliding Ripples* An Overview

Lily Arul Sharmila

T.V. Reddy, a reputed Indian poet of contemporary era possesses an uncommon share of good sense and his forcible expressions have secured for him the reputation to a high degree from his readers. He has a penetrating insight into life around him and a happy talent of correcting the popular opinion upon all occasions where it is erroneous. This he does with the fearlessness of a man who entertains ideas for himself. A close examination of his poems is bound to reveal some basis for his harshness and severity. In his petulant, argumentative moods he begins his criticism. The diction is harsh so as to treat the evil attitude of the predators contemptuously.

In a broader sense, a single body of written works, artistic works, lend the best expression of thoughts. His literature has the potential of value judgment, superior with lasting artistic merit. His works of imagination are characterized by excellence of style, expression and themes of general interest. Printed material gives a particular type of information. Writings of imaginative or critical characters have permanent value, an excellence of form and great emotional effect. Writings of particular time, place, have lasting impressions to evoke beauty and imagination. The main focus of the poet is on cultural study and structure. Though his poetry is in the broadest sense is an activity of the imagination, it realizes the ideal. The immediate object of his work is truth. His poems published under a collected title, *Gliding Ripples* accommodate the actual presence of a specified substance, the profound truth.

He talks with condor to his readers. He remains always at the readers' level and enters into a dialogue with them on a footing of perfect equality. His instinctive reactions are submitted to the social critique. There is no pedantry in his judgments on the political activities, economic measures and social scenario and whatever he says, he upholds in a clear picturesque style, as a creative writer cannot be indifferent to the temper and taste of his age. His poem, "Burning Thoughts" muses on the state of the contemporary world. "My flaming thoughts / wishing to create a new haven ..../ burning nation in a world of fire / chased by thirsty flames /and hungry fires of fiery souls." (*GR*, 25) His psychological insight into what reproves the readers makes him an accomplished poet. The poems are very ambitious discourses concerning the progress of human society. According to the poet, in order to be successful man must adapt himself to a system that submits to higher principles in life.

The objectivity shows itself in the choice of subjects far from personal preferences, interests and situations in the life of the writer himself. He is at once a painter and a subtle analyst. He knows no monochrome, but that is reflected only from the related things around us. The poet's pictures of life are faithful clones, accurately and directly executed. The pictures are poeticized by the overriding passion, a strong feeling, intense emotion and compelling action. His poetic zeal awakens thoughts which instantly transform themselves into intellectual life. As Coleridge notes, in *Biographica Literaria*, "There must be not only a partnership, but a union; an interpenetration of passion and of will, of spontaneous impulse and of voluntary purpose". Graphic descriptions and depicted visual conceptions are unified into a direct mystical awareness. As Wordsworth expresses in *Preface to Lyrical Ballads,* "The poet thinks and feels in the spirit of human passions. Poets do not write for poets alone, but for men."

The poem "Countryside" illustrates the poet's zest for social realism which is fully corroborated by the choice of compound words such as barren lands, vanishing sands, elusive clouds, depressed crowds, dried streams, dying dreams, subsidized rice, cooked up lies. A social critic endeavors to strengthen the social fabrics. "Election season / in exile reason/ Promises tall and false on village walls/ leaders' cut outs/ factories lock outs./ Once a sylvan scene/ now sick with no sheen;/ once with vernal bloom/ now only deepening gloom."(GR 19) A breach in the environmental ethics is contemptuously treated.

There is beauty in the sentiments and images. The poetic discourses have dramatic significance animated by reciprocal contention on social reality of the contemporary world. They are tediously instructive. The huge dimension affords space enough for elaborate descriptions, long speeches and moral discourses. The highest aim of his poems is to produce maximum effect on the society. The drama of human existence is dull and desultory and the special power of the poet lies in displaying the vast play of life, illuminating it with the light of splendid intellect and enforcing constant harmony and chance which make human life fresh and lively.

Therefore, to understand the poetry of T.V. Reddy, one must know what he conceives of life to be. His primary concern is culture, a way of living, ordered and patterned with coherent system. In the industrial ages, code of conduct in all matters generated from one generation to another ensures the continuity and the advancement of the cultural heritage of the nation. The conditions today are very different. Concentrating on huge production with machinery, stumbled in cosmopolitan cities, men have ceased to have that feeling of solidarity and shared ideals which were cherished in the past. What brings them under one federation is their industrial colonies which are not of any common cultural bond. Their tastes and habits have also degenerated. As F.R. Leavis says in his *Culture and Environment,* "we might in a healthy state of culture leave the citizen to be formed unconsciously by his environment if anything like a worthy idea of satisfactory living is to be saved, he must be trained to discriminate and resist.

The poem "My Village Bus" pictures the scanty means of social livelihood. Seeing the uncared villages, the poet lashes at the Government's negligence. "Omnibus with ominous signs / Parched tyres and broken window glasses/ Clothes absorbing dripping drops of sweat/ Seats worn out, smelling fishing pits,/nostrils struck with sultry stink of armpits."(*GR*, 20) The poet narrates scenes and live narrations from wedding bells to divorces:

> tongues lose the tang, brains became bricks.
> amid words of abuse from drunken lips,
> rending cries of suffocating children echo
> Loud talk of a khaddar leader fans his puffs.
> He heaves a sign of relief at his cash balance.
> Front mirror, though foggy grey with cracks,
> nothing seems to faze the undaunted driver's gaze.
> May he drive for ever safe with Lord's grace! (*GR*, 20)

The poem moves towards the central situation i.e. the struggle or the predicament of life involving the embodiment of divergent points of view on modes of living. He says in the poem 'Let us be Human': 'Frenzied men wage power wars/ which they proudly call Holy wars/Let us strive to be human/ and drive the spirit inhuman.' (*GR* 28)

The words in the poem, "Bleeding Words", colour up the poetic work of Reddy. He writes with felicity and clarity. His thoughts are measured by their propriety and proportion. He is the poet, a perpetual fountain head of sense that can speak on all subjects. Reddy, a man of wonderful foresight and acumen, suggests an efficacious alternate remedy for the social ills. Let us see how he conveys his thought in the thought-provoking poem 'Bleeding Words':

> "Barriers beyond the ethnic hell,
> Emotion, powered by remote control,
> blind beyond the ken of Satan's reason,....
> It is time to heal and free the battered word
> from grisly hands to free the embattled world." (GR, 26)

The ideal exercise of the poet is to perceive the world through his sense unimpeded by the combinations brought by philosophical seriousness and celestial experience for the evolution of principles to guide man. "Time Spares None" speculates,

> "Time is a big leveler ...
> evil forces soon may rise
> only to pay a heavier price;
> a dictator or a cruel tyrant
> with all his power and rant
> cannot escape the gallows
> when Higher Justice bellows." (GR, 27)

The poet probes the imaginative processes which result in the genesis of poetic dialectics. The transcendental principle, the self revelation and the state of poetic mind trace thoughts, facts and ideas from a higher angle. There are moments in a man's life when his sudden spontaneous inclination reacts to a direct influence in such an organized way that the mind has life's experiences. T.V. Reddy's poetry is an artistic reflection of the uniquely ordered state of mind to affect something for a change. With T.V. Reddy, the basic issue is propriety and scholastic speculation or notional philosophy.

The world of mankind is not ministering the things which are not reported to the people. They are not sober and they fully rest their hope upon grace. They conform themselves to the former lists in their ignorance. They are not redeemed of the corruptible things. With their aimless conduct they fail to purify their souls in obeying truth through the spirit of sincere love of their fellow human beings. They fail to love one another with pure heart. All are born of corruptible seed. All flesh is as grass and all glory of man as the flower of grass. The grass withers and flowers fall away. But truth endures. Man does not lay aside all malice, all deceit, hypocrisy, envy and all evil speaking. Man is called out of darkness into his marvelous light. They speak against one another as evil doers. Man is expected to submit himself to the ordinance of the Divine. By doing good, man can put to silence the ignorance of foolish men. Men seem to be committed to tread the path of sin and deceit which are invariably found in them. They walk in lewdness, lust, drunkenness, revelries, abominable adultery. The humbled are exalted in due course of time. Man needs to be vigilant and sober. In the poem 'Idols for the Idle' he writes: "With dilution and pollution of culture/ Radical revolutions to rob and grab ... / Crazy idle brains worship false Gods" (GR 16)

The poet accuses the plotting and executing of extremist's activities. Hypocrites, gangsters, scamsters and criminals are now in line for the covetous claim. The poet wishes to bring a change so as to make the people cultured and sensitive. Competitors stand to seek the sprucely bride's jeweled hand; for them fortune is as blind as justice.

Truth is the necessary part of existence. Truth concerns man's relation to society. The ultimate excellence lies in man's adherence to truth. Every poem in this brilliant collection echoes noble sentiments of the poet. The poet cries for the benign quality of man and sublime functioning of social structure as an efficient poet tries to make man wiser and better. His creative principle is based on a certain philosophical seriousness and his poems are the outcome of a deep union of feelings and profound thoughts. He perceives objects, persons and things with his powerful analytical mind, with a keen and observant eye for details and conscious use of his imaginative faculty.

"A Broken Life" relates the pathetic life of a man who lost his son in war – 'the body did not come, shadow returns;/All these cups and drops fail to trace/ the missing son, the missing rays,/ and draw his broken heart's ECG;/ The graph of the curling fumes of tea/ fail to draw his life's ship wreck,/ while the mirror on the wall micks/ at the broken pieces of his lifeless life'(*GR*, 15). His eyes lost the real light.

In the poem, "Idols for the Idle", the poet says that as a little boy at the village school, 'my mind absorbed from my teacher/ Visions of legendary idols,/ Sri Rama, Harischandra, Hanuman,/ Krishna, Buddha, Christ, Kabir,' and historical figures – Asoka, Akbar, Sivaji, Napoleon, Lincoln, Vivekananda, Aurobindo, Tilak, Gokhale, Gandhi, Subash Bose and Patel kindled the spirit of National Song.

"Our Bureaucrat", coloured by the vision of the poet, stimulates the readers' interest for perfection:

> Heavy with choking scent this important car
> races like a shooting star to the Blue Moon bar,
> with hurried steps he enters the spacious hall
> amid Cabaret dance, lights and lively ball.
> Navigate the menu file to eat, bite or nibble,
> Heads heavy with pride
> Corrupt file is purged with green greedy ink. ...
> Where words fail, voluptuous looks gain.
> Misty minds with painted lips to train;
> He drinks and drinks until his eyes sail and fly.
> The bureaucrat floats with his vision twenty
> of spicy touch of the damsel's kiss in twenty;.
> The master's voice snores in the magic land (*GR*, 22)

The readers are bound to derive the delight of the implication of the sarcasm present in the poem "Our Bureaucrats". Without preparation a system would adequately lead to confusion. People need to shed hypocrisy to understand the dynamics of the changing society. Everyday thoughts and actions become the story of their future. They dare to tread upon new areas leading into many unethical practices. The poet draws our attention on matters of such fundamental significance to one's character, shows inspirational steps and enables us to have a strong understanding of purposes and an experience through spiritual travel so as to appreciate and imbibe the enriched culture. But people are caught unawares in intricate situations with a sudden quirk of fate which brings a severe blow.

T.V. Reddy, in his poem "Erase the Borders" expresses his universal love for the humanity and broader outlook leading to peace and harmony in the world on one side and on the other his contempt for hate and hostility and border disputes and wars that drive away peace. The poem has topical significance as our country faces the sounds of killing guns at the borders with our neighbor and the poet has in his mind the unending tensions in the borders with our neighbours. With a feeling heart he writes:

> "Let frenzied fears and tears fly
> Free from missiles keep the sky
> Let fantastic fires cool down.... (*GR*, 11)

"Path of Life" is a poem that shows man's heroic spirit to march "on the pricking flowery path of life/ fraught with testing stress and strife/ ... While on the path pieces of glass peep/ serene gems lie many a fathom deep." (GR 31) The poet voices for global peace. He makes a clarion call to the mankind for following righteous path of justice. He makes a plea to the human world to come out of darkness and come into light and get illumined. In this context, one can recall Abdul Kalam's words – "There are two main causes of familial conflict. Wealth and behaviour – Man's attitude and behavior are immensely affected by the expansion of the world of material objects. Money is the main means of obtaining these objects……." (154)

There is a deep union of feelings and profound thoughts in his poems maintaining a fine balance of truth in observation. The poet discovers the truth in the phenomena he observes. The poet makes a self revelation and the union of his soul with the external world is much explicit. His art illumines what is dark and raises what is low.

Reason and good sense becomes the yardstick to assess his literary merit. The beauty of his art lends literary mechanics which act as tools to establish social principles. The test of a good literary work is its capacity to reveal poetic intuition and to inspire; and expression of emotion is more important than an enlisting of physical properties. Reddy's poetry is not only a self expression but it also lays an impact on the readers with the suggestive ways for improvement. The silent influence of the poet comes from his moral stamina that inspires the readers with refined feelings. All these make his poetic work richer, fuller, grandeur, beautiful and sublime. The feelings of the poet are powerful and genuine, sane and sensible, righteous and everlasting. His poetry is a pursuit of truth of man's life and an insight into the knowledge of this world.

The eternal truths of life are expressed in crystal clear terms in the poem "What is there for Pride": 'Vicious lust for power and wealth / To grab the crown with sword or stealth;/ When time calls and gives a sign, / tyrants fall, and fades their reign;/When Fate summons depart we must,/ All this parading power goes to dust.' (*GR*, 12)

Creativity is a passion to the poet and his poems are the off springs of that creative urge and they demonstrate that positive spirit to voyage to newer shores to realize higher dreams of glorious tomorrow. The poet's mental process of wishful thinking involves stimulation of a higher goal, sometimes an improbable reality. Mind is a powerful medium with which one can process, programme and progress with thought process in a positive manner. Our world is full of unnecessary conflicts that drive people half insane. Victory feels hollow, gains seem irrelevant and so life is disappointing. But it is not too late to rescue everything to shape up things to come. No need to fear about the future but we should explore the full potential of every opportunity to shun the risks in the world. A silly situation is merely a passing phase; so man must look beyond frustration, breathe deeply to trust the world to do its best for him. All the apparent problems would lead us actually towards something better. Thus T.V. Reddy succeeds in his poetic art to unify ideas, to promulgate truth, to universalize his ideals and to promote world view and universal vision.

Works Cited

Coleridge, S.T. *Biographia Literaria*. From *English Critical Texts*, Ed. D. J .Enright & Ernst Chickera, London: OUP, 1962, 216. Print.

Kalam, Abdul.*The Family and the Nation*. New Delhi: Harper Collins, 2008. Print.

Leavis, F.R. *Culture and Environment*. London: Chatto & Windus, 1933. Print.

Prasad, B. *An Introduction to English Criticism*. Mumbai: Macmillan Publishers India Limited, 1965.Print.

Reddy, T. V. *Gliding Ripples*. Publish America. Baltimore: USA, 2008. Print.

--- ---- ----. *Golden Veil*. New Delhi: Authors Press, 2016. Print.

--- ---- ----. *Thousand Haiku Pearls*, New Delhi: Author Press, 2016. Print.
---- ---- ----. *A Critical Survey of Indo English Poetry.* New Delhi: Author Press, 2016. Print.
Wordsworth, William. *English Critical Texts*, Ed. D.J. Enright & Ernst Chickera, London: OUP, 1962, 176. Print.

17

Social Consciousness in the Poetry of T.V. Reddy's *Golden Veil*

V. Suganthi

T. V. Reddy is a renowned poet, a notable novelist, and a reputed critic in English. Born in a village near Tirupati of Andhra Pradesh in India, he has held many positions of high importance. Apart from 12 collections of poems, he has produced two novels, and three critical books of which two are on Jane Austen. Many honours and awards including the International Eminent Poet and International Award of Excellence in World Poetry have been bestowed upon him.

Literature guides our life. Any life without aim is like a boat without an oar. It is the goal that decides the course of human life. T.V. Reddy is a poet who is concerned very much with the human life and humanistic values. The potent themes of his poetry are nature and the divinity in nature and death and suffering. His *Golden Veil* is his tenth collection of his poems. This research article attempts to analyze the poems that appear in *Golden Veil*.

The first poem in this collection "In the Shell of Solitude" talks about one who shuts himself up in a shell of solitude. It is not that he prefers it or because he likes it, but because it is his nature. He is unused to the ways of the world and the hurly-burly situation. It is a forced solitude upon him, for he feels that he is "... deprived of the dreamt of touch/ of the long cherished blooming moments" (GV 9). He wants to come out of it, but he fails in his attempt to break the walls. He compares his life in solitude to a life in one's mother's womb. He says, "I fail to cut the tumescent umbilical cord/and free myself from the dark gloomy cell..." (*GV*, 9). When there is such a strong hesitation on his part, he cannot expect any help from the Almighty also. So he does not pray to God. He now realizes that what people say about him is true – that he has been shy and timid from his birth. He is not able to reason out why, but he can only sigh now. He regrets being what he is. Though he cannot transform himself now, because of all these characteristics are in his cells, inbuilt and cannot be got rid of, he realizes he has to be a little bold. He also realizes that he cannot go to anyone else except to Him, the Omnipotent, the Omnipresent; he needs His grace without which nothing can be done, nothing can be got, no peace of mind can be achieved; he cannot shine. It is only courage and blessing of God that make man a legend, change a mortal into an immortal being, a lizard into a dinosaurs or a lion. Even works of art like the poem live forever only with His blessings.

> Yes, I need the kind rays of the higher Grace,
> Bereft of it these lives and lines can't blaze.
> Courage often makes a common man a legend
> Or one has to live and crawl as a lone lizard. (*GV*, 9)

Many visible and significant cultural changes have taken place in India since independence. Across the nation, the lifestyle and attitude of the people have changed. This includes the change in the attitude of the younger generation towards the older generation. The agony of being left alone and left out in old age is brought out in his poem "Old Napkins". It reflects the mindset of the people of today who value things and use people. Even one's parents lose their value once they stop earning, when their kith and kin do not feel the necessity for them anymore, when their kindred do not depend on them any longer, when their children become self-dependent or rather do not depend on them anymore and they become a troublesome burden to their shoulders. Old men are treated like old napkins and used tissues that are considered as waste and thrown, disposed, and dumped into dustbins.

Until recent years, when joint family system was prevalent in the Indian society, it was the care and guidance of the elders at home that molded and shaped the children. There had been great affection and understanding between grandparents and grand children. But today, gone are those days and those ways of life. When the old people try to correct the children, the parents feel that the feelings of the children are hurt and the old men are cruel. But they never try to understand how the feelings of the elder generation are hurt and burst. The poet feels that the parents should not close their eyes to the faults of their children. They should not fail to advise them and lead them in the right path at the initial stage itself. It is the duty of the elders and if the elders fail in their duty, children will sink and stink in their lives. It is like - spare the rod and spoil the child. The poet makes use of a comparison here – he compares the erring children to stray cattle that graze in another's rice field. He also compares the children to leaves and buds that are infested. As pesticides are applied to get rid of the pests, corrective measures should be applied on children. This poem, apart from bringing out the agony and the feelings of neglect in the hearts of old men, brings out the concern, care, and anxiety of the old men for a better and dignified future of their grandchildren to be good human beings:

> Children can be free till they do not go astray
> Parents should not wink, they should think
> Correction at the initial stage is the only way;
> If elders fail to advise, children will sink and stink. (*GV*, 10)

T.V. Reddy finds God and the ways to His abode a mystery in his poem "Unsolved Mystery". He lives in a technological world where everything is brought to the palm of men, and sitting in one's room one can watch the world and talk to people living in distant corners of the world. One need not go outdoors and travel to know about people and lands. The whole universe and beyond is brought to one's palm:

> Sitting in the closed room, the whole world I watch
> I see and talk to people on the other hemisphere;
> This vast parabolic earth in my palm I hold and catch,
> In hours I can reach any part of the world without fear. (*GV*, 11)

He could even feel the taste of the dust of one's motherland and little baby's smiling face in the shining moon. But even these grand leaps in technology fail to solve the unsolved mystery of God. It only deepens one's thirst to know Him better, know Him soon. Technology fails in this regard and the poet closes the poem saying, "All the technical strength fails to find to His abode the way/The more we grow the more the territory of hell and its sway" (GV 11).

> Here one who lives on honest means is a born fool;
> Only those who hate and cheat grab and rob rule,
> Robber kings reign in royal robes and crazy crowns,
> While pseudo-scholars shine inn convocation gowns,
> Powers at the centre thrive in shearing and sharing (*GV*, 12)

The righteous people have lost their confidence and courage to live in this evil-haunted materialistic, power-thirsty world. The anarchic forces are let free to rule. Whatever be the party of a politician, all politicians belong to one common party – the party of corruption and devil's game. They are all power-mongers, rotten to the core. They use caste and creed not only for their votes, they use them also to divide the people and rule them. When people stand divided it becomes easy for the politicians to indulge in more corruption without the fear of any question from the people, for, common men themselves will be busy talking about and quarrelling over their caste and community. People who had been unbiased

> on elusive lines of caste and creed, breed and zone
> by burying ethical frame of mind and spiritualism
> by the new found weapon of pseudo-secularism. (*GV*, 12)

A true leader who is not corrupt, not after power, not after money, and truly concerned with the welfare and progress of the people is the need of the hour. He should have the courage and the strength of mind to drive away all the evil from the land with a sweep of the wand. Only a person who has great moral strength can do it. So another Mahatma, another Kamarajar, another Mandela, another Lee Kuan Yu are the need of the hour to make India a corruption-free country. A Saviour is the need of the hour.

Smile is the curve that sets everything straight. It is contagious. It blesses both the giver and the receiver. It sets the mood of the day bright and gay. It is not artificial; it comes out of one's heart. Such a smile dispels all sorrows and darkness of one's heart. It chases away all pangs and pains, all stresses and strains, all wiles and gules. It is a magic wand that changes everything gloomy into brightness. "Smile, the Saviour" is a poem of light-hearted spirit that talks about smile – nature's blessing to mankind. "It is the shield guarding us from gloom till the end/To mankind Nature's precious gift a real godsend" (20-21).

There is an echo of the American poet Robert Frost in T.V. Reddy when he talks about choosing the right path in his poem "Choose the Right Path". Where in Frost there are two roads diverging in a wood, in T.V. Reddy the path splits in two.

> One seems smooth and safe, leads to majestic metro lights,
> the other, zigzag climbing track up the winding craggy hill;
> One, feast to festive lights teeming with tempting sights,
> the other, a hard and arduous climb through haunting nights. (*GV*, 16)

Frost chose to choose the untrodden path. T.V. Reddy's inner voice, his conscience "... urges me to climb higher above this clay;/Search for Truth, an uphill task, leads to lasting bliss,/We are not sheep to graze and relish ephemeral kiss" (lines 23-15). In this poem the readers see that nationality does not have any impact on the attitude of the people, be they Americans or Indians. Adventurous people, people with individuality who do not accept a readily available smooth path, who cannot be made to follow others, who are ready to face challenges will find their own path, make their own path. They cannot be wearied down by any obstacle on their path; even giant-sized problems become mole hills for them. The poet's travel -

> ... continues from dawn to noon
> No shade; I walk in severe scorching heat
> It is not the end, I hope to reach it soon.
> As throat dries up, reluctant are my feet (*GV*, 16)

Unmindful of any trouble, unmindful of everything that goes around, they carry on their mission. In T.V. Reddy's poem "Choose the Right Path" readers can see such a spirit which is after adventure, which prefers to tread upon the untrodden path. Though at first

> To the easy one, the path pleasant cozy one, mind leads,
> Instant fruits and sweet comforts it dreams to reap;
> Mind is averse to austere steps as in pain it bleeds,
> It runs to seek all pleasures and treasures in one leap. (*GV*, 16)

At the end the poet lands up choosing the difficult, rough one, saying, "We are not sheep to graze and relish ephemeral kiss" (line 25).

Man is mortal. His life is like a day. T.V. Reddy's poem "Soon the Sun does Set" drives home the meaning that the whole life of a person is like a day from sunrise to sunset. As a baby is born, a new life, a new breath comes into the world. Birth is like sunrise. There is always a new leaf to turn, a new experience. Days pass by quickly. And one becomes old day by day. There is no use recollecting days of one's prime life.

> The sun is at the meridian hour in full glory
> The rays are sharp, they strike the skull
> Soon the sun would set, retire hurt and gory
> Before storm or sleep there is the dull lull. (*GV*, 18)

Then there is "... a jerky slide/The sun is past the meridian line, rays are slant/Soon he would set without heat, rage and rant" (lines 10-12). One attains his old age, age of wisdom and sagacity. His feelings and passions are mellowed down by age. The youthful days become moments of memory and pages of history. He has become old.

> You are tired, my child, you are grown too old;
> No use in groaning and gasping for bad breath
> Better not to breathe on the burning pure of pest
> The old frame is laid to rest with a formal wreath
> The sun has set for good with the hope of rest (*GV*, 18)

The proverb says, "A bird in hand is worth two in the bush." Though this proverb goes well with the saying "Cover all, lose all", the poet gives a lively twist to this famous proverb. He interprets it in terms of freedom, in terms of liberty. He says that not even a thousand or more birds in the cage can equal one in the sky at any point of time. Its freedom gives it beauty; its freedom gives tune to its song. The patriotic Tamil poet Bharathiar says, "Vittu viduthalai aahi nirpaai antha chittuk kuruviyaip polae", which means "Be as free as the sparrow that has no ties". One is reminded of Shelley's *Ode to Skylark* in which the blithe or happy spirit flies upward, singing happily filling all the earth and air with its song. What is the factor that brings such happy note into the song of the skylark? It is that the skylark is free – free to lead its own life in the way it chooses. It is not caged. Its freedom is not narrow or limited. It reflects the spirit of Hinduism that talks of the freedom of the soul.

T.V. Reddy's poems are of contemporary significance. They talk of contemporary problems and issues. His poem "Water is Dearer than Blood" is on the issues of water. He is not concerned with whether blood is thicker than water or not, what he is concerned with is that water is dearer than blood to him. He is born and living in a land that suffers from water scarcity. To get even a single drop of drinking water, one has to dig a thousand feet deep. But "of late more often it proves a losing gamble,/an abortive step throwing in economic shambles;" (lines 10-11). Water problem leads to enmity of states and of people. Politicians make it water politics and derive benefits out of it. They give election promises which are empty words that do not bear fruit.

> Deceptive clouds of election promises don't rain,
> Let drops of honesty wash our myopic minds
> And ease our hearts and cleanse our corrupt hands. (GV, 26)

Even the villages which are considered to be the store houses of grains and where there is greenery everywhere are no longer so. There is drought and famine in villages also. And politicians use it as an opportunity to divide and rule the people. When people are in some problem, they will not be conscious of it and bother about what is happening in the social and political life.

> Village is hard-hit with lack of water, lack of order,
> thrown in the tiger's grinding jaws of factions,
> bastards born of dirty elections and petty politics,
> words and acts lead to clashes that spill pools of blood;
> they spread cold wars with cold blood that yields
> not a drop of water but only hate and heat it breeds (GV, 26)

The poet is critical of the politicians and their deeds and he is reminded of the good qualities that are attached to water. "Road to water leads to life, not to pools of blood,/road to life lies in peace and smiles, not in lies" (lines 24-15).

The same theme of barrenness continues in the poem "Our Thirsty Land" also. It is a land of changing moods, changing seasons, changing scenario of green plants and barren land. The rain is rare in this land and added to it there is no storage tank to store and save the water got during the rare rainfall. There are no leaders who have far-sightedness and who is a visionary who thinks of the country and its future generation. Though there is no rain, people still plant in their fields expecting rain but not hoping for it. The poet says

> We are regular victims of heat and hot waves
> And total aliens to foggy morns and cold winds,
> To freezing kisses of the northern snow-clad peaks;
> No sincere scheme, no clean framework to develop
> We continue to be drought and hunger-hit (GV, 43)

Then the poet continues to talk about the economic gap that exists in the country. The poor become poorer and the rich become richer:

> People at the top and bottom reap all fruits,
> those in the middle bear all the breaking weight;
> Small farmers reduced to hungry coolies
> With no hope to rise, they weep and bleed (GV, 43)

Not just this, the farmers can no longer plough their fields, they sell their lands and become coolies. He does not approve of the nursery rhyme "Rain, rain, go away". Instead the poet writes

> Rain, rain, humbly we pray you not to go away
> Please do not wait to come another day;
> We cry and die for a drop of rain like chakora
> To feed our children; let not our prayers go in vain. (GV, 44)

Though T.V. Reddy does not follow any particular rhyme scheme, throughout his poems rhyme casts its spell on us and there is still a rhyme scheme in most of his poems that adds music to his thoughts and makes his poems lively and interesting to read giving it a musical quality. When a pen bends to write, this society should stand upright. The mighty power of the pen of T.V. Reddy can be felt in his poems which are the guiding stars for a righteous worldly life for a heavenly afterlife. The poems bring out T.V. Reddy's social consciousness and his concern for the society and its welfare and future.

Works Cited

Reddy, T. V. *Golden Veil*. New Delhi: Authors Press, 2016. Print.
Shelley's Poems. *The World's Classics*, London : OUP. Print.
Yogendra. *Culture Change in India: Identity and Globalization*. Jaipur: Rawat Publications. 2000. Print.

18 Nature, a Healing Heaven: An Ecological Reading of T.V. Reddy's *Golden Veil*

R. Janatha Kumari

T. Vasudeva Reddy occupies a significant place among the Indian poets. An exemplary academician, Reddy is a renowned poet, critic and novelist of international repute. His poems unveil the inner essence of life. Death, poverty, pain and cultural decadence are some of the eternal issues which the vast majority of people face and experience in real life. Reddy could paint a realistic picture of the contemporary society in multiple shades and colours as seen by his intellectual mind. *Golden Veil* tries to unveil the exciting, emotional, invigorating, futuristic and humanistic persona in Reddy. The poetic collection is rather a beautiful portrait of colourful, soothing and lovely nature in spicy and elegant verses. It is a lullaby for the readers to lull ourselves on the lap of the immaculate nature.

Literature and nature have been intimately interlinked in the long history of literary production throughout the world, especially when oral as well as textual forms of literature are taken into account. Right from Wordsworth onwards, nature poets have expressed their desire to go away from the hullabaloo and crowds of urban settings as they rightly felt that "urban life disturbed a man's peace of mind, unnecessarily filled a man with fatal tensions and worries and hence one wants to have a break from all these and get back his pristine peace of mind" (qtd. in Sivaramakrishna 117).

Poetry is a single eternal stream flowing with crystal clear waters of reality and imagination, consciousness of the self, society and surroundings. To Reddy, writing poetry is purely creative and it gives the poet so much pleasure and happiness. A poet is the member of the society and as such he is always aware of the social surroundings and the environment in which he lives. T. V. Reddy has been a keen observer of nature and human beings. Life in the society, situations and experiences in social life become natural themes of his writing. His love of nature is most probably true and gentle.

In the poem "Nature" Reddy advises us to live with nature and enjoy the plenty of gifts. He is much proud of this wonderful nature which envelops us and showers bounteous gifts on us. The poet is quite aware of god's plenty that he begins the poem with "Live in Nature, live with Nature/ move in nature, merge with Nature/ Nature is our mother and teacher/ nurse, guide, friend and preacher" (1-4). The poet pens down a long list of precious things nature bestows on us.

> Nature gives us fresh water …
> Nature gives us fresh air …
> Let us feel as a bird fresh and light
> It keeps us healthy and makes our mind bright
> Nature gives us birth, our birth and berth
> We need to be grateful till our last breath (*GV*, 83)

The profound relationship between men and the landscape is described practically in all Reddy's poems. Human being is not only a part and parcel of Nature but also a product of nature. This is too true to such an extent that human beings are moulded physically as well as mentally and emotionally by natural atmosphere. Bijay Kant Dubey in his poem "T. Vasudeva Reddy as a Poet" speaks of Reddy, as "a romantic twilight" (7) and "a poet of the sunset and the dark footfall" (24). The poet paints the beauty of nature with all its beatitudes in the poem 'Our Thirsty Land': "A land is girdled with hills or woods/ crescent-shaped range of hills/ green cover of woods and changing moods/ sometimes green" (43) and it presents the serene beauty everyone longs for. In the poem 'Beyond Neon Lights' the poet describes moonlight as the light of happiness and contentment.

As a lover of nature, Reddy's poems brim with images of nature. The age old story of suppression, slavery and hard labour turns a new leaf in the poem 'A Bird in the Cage'. A free bird "From bough to bough it flies singing free/ from wood to wood, from tree to tree/ It tows the sky in sheer joy and flaps its wings/ With the gently blowing wind it flies and floats" (5-8). The poet speaks of the freedom enjoyed by the bird when it was left free to live with nature rather than caged. The concept of freedom literally suits to humanity.

Earth is a great planet which provides us with everything such as food, water, medicines and materials for shelter. Earth has been deified and endowed with all the motherly qualities in Vedic literature. In *Atharva Veda*, Mother Earth is described as sacred: "O Mother Earth! Sacred are thy hills, Snowy mountains, and deep forests" (qtd. in Sivaramakrishnan Xii). Earth is glorified with all tenderness and loveliness of a mother in *Mother Earth*. Reddy questions the madness of man in ravaging this sacred mother Earth. A mother never betrays her children. We rely on our mother for everything. "We live with solid faith in our mother Earth/ Mother never deceives or wrecks her children/ it is there in our blood and veins from birth/ but who will save the Mother from this madness" (9-12). It is always better to live a life merged and mingled with nature It will bestow you with reward of health and happiness. The poet is proud of the resources of our mother Earth. He pens, "Green manure would chase the prowling pest/ Fresh plantation may yield more with our toil" (15-16).

The poet evidently proves the influence of nature on our lives through his verses. Painting the beauty of the landscape is an art that Reddy feels proud of and in this aspect very few can equal him. The poem 'Watching the Field at Night' (68-69) expresses the poet's welling heart to see the pleasant wide stubble field looking cool with quiet moonlit meadows, while 'Green Canopy' deftly portrays the poet's heart which leaps in joy to be with nature. Tired of the humdrum of daily work, the poet "seeks shelter in the wood" (66) and "walking on the leafy banks of forest brooks" (66) is his dire need. The wide sloping rock on the hillside allures the curious eyes to rest on the naked breast of nature and to forget discontent and disappointment.

God's plenty is pictured in the poem *Alone as a Bird*. Life is blessed with all its freshness and fertility. "Eyes could not move from this sunflower field/ Flowers and flowers, large and yellow, rich in yield/ In the drought-hit land, an oasis fresh and fragrant/ beside the mango grove with trees green and vibrant" (39). The land is alive with trees, birds and animals and the tiny patch of golden field becomes "a healing heaven" (6-8) for the suffering humble folks. As the mild evening breeze gently waves and glides, nature appears as though she is dancing and celebrating the bliss. The poet is mesmerized by the beauty of nature. While the "fair flowers dance to the tunes of setting rays" (10) "My feet refuse to move from this yellow patch of land/ as the golden beauty casts its spell with a magic wand' (39). The description of the beauty of nature acquires a higher dimension with the constant flow of music of the lines.

The poem *Sylvan Scene* sketches the charming scene of the "roses, tulips and flowers of purple and yellow colours" that "enthrall the hearts of thousands that watch and vie" (40). The writer adroitly presents the golden glory of the eternal green sylvan scene, the crescent moon that peeps from the golden sky, the sparrows and pigeons which flap and chirp in the ravishing bliss from the space above. It is an excellent poem speaking how Nature guards our life. "Trees tall and stout stand as constant sentinels" (60) and protect our earth at the time of natural calamities. The poet compares the river bank to the neck of a woman and the flowers and plants as precious rubies and sapphires. "Studded with countless rubies and sapphires of flowers/ and plants as a priceless necklace banks dazzle the eye" (60).

Riverside skillfully pictures the beauty of a river, "full with flood water" (42) after a decade. River bank is bright with light and "cool and dear as a mother's heart". Nature always plays hide and seek. The sun hides behind the western hill and tender twilight kisses the barren land hoping to see life there. Trees that stand as guards provide shelter to the birds, and "...tired birds reach their familiar trees" (42).

Reddy could give delicate and subtle expression to the sheer aesthetic delight of the world of Nature. Being the poet of the ear and the eye, he is exquisitely felicitous. Water has been endowed with vital significance all through human history. Water is an oft quoted theme in his poems. Water always delights the poet with its sweet melody and its life giving power. During rain, water comes from the nearby hill giving life to the entire plain. Life seems meaningful and beautiful like the flowers of the fairer bunch. Company of nature gives joy to the human heart and he looks upon nature as exercising a healing influence on sorrow-stricken hearts. *Riverside* registers the musical composing of the flow of waters that "... move and glide" (42) and attract the human beings to "... walk and feel the kiss of the breeze" (42) whereas "Sylvan Scene" invites us to listen "to the melodious tunes of water that glides and races" (42) and to the "music of the rustling leaves" (9).

Ruskin Bond stresses on the importance of living in harmony with nature. Reddy belongs to this creative group and he is no exception; he started growing right from the childhood in the lap of nature. He himself, in one of his interviews with Goutam Karmakar shared the inspiration and influence, nature had in his life. He avers: "some of the scenes and situations that I had seen and experienced as a school going boy certainly do have their impact on a few of my poems" (qtd. in Karmakar 84). The poet's love for nature developed in his childhood days. "Our School Days" is the poet's simple record of his nimble deeds. Even in his school days, he walked "though sands and mango groves" that "added a fresh glow" (73) enjoying the sweet songs of the koel.

T. V. Reddy's poetry presents the graphic picture of the rural Indian life which is the life of Indian villages, mostly agriculture in character. In his presentation of rural settings, Reddy re-creates "the rural ethos and depicts the village, the farmer, the tiller, the corn-reaper, the thirsty fields, the snake charmer, the sparrow and the simple men and women of the village" (Venkataramana, 107). "Erstwhile Farmer" is the mark of a simple rural village life. Beneath the tall and stout tamarind trees, "a few huts of mud walls with thatched roof/ rise as signs of erstwhile simple rural life" (76). The poet pictures the simple life style of the farmers. Their life is entwined with nature. The rural huts with mud walls and mud flooring shine with clean and healthy cow dung coat. Men bathe under the neem tree and "On that limited water the little garden lives free" (76). The lighthearted cheery life is pictured here.

The poet represents the daily life of an ordinary peasant, a common scene witnessed in a village. The farmer "With his pair of bulls ... goes to field at sunrise/ His spouse brings for his breakfast water- soaked rice/ his usual healthy stuff heavy with mango pickle" (76). The hard labour of the farmer working like a bull with the bulls from dawn to dusk finds a realistic portrayal in the poem. After the bath and night meal and a brief talk, " his tired limbs after the daylong toil fall asleep/ on the hard threaded cot of old wooden stock/ his spouse closes the door for the day to sleep" (77).

Reddy's poems reflect the contemporary reality of the society. He prefers to write on natural and social themes, the loss of values in life in general and degeneration in all walks of life. Moreover, as a responsible citizen, he holds the mirror to the reality of social life and exposes all pervasive evil of corruption that has crept into every field of human life. The drought and the suffering lives of the farmers of the nation find a pertinent representation in Reddy's poems.

Nature, a Healing Heaven

The poet speaks high of the farmers and their hard labour in the poem "Today's Rural Life". Life is meant to live. But the farmers sacrifice their life and labour, thereby helping others to live and wait for a new dawn. "Here the farmers look at the skies/ their bowed heads heave endless sighs" (62). Their hearts shoot out arrows of pointed queries: "Our fields how can we cultivate?/ Heat and hunger our hearts can't calibrate" (62). The farmers long to see their fields green, look at the sky without even winking, waiting for the rain. "Cows, bulls and sheep move feeble and lean/ Ponds, tanks and wells die with thirst/ for a spell of long-awaited rain to burst"(62). The poet is very sad at heart to see the streams and canals where he learned to swim once "have lost their address" (62) and now they do not exist at all. "We, the marginal farmers now fail and fall/ At the dry well or the mocking margin wall" (62). They are unable to feed the cattle, for the fields are barren and dry. The issue of farmer's debt and death due to drought, spoken around the nation, finds a reference in Reddy's poems in its true colours:

> If farmers live they live by selling their land
> with water, power and labour rates sky-high
> Farming drowns us in debt and death well nigh (62).

The burning and aching hearts of the farmers is best depicted in the poem "Today's Rural Life" where we see the poet brooding over the past. Fields have turned dry and barren like a desert devoid of life. The farmers earnestly cry over the bygone pleasant days and ask themselves: "Can we ever breathe the rich harvest breeze?/ Can we ever see the good olden days with ease?" (62).

The hot summer finds its portrayal in the poem "Summer Sizzles". Reddy describes the months as scorching. "With March marches the cruel sun/ April indeed is the cruelest month/ paving way to the frying fumes of May" (64) and "mighty May's midsummer furnace" (6) embrace the people with searing heat. Old men like autumnal leaves wither and the streets were deserted because of spilling heat. Shower remains a day dream for the farmers. The peasant's dilemma is pictured in such a way that it evokes sympathy.

> Fields crack as farmers' hearts crack!
> Monsoon loves to play hide and seek
> Crops die s dismal death as aborted babies
> Women walk miles for a pot of water
> Cattle perish in hunger and acute thirst
> As summer sizzles our heart boils and burst
> Jilting June and July reel and roll in heat
> Hands in glove chasing the hot winds (64)

Reddy militantly advocates the people not to cause damage to the natural resources. He is sad at heart for man's greedy nature that made the "Larger part of the hills bare and bald". "Mansion in Ruins" presents the dilapidated house. "At the outskirts of the village alone it stood/ All rains and winds for ages it withstood" (34). It sorrowfully speaks of the heaving "sighs of poor farmers who lost their lands to the mutt" (34). Elsewhere he highlights the devastating debts of the farmers and the comfortable life of the upper class:

> now sky-high costs drown farmers in crushing debts
> With freebies workers sit and sip the honey of bees
> Erstwhile hamlets of hard work turn into idler's nests"

It pitifully mourns for the hungry and desolate farmers for whom "sight of rainfall is a rare event of joy" and rain has become a dream in pensive pain. The farmers walk miles for a pot of water. They plant seeds and wait for the rain in vain. They "are regular victims of heat and hot waves". The farmers continue to live in drought and hunger. The situation compels reader's sympathy: "With no hope to rise, they weep and bleed" and "small farmers are reduced to hungry coolies" (43). They are forced to sell their piece of land and leave their place "in search of green pastures to feed the flock"; they "cry and die for a drop of rain" (44) "to feed our children; let not our prayers go in vain" (44). Therefore, it is our duty to preserve the purity of nature. By harming it, we harm ourselves. Already a greater harm has been done and it is time to protect nature so as to protect the human race. As children of nature it is our duty to protect the bounteous nature, the precious god-sent gift, as nature is our mother, guide and philosopher.

The poem "Water is Dearer than Blood" is in fact an elegy on drought. Reddy, a poet born and brought up in the land known for rivers and lakes strikingly records the importance of water, which is the true elixir of life. He stresses on the fact that water is dearer than blood in this rainless land haunted by drought. Though one drills 'thousand feet deep' into earth, one cannot hope to get a drop of water, because "water is a rarity, rain a rare spectacle" (26). The poet lucidly presents the significance of water in our life and pleads – "Let drops of honesty wash our myopic minds" (26); he advises the villagers, hard-hit with lack of water, to bid goodbye to factional fights because they yield -

> not a drop of water but only hate, and heat it breeds;
> Road to water leads to life, not to pools of blood;
> Road to life lies in peace and smiles, not in lies." (26)

"Seeded Soil" is a remarkable poem in four stanzas of four lines each with rhyming lines and it spreads the light of hope amid the darkness of disappointment crushing the helpless farmers. While presenting the disappointment of the farmers it motivates them at the same time with rays of hope. Farmer's "solemn prayers for rain go in vain;/ In the furrowed field groans the betrayed grain (78). A few seedlings boldly rise to see the light but "Soon sun-burnt the shoots fall into dusty night" (78). A soothing word or deed can heal the burning heart and revive it afresh. The futuristic thought of the poet urges him to think that a rainy drop can wake up and make the burnt plants breathe afresh: "Beneath the soil seeds lie buried with the sheath; / Poor farmers' dreams and seasonal hopes fall" (78). It is not an exaggeration to say that this poem is one of the best poems in Indian English on the rural scenario for the faithful presentation, veracity of factual information, powerful imagery and the amazing word music.

Reddy painfully records the vagaries of vicissitudes of life he experienced in his life and how his experiences gave him strength to overcome such difficulties and to be hopeful. "Track without a Trace" is a powerful sonnet that reveals a part of his self and how he faced and braved the "Vagaries of wily winds and storms" (73). "Look at the Stars" portrays the obstacles that lie in the path of life and the poet says "Dark clouds and stormy winds might try in vain/ to arrest the bright twinkling touch of starry light" (45). "Dumb Toys" states the muted situation of the societal members who struggle to reach the destination of their journey in life. Life is a voyage where the poet discloses the secret of his journey in the turbulent sea of life, "braving the wild world of whales and crocodiles" (35).The poet pens that "we are all dumb toys or struggling ants/ to sail or sink to the whims of sealed fate/ our voices are muted" (35).

In the poem "Let Me Stand Erect" which is almost subjective, the poet teaches the world to withstand the stormy winds of stress and strain and to " march through varied shades and stars of injury" (37) and "From the clouds of rage and envy" to "emerge like a star" (37). "Soon the Sun does Set" instructs to work hard at the right time and to be courageous to face all shortcomings. The poet is of the view that there is no use in groaning and gasping for the past things, but to be "brave to turn a new leaf" (37) for the dawn is near. The old frame is laid to rest with a formal wreath/ the sun has set for good with the hope of rest" (37).

According to Aju Mukhopadhyaya, "Reddy's poems are charged with intense humanism as the poet bemoans the loss of values so as to dream for harmony and a better future" (Mukhopadhyaya, 96). He is a poet with humanistic vision who envisages a new beginning and brings cheer to the lives of all who feel forlorn and dejected. His poems mark the majestic print of hope that makes anyone come out with a smiling spirit. He emerges in most of his poetry as a social being concerned with the fall of values and happy with the progressive rising trends of standards in human life especially in Indian content.

"No More Tears" bravely advocates the folks to brush away the tears and "trace the end of the soothing spring" (20) and prepare ourselves for a fresh beginning. "Star is a Star" is a twinkling spark of radiance that illuminates the life in "this dusty earth/ or in vast expanse of azure sky" (29) and sprinkles hope to attain the peak of glory. 'Flowers Shall Bloom' is a poem that urges the mankind to shed away all hopelessness, for, "Life is not an endless autumn, it has its spring/ Flowers shall bloom and koels are sure to sing" (65).

Nature has a befitting role in each one's life. It plays a pivotal role in shaping a man's personality and life. Wordsworth opines that, Nature is a teacher from whom one can learn a lot and without which any human life is incomplete and vain. "Learning is Life" is an enlightening poem in the form of a lesson for all ages to come. It illustrates that there is much to learn from the various objects of nature. The trinity of earth, sun, moon and stars convey their perpetual message in natural ways:

> Let us look at this amazing globe
> and learn from tree and leaf and fruit and flower
> from ant to elephant, dog or deer and lion
> from crow to cow, reptile to fish, let us learn
> From all the five prime elements of nature,
> fire, air, earth, water and sky, let us learn (81-82)

The poet is an optimist who accepts both sides of life with a welcoming note. He acknowledges life with all dualities like happiness and grief, heat and cold, fame and shame and lead a contented life "with what we get; / Let us not expect high" for it leads to despair (81).

Reddy believes in god and he firmly states that it is *karma* that shapes our means and ends So let us learn and receive the good from everyone to lead a life of righteousness and to save ourselves from fall. He hopefully says god shall shower his mercy with all that befits us. His poems exhibit his ample love and appreciation of nature and sympathy for the noble cause. Reddy requests the mankind not to neglect Nature, as we are the children of that great Mother. He wants his voice to linger in the hearts of the people. In "Let Us Sing as One", Reddy sings the "sweet symphony" of his "art of life" (25) and leaves "a few humble lyrical notes" for us "to recollect" (32) and live the life meaningfully merging with nature,

Works Cited

Reddy, T. V. *Golden Veil*. New Delhi: Authors Press, 2016. Print.

Karamkar, Goutam. "Interview: Dr. T.Vasudeva Reddy." *Contemporary Literary Review India*. Vol.4, No.1, Feb. 2017. 84-91. Print.

Mukhopadhyay, Aju. "Thrust and Trend in Vasudeva Reddy's Poetry." *Galaxy: An International Multidisciplinary Research Journal*. Vol.5, Issue. 4, July: 2016. 66-71. Print.

Sivaramakrishnan, Murali. & Jane, Ujjwala. "Ecological Criticism for our Times – Literature, Nature and Critical Inquiry". New Delhi: Authors Press, 2011.Print.

Venkataramana. "T.Vasudeva Reddy, The Poet: The True Son of Indian Villages." *Labyrinth* – An International Refereed Journal of Postmodern Studies. Vol.3, Issue. 3, July: 2012. 107. Print.

Dubey, Bijay Kant. //http://poemhunter.com//> 12 July 2017.
   <//http://www.boloji.com//> 22 July 2017.

19   Ecological Concerns in T.V. Reddy's collection of poems *The Broken Rhythms*

Sr. Candy D Cunha

Nature is a constant support for the development of human being. It juxtaposes various themes such as environment, ecology, green earth, nature, planet, universe and the world at large. Nature has served as an important subject for many poets across the country. Nature not only unfolds the music and beauty of the pretty backdrop of the natural world but also mirrors its pains and struggles. The romantic poets like Shelly, Coleridge, Keats, Wordsworth, Byron, etc. celebrated nature through aesthetic expression. They found joy and contentment by being one with nature and reflecting upon it. They looked at nature as the expression of beauty of the Creator's handy design. Nature gave them comfort and solace. They reciprocated their love for nature through nature poems that brought out the rhythmic expressions and musical qualities. Their poems revealed beauty and happiness and above all the principles of human nature.

The present century is unquestionably facing serious ecological crisis. Nature which was cherished and praised by the great romantic poets is gradually ruined and distorted by the irresponsible use of the advancements in science and technology, and with the herald of the global era. The world is facing many ecological problems due to the selfishness, lack of understanding and reckless behavior of many people towards mother earth. Many ecological thinkers, poets, and writers try to voice their concerns through their writings.

All these writers try to provide a ray of hope for future generations. Their tireless efforts and good will on behalf of the environment can be deeply seen in their works. Rachel Carson's *Silent Spring*, published in 1962, served as a main resource material for ecological thinkers. She challenged her readers to reflect upon the dangers posed by an indiscriminate use of chemical biocides. She urged humans to care for nature with responsibility and admiration and to draw life from it:

> Those who contemplate the beauty of the earth, find reserves of strength that will endure as long as life lasts. There is something infinitely healing in the repeated refrains of nature - the assurance that dawn comes after night, and spring after winter.
> *Silent Spring* (1962)

The ancient philosophy of India has its deep roots in ecological realms as it speaks of culture, traditions, beliefs and a holistic way of living. Looking back at the former periods, we notice that the ecological unsteadiness began with the industrial revolution. The eighteenth century witnessed the gradual change of climatic conditions as it succumbed to the new phenomenon of setting up of many factories and industries. As a consequence, human being's relationship with nature changed forever.

The attitude of humans towards the sacred nature deteriorated slowly and led him to falsely imagine that he is the supreme ruler of the earth. This anthropocentric attitude made him feel that he is the most important species on earth and nature could be used as he pleased. Natural resources were exploited as science and technology began advancing. Many western countries tried to use industrialization solely for unplanned growth. Many societies adopted the idea of progress which aimed at a healthier, happier and prosperous life. In the bargain, environment became the victim of human being's progress. Natural resources like minerals and coal are used in factories. The smoke that emanates from them causes heavy pollution and it leads to the damage of the environment. If wood, instead of being recycled, is used in the wrong way, it gradually changes into non-renewable fossil fuels.

The nineteenth and twentieth centuries witnessed several scientific discoveries and new technologies which led to rapid industrialization in many western countries. This brought about the rapid exploitation of natural resources. With the invention of the engine and the automobile, the consumption of fossil fuel in industries and for transportation increased rapidly. Huge machines which were made for sawing and felling trees were used in forests for converting them into industrial wood.

Thousands of dams were constructed with the invention of concrete, and river water was diverted for agriculture and power production. Food production was increased with the help of chemical fertilizers and pesticides, but they also polluted water and degraded the soil. For irrigation, ground water was extracted in huge amounts with the help of pumps. Many species became extinct. Millions of birds, whales, fish, and animals were hunted down and destroyed by using powerful guns and big ships.

As the ecosystem is severely degraded in many ways, the question remains: "Will nature restore the ecological balance over time"? The earth has existed for over five billion years, and human generations for about three to five million years and civilizations for about 10000 years. Many of these generations have often contributed to the degradation of the environment but still mother earth survived these crises.

The last third part of the twentieth century witnessed several problems of ecological backlash that mounted feverishly. Undoubtedly, science has brought in wonders to the world in helping humanity in many ways. Humans need to understand also the darker side of science, as it has the potential to wipe out humans from the face of the earth. The products of science like the nuclear, biological, chemical weapons can destroy the human race for ever. The former Prime Minister of India, Manmohan Singh, in his article on Science, Religion, and Spirituality states:

> Concern for the environment has followed hard on the heels of the concern about the destructive potential of the weapons of mass destruction that twentieth century technology has gifted to the people of the world (T. D. Singh 2005:158).

The present era has been exploring nature, often making rapid development and progress. But, unfortunately, many of the traditions, their meaning and effectiveness are being lost, leading to the destruction of nature. Indian environmentalists, both ancient and modern, have voiced out their true love and care for nature through their very living. The wisdom contained in Indian ecosophy reminds every one of the great concept of nature as the supporter and sustainer of life. This can be seen clearly in the thinking, ideas and principles of Indian environmental thinkers.

Some of the great Indian environmentalists of the pre-independence period and the present period like Rabindranath Tagore, Mahatma Gandhi, Vandana Shiva, Ramchandra Guha, Krishna Srinivas, Arundhati Roy, Mahaswetha Devi, T.V. Reddy and many others have contributed immensely to the study of environment.

T.V. Reddy is a renowned poet, critic and a novelist who has gained international name and fame. He occupies a significant place in Indian writing in English. His poems unfold the inner essence of life. He did his M.A. in 1966. Since then he has been contributing to poetry. He received an International Eminent poet award in 1987. He received best poetry award for his third book *Fleeting Bubbles*. His poems appeared in French journals in Paris. He was recently awarded an International award for his

Excellence in World Poetry in 2009. Some of his popular works of the early phase are: *When Grief Rains* (1982), *The Broken Rhythms* (1987), *The Fleeting Melodies* (1989), *Melting Melodies* (1994) *and Pensive Memories* (2005) The present paper is an attempt to explore ecological concerns voiced in his anthology *The Broken Rhythms*.

As the title *The Broken Rhythms* itself suggests the picture of broken melody and potentially it is to be understood as a symbol presenting the broken rhythm of life. A broken rhythm cannot provide a full fledged synchrony. Similarly the ecological concerns mentioned by the poet in his anthology also lack an ecological rhythm. Most of the poems in the anthology are eco-centric. They aim at restoring ecological harmony and balance.

The poem "The Naked Tree" is a symbol of brokenness and pain which nature undergoes due to the various atrocities done to her. The tree represents life. It is full of beauty and grandeur as it gives life to the humans and also to other creatures in creation. Trees protect humans and other creatures from various disasters and afflictions. The poet feels very sad to describe the pathetic condition of the naked tree. He uses various figurative expressions to compare the pitiful status of the tree. He urges mankind to revere the naked tree as it was once upon a time a giver of life.

> Don't turn your eyes
> from the naked tree;
> it is as dry and stark
> as the skeleton of a cow
> whose carcass is punctured
> by the steely beaks of vultures
> tired of giving life. (*BR*, 4)

The poet reminds humans that even though the tree is not in a healthy condition of giving life, still its past glory of serving mankind is to be kept in mind. The tree was a great provider for the mankind. The fruits of the tree were cherished and consumed by humans. Now that the tree has lost its greenery and has become old, it is neglected by all those who enjoyed its fruits in due season. The poet feels extremely sorry for the tree which bore all the blows from humans who enjoyed its fruits. He tries to remind mankind of their irresponsible acts towards the tree:

> Betrayed by those that relished
> Its fruits in raptures
> The mango with all its past glory
> Succumbs to the unkind blows (*BR*, 4)

Valuing nature is the most important environmental attitude. As human being often gives great importance to his own beauty, status and lifestyle, so also nature has to be regarded as part and parcel of his daily life. It is only when human being feels that he is only a minute part of the complex web of life, then true appreciation for nature begins. Human being needs to understand that he belongs to the huge global community which includes 1.8 million known living forms. As each one forms a unique part of creation, so too, every other living organism forms an integral part of the universe. Therefore, human beings must recognize their great responsibility towards nature and value the diversity of life and foster stability upon the face of the earth.

> At the bottom, every man knows well enough that he is a unique being, only once on this earth; and by no extraordinary chance will such a marvelously picturesque piece of diversity in unity as he is, ever be put together a second time.
> Friedrich Nietzsche (Quotes 1844:1900).

"The Milky Way" is the other poem which emphasizes nature as the powerful tool to introspect on certain realities of life. The poet mentions the name of the great philosopher Sophocles who found wisdom and great understanding from the Aegean Sea. The poem also describes the various phenomena in nature like the Milky Way which refreshes sad souls.

> On the shores of Aegean sea
> Ages ago Sophocles watched
> The hoary sound o weird waves
> And the vast dark expanse, a crux;
> Bulwark of brightest brains.....
> As it gazes at the Milky Way
> That keeps darkling souls at bay (*BR*, 5)

The poet assumes that humans hardly see the truth hidden in nature. He compares the musing mind of human like a summer tyre which bursts in friction if it discovers the truth. The poet tries to make a beautiful impact of nature upon the life of man. The poet also brings to light the Vedic Rishis who drew strength from nature by deeply meditating upon the great truths hidden in nature. By way of conclusion, the poem tries to shed a ray of hope on the human who has failed to draw insights from nature. Nature can give joy unspeakable, in leaps and bounds to human soul.

> Vedic Rishis cracked their brains
> retreated in despair to forest
> and spent their breath in penance. (*BR*, 5)

The poem focuses on nature as a healer. Great wisdom can be drawn from nature. It has the power to transform the attitude of human and make him into a great person. Nature can provide the entire humanity with eloquence and wisdom to move and act wisely in this world to make this earth a better place.

Through the poem "Toiling Ants", the poet invites the readers to learn from nature. The tiniest creature in nature performs its duty with toils and pains. The toiling ants teach humans to work in unity and dedication. The spirit of perseverance and endurance can be grasped through the poem.

> As I looked
> through the window
> of my mind
> at the marching troop
> of tiny toiling ants (*BR*, 3)

The poet reminds human to open the window of his mind and observe the tiniest creature in nature that are totally loyal and committed to their work. They are like an eye opener to the humans. It is the duty of man or woman to learn from nature and the smallest creature in it.

The next poem in the anthology is on "Farmer". In this poem, the poet tries to elevate the relationship of a poor farmer with nature. His simplicity and true desire to endure struggles in order to produce the harvest of joy are seen in the following lines:

> With a loin cloth around his waist
> And a soiled, the only cover
> For his sun-burnt back,
> He drew his wearied feet
> To his field- a still-born child (*BR*, 9)

The farmer has an immense dependency on nature. He soils his hands in the earth to pull out the thorns and weeds. He is very close to nature. He waits for a drop of rain looking at the sky. Nature is the constant companion of the farmer. Despite many difficulties and discouragements, the farmer continues his good works by counting on nature for his survival.

> With full many a thorn and weed
> Still he pulled on the drudgery
> like the dumb bull that ploughed
> looking everyday up into the sky
> for the deceptive clouds with a sigh. (*BR*, 9)

T.V. Reddy tries to convey the message of broken rhythms through the disfigured images in nature. He proposes the need for a paradigm shift in understanding and dealing with ecological problems that our common home is facing. We need to rediscover the earth as our home, our dwelling place, as more than our simple environment. It is only when we start caring for our common home that we will be able to listen attentively to the groaning of the earth and understand the pain that she is going through.

The select poems in the anthology are about the wounded earth with bandages and wounds. The poet reminds every one of the greatness of mother earth that gave birth to her children and nurtured them with care and breast-fed them with a plentiful harvest. The poet feels pained that now in turn, the children of the earth have turned against her and have exploited her and have stripped off her green garment, making her to feel immersed in sin and shame. The paper is an attempt to present the ecological concern present in the select poems of T.V. Reddy.

Works cited

Carson, Rachel. *Silent Spring*. London: Linda Lear, 1999. Print.

Catton, William. R. Jr. *Overshoot: The Ecological Basis of Revolutionary Change*. Urbana: University of Illinois Press, 1980. Print.

Nietzsche. https://www.goodreads.com/author/quotes/1938.Friedrich_Nietzsche?page=4/

Reddy, T.V. *The Broken Rhythms*. Madras: Poets Press India, 1987.Print.

Singh, T.D. *Towards a Culture of Harmony & Peace*. Delhi Peace Summit, New Delhi: Anderson Printing House, 2005. Print.

20
Echoes of Native Ethos:
A Study of Indian Sensibility in T. V. Reddy's *Echoes*

Gobinda Sahoo

Indianness is an element of Indian writings, which shows Indian thought, its setting and scenes, language and locations, myths and legends, philosophy and society, which makes Indian an Indian. K. R. Srinivasa Iyengar opines: "Indian writing in English is but one of the voices in which India speaks."(3) Further he asserts "Indians have written - and are writing- in English for communicating with one another and with the outside world, for achieving self-expression too artistically, using English, if necessary, or necessarily, in an Indian way." (4) And these writers through the process of Indianization have molded the language to suit their communicative purpose. Indianness in literature has a native appeal on Indian readers, whereas for alien readers the feature makes it exotic by way of giving a deep feeling to encounter real India. Indian English poets now are giving importance to various subjects of day-to-day life dealing with the socio-economic-political problems of the society.

> "Their poetic outpouring to various subjects, their nostalgic attachment to the roots of Indian culture, myths, customs and rites, their marathon efforts for picturizing the tone and temperament of Indianness, their new poetic and structural devices to make the feelings quite equivalent to the form are really very encouraging and worth appreciating." (Amar Nath Prasad, 34)

Like the reflections of Indianness found in many contemporary Indian English poets, it is abundantly found in the poems of T. Vasudeva Reddy. His poems are deeply rooted in the traditional Indian sensibility and it is yet strikingly modern in expression.

T. V. Reddy is thoroughly a poet of Indian sensibility. The present study deals with the echoes of native ethos, the reflections of Indianness in his collection of poems viz. *Echoes*, published in the year 2012. India is a land of scenic beauty. A keen study of the collection reveals that many poems in it reflect the poet's longing for natural beauty around him. He does not merely give importance to the natural sights but he is also captivated by the sound, smell and feeling of numerous miracles of nature. He is moved by the 'gentle zephyr of cosmic music/ soft, inaudible and eternal'. The soothing aroma, which he describes as 'invading flood of fragrance' of different flowers, has its impact on his olfaction, the sense of smell. The gentle rustle of lush leaves, the soft whisper of woods, the songs of birds, the helpless whine of animals, the roaring beauty of the ocean, and soothing melody of rain – all have their profound impact on his sense of hearing. All these form the music of nature which is irresistible to his aesthetic imagination.

The striking and eye-catching sights of nature - the earth kissing the sky, the mesmerizing colourful celestial rainbow, the sparkling jeweled beauty of the vast starry sky - have a deep impact on the poet. All that he sees, hears, smells and touches have indelible impression on him and they get reflected in his poems. He concludes the poem "Nature's Play" thus:

Echoes of Native Ethos: A Study of Indian Sensibility 131

> I hear the resounding sound
> Of the tyrant's pounding feet,
> the thunder and the stormy wind,
> eternal music of oceanic waves
> the icy touch of the Himalayas.
> Nature's play of balancing
> is superb, a wonder, a marvel,
> a mystery we can never unravel (15)

In the poem "A Summer Trip" the poetic persona wants to visit the northern tourist destinations like Haridwar and Rishikesh. The poet is captivated by the scenic beauty of the flow of the river Ganga from the Himalayas to the plains downwards. He considers crossing the river Ganga on the Lakshman Bridge as:

> a solace to the disturbed mind
> and indeed a balm to the aching body (59)

The poet is enthralled by the charm of the musical flow of the racing river. He writes:

> The hills ring with the flowing music
> of the rise and fall of the racing river,
> echo the range of scenic splendor;
> on the higher hills of biting cold;   (59)

The poet gives a comparative picture of tea gardens in the south and north of India and the pleasure of tasting a cup of tea. He says that Kerala tea shop is a high landmark. He might have given reference to the tea of Munnar hill station of Kerala or a favorite tea shop maintained by a Keralite in his native town. On the other hand the tea of the north is distinct for its flavour. Towards the end of the poem the poet expresses his intense personal feelings. In India many temples are found on the hill stations. T. V. Reddy thinks that Gods may prefer to live and move on the hill stations, as the places are the centers of solace and tranquility, peaceful atmosphere and bliss free from pollution in a country like India.

T.V. Reddy expresses his concern for the degrading state of forests in "A Journey in the Jungle". He states even the Himalayas are not as green as they used to be earlier. Owing to the global warming, snow is melting fast and the Himalayan range is losing its luster and radiance. It has started losing the density of its past greenery, beauty and 'freshness of the old Paradise'.

The poem "Plants" in four stanzas of four rhymed lines each is an aesthetic presentation of the botanical growth and life of plants in general with their budding and flowering stages marked by blooming smiles and dancing of rustling leaves. Growth of plant is described as overcoming the hostility of spoiling weeds and aggressive reeds and T.V. Reddy deftly presents the reality that even for plants life is a struggle. Then it leads to the advent of buds. With the emergence of spring new foliage blooms and flowers emerge out of the buds that 'smile as full moon'. The reference to spring and autumn seasons speak of the poet's love of nature and seasons and his attachment to natural beauty of the country with the changes brought in by the changing seasons in the beauty of the natural surroundings of the countryside.

T.V. Reddy gives a panoramic picture of places of pilgrimage, their importance and their scenic beauty in the poem "A Summer Trip". He gives reference to the cooler tourist destinations in Northern India in order to take respite from the scorching heat of soaring temperature in the south and middle India.

> from the pitiless hammering sun

> and his smarting whipping lash
> in search of a cool breezy wash
> of the burning body and mind
> in the northern streams that run, wind
> and hop from the mountain range (59)

He gives references to pilgrimage to 'Haridwar or Rishikesh, a tapovan' (59) where the sages in ancient age had won divine peace. The Ganges that descends from the Himalayas to the plains is marked by cool and refreshing water which may be called life-giving under the hammering sun of the summer. He portrays the scenic beauty of the sacred hilly place at the foothills of the Himalayas and says crossing the Lakshman Bridge (known as Lakshman Jhula) on the river Ganga is 'a balm to the aching body' (59). Highlighting the spiritual significance of the pilgrim centres, now the tourist destinations, he mentions the prominent places like Rameswaram, Tirupati, Badrinath, Varanashi, Kedarnath and Haridwar.

"A Journey in the Jungle" also gives a panoramic view of the rural phase of India. Reddy's reference to 'the parrots singing in the swinging boughs', 'the chirping sparrows', 'height of the Himalayas' give the readers a local feeling of natural sights in India and the poet's love of the beauty of nature which has an irresistible charm on the poet.

T.V. Reddy has been a champion of the use of Indian traditions and ethnicity in his poems. The social practices have amply been used as themes of his poems. The poem "Reflections of a Crow" gives a picture of the age-old belief of the Hindus in India. The poem has been presented as reactions of a crow which is served with *pindam*. It is a social practice in India among the Hindus that, during death anniversaries food cooked in memory of the departed souls is served to the crow, which marks the end of the ritual. Only after that the members of the family take the food. The crow considers the people with such belief as 'poor souls' who see the souls of their departed loved ones in the crows. The crow could not make out whether they are learned fools or they use the crows as foolish tools to achieve their goals of paying tributes to their loved ancestors.

In the poem "A Cry in the Jungle" (86) T. V. Reddy gives reference to the great freedom fighters and statesmen like Gandhiji, Netaji and Sardar Patel, in order to bring a comparison with that group of so-called politicians who are power-mongers and corrupt in nature.

In the poem "A Summer Trip" (59) T. V. Reddy strongly opines in the voice of the poetic persona that it is the spiritual belief of the people of India that binds them amidst diversity. And the flow of the Ganga is described to be an eternal one. He writes:

> Spiritual quest is a common bond
> that binds all the people of this land
> from the seas to the northern snows;
> it has a gravitational pull to attract
> while in the Ganges eternal dharma flows (60)

T. V. Reddy's poetry abounds in social consciousness. He gives a vivid picture of the trauma of Indian society. With its glorious cultural heritage and wealthy race the country is facing multiple problems, some seen and some unseen or felt, some natural, some man-made. The ruler, who one day was supposed to be the representative of God, is the leader of a coalition government sans ideology. The parliament which is supposed to be a sacred temple of democracy is a meeting place of robbers, criminals and people full of tricks. It has turned into 'a house of hostile pulls and pricks'. The words of the people 'should bloom and blossom/ as fair flowers in the green garden/ to spread pure healthy fragrance' (45) else they prove to be fatal. T.V. Reddy gives a picture of the canvas of Indian nation, as he foresees the consequences of a country where the relation among the inhabitants are hostile and ill like:

> vomiting vicious drops of poison -
> robbing, raping and looting,
> killing, burning and shooting
> with bullets from bullet proof cars (45-46)

Reddy with profound confidence believes that the bloodshed as recorded in history may be far many times less than what was not recorded in the pages of history and what is seen in the modern world through internal wars, bloody revolutions, the killing spree of Jihadi and terrorist organizations etc.

> History knows only a few stains of blood,
> pages beyond it stand and stare unseen
> with their kin untraced in the gory flood;
> unseen leaves are drowned and buried
> in streams of blood dry in cold dust
> beneath which ruthless swords die in rust(46)

We have forgotten the 'eternal words of peace, love and ethics for righteous path and noble life' which were pronounced by Ram, Krishna, Buddha and Christ millenniums back. At the end the poet cautions one and all that if peace and grace do not emerge from words, they may get converted into hacking swords in cruel hands.

In the poem "Change" T.V. Reddy brings forth the change that has occurred in the Indian society. In earlier days it was only poor people who were hungry for want of food. But now with the change of time it has shifted to the power hungry leaders. In a very simple and lucid manner the poet asserts that the common people still remain helpless tools.

> common people remain helpless tools,
> flow with the wind like yellow leaves,
> they simply sit and see as willing fools
> in search of a bunch of shining sheaves (49)

Hunger lies on the lap of those who labor for two loaves of bread daily, but the hunger of political leaders leads them to trips to foreign countries. Here power-hankering political leaders have been compared to the hungry wolves that 'resort to wicked ways'. Agitations and demonstrations nowadays are done with the involvement of unlawful elements and hired ruffians and idle people of the so-called backward and oppressed classes who march 'in fleets of AC cars with burning torch.' The poet questions: can such parades bring a revolution? Revolution is the consequence of nobler evolution. If the leaders of a country indulge in such foul ways to achieve their selfish goals, there is no chance of the rise of the nation. Progress of a nation depends upon the progressive mindset of the people in any age.

The poet expresses his concern over the degenerated state of the society in the poem "This System". Many people raise their voice to bring changes in the society, to change the entire system in order to establish the cherished dream of the thinkers. The progress of the society is nowadays counted in terms of super markets, I-MAX (Maximum Image) theatres, hi-fi educational institutions with multiple professional courses.

Education is sold and purchased as commodities in the society where there are multitudes of scams related to all the five elements. These five elements are known as the *Pancha Maha-Bhoota*; the Earth or *Prithvi*, water or *Jal*, Fire or *Agni*, Air or *Vayu*, and Ether or *Akasha*. These elements have their characters and celestial functions. According to Hinduism these are the basis of all cosmic creations. According to Indian Philosophy and *Ayurveda*, the human body is supposed to be made of these five elements. Reddy indicates that scams linked to these five elements ultimately means scams of self. On the other hand, the western countries are inclined to look to the Eastern countries and particularly to India and consider her as the spiritual guide. But the people of the east have developed a false sense of fascination coupled with pride for the Western culture ignoring the rich cultural heritage of India and amidst chanting of mantras of the past, they go on amassing wealth through corrupt practices. The poet lashes out at this callous attitude severely.

"Wings of Dragon" gives a vivid picture of India struggling in the trap of corruption. There is no sphere in Indian society which is free from corruption that 'marches with a heroic hand'. India was considered a sacred land with rich cultural heritage and ethical background. But now the scene is changed and no sphere is free from the deadly dent of the dragon that covers the sub-continent. The higher the position, higher is the level of corruption and it is an uphill task to change the attitude of the officials. Reddy expresses his deep concern for all people, rich and poor alike, who willingly let themselves fall into the tempting trap of corruption and relish to love this vicious practice. At the same time he is grief-stricken at the growing corruption spreading its wings on all the spheres, political and education, cricket and defense, construction and excavation, commerce and bureaucracy.

In "Comfort Zone" the poet recalls the open defecation practice of the rural folks when he was a child. In order to ease oneself, one had to get up early before sunrise and go to the fields with running water at arm's length. He lashes at the unhealthy condition of the toilets in public places and the hopeless way in which they are maintained. Though we have toilets in both urban and rural areas including in public places they are neither properly used nor well maintained.

"Empowered Woman?" is a poem that presents a vivid picture of a working lady. She has to work right from early morning before sunrise to late night. In the morning her face glows like 'Minister's khadi cap' but in the evening her fatigued face is transformed into a 'weak withered vegetable stalk (51)'. The poet has the extraordinary talent in the use of right imagery and it is quite evident in the portrait of the working woman he has painted. She has to get her two naughty children ready for the school. Then she has to rush to the office, where she smiles artificially to her co-workers. She works there half-heartedly and sharp at 5'O clock she leaves the office. The bus in which she returns also remains crowded. What drives her move to her home in haste is 'to refresh her restless waiting kids/ and her passive unconcerned husband.'(51). Late in the night she rests 'the mass of her aching limbs' on her hard unfeeling cot. This is the regular hectic schedule of a working lady who is 'patience personified'.

There has been an abundant use of Indian myths and legends in the lyrically rich poems in the anthology *Echoes*. Through the path adopted by Buddha in renouncing the world, despite all abundances, the poet puts forth the flashes of glowing pages of Indian history. In order to cherish truth prince Siddharta had to renounce his wife, child, palace and everything, seeing disease, decay and death. And he turned Buddha. His life and teachings were so heart-touching, soothing and lovable that criminals, even cannibals, turned his followers. Buddha has been termed as a great guide who 'showed the path of Dharma / to reach Nirvana by treading the Eight-fold path' (96). Reddy gives the chronological development of Buddha from Siddharth.

In the poem "Sri Aurobindo" (99) T. V. Reddy gives a picture of how the minds and attitudes of the followers of Sri Aurobindo are enabled to capture the 'divine drops of honeyed essence' and the minds transform 'to reach Supramental state' with the light of spiritual bliss. Reference to Buddha, Sri Aurobindo and the Mother is a way but to reflect on the spiritual history of India. Reddy seems to have been influenced by Sri Aurobindo's philosophy, his theory of evolution and his interpretation of *Bhagavad Gita*.

In the poem "Lord of the Universe" (100) the poet's reference to the Vedas and the Upanishads, where it has been mentioned that the 'Supreme Power and Force' is nameless and formless but limitless, give light on his deep knowledge of Indian philosophy and religious scriptures. He also asserts that God is above life and death.

"Nothing Follows" (101) is the last poem in the book and this poem is steeped in Indian philosophy and thought. T. V. Reddy says that the air, the water, the land do not belong to us. We are not what we are and we don't own what we think to own. But the entire universe is ours and we occupy every atom, every line. The entire world is a mere illusion, a synthesis of shades and our life is but a journey after the mirage which we strive to fetch. Throughout our life we care not for loss of our name and fame for the sake of earning money. But by the time we realize the reality of life literally, we are left with nothing in our control; our eyes are forced to close for ever. By the end of the poem the poet furnishes a set of suggestions for the human society to follow. It is vital for all in the society to do some good before we are trapped by the final journey. In the final journey to the funeral, a dead body needs four shoulders or hands. The journey remains the same for all the people, rich or poor, ruler or the ruled. We come to this earth empty handed and leave in the same state. Thus, we must not have any sense of hate or hostility or loathsomeness in our life. And before the final adieu we must do something meaningful and leave a trace of the fragrance of the small good act to remain as reminiscence when we depart from the world. The poet writes in simple but memorable lines to stay in our minds with their everlasting message:

> We may win, reign or lose empires
> listen to the music of flutes or lyres
> and sit on the golden thrones with stones,
> but our last place is the pit or pyre.
> When we come we bring nothing
> When we leave we carry nothing,
> then why this petty play of heat and hate;
> before we depart let us do a bit of good
> leaving a trace of fleeting fragrance (102)

Creation of a new idiom i.e. Indian English idiom has been a striking feature of writers in Indian English. In order to give authenticity and identity to the Indian English language there has been a demand for creation of an Indian English idiom. Many poets of post-independence period like Nissim Ezekiel, Kamala Das, Jayanta Mahapatra, Shiv K.Kumar, Keki N. Daruwalla, and others have attempted to create a new idiom for Indian English. Contemporary poets are no exception to this group and T.V. Reddy is one of the potential contributors to this new development. He uses a number of Indian words like *'pindam'*, *'Nirvana'*, *'Dharma'*, *'Karma'*, 'Bodhi tree' which make the poems thoroughly Indian in sensibility.

The imagery and idiom, situations and locations, allusions and philosophy of India have found significant place and ample expression in the poetry of T.V. Reddy and all these aspects make his poetry quite remarkable leaving an everlasting impression on the minds of the readers. Among contemporary voices in Indian English poetry he has distinguished himself as a poet par excellence with his rich idiom, simplicity of diction, spontaneity of expression, lyrical line and enchanting melody. His poetry is deeply rooted in the age-old Indian tradition and culture and as such in Indian sensibility. Thus all these textual evidences lead to the conclusion that poetry of T.V. Reddy bears the unmistakable stamp of Indianness with regular echoes of native ethos, which constitutes the bedrock of the thematic structure of his poetry.

Works Cited

Iyengar, K R Srinivasa. *Indian Writing in English*. New Delhi: Sterling Publishers Ltd, 2014. Print.

Prasad, Amar Nath. "*Indian Poetry in English: A Bird's Eye View*". *Critical Response to Indian Poetry in English*. Eds. Amar Nath Prasad, Bithika Sarkar, New Delhi: Sarup and Sons, 2008,

1-37. Print.

Reddy, T. V. *Echoes*. New Delhi: Gnosis, 2012. Print.

----

21   Manifestations of a Fractured Soul in T. V. Reddy's *Pensive Memories*

J.S. Divya Sree

Since ancient times, man has been trying to express his emotions and feelings, and his observations on life and the world through various media. Many great writers had already proved that poetry is the best medium to express human feelings and experiences. T. V. Reddy, as a poet, has used the platform of poetry to reach the inner minds of the readers, unsettle and disturb them so that the readers think about life and world. With their elegant style and rhythmic quality, his poems have always rendered a new focus into life. The present article is about how T. V. Reddy treats various themes on man, nature, society and philosophy in his poems in the collection *Pensive Memories*.

Man's suffering has always been a spark for many a great writers to provide the common people with some of the great pieces of literature. Almost all the poems in the collection *Pensive Memories* contain that element of suffering of man at physical, emotional and spiritual levels. Deep speculation on life and society marked by the poet's reflective nature are the keynotes of the poems in this collection. Man's suffering in general, the inevitability of death, unbearable loss of the loved one, the crude portrayal of rural and urban setting, and the futility of power and authority are the major themes dealt within these poems.

The poem "The Dull Evening" deals with the suffering of both man and nature during midsummer time. The nature, animals and humans are tired by the evening which is described as "dull, eerie and dreary". Cattle are thirsty and are in a persistent search for a drop of water. They see mirages all through their way home but those mirages cannot quench the desire of their parched tongues. The use of the phrase "parched tongues" reveals the intensity of their desire. The roads are dusty and the condition of the trees on both sides of the road is more pitiable. The image of trees as "hapless bony skeletons/ waiting for Christ's resurrection" creates an element of pathos in the mind of the readers. Here, the poet compares the rain to Christ's resurrection. In other words, the rain has been imparted with the god-like image, but it refuses to get resurrected. They are at the mercy of "eerie elusive sepulchral clouds" for the restoration of rains.

The scene gradually moves on to the cloud of dust rising out of the cattle's movement and "the wide patches of smoke" from the poor village hamlets. The smoke from the huts is the result of the hard work of the village housewives who lit the kitchen fire with their "loud painful pitiful… /…coughing lungs" (19-20). The village women toil hard even destroying their health to serve their husbands. They wait for their husbands to return from fields with "moist eyes alive with a flicker of hope". They are out of energy after the whole day's work but a spark of hope let them alive. This poem, as the title suggests, is about a dull evening; but the poet uses the evening time to showcase the real life of village women. The poem is structured in a cinemascope manner where one scene rolls on to another. The images are so well used and special mention is to be made for the use of alliteration in this poem: "sweating, sighing and stinking"; "sullen, sultry, shadow"; "grisly ghostly"; "bare and bald"; "from the fuming fallow furrowed fields". The poem is a realistic presentation of the village life after the sun-set and we see before our eyes a living picture of rustic life through Reddy's marvelous word-painting the effect of which is enhanced by word-music:

> The cloud of dust rising from the herd
> merges with the wide patches of smoke
> emitted from the poorly feebly thatched huts
> the result of the loud painful pitiful play
> of the coughing lungs of rustic housewives
> waiting for the return of their tired men
> from the fuming fallow furrowed fields
> with moist eyes alive with a flicker of hope. (*PM*, 18)

"The Crow" is a poem that speaks about the qualities of the crow and the attitude of humans towards it. Humans are seen as the sophisticated creation of God with their intellect, and their ability to use power. In this poem, the poet tries to distinguish between the crow and the man. The crow clad in black is called "the alarm bird" awakening the world from sleep. With the crow's alarm, the village is roused and the women have started to work in the house. The day's toil of housewives starts with cleaning of the house and the surroundings with cow dung water, decorating the front yard with flour designs and lighting the oven. The crow is "the unfailing friend" of the village people who, at their call, comes to gulp the grain and crumbs. The crow is given special importance on occasions like that of funeral. During the funeral ceremonies, it has been given the position of the special invitee. According to the belief of the villagers, the crow is the symbol of the dead ancestors coming to taste a few bites of the funeral morsel. It is also believed that those who do not give food to crows will not be given seat in heaven. At the same time, the poet expresses his wonder at the discrimination man shows to the crow.

On the one hand, people adore the crow as the carriers of the souls of their dead ancestors and on the other hand, some people discriminate the crow based on the colour of its body. The poet calls this discrimination "apartheid policy" applied with folly. Then the poet compares the values of man and crow. He says that the crow represent human values that have become extinct in man. Unlike the man, the crow is not corrupt in its voice and action. The poet also points out the fact that when one among the crow's species falls and collapses, all in the tribe surround the collapsed one and expresses their grief. This is an indirect indication on man's selfish and self-centered nature. Man has lost the ability to empathize with the fallen fellow beings. Even though the crows are dark and are marginalized on this basis, they are humane. In the modern world of competition and complicated social relationships, the crow will show us the right meaning of living.

'Migrating Birds' is a poem that expresses the concern of the people who have to migrate due to famine. The poem narrates the pathetic migration of people to distant places in detail. The people migrate with their belongings placed on their heads and shoulders in "silent shadows with sunken eyes". They are in search of green pastures where they can cultivate a prosperous future of their own. While men hope for a better workplace to settle down, the women follow the footsteps of their men with children. The children do not have the strength to smile or cry but "a faint flicker of horizontal hope" can be found in their "passive eyes". They have to face the hostile climate all through their way to new lands. The old men and women who cannot move are left behind, and the phrases "heavy hearts" and "hunger-hollow eyes" provide us with a neatly drawn picture of the poor old people. The migrating birds reflect on their past life with grief but their "weak and weary wings" cannot take them far away land free of misery and poverty. The comparison of people moving from one place to another because of a calamity to migratory birds indicates the poet's creative and imaginative power.

"A Lone Bird", "The Healing Echo", "Veil of Death", "A Pair of Doves" and "To My Other Half" are poems that are based on the death of the poet's wife. In "A Lone Bird", the poet compares himself to a lonely bird which has lost its beloved. Being ten years older to his wife, the poet expected that he would make his exit from the world before his wife. Unfortunately, fate played a game with the poet's life by taking her away in "airy chariot". Poet calls the sudden demise of his beloved as "a sad unnatural process". He also finds that the Gods liked her so much that they brought "an abrupt end" to her life. As a loving husband, the poet is now waiting for death to reunite the separated couple in heaven. He compares himself to a chatak bird. Like a chatak bird waiting for a drop of rain to quench its thirst, the poet is waiting for the destined chance to meet his other half.

The poet's heartfelt desire to live in his wife's memories till the last breath is the essence of the poem 'The Healing Echo'. The poet wishes to live in the past memories of the healing echo, his wife. With a smiling face and love, she had "lent light to his dull inert life". The void of his life had been filled up by her with harmony. Till his last breath, he wants to be alive in the memory of his gentle love. Her voice, eyes, and smile are all those which he wishes to sense "till I (he) breathe".

> I know it is a dream; still I love it
> O Lord, make it real after my exit. (PM, 25)

Thus ends the poem. These lines are enough to explain the dedication and love of the poet to his wife.

'Veil of Death' is a poem that elevates the poet's love for his deceased love to another level. The poet says that a thin veil of death stands between the mind and the body. He is so desperate that he craves for death to take him away from the world of duties and responsibilities:

> When half of the self is gone
> why should I care for the end? (PM, 34)

A parent bird leaves its abode once its young ones become bold and free. Similarly, the poet also waits for "the stark stony end" to rescue him from this lonely world. The poet feels that his "fractured soul" will rejoice to meet his other half waiting for him in an unknown place.

The poet uses the metaphor of a pair of doves to show the intensity of the bond of love between his wife and himself. Through the verse narrative "A Pair of Doves", the poet has drawn a brilliant picture of his own family. The male and female doves lived in a happy home, "a mini Paradise". With love, trust and mutual understanding, the doves led a joyous life. Unfortunately, the female fell ill and died. The male dove enthusiastically waited for its beloved to open its eyes. The young ones grew up and flew away but the male dove waited for that eternal call that might re-unite the lovers. With utter desperation, the poet asserts that "with Eve's exit, Adam lost his Paradise" (41).

"To My Other Half" is written in the form of elegy. It begins with general philosophical assertion and gradually leads to grief on the loss of his beloved. The poem states that the life in this world is "ephemeral and momentary". It is only a fleeting bubble and according to the poet, when his better half has died, it means that half of breath is lost. The poet continues lamenting that his lonely life is of waste without her. The death of his wife is "an atomic explosion" to him. Her dead body has joined the five elements of nature but the heart of the poet is left behind with "a burning pyre" and "an endless saga of sheer sorrow". Then the poet describes nature's mourning at the death of his beloved. Clouds roared, and streams and rivers overflowed with tears. The sun the moon and stars hid themselves behind the clouds and the sky expressed its sorrow with the burning meteors. He asks the moon not to pity at his life without his beloved. He uses the metaphysical conceit of "two lunar spheres" to describe his wife's eyes. The light of those eyes were put out by the cruel hands of fate and as a result, the light of his life is also put out. He remembers with love how she filled his life with happiness and prosperity, and asks the reason for leaving him alone in the world:

> O love, your lively loving presence
> lent my average life a rich fragrance/...
> created million melodies in life's voyage

> churned sweetest drops of honey,
> tuned the lyrical strings of my heart
> and solaced my tired sentient soul
> with your radiant smile and balmy touch;
> Why have you vanished from my life?   (49)

His life without her is like a toy without a guide and he is not at all confident in leading his life's "heavy cart" to the end. When they were together, their life was full of liveliness and serenity whereas after her death, it has become a desert. Towards the end of the poem, he considers the demise of his wife as a kind of punishment from Lord Shiva. He bemoans that he does not have the power of Saadhvi Savithri who brought back her husband from the clutches of Yama (Death) through worship and devotion. So instead of bringing back his wife, he craves to reach her soul in heaven. He justifies his belief in the reunion asserting that their relationship was made of *Saptapadi* bond. *Saptapadi* refers to a rite in Hindu marriage ceremony where the couples vow to share their life, joy and sorrow in their married life. The poem ends in an optimistic note that even though they are separated in the physical world, their hearts will unify in the heaven.

"The Lotus Palace" and "Tsunami" are poems that convey the transitory nature of art and the insignificance of human life. The Lotus Palace is a monument in Hampi Vijayanagara that got its name from the lotus bud curved on its dome. The palace is one of the structures, which remained undamaged when the city was looted. But here in this poem the Lotus Palace refers to the Royal Palace at Chandragiri, the last capital of Vijayanagar Kingdom. It was built in 1000 AD and it still retains part of its glory even after the Mohammedan invasion. The Lotus Palace is portrayed as a 'dumb witness' to the degraded glory of the noble life. The engravings on it have marks of prided lust and royal luster down the ages. It has been once a Paradise envied by others and "blind and unwise" hands have caused the ruin of the tower. The rooms, once used by royal ladies, are now occupied by spiders and bats. The carvings of gods and goddesses are now mutilated. Even though the Palace has lost its past glory, it still has faith in time:

> Royal rooms studded with spider's web
> in nocturnal internet with bats' racking rub;
> The chiseled gods and goddesses scattered lay
> Mute and mutilated at an unholy havoc's bay;
> Lotus with lovely petals shines and smiles
> With eternal faith at the passing clouds,
> Changing shades and marching miles.   (40)

"Tsunami" is written on the 26th December 2004 terrible tidal wave that caused vast destruction. The poet traces the origin of the tsunami and calls it "monstrous" that rose from unknown dark depths. The places which once allured the minds of men have become similar to a grave. People irrespective of age, gender and class were crushed and washed away by the waves. The poet inquires:

> Are they beaches or bleeding open air mortuaries
> Sylvan seaside scenes or corpses-filled foul sanctuaries? (56)

Beaches have been transformed into "bleeding open air mortuaries" and this suggests that all forms of beauty created and maintained by human beings are silly before the outrageous Nature. Nature is beautiful and can be beautified by man's creativity. But once Nature lets loose open its fury, then it is impossible for the humanbeings to overcome. After the tsunami attack, many rescue attempts were made but poet feels that no rescue ships or planes can restore the victims to harmonious life. The words "bereaved souls", "battered", "bruised", and "beaten" describe the shattered minds and lives of the tsunami attack. Borrowing Shakespeare's words ("flies to wanton boys") to compare the insignificance of man before Nature proves the poet's elevated imaginative power. For humans, ants are too small; similarly, we are also too small from Nature's perspective.

T.V. Reddy in his *Haiku* attacks the contemporary political, educational, professional and social society. Starting from poetic insight on a sleepy night, the poet delves into the issues that need grave consideration, and ends with a reflection on his deep philosophical thought. This philosophical thought can be regarded as a probable solution to the problems that upsets the poet. The poet mocks at the servitude of politicians to the public that only ensures their political power. The political power granted to them by the public is used to enslave them for "full five years". A man who openly declares that dowry is a crime receives ten million as his son's dowry. The poet also satirizes a modern woman who went on a tour against dowry and came back home to pester her daughter-in-law in the name of dowry. Harsh arrows are aimed at politicians who are unethical and corrupt.

> If you get elected for one time
> Your life and progeny are sure
> For generations to be secure (*PM*, 59)

These lines are a testimony to the inglorious nature of contemporary politics. The poet also mocks at the leader's proclamation to transform his state into "a land of gold". In his attempts to make his "magic vision" practical, he forgets the poor ordinary masses living in his own state. Not only politics but religion has also become corrupt. With wealth in the hands of politicians and priests, they can rule over the political and religious systems.

The poet also makes a grating criticism on doctors. When the poet says that doctors who got their degrees out of people's money are now interested in accumulating wealth, the readers are given a picture of heartlessness of the doctors. The line "stethoscope widens economic scope" clearly indicates the poet's contempt for the amoral physician community. The teachers are also without any principals. Teachers' inertia and their pretension to be knowledgeable affect the dreams and aspirations of students who are compared to wingless birds. The doubt whether schools are educational institutions or financial companies is a doubt that exists in each and every one of us. Managers of educational institutions act like bill collectors and therefore guide students in a wrong direction. But the sad state of affairs is that with all these negative aspects schools are growing in our society like mushroom. The public works department is also equally corrupt and irresponsible. The condition of the poets is too miserable without any word of appreciation for their work. Here is the poet's philosophical dictum:

> The greatest art
> on this museum of earth
> is the art of life. (*PM*, 61)

In this world, the brightest light after the sun is reality – which the poet calls "the light of the eyes". The only solution to these problems is to make ourselves pure and clean.

As a poet, T. V. Reddy occupies a prominent place in Indian English literature. His keen observation of nature, speculations on life, harsh criticism of social institutions and use of alliterative verse makes him stand apart from his contemporary poets.

Abbreviation: PM: Pensive Memories

Work Cited

Reddy, T. V. *Pensive Memories*. Madras: Poets Press India, 2005. Print.

22   T.V. Reddy's *Quest for Peace* and T.S. Eliot's *The Waste Land*: A Comparative Study

Poonam Dwivedi

T.S. Eliot composed five sections in *The Waste Land* and T.V. Reddy has gone for seven sections in his *Quest for Peace*, a longer poem impregnated with ideation of sojourn of solitary soul sailing in the sky hovering over the cities of Indian sub-continent. The watchful eye of the soul relates the tale of the city, its environs, episodes, reportage, skirmishes and conflict of interests of the corrupt characters. Although Eliot's *The Waste Land* has titles for its sections like "The Burial of the Dead," "A Game of Chess," "The Fire Sermon," "Death by Water," and "What the Thunder Said", all the seven sections of T.V. Reddy's *Quest for Peace* are untitled. The substance can only be gauged from the narrative which is summarized as 'Soul Set on Sojourn,' 'Soul's Search for Truth', 'Nostalgia of Soul,' 'Soul's Yearning for Peace,' 'Soul's Idealism' 'Soul's Pilgrimage,' 'Soul's Quest for Peace Ends in Spirituality.' But ending of both the legendary poems is a clear convergence in the confluence of Vedantic thought followed by Peace (*Shantih*) repeated three times.

In *Quest for Peace* a hypothetic soul sans the cage of the body sails beyond the dynamics of space and time; it desires to have a sojourn and a resting place to experience peace which is the seminal spiritual spark glowing in T.V. Reddy's *Quest for Peace,* an epical poem of 1665 lines written in Khanda-kavya style of Indian poetic tradition and ethos. Each and every line is complete in its meaningful mysticism and at the same time the quatrain stanzas maintain rhyme and rhythm but certainly not at the cost of unwanted verbosity or thematic sequence. The sense and sound of the epical poem is not broken for the sake of critical appreciation, but it has to be bifurcated. I have chosen to take up first 60 lines for the sake of its decoding and prodding vis-à-vis the long legendary poem of T.S. Eliot's *The Waste Land*.

We may rightly place the *Quest for Peace* as one of the best works of all modernist literature like T.S. Eliot's *The Waste Land*, Joyce's *Ulysses* and Stephen Gill's *The Flame*. Although in those three other great works rhyme scheme has been randomly followed, T.V. Reddy follows the rhythm and rhyme scrupulously while progressively developing the thematic substance of the long poem. If we compare the sections of *The Waste Land* with *Quest for Peace*, the magnitude of the latter is more striking not only because two more sections have been added but due to longer scope and vastness of content of the sections penned by T.V. Reddy.

To dive deep into the poetic skills of the great mystic poets, let us examine the background of the contemporaneous world when *The Waste Land* was composed. The First World War had ended after leaving a degraded, decayed and demoralized society in Europe. Eliot's sensitivity has tried to reconstitute and rejuvenate the society wallowing in degeneration, but any diagnostic treatment needs a descriptive and elaborative scanning of the ailment. The narrative in such circumstances cannot be called pessimistic and pensive, but it has to be full of agony, anguish and righteous indignation seeking necessary correction and improvement. The evocative exhortations and emotional explorations of the poets, thus, become long poems as it has happened with T.S. Eliot and T.V.

Reddy. Both the great mystic poets have unflinching faith in ancient glory and rich heritage to resurrect and replenish the wasteland, a land that has become a burial ground, a land covered with garbage that has turned it into a rats-ridden stinking place.

> Let us have the first quatrain of the poem of T.V. Reddy:
> "For this single soul's ceaseless flight
> this is a brief linear landing place for rest
> to refuel its teasing tank with inherent right,
> and refresh with clean air free from pest. (*Quest for Peace*, 1-4)

The mystic poet has narrated the solitary journey of a soul by using the word 'single' and 'soul's ceaseless flight' which denotes that the soul has taken the endless journey all alone; and the sojourns of births and reincarnations of the soul do take place after death. The soul is indestructible in Indian ethos and its ceaseless flight goes on even after the demise of a person on the physical plane. A subtle reference connects the mythological divine bird Garuda which is invariably related to *pauranic* stories and legends regarding soul's transportation to several invisible worlds and realms including the hellish river Vaitarini. Eliot has also fired his first salvo in the first section "The Burial of the Dead" in his long poem:

> April is the cruellest month, breeding
> Lilacs out of the dead land, mixing
> Memory and desire, stirring
> Dull roots with spring rain ("The Burial of The Dead", *The Waste Land*, 1-4)

Everything seems to be either dead or dull, a beautiful symbolism of the devastated land which is in need of a soothing touch of spring rain.

T.V. Reddy's invocation of the ancient anecdotes to resurrect the dead souls living in the present day world is to be found everywhere in the poem just as there is the focus of T.S. Eliot on the ancient tale of fertility rituals vis-à-vis modern thought and religion in the guise of Fisher King. The mythical aphorism remains the spine of the thematic structure of both the poems of significant length. Fisher King has been wounded in the genitals and his lack of potency is supposed to be responsible for his country turning into a waste land. Reddy's solitary soul sailing in the sky seems to be a sojourn after death; otherwise the soul remains in the cage of the body which is revealed in the later part of the poem.

Eliot's emphasis and search for panacea for all the ills of the country has to be read between the lines to restore the vitality and potency of the Fisher King; similarly for T.V. Reddy, the ambrosia for the nation's survival may be traced in the ancient wisdom as enshrined in the scriptures.

The life is just a 'brief linear landing place for rest' as the earth is not considered to be a permanent abode of the soul. The world is impermanent and perishable, a transient abode metaphorically said to be an inn for resting for a while. The whole poem is agog with Indian beliefs and mystic teachings of the yore as presented vis-à-vis the face of contemporary metropolitan culture and mega malls. In the last two lines appended below, the mystic poet attacks the polluted environs of modern day living with the introduction of 'pest' and 'teasing tank' for refueling. The journey of the soul is spoiled by the presence of impure and filthy atmosphere of the sacred places. There seems to be no place for the pure soul to rest and the search goes on in the poem as it advances. The searching soul seeks the abode of peace but there is no such place where it is not 'full of foul fear.' The lamentations with prefix of 'Alas!' occur at many places to bring down the curtain of a thought or relief as it happens for a short interval:

> Alas! A loss for the searching soul to rest here,
> a stage far from peace, full of foul fear.   (*Quest for Peace*, 5-6)

T.V. Reddy has adopted a pattern of writing for the mystic poem which seems similar to Kalidasa's *Meghdootam*, wherein the personified cloud hovers to see many places during its sojourn to the city of Ujjain. The searching soul of the mystic poet looks at the sacrosanct place of the Lord's Temple in the Eastern Hills. The exact naming has been avoided by the poet intentionally so that nobody should feel hurt in sentiments due to the outpour of mysticism and pragmatism with veiled criticism of the poet, who has used the literary device of legendary fables to browbeat and expose the caprice, greed and cut-throat competition in the pursuit of capitalism etc.

> This fabled ancient eastern hilly place
> relished once the Lord's supreme grace;
> Eons ago it was the sacred spot of His choice
> on this earth hallowed with His divine voice
> that Gods and humans had cast a spell,
> now exiled by the metropolitan pell-mell (*QP*, 7-12)

The opening two stanzas of the first section describe the ultimate 'Waste Land' as Eliot perceives it. The wasteland is cold, dry and barren, heaped in garbage. It is not like a desert, which has its own beauty in mounds and dunes with footprints as it burns with heat; the clogged water of river is static except to see a few scurrying rats. The stagnation stinks and its ugliness stands implicit in contrast to the 'Sweet Thames' of Spenser's time.

T. S. Eliot in an ode to the River Thames in *The Waste Land* wrote that it is indeed, oil and tar and other industrial pollutants for years plagued Britain's rivers, right from the 'Great Sink of 1858.' The celebrated poet recalled the horrifying past when the human waste choked London's Thames. The famous lines still ring the warning bells for water and environmental pollution happening across the globe:

> The river sweats
> Oil and tar
> The barges drift
> With the turning tide
> Red sails
> Wide
> To leeward, swing on the heavy spar
> ("The Fire Sermon", *WL*, 266-272)

In the *Quest for Peace* the protagonist is a dissatisfied soul that narrates in the next lines the sordid state of affairs of the modern world. The poet has chosen the poetic device of profound alliteration in describing the poignant and gory tales of the so-called present day development and progress as reflected in the ancient cities of civilization. The words like 'human vultures'... 'without culture' 'busy to their bones as bees'... 'sucking human blood to the lees' 'parched rags'... 'borrowed tags' and alike 'broken doors, frames and bones'... 'cracking walls and roofs and crushed tones,' tell the story of the trampling foot prints of man:

> mindless terrorism spilling pools of blood,
> every minute ticking in its streaming flood,
> while bridges widen the yawning grisly gulf
> wiping out the blooming petals of self
> to lengthen the elastic life of sinful courses
> with the hideous help of infernal sources. (*QP*, 69-74)

The first section of *The Waste Land* begins with a desolate riverside scene: rats and garbage surround the protagonist. Symbolism is at its best- the speaker proclaims himself to be Tiresias - a figure from classical mythology who has both old man's wrinkled face and breasts of a female and who is blind, but has the ability to look into future. He is a mystic figure, portrayed as:

> "I, Tiresias, though blind, throbbing between two lives,
> Old man with wrinkled female breasts, can see
> At the violet hour, the evening hour that strives
> Homeward, and brings the sailor home from sea,"
> ("The Fire Sermon", WL, 218-221)

The section comes to an abrupt end with a few lines from St. Augustine's Confessions and a vague reference to the Buddha's Fire Sermon regarding 'burning' which is repeated four times; however, reference to 'nothing' repeatedly speaks volumes about the Buddhist philosophy of '*Shunya*'(The Void). The readers and critics are left perplexed with the riddle of 'nothing', but the Buddhist philosophy has its base in 'nothingness' just as the Vedantic thought ends with 'neti, neti, neti' 'not this, not this, not this.' In fact, to describe the indescribable, one has to take the help of the negative tool of elimination; otherwise the glory of the ineffable Absolute becomes limited to the words of eulogy. Eliot has reached that state of consciousness:

> What is that noise?
> The wind under the door
> "What is that noise now? What is the wind doing
> Nothing again nothing.
> "Do
> You know nothing? Do you see nothing? Do you remember
> Nothing?"
> ("The Burial of the Dead", WL, 117-123)
> "La la
> To Carthage then I came
> Burning Burning Burning Burning
> O Lord Thou pluckest me out
> O Lord Thou pluckest
> Burning   ("The Fire Sermon", WL, 306-311)

In *Quest for Peace* almost two-thirds of the inference of contemporary culture comes from the newspaper reports published from time to time. There is a plethora of happenings which find their proper place in the poem to depict the scenario of the present day living. The suffocated and wretched soul living in contemporary culture of exploitation and plunder, violence and cut-throat competition, savage human behaviour compels the poet to open the window for a fresh breathing and seeing. The pithy portrayal of the pathetic tale of modern society has found an emotional narrative in a long poetic breath which finds its next inhale after completing the journey of the soul on crossing of sixty milestones. The stanza of the poem, thus, ushers in a whiff of oxygen to the gasping man:

> where desire and death vie with each other
> with equal force the voice of truth to smother (QP, 57-58)

Finally, the chaste soul finds 'voice of truth' almost smothered with equal force. The duel of desire and death ceaselessly has been going on in the arena of modernity and the world cheers the bout with boisterous applause. The three dimensional graphic has been presented by the mystic poet after the completion of his first breath of 60 seconds; then and there begins the presentation of the pathos of the marginalized, the fallout of the environmental pollution, exploitation of capitalism, leftist obstructionism, scourge of reservation, monstrous corruption, ugly face of bribery and its volcanic eruption and the widening gulf between the haves and have-nots. With the signature seventy lines of mystic poetry with its stunning sweep, the searching soul halts for a while and adverts to new sojourn:

> Let us free this city from heat and hunger,
> at its security let none raise his foul finger;
> the existing power blocs have monopoly total,
> as great as medieval Western authority Papal. (*QP*, 84-87)

The mysticism of the poet is not only confined to the speculations of philosophy but it has within its fold the layers of universal hunger and power struggle between the super powers to monopolize the mankind. The Papal conflict of 'State within a State' of the medieval times makes sense to exhibit the scourge of starvation even after so many centuries of resolve to end human hunger. After blasting the conceptual expression 'His Holiness', the poet focuses his attention to His Highness, the political jugglers, money multipliers, hired killers, parasites, thugs and pubs, who have spoiled the generations with their paraphernalia of cronies and cranks. The high rise structures do have 'raucous rupture' and the darkness is being hailed by the plunderers through prism of their selfish interests and greed and the whole world seems to be a paradise for the self-centered eyes.

While Eliot refers to the mythic tales of ancient Egypt to Arthurian England, Reddy refers to the Vedic and Vedantic canons. The modern thought does not believe in the mythological figures and their monopoly of admiration and veneration. But both the poets have attempted to rivet to the twain of the past and present, Western and Asian poetic didacticism and diction.

Autobiographical element always creeps in such an emotional work as after all it is a journey, may be poetic in tone and tenor, seeking poetic justice, and may be christened as *Quest for Peace*. The fragmentary thoughts of the Bible and the Vedas suggest that both the poets never wanted assorted and scattered anecdotes and aphorism to be inanely borrowed and included, instead the poets were very eager to consolidate the allusions in coherence but at the same time never wanted to adhere to a didactic and puritanical style.

Both the poets have disowned the reader at several stages to be left high and dry in the face of their erudite scholarship that surprises with its integrated creative attempt to present a mimetic account of contemporary life in the world of contradictions. Although Reddy's long poem opens with the soul sailing for quest of peace and later on it converts into personalized experience, again in the middle of the long poem the soul searches for its contextual coherence. If symbolism is to be taken into account, Eliot's 'regeneration' at the opening in the month of summer is meaningful as the dried roots sprout after the spell of winter. Reddy is also emphatic to relate the pathetic scenario to build up the tempo for a poetic onslaught of sarcasm soaked in irony.

The personal experience of both the poets creeps in and the nostalgia peeps through the stanzas in the long poems. The juxtaposition of the past and the present becomes a necessity to highlight the decadence in the society. Nobody has seen the past but its glory has always haunted the souls throughout the history. The contemporary tales in the history have always been critical of the state of affairs but the past of course comprises of a collected collage of the continuous contemporaneous culture.

The mystic poet after completion of 120 lines, turns into a creative genius of idiomatic aphorism like 'blood of butchered bodies in cruel showers' being washed away, 'mercury of morals to bottom level slips and dips' and again the beautiful line 'crowded bars, rising stars, tempting lips and zips,' all have been soaked in the emotional outpour which finds mention in the poem to sum up in 'a city of burning lights, fights and dark delights.' All bad lights have been focused on the slighted sights by the poet's creative righteous power reigning everywhere from remote village to the civilized capital including the fashion shows, rapes and gagging. The whole scenario presents a hellish canvass of criminality to be witnessed in the midst of progress and civil strides and strikes. Even Guru Dutt's legendary Pyasa song fails to match the description of Reddy whose lines (*QP*, 170) excel the former's lines which are quoted here: "Jinhe naaz hai Hind par voh kahan hain…" The entire poem *Quest for Peace* reveals the supreme gift of the sense of sonorous sound which is the unique forte of T.V. Reddy.

Eliot's sense of sound has a unique role and the poet succeeds in exploiting its remarkable role in the presentation of the theme. These forms of presentation also have a significant place in the poem as theme-driven sections proceed with the usual assortment of various line lengths and random rhythmic progression. "The Fire Sermon" has the input of musicology to sound better because of the wedding song, a ballad and nightingale's chirping, and all these notes of symphony contribute to the making of an exalted piece of literature.

For T.V. Reddy a ray of hope and positive signal comes at the end of the dark tunnel after completion of the initial mystic breath. The optimism at last survives all the onslaughts of contemporaneous corrupt practices that hamper the progress based on 'bear all to fare well' syndrome:

> To survive the nomadic onslaughts of erasures
> let us fortify and energize our heart's enclosures (*QP*, 205-06)

The poet does not stop and halt in condemnation of the acts, behaviour, and conduct of the politicians, merchants of death, all-round masters of Satanic brains that know the knack of minting money through trumpeted Vision 2020 and the propagators of the creeds of Divide and Prosper and *Chaturvarna* Caste system. A positive spark emerges from the pen of the poet after 280 lines where eulogistic reference to Vedantic thought is given:

> after five millenniums nation still wriggles,
> in the age-old iron structure bleeds and struggles;
> our great Upanishads see the glow of god in all
> while the corrupt pundits caused the murky fall (*QP*, 291-94)

The poet becomes nostalgic of the past, but at the same time the series of historical blunders that happened teases and dampens the spirit of the mystic poet and his comparison of 'White Raj' with 'Native Raj' and 'Personal Raj' is relevant and profoundly suggestive. The concept of 'Raj' has been expanded by the poet to the meaning of proprietorship, autocratic rule and fiefdom of the politicians and bureaucracy. They have all combined and conspired together to reduce the great nation to a backward state in all respects - 'Nation is hurled into a foul and fallen state.'

Pollution of rivers and reference to Varanasi where the impure water of the holy Ganges flows reveal the aching heart of the mystic poet and his painful awareness of the dangerous level of environment pollution. The poet is not an atheist and he is a blind believer, but his faith is not ritualistic and as such he relishes laughing at his sleeve at the dogmatic style of our people. There is continuous shifting of stance by the poet in the lines because there seems to be a volcanic eruption in his heart and mind. The lava flows rapidly and the gush takes in its flood all the dirt, filth, garbage that has been piled up by the politicians, media, corrupt bureaucracy and other centers of power and position. The poet does not want to miss an opportunity to make a reference to Anna Hazare's Movement and so-called 'anarchy' as termed by the establishment. There is a regular and reiterated attack on the dynastic politics though the system of princes and princely privileges had been scrapped. The coinage of the word 'son-stroke' is a brilliant innovation of the poet. The assertion of the poet comes to the fore when he says that he is a believer in democracy, but hates the dynastic politics and parachute landing of the sons on the political stage of stardom:

> We believe in our age-old doctrine of Fate
> and Karma which indeed is great at any rate;
> the poorest old fall like leaves with sunstroke
> while the leaders at the top with 'son-stroke (QP, 349-52)

The portrayal of stark realism in its nudity is the high watermark of both the poets of creative excellence – T.S. Eliot and T.V. Reddy. T.S. Eliot in the third section "The Fire Sermon" presents the prevailing conditions of that time with the sorry state of affairs in London and the sordid plight of the Thames with all the garbage of the city dumped in the river. The description of the guttered river is miserable:

> The river bears no empty bottles, sandwich papers,
> Silk handkerchiefs, cardboard boxes, cigarette ends
> Or other testimony of summer nights. The nymphs are departed.
> Sweet Thames, run softly till I end my song,
> Sweet Thames, run softly, for I speak not loud or long.
> And bones cast in a little low dry garret,
> Rattled by the rat's foot only, year to year
> ("The Fire Sermon", WL, 177-186)

T.V. Reddy's *Quest for Peace* also touches all aspects of modern life and there are no vagaries of life left untouched by the poet in his long poem. It has extended its wings to the space of foreign policy of 'non-alignment' and has given the sketch of a new dawn of the 'new alignment' to ponder over the circumstantial change in the international arena. The economy of the country vis-à-vis the budget and its stakeholders has been discussed elaborately in a gutsy style. The poet is concerned about the budgetary allocations:

> and a lion's share of our budget is lost as a whole
> mysteriously without a trace in the black hole; (369-370)

The mystic poet's observation covers the nature of our general elections and the politics of offering sops and freebies at the time of elections by the political parties at the cost of public exchequer, which pinches the heart of the poet. The sloganeering and 'disinformation' coupled with 'misinformation' seems to be the curse of our leaders. The biting criticism in poetics comes in the following lines which are quite meaningful and strongly convey the deep message:

> belching with fat salaries from public money
> sucking common man's sweat as sweet honey;
> in global meets they recite the scripted lines
> and pose tall and stout as strong alien pines (QP, 393-396)

The mysticism of the poet is blended with realism and existentialism with which the poetry is laced profusely in the middle of this minor social epic. The liberalization of the economy has been widely discussed and the role of red radicals in resorting to violence and in obstructing the progress of the country comes alive like a journalistic presentation covering the incidents and events in minute details. But the poet maintains the gusto of poetic fervor and flavor even in the face of writing against the writers:

> Popular ballad singers step in beggar's guise
> with pseudo writers to grab land being wise;
> these revolutionaries self-seekers create unrest,
> at the spill of human blood they evade acid test;

> hostile to democratic ways they always oppose
> constructive steps with a red intellectual pose (*QP*, 456-460)

More thrust to this thesis on the study of society comes with the comparative study of the big fat leaders pitted against the marginalized populace of skinny and shabby countenance. The graphics of the have-nots and downtrodden have been drawn by the poet with apt words and the poetry is verdant in its exposure which is heart-rending and painful to contemplate:

> Always we look so pale, stale and small
> though our leaders steal and swell in size
> and look in imported cars smart and tall
> with drunken eyes feigning to be fully wise,
> always bragging their heinous heroic acts
> drowsily dipped in false fabricated facts; (*QP*, 471-76)

Self-explicit and explanatory, captivating with beautiful alliteration, the above lines portray the falsity of the world which is beyond the understanding of common men. Vast majority of population sleeps without food at night and they have no work to do as the scourge of un-employment and under-employment has taken millions in its jaws. The poet has the moral courage to express that the media has also played a negative role and it has forgotten the ethics and now it 'stinks with foul pranks, pricks and tricks.' The stanza has its own charm to be reproduced here as it conveys the heart-felt groaning of the poet:

> our sipping sails with the skipping of stinking pages
> stuffed with misleading news and false images;
> gone are the glorious days of media ethics,
> now it stinks with foul pranks, pricks and tricks (*QP*, 501-04)

The poet has summed up the second part of the epic poem with the clarion call for the original creativity and to shirk from the borrowed ideation in the academia and in the corridors of higher education. The glittering laces of erudition haunt the poet when he is confronted with the office persons to get a file cleared as he has to 'wait for years till palms are greased in style' and ends this part in grief and lamentation by saying:

> Like hungry wolves they consume at our cost
> and show us bare empty hands to go at last.(*QP*, 523-24)

T.S. Eliot's *The Waste Land* may have been forgotten by a class of people who indulge in exploitation to reduce the society to a debased hovel, a degenerated cultural hub and a narrow field of marginalized human resource, but the persons with futuristic vision and humanism at heart always feel awe struck to read the revolutionary ideation ending in equality, liberty and fraternity. As the second section of *The Waste Land* is a prophetic, apocalyptic invitation to journey into a desert waste, where the speaker will show the reader 'something different from either/Your shadow at morning striding behind you/ Or your shadow at evening rising to meet you; / [He] will show you fear in a handful of dust.'

T.V. Reddy has a global vision to restructure the edifice of humanity based on the principles postulated by Eliot and other European thinkers of French Revolution. Both the Western and the eastern thought find their place here and the twain are fused together meet in T.V. Reddy's unified approach of humanism. The Ganges and Thames meet in his poetry with equal gush, meaning and sacredness of purity as a man can imagine and the geographical boundaries are happily erased in the pursuit of peace. The poet presents this soothing picture in the marvelously composed lines bubbling with vigor and vitality and he has proven to be a tough fighter while upholding the banner of principles as he proclaims:

> Let me remain my simple self till I die
> trying to tread the perilous path of truth (QP, 1329-'30)
> I will walk and walk with bleeding feet,
> a determined pace, an uncertain fight (QP, 1333-'34)
> The Ganges roars in floods, fumes and flames
> and widens its seething sphere to the Thames;
> Lord Siva atop the snowy peak raves and rages
> in His Sivathandava the dance that blazes (QP, 1343-46)

T.S. Eliot is nostalgic right from the very beginning and his sledging with friends on the river side and near the mountains has been used to portray the ugliness of the waters; similarly as the long poem proceeds Reddy recounts his nostalgic moments and relates his personal experience of the inner quest for peace and embellishment of the soul. The outer world takes rest now and the inner world takes the stage and the tuning is set by the poet with the opening lines of new untitled section:

> I wish to renovate my sinking heart
> with the material of my own aesthetic art
> along with my old weak ancestral house,
> which once my thoughts used to rouse (QP, 525-28))

The stanza conveys two-pronged sensibility - one leading to personal choices and aesthetic sense and the second is to connect with the heritage; the source of inspiration comes from the inheritance of spiritual gain, the gain may be small, old and weak. The rupture of relationship in the towns has forced the poet to go back to his memorabilia and be lost in that thought of inspiration. All educational qualifications and equipped intellectual erudition of the poet finds mention in the verses which, although personal, have the cascading effect on the readers.

The relationship with Gods and demi-gods and the pursuits of spirituality to find peace have been discussed by the poet elaborately, since these random feelings often trouble the students in that idealistic state. However, suddenly the poet finds the traces of 'serfdom' in a democratic system and he jumps to add:

> In the light of this democratic freedom
> We stoop to embrace the teasing serfdom. (QP, 619-20)

Anna Hazare's "Lokpal movement", "Grow More Green", and blaring of the T.V. Channels with discussions on topics of human interest, preferable politics and insecurity of women have been elaborated in the lines of the poem. The poet wants revolution but not with 'borrowed blood' which is significant as it denotes that it must be indigenous and native and not financed and orchestrated by the alien forces and foreign powers. Then theological revolution has also been discarded in the next line by the poet since religious bigotry is inherent in such religious revolutions. The contemporary knowledge and information of the poet is matchless and laudable. The revolutions of Cairo at Tahir Square and the tragic event of Tiananmen Square have been highlighted in a revolutionary tone when he says- 'like a mighty thunder to consume cruel forces.' (Q P, 755)

T.S. Eliot's wide and frequent usage of 'bones' and 'thunder' can be seen on a different scale in Reddy's long poem and quite often Reddy also looks to the skies for justice for the teeming millions. The visionary poet's looking to the skies for solace cannot be called 'escapism', but certainly a solution might come from such meditation and higher vision looking at the void. The soaring soul in the sky has developed a feeling of disgust to see all the sordid state of affairs mentioned in the three parts of the epical poem, but now the soul wants to have rest and desires to nestle in the arms of peace.

The searching soul thinks of the scenic beauty of Char Dham in the Himalayas, Gangetic Mountains, then adverts to have a look at the South Indian temples such as the richest temple at Tirupati. Kedarnath Temple's tragedy comes to the mind of the poet and again the brooding begins as he reflects over the sufferings and exploitation of the pilgrims. The discrimination in charging and collecting prescribed amounts for a glimpse of the god and preferable treatment in terms of money and all such commercial aspects in religious centres shake the soul of the poet. The imagination comes to the rescue of the poet when he feels disgusted with the corrupt world and wishes to be a bird which can fly freely 'from tree to tree.'

T.V. Reddy's soul wants to be shackle-free so as to have an aerial view of the land and sea. The sheer enjoyment of the hovering soul in the sky is indeed a glorious narration that speaks of the poetic excellence of Reddy reminding us the message-bearing cloud of the immortal poet Kalidasa. But again there comes a shift in the mind of the poet and his soul flies to the alien lands to see the sad plight of the famished faces of youth seeking jobs and facing the recession in the countries and the blasting of Twin Towers and the World Trade Centre. The terrorism and un-employment trouble the mind of the poet and he is so upset that he realizes the limitations of the governance.

Eliot and Reddy are aware of the limitations of an individual to bring complete transformation of the society and as such they exhort themselves to do a bit of service and contribute their mite at least to salvage their souls. Eliot moans, groans and yearns:

> I sat upon the shore
> Fishing, with the arid plain behind me
> Shall I at least set my lands in order?
> London Bridge is falling down, falling down, falling down
> ("What the Thunder Said", *WL*, 423-426)

Reddy wants to restore order on earth and to make it a livable place. His sailing soul in quest of peace finds solace at last in the philosophic realm of spirituality, where the Almighty is supposed to do justice to all beings with its omnipresent and omnipotent elements of Nature such as winds and waters. Everything shall be shown its place and the Nature's order shall prevail. The devastation unleashed by the Nature shall gradually lead to the resurgence of peace process and tranquility. The usage of words like 'swept like lambs in flash floods' and 'like leaves people may shiver' tell the tale of fatal blow of the Nature to restore order in the long run. The situation reminds us of Lord Byron's eulogy to the mighty oceanic waves:

> Roll on, thou deep and dark blue Ocean—roll!
> Ten thousand fleets sweep over thee in vain;
> Man marks the earth with ruin—his control
> Stops with the shore...
> (Lord Byron, *Childe Harold's Pilgrimage*, Canto IV (1818), Stanza 179)

The might of the ocean has been recognized by Eliot while relating the story of Plebes the Phoenician in the fourth section "Death by Water" which is very interesting to show the human ego its right place:

> Phlebas the Phoenician, a fortnight dead,
> Forgot the cry of gulls, and the deep sea swell
> And the profit and loss.
> A current under sea
> Picked his bones in whispers. As he rose and fell

> He passed the stages of his age and youth
> Entering the whirlpool.
> Gentile or Jew
> O you who turn the wheel and look to windward,
> Consider Phlebas, who was once handsome and tall as you
> ("Death by Water", WL, 312-321)

The ultimate quest of the mystic poet T.V. Reddy is to 'Arrest the juggernaut of Maya' and then only, he feels, quest for peace may end. The juggernaut of *maya* tramples heavily on everything on its way in human life. The chase of the mirage of money and the entailed miseries have been elaborately depicted, narrated and discussed by the poet in a very interesting and mind-blowing manner. The veil of *maya* has been lifted in the end by narrative device of presenting its monstrous heads of hydra and devilish designs. Humans are nothing more than puppets in the hand of fatalistic strokes. The shuttling of mankind between the idealist society and pragmatism has left the poet perplexed in his quest for peace. But after having all round discussions on each and every spectrum of its fall out, the poet has a glimpse of light at the end of the dark tunnel. The optimism of the poet can be witnessed from the memorable lines beginning with 'Roaring clouds for ever cannot rule the skies', and ending with 'wails of grief give place to waves of peace' and it reminds us of the optimism of Robert Browning:

> And the elements' rage, the fiend-voices that rave,
> Shall dwindle, shall blend,
> Shall change, shall become first a peace out of pain,
> Then a light, then my breast,
> O thou soul of my soul! I shall clasp thee again,
> And with god be the rest! ("Prospice")

> "Roaring clouds for ever cannot rule the skies,
> with the sunrise the negative darkness flies;
> like leaves people may shiver under hurricanes
> and be swept away like lambs in flash floods
> when nature's fury turns multitudes into manes,
> but soon calm follows with patches of peace,
> wails of grief give place to waves of peace"(QP, 1650-56)

Eliot's childhood reminiscences about a "hyacinth girl" and a nihilistic epiphany are a few instances of love-making and expression amorous in the otherwise serious poet. There is no sexual encounters and love-making of intensity. Reddy has also scrupulously avoided references to sensuous love and its charming pranks and its absence is quite conspicuous. The principal urge and utmost yearning is to have peaceful world and solace of the soul. A passing reference in the midst of 'mirth' and 'peace' comes to stay and unlock the riddle of Reddy's life of love, but suddenly he remembers the 'fake' world and its double speak, acts and gestures:

> Let us try to make this restless earth
> a livable place of peace, love and mirth."
> Before we make unawares our sudden exist,
> let us do some good even in small digit;
> before it is too late, let us soon awake
> or our acts and gestures become fake (QP, 1142-47)

The finesse in exposure also comes from the pen of T.S. Eliot when he describes the fake world of that period like 'unstoppered, lurked her strange synthetic perfumes,/Unguent, powered, or liquid—troubled, confused,/And drowned the sense in odours; stirred by the air'. T.S. Eliot drew most of his philosophy from Christianity which is obvious in the contexts of the agony in the garden, the unrecognizable companion on the road to Emmaus, the allusions to St. Augustine in spiritual crisis and in references to Buddhism and its gift of three-fold gospel of peace and ultimately in the ending of the epic poem with the triple Vedic commands of the Thunder.

T.V. Reddy prefers to expose all the professionals who are habituated to double-speak and double action that lead to dual lives. Satirical vein comes first and the elevation of the soul to spiritual heights comes later for the reader. Ultimately both the poets scale new heights and touch the horizon of thought as disclosed by the heavenly Thunder, but interpretation of the Vedic thought has been elusive to the West because of their lesser acquaintance with the Indian scriptures and oriental spiritual thought. It is here that Reddy stands on a stronger ground and now let us aesthetically relish the poetical experience of the ironical and satirical vein of T.V. Reddy's poetry:

> Time mocks at our upstart human race,
> a dot in this vast immeasurable space;
> ...
> pseudo Professors preach lessons of hate
> And change the youth to unruly mob irate (QP, 1148-53)

Eliot has not spared the literary fakeness and pseudo behavior of intellectuals who by quoting Shakespeare try to prove themselves to be elegant and intelligent. Shallow-minded persons pretend to be scholars with all wisdom and prudence in the world by reciting a few quotes from the great bard. Eliot mocks at such fake persons:

> Oooo that Shakespearian Rag—
> It is so elegant
> So intelligent
> "What shall I do now? What shall I Do?
> 'I shall rush out as I am, and wall the street'
> 'With my hair down, so what shall we do tomorrow?'
> 'What shall we ever do?"
> The hot water at ten   ("A Game of Chess", WL, 128-305)

T.V. Reddy, a devoted teacher by himself, does not spare members of his profession and takes to task such teachers and professors who feign scholarship though in actuality they are intellectually shallow; though they are wiseacres they feign to be wise. The hollow personalities are unable to inculcate righteous knowledge which the students aspire, desire and want in their earnest efforts:

> Can there be a greater sin or shock
> than teacher's misdirecting a tender flock?   (QP, ls.1156-'57)
> ...
> When lawyers in high Courts turn violent
> like street ruffians, justice is sadly silent;
> In total silence justice flees to forest
> In search of justice and heavenly rest (QP, l1172-'75)

Eliot has lamented the habit of non-thinking and staying away from contemplation as he always gives utmost importance to the faculty of thinking as revealed at every stage in *The Waste Land*. The poet feels unhappy because the whole land has been reduced to a wasteful stretch due to nonperformance of mind. When there is no thought, no ideation, there can never be any progress and innovation. The borrowed ideas cannot help to restore the glory. It is always the ingenuity of brain and that can be achieved by thinking. Eliot's thinking syndrome is very important as T.V. Reddy has also stressed the need for meditative mind that alone can ignite new ideas. Eliot says:

> My nerves are bad tonight. Yes, bad. stay with me.
> Speak to me. Why do you never speak? speak
> What are you thinking of? What thinking? What?
> I never know what you are thinking. Think
> ("A Game of Chess", WL, l111-114)

T.V. Reddy shows the path of righteous thinking with his preferred instructive verb 'let' and that always contains his message and wishes for the readers. The style of Reddy has unique appeal in the sense that the spontaneity of expression as well as its in-built melody casts an irresistible charm on the mind of the reader and as such the lines expressing message become everlasting and memorable. Here Reddy stands unique among modern poets and in this respect there is hardly a poet in Indian English who can be compared with him and it is not an exaggeration to say that even the lines of Eliot are not as memorable as the lines of Reddy:

> Let us focus our mind on Krishna's gospel
> and tread the righteous path in His spell (QP, 1217-'18)
> Time's razor edge is on my neck and lungs,
> give me the last chance to mend or end. (QP, 1271-72)
> I wish to express my bursting word
> before it droops fast feather by feather
> and drops vertically as a wingless bird (QP, 1279-80)

The hypocrisy of man has been exposed by T.S. Eliot in *The Waste Land* by using the metaphor of 'corpse' to be planted and the harvest to be reaped. The filth and dirt has been thrown on the face of the fake man, who is friendlier to a dog than to humanity. The lame excuses, exploitation and lack of sensitivity are tools of the modern society to befool the innocent. In *The Waste Land* the section in which the speaker walks through London populated by ghosts of the dead is mostly surrealistic. He confronts a figure with whom he once fought in a battle that seems to conflate the clashes of World War I with the Punic Wars between Rome and Carthage. The speaker asks the ghostly figure, Stetson, about the fate of a corpse planted in his garden:

> That corpse you planted last year in your garden,
> Has it begun to sprout? Will it bloom this year?
> Or has the sudden frost disturbed its bed?
> Oh keep the Dog far hence, that's friend to men,
> Or with his nails he'll dig it up again!
> You! Hypocrite lecteur! –mon semblable, --mon frère!
> ("The Burial of The Dead", *WL*, 171-76)

T.V. Reddy outlines the search for peace and prosperity and the search tends to become endless that it even touches the horizon. But it is elusive and we chase the mirage in the desert of life and go on struggling with all the tools of ethics and non-ethics. He poses a question to the humanity as well as to the eternity and divinity:

> Is search for peace a wild goose chase?
> At the horizon can't we find its trace? (QP, 1347-48)

Similarly Eliot minces no words to address the 'son of man' who has collected heaps of broken images which are lying under the fierce sun. All the strenuous efforts of man end in wasteful and futile exercise:

> What are the roots that clutch, what branches grow
> Out of this stony rubbish? Son of man,
> You cannot say, or guess, for you know only
> A heap of broken images, where the sun beats
> ("The Burial of the Dead", *WL*, 19-22)

T.V. Reddy exhorts the immortal spiritual Lords representing world religions in a unified prayer to portray the message of universality, because the *Quest for Peace* is abound with international situations and connotations. The love and joy are the necessary ingredients of man's life. Just as Eliot tried to unify world religions such as Christianity, Buddhism and Vedic thought and has presented a relatively acceptable faith out of the conglomeration of various creeds, similarly Reddy has skillfully attempted to unify the different threads of diversified pantheon of gods to achieve the common destination i.e. the long cherished peace in *The Quest for Peace*:

> Let Rama, Buddha and Christ be our models
> To tread their path with a will without hurdles;" (*QP*, 1383-'84)
> "Where bombs and bullets fail to conquer
> A little love will do with a kind generous act
> Pregnant with power flinty hearts to stir
> To bring peace and smiling joy with tact   (*QP*, 1391-'94)

T.V. Reddy has been blessed with the inborn poetic capability to touch the skies and descend to fathom the ground realities of life. It may be possible due to his vast experience of wide reading of literature as well as journals, fertility of imagination, resourcefulness of mind and keenly perceptive eye to see on one side the smart street boys indulging in intimidation and illegal activities and on the other side the degeneration that has set in the universities where persons without any quality or scholarship easily find entry. Reddy sees no difference between the two as far as their behavior and conduct is to be tested on the touchstone of ethics and aesthetics. In fact unruly conduct of the duo pinches the heart of the poet:

> Mushrooming gangs of petty muscled leaders
> From all sundry streets and slummy lanes   (*QP*, 1423-24)
> Universities, where once angels feared to tread
> now invite wolves and foxes to market bread   (*QP*, 1449-50)

T.S. Eliot leaves no stone unturned to attack the non-thinking intellectuals, who are busy in rat race rather than in the pursuit of knowledge and yearning for intellectual excellence. Eliot's 'A Game of Chess' is a sarcastic attack on the society in which no one has the guts to take a moralistic stand, no one to bear the brunt of violence in thought and action, and no one to take cudgels against the unlawful elements. The common mind seems to have become empty in the eyes of Eliot and people seem to be dead and the sparkling eyes have lost their vision; to sum up, it can be well said that the society of his time could not match the expectations of the poet, nor could it rise to the level of understanding the idea of visionary intellectualism.

> "I think we are in rats' alley
> Where the dead men lost their bones
> ...
> I remember

>Those are pearls that were his eyes.
>"Are you alive, or not? Is there nothing in your head?"
>("*A Game of Chess*", WL, 1115-126)

T.V. Reddy does not want to miss any opportunity in exposing the vices in the society and in laying bare the stinking corruption in all the wings of the Government. He is more direct and vitriolic than T.S. Eliot in aiming his shafts of satire at unsocial forces and he has left no event unobserved or unreported to tell the reader about the horrors in the global scenario and about the feeling of disgust the poet has in his mind to read the newspapers which are full of disturbing news presenting plunder and murder, terror and violence. His reference to the 'recent shocking terror strike on the Hotel Taj and Nariman in Mumbai, India's financial capital, proves 'the grisly global power of Satan's Raj and monstrous thirst for blood and life vital' and reveals his awareness and deep concern for the safety of the people threatened by the unlawful forces and the unwanted and unnecessary violence unleashed on the innocent public. Again his observation stretches to global level when he speaks of the series of bomb blasts that occurred in places such as Delhi High Court and Sri Lankan cricket team also was made a target; he refers to our strained relations with China and American economic recession; Norwegian Breivik's mass killing and terror attacks at Madrid and London also find prominent place in his tapestry of terror attacks. (*QP*, 1475 & 1492)

Reddy's elaborate sketch of 'the richly reckless feckless sinning city' moves more or less on the same lines of the portrayal of Eliot's 'unreal city' and in both places 'death' looms large on the head of humanity and mankind heaves awful sighs. In Eliot's poem the setting is created with subtle poetry where it is pitted against the cross and tangent verses, but the substance remains the same as much as the sensitivity of the poet. Subtlety of Eliot's description can be perceived from the lines:

>Unreal City,
>Under the brown fog of a winter dawn,
>A crowd flowed over London Bridge, so many,
>I had not thought death had undone so many.
>Sighs, short and infrequent, were exhaled,
>And each man fixed his eyes before his feet.
>Flowed up the hill and down King William Street,
>("The Burial of the Dead", WL, 60-66)

Reddy's Style of writing as well as his poetic diction is different from that of T.S. Eliot. In Eliot's poem we find 'questions' rose with signs of interrogation at several places and the interrogatories of Eliot are conscience-keepers. Reddy urges the people with a sense of urgency and earnestness with expressions of intimacy such as 'Let us not stand'; but Eliot refrains from making such exhortations. First, the reader is shaken from toe to toe and then the poet poses a question to shake the inner conscience of the reader. Reddy is direct in attack and straight in talk to walk all the way with the reader in reaching the goal. While Eliot is entirely different and objective in his approach, Reddy wants to take the reader along with him and there is personal urge. While Eliot's lines ring with an echo of evasiveness, Reddy's lines are packed with the intensity of intimacy and personal urgency and immortalized with the irresistible charm of its musical power:

>Let us not stand and stare as idle star gazers,
>let us move and prove to be true torch bearers,
>let us march and burn all vicious forces dark,
>on this nobler human mission let us all embark (*QP*, 1590-94)

T.V. Reddy and T.S. Eliot are mystic poets of excellence and their mythic references make their poetics surprise us with riddles and perplexing propositions. Eliot in the Section V- 'What the

Thunder Said' has taken liberty to blast the mundane living of playing chess game, indulging in protocols of nicety without its meaningful intent, while the frivolities of life and wasteful indulgences stand exposed. Similarly Reddy laments over the dying traditions of our culture and ignoring of spiritual discourses, rich heritage of higher thinking and simple living; the middle ages have proved to be a scourge and curse for this ancient rich culture which was destroyed and disfigured by foreign invasions and religious conversions by force. Reddy's lines express agony and anguish and he makes use of the weapon of irony and satire in exposing the social ills, while Eliot is seen indulging in sarcastic ways by repeating the same word 'goodnight' several times:

> We are victims of our vicious inheritance,
> not the luminous one of our eternal Upanishads
> but the hybrid one of the corrupt Middle Ages,
> it erupts like volcano and explodes our defense (QP, 1560-'63)
> And if it rains, a closed car at four
> And we shall play a game of chess,
> Pressing lidless eyes and waiting for a knock upon the door.
> ("A Game of Chess", WL, l136-172)

T.S. Eliot has turned totally Vedantic and the wisdom digested by him has been spelt out in the poem *The Waste Land*. In fact the crux of all philosophies merges in the Vedantic thought which envisages a pupil to contemplate as to who is behind all your breath, who hears beyond your ears, who controls your mind etc. which is answered in one liner *Tadvanam*- the unknown Almighty! Eliot's spirituality touches heights and it seems difficult for the critics to catch his frequency when they say that Eliot's 'Shantih, shantih, shantih- is perhaps the peace of exhaustion rather acceptance. Eliot's experience of blissful peace is unspeakable:

> Who is the third who walks always beside you?
> When I count, there are only you and I together
> But when I look ahead up the white road
> There is always another one walking beside you
> Gliding wrapt in a brown mantle, hooded
> I do not know whether a man or a woman
> —But who is that on the other side of you?
> ("What the Thunder Said", WL, l359-365)

To T.V. Reddy the groping soul in its brief sojourn is still looking for a suitable space to land but in the analysis of the poet it may be surmised that the great souls of Alexander, Ashoka, Napoleon, Shivaji, Vivekananda must have bloomed somewhere. The life after death haunts the soul and the groping soul is puzzled. The body's burial or burning has no meaning and the creative clay reminds of a person while the self remains a mute witness to the whole play of life. The lines are pregnant with deep universal philosophy with its stress on the transience of life on the earth:

> This choice land is a strange landing place
> for the puzzled groping soul's brief sojourn
> soon to fade without a visible face or trace
> with a simple inevitable act to bury or burn (QP, 1584-'87)

> "...Alexander, ...Ashoka, ...Napoleon, ...Shivaji, ...Vivekananda, (QP, 1618-24)
> ....
> This life is the supreme gift of the One Supreme
> to bloom into life divine, not to fade as a bad dream;

> What we do shapes our ends on this creative clay,
> The Self in us is a mute witness to this mixed play
> *Dharmo rakshati rakshitah!*
> Ohm, Santhi! Santhi!!Santhih!!! (QP, 1660-1665)

T.V. Reddy succeeds in the above lines in enshrining the essence of this ancient *Sanatana Dharma*, which has come to be known as Hinduism and revealing the two great concepts of *Karma* and the Lord as a silent witness of our thoughts and actions. Moreover it throws light on two aspects of the ancient Vedic wisdom in the last two concluding lines of this minor epic *Quest for Peace*. One is 'Dharmo-rakshtih-rakshatah'- which means whosoever protects '*dharma*', in reciprocity with equal force '*Dharma*' protects the person. But the decoding of '*Dharma*' remains a riddle for the commentators and interpreters. Some critics call 'dharma' to be 'duty' and sometimes its literal meaning is taken as 'religion' and many a time 'dharma' is interpreted as 'natural behaviour' of a person or thing, animate or inanimate. But one thing is evident from the usage of the aforesaid adage; that is, the energy bounces back from the action done to protect any kind of 'dharma.' May be the positive energy bounces back with equal force and negativity depletes the energy reservoir.

The second one refers to *Santhi*. T.S. Eliot has used the aphorism of '*Shantih*' three times and it may be concluded that the '*Shantih*' he wants in thought, speech and action. Beyond the three dimensions of personality of a person, there is nothing to be explored. The thoughts are swift to spread worldwide while speech has limited audience, and the action has the effect of a ripple. T.V. Reddy has added the prefix of '*Ohm*' before '*Santhi*' being conversant with the primordial sound of the universe with which our prayers commence; it may be prayer for prosperity or joy or peace. By prefixing '*Ohm*' Reddy has given a sense of fullness and completion to the concept of *Santhi* which is beyond the level of understanding of the Western poets and scholars. It is really a matter of joy for humanity to have peace at last after talking about *The Waste Land* and making an earnest attempt to acquire peace through *Quest for Peace* as the soul soars in the skies filled with the ceaseless cosmic music of the mellifluous lines of Reddy.

Abbreviations:

QP: Quest for Peace; WL: The Waste Land

Works Cited

Eliot, T. S. *The Waste Land*. http://www.bartleby.com/201/1.html

Reddy, T. V. *Quest for Peace*. New Delhi: Authors Press, 2013. Print.

23 Nature: "Fairest Eve in Eden" in T.V. Reddy's *Thousand Haiku Pearls*

K. Rajamouly

Amazing abundance of nature description fills T.V. Reddy's marvelous haiku work *Thousand Haiku Pearls* which has vastly enriched the treasure house of Indian poetry in English. Nature is so beauteous and bounteous for T.V. Reddy that it attracts his deep attention towards its charms and rhythms, beauty and music. He as a poet and man loves to live and move in nature and become one with nature. His love for nature is not only due to his temperament but also to the background of his native region. He was born and brought up in a village surrounded by green fields and groves, hills and forests, rills and rivers. It is natural that his main focus is on nature and man in nature. One of the nucleus themes of his poetry is nature, "Fairest Eve in Eden".

For T.V. Reddy, nature is the treasure of pleasures and the storehouse of raptures to free him from the stresses and strains of hard realities of life in his contact with it. He finds it fresh and fabulous, slim and shy, sensuous and all soothing, refreshing and rejuvenating him:

> Nude lush green garden
> Feels fresh, slim, shy, and sensuous---
> Fairest Eve in Eden (*H*, 83)

The poet visualizes angelic qualities in nature. This is evident in his use of the words: 'nude', 'fresh', 'slim' and 'shy' in the triplet. He comes closer to Wordsworth in the description and adoration of nature.

Nature is a green garden to offer the poet sensuous bliss, a mellifluous melody to delight his ears, graceful breeze to fill his heart with pleasures, a freshly blooming daisy to feast his eyes, a cool bower to shower on him solace, a heaven to fill the earth with beauties and a lovely mother to satiate his aesthetic hunger. It bestows on him all pleasures, turning the life of man fresh to lead afresh:

> Life begins afresh
> Nature is as fresh as a bride;
> Spring in the ride (*H*, 626)

Nature is not an abstract idea or a lifeless object but it is a life-giving force and has actions to perform. For T.V. Reddy, nature is an active agent to attract man with its charms and rhythms and he is bound to respond to it as per its impressions on him. For him, Nature, the personification of nature, is for the incarnation of beauty and divinity. Her angelic qualities in bounty leave him enthralled:

> My heart knows no control
> When Nature's boundless beauty
> Enslaves my soul   (*H*, 324)

Like Wordsworth, T.V. Reddy gives the divine status to nature. He feels that Nature has 'the kinetic power of the Lord'. He treats nature as mother and guide. Nature is kind, lovely, benevolent and cordial to him and so he must be grateful to her:

> Thanks to Mother Nature
> The kinetic power of the Lord
> The only ruling God.   (H, 984)
> Nature is our mother and guide;
> Let us not be ungrateful wretches
> By exploiting her with pride.   (H, 644)

As man and poet, T.V. Reddy sketches the lively pictures of nature for the reader to visualize its beauty and enjoy the enchanting scenes feasting the eye. His wide range of nature's picturesque descriptions marks his comprehensive vision and reveals that he loves and worships nature in the heart of his heart. His mind and heart crave for unraveling the mysteries of nature. Even minute objects of nature leave indelible and memorable impressions on him as a poet and man:

> Blades of grass dance
> and to the stir of gentle wind that fans---
> gesture of Lord's grace.   (H, 964)

T.V. Reddy finds beauty even in the blades of grass. He has revered impressions of nature like Wordsworth and other Romantic poets and as such every blade of grass with the beauty of all the graces of its dance leaves deep impressions in spite of its minuteness and smallness. Nature has rhythmic harmony and idyllic beauty. T.V. Reddy goes to nature to be a willing thrall to its soothing effect. As a result, he finds indefinable pleasures at the sight of nature. His experiences reveal the fact that it makes him sail on the wings of imagination in ecstasy. When he looks at moonlit night and other objects of nature, his impressions turn creative and imaginative for their gushing on paper from his pen:

> Cool moonlight
> lights our poets and their hearts
> a creative night.   (H, 245)
> From the ashes of the sleepy night
> Rise luminous flashes of poetic flight
> And piercing rays of light.   (H, 101)
> The happiest thought
> is the simple artless thought
> Of being pure and clean.   (H, 134)
> Creative pen springs
> With silken touch mercury flow;
> peerless pearl glow.   (H, 479)

Nature has not only pleasant sights but also delightful sounds like the singing of birds, rustling of leaves, the blowing of the breeze, buzzing of bees and the flowing of rivers to attract all creatures. The rhythmic harmony of nature is beyond description in one's words:

> Flute of reed
> Triumph on spell-bound cattle---
> Words fail to read.   (H, 51)
> I see bees hum.
> spring flowers dance in sum;

> the earth smiles. (H, 267)
> Birds flutter wings
> Merry leaves rustle and greet in spring,
> Children's chaste smiles. (H, 269)
> Leaves rustle
> To nature's musical rhythm
> To the wind's bustle. (H, 247)

The sights and sounds of nature therefore fill the earth with a rich variety of beauties for the gaieties of man especially the poet. For T.V. Reddy, nature is inspiring, soothing and enthralling. Wordsworth finds soothing experience and healing powers in nature; it is a common feature in both the poets who share love of nature in equal measure. The sights of idyllic beauty of rural surroundings and rhythmic melodies of nature fill Reddy's heart with joy inexpressible.

Every poet has a poetics of his own. T.V. Reddy marks a distinction as a poet of nature. He draws copious imagery and comparisons from nature which forms the major characteristic of his poetry. He studies plant life in relation to man's life and nature in all respects. There are certain striking comparisons between the functional state of plant and that of man or animal and this is brought out in the triplet:

> Palm trees tall
> queue in a long line on the road---
> Soldiers stand as a wall. (H, 81)

Life is beautiful in conjugal life. When they are born for each other and made for each other, there is no place for any tear or fear in their living together. This truth finds an earnest expression in the haiku:

> My loving wife
> If she were alive---
> vernal moonlight. (H, 60)

T.V. Reddy finds the quality of sage-like purity in the spell of moonlight. How appropriate it is for him to compare! The beauty as well as the propriety of the image is matchless:

> Moonlight casts its spell,
> It is as pure as a spotless sage,
> a milk-white page. (H, 561)

The poet talks of soft communication skills and their soothing effect. He hates harsh words and false talk for they result in unrest. He draws an apt comparison,

> A violent word
> Cuts the heart from the world---
> Wild fires in the forest (H, 91)

The poet extensively explores the possible areas of comparisons to make the point crystal clear through the sharpness of the natural image. The over-growing evils of man are compared to the outgrowth of weeds:

> In the garden of thoughts
> Destructive evil is only the weed;
> Crush it in the seed. (H, 22)

T.V. Reddy aptly compares the mushroom growth of corporate management schools to the weeds in the garden of plants:

> Management schools,
> Beehives with stinging rules --
> gardens of weeds.   (H, 85)
> Vultures encash
> and trade in admissions academic;
> fast spreads the epidemic.   (H, 59)

The poet compares fake leaders to wolves in lamb's skin as they are for deception, corruption and exploitation and it reveals the inborn poetic talent of the writer in presenting natural images:

> Legendary heroes, our icons,
> are dislodged by fake leaders on lawns---
> wolves in lamb's hide.   (H, 30)

The greatness of a poet lies in the use of apt comparisons. Here is the most appropriate comparison of the leaders with the spider that weaves a web and swallows insects that come to it innocently and unexpectedly:

> Spider on the web---
> Leaders' greedy arrogant rub
> on people's destiny.   (H, 58)

T.V. Reddy believes in hard work and commitment to work as work is worship. The ant is symbolic of hard work. It serves as a giant and as a model to men of indolence:

> World philosophy
> navigates around the tiny ant
> that defies all.   (H, 32)
> Ant is the day
> is a giant, management guru---
> as night an atom of clay.   (H, 34)
> Ants in a line
> march as a formidable troop;
> They inspire and shine.   (H, 558)

T.V. Reddy applauds the laudable quality of ant's hard work and orderliness while mocking at man in the way Robert Frost shows resemblance between the ant and man. He refers to the ant as 'he' but not 'it'. He humorously comments on the ant's departmentalism in comparison with that of men in his poem:

> It couldn't be called ungentle
> But how thoroughly departmental ("Departmental")

T.V. Reddy indirectly mocks at man for his non-commitment to work by drawing comparison between ants and men and making a mockery of the tribe of lazy men. Every object of nature leaves the poet impressed in the manner of Wordsworth and other Romantics as nature has life, joys and love to be benevolent to man. He comes closer to Wordsworth on one hand and Robert Frost on the other.

As a poet and man, T.V. Reddy experiences the feel of all the seasons, especially summer. He as a regional poet presents its impact on him in the hot region of Rayalaseema to which he belongs. His poetry reflects rural life to characterize down-to-earth realism. There is an extensive delineation of

Nature: "Fairest Eve in Eden" in Thousand Haiku Pearls

summer in T.V. Reddy's poetry. On one hand, the poet treats the summer season as his friend for it brings the rainy season with it, freeing him from scorching heart -

> Even in the scorching heat
> a good friend follows thy heart beat
> a rain drop in summer. (*H*, 24)

Summer gives a fresh lease of life and presents the renewal of life to farmers by summer showers of rain, for their life is a gamble in rain:

> Summer showers
> give a fresh lease of life to flowers---
> Rebirth to plants. (*H*, 495)
>
> Summer showers of rain
> chase farmers' fears and pains
> Renewal of life. (*H*, 589)

The poet has positive attitude and optimistic outlook to expect happiness after troubles, joys to come after sorrows. He opines 'Life is not for tears;/It is to see fairer flowers to bloom,/not to wither in gloom' (*H*,718). He prepares himself for bearing the scorching heat of the sweltering summer while waiting for rain, the 'guest' who is welcome (H.524).

T.V. Reddy feels sorry for 'withering trees and parching throats' due to the scorching sun in summer when the season becomes almost 'a pest' (524). Creatures fail to beat the heat of summer:

> My heart full of fears
> not a drop to put out fires---
> Summer arrives. (*H*, 71)
>
> Mid-summer---
> Roads and heads radiant heat;
> Wings fail to beat. (*H*, 40)

The poet humorously comments on the deserted roads in summers, comparing them with a shining bald head, as people do not tread the roads at noon in the season due to simmering heat. To tread the hot roads is like a circus feat:

> Burning rays of the sun,
> Deserted roads to tread---
> a shining bald head. (*H*, 43)
>
> Summer heat,
> a feat for the burning feet---
> a hot game of balance. (*H*, 64)

Workers and farmers sweat and get tired soon. Leaves wither and beauty fades due to scorching sun. Birds such as sparrows fall dead as leaves due to scorching sun in summer:

> Day is too long
> Workers full of sweat and fatigue;
> Summer is too strong. (*H*, 140)
>
> Summer sun
> for toiling peasants at noon no fun
> Tired to the bone. (*H*, 191)
>
> Summer heat wave
> Urban life halts and heaves---

>   Withering leaves. (H, 346)
>   Burning rays of the sun
>   Poor sparrows fall like leaves
>   Deserted roads burn. (H, 213)

The poet welcomes rainy season having its positive side as the people wish early rains to be away from the burning sun and simmering heat. As a sign of joy, rains renew life in the form of germination and the lake looks alive with sufficient water:

>   Showers of rain
>   On the lake of delight the fish
>   They dance and kiss. (H, 212)
>   Downpour of rain
>   Shivering peepal leaves collapse,
>   in nirvana feel no pain. (H, 211)
>   A brief summer shower---
>   cattle feel renewed power
>   with glowing eyes. (H, 231)

The poet at the same time feels sorry for the fury of the rainy season. Hailstorms disrupt all. Trees fall down in storms. One cannot escape the devastating force of storms and cyclones:

>   Raining all day ---
>   a deserted water sheet of landscape;
>   hunger haunts the way. (H, 67)
>   The aged tree falls
>   The wreck of the stormy wind
>   Nature's fury blind. (H, 214)

In the cycle of seasons, winter seems to have its own significance as per the thinking of the poet. He describes seasons but draws no corresponding likeness between the seasons and the stages of life of man. He surveys the effects or impressions of the seasons on man:

>   Winter night
>   glows with glowworm's light---
>   Nature's wonder. (H, 142)
>   The winter sun
>   Invites us with a mild balmy cool,
>   flowers and leaves are one. (H, 290)
>   Cold winter is dead,
>   Welcome to the songs of spring;
>   Tunes of joy let it sing. (H, 601)

Autumn or fall is the season like the evening of a day. While the fast falling of leaves is compared to the movement of descending arrows, the passing of days is beautifully described as falling of leaves from the branches. With an appropriate image T.V. Reddy presents its graphic description in his triplets:

>   Evening in autumn ---
>   Feeble leaves fall in a column,
>   Volley of dead arrows. (H, 147)
>   Days pass fast

Nature: "Fairest Eve in Eden" in Thousand Haiku Pearls

>   Like leaves falling at last---
>   Autumnal effect.   (H, 320)

Nature welcomes the cycle of seasons, for trees have to wear new leaves. It paves the way for rebirth of greenness on trees in the governance of time.

>   Autumn arrives
>   Leaves decay to spring again
>   With life, afresh again.   (H, 221)
>   Chastening autumn
>   We feel weak and naked trees
>   Awaiting fresh lease.   (H, 352)

For every poet spring is the best season as it is full of enchanting beauty and attractive gaiety. Nature appears in abundance in the season:

>   Early spring
>   Lawn is spread with dew drops
>   Pearls smile and spring.   (H, 335)
>   Spring showers---
>   Sunny fields full of flowers
>   Gets a fresh lease.   (H, 300)

Wordsworth's love of nature is evident in all his nature poetry. The opening line of *The Prelude*, 'O there is a blessing in this gentle breeze' reflects his passion for nature. So is the case with T.V. Reddy whose love of nature gets reflected in his poetry.

T.V. Reddy extensively describes almost all objects and bodies of nature. Grass, plants, trees, beaches, hills, winds, breezes, rains, rivers, dews, snow, clouds, the rainbow, dawn and dusk, day and night, sunrises and sunsets, sky, sun, moon, and so on, for he loves nature as a nature poet. His poetry reflects his personal, local and regional scenes as a regional poet:

>   Canopied tree is cut;
>   the hand that helps is removed;
>   way of the world is that.   (H, 228)
>   Penance of the tree
>   yields a huge load f fruits;
>   patience of roots.   (H, 229)
>   On the sandy beach
>   I walk and walk with eyes blank
>   For some feeling tide to reach.   (H, 230)

T.V. Reddy paints the rainbow in his pen picture with wonderful colours and makes it glow in the light of his imagination:

>   Formation of rainbow---
>   an event beyond words a wonder
>   as the sound of thunder.   (H, 607)

For the poet, breeze presents a fresh lease of life, 'breeze dispels fear' (H-162). It fills him with all blissful solace and charming smiles,

>   Breezy beach
>   shines within lovers' reach,
>   smiles at seagulls' sunbath.   (H, 163)

> Morning breeze
> Old man walks on the beach'
> gets a fresh lease.   (H, 301)

T.V. Reddy's remarkable word-painting is virtually a visual feast and his excellent descriptive pictures are so fresh in our minds that we the readers are enabled to visualize the scenes of sunrise, moonlit night, snow fall etc. feasting our eyes and making us to become one with the scenes:

> Morning rays of the east
> chase the chill dark shadows
> and fill the globe with feast.   (H, 108)
> The scene of sunrise
> is a vermilion mark shining wise
> on mother earth's forehead.   (H, 144)
> Flakes of falling snow
> Shines the high range of silver carpet,
> A soundless cold trumpet.   (H, 256)
> Scarlet is the western sky
> below the blood-smeared cry
> of the sinking sun.   (H, 325)
> Moonlight in summer
> a mute mystic musical murmur
> a solace to the heart.   (H, 148)
> Moon in full bloom
> Bride invites to her room--
> two moons await.   (H, 68)

The painting is done with appropriate colours and the night in T.V. Reddy's poetry is wonderfully presented and it is compared to a pregnant mother waiting for the sun-rise to give birth to a child, another son-rise:

> Pregnant night
> bearing the weight of the universe
> delivers sunlight. (H, 358)

As the poet of nature, T.V. Reddy relishes sensuous pleasures in flowers - roses, lotuses, lilies, jasmines, hovered round by butterflies. When a poet refers to a flight of butterflies or bees hovering around the flowers, we can say that flowers invite them to suck the sweet substance of honey:

> Butterflies
> suck the sweetness of flowers;
> the spring flies.   (H, 186)
> Flight of butterflies
> laying kids with noisy cries
> Roses smile.   (H, 274)
> I see bees hum.
> Spring flowers dance in sum;
> the earth smiles.   (H, 267)

The poet adopts love-hate relation for bees. He likes to hear the singing, the buzzing of bees but hates their stinging:

Nature: "Fairest Eve in Eden" in Thousand Haiku Pearls

> I hear bees sing
> When I go near, they sting;
> Life is precious.   (H, 268)

Nature bestows on T.V. Reddy floral tributes, welcoming him to taste the glimpse of varied flowers. It is the most enjoyable sight for him:

> Flowers blossom
> add new aura of fragrance
> To my pining bosom.   (H, 227)

As a poet and man, he realistically perceives the beauty of the dimpled cheeks of a bride in the charms of blooming roses. He explores an excellent analogy between the beautiful roses and the rosy cheeks of a bride as he finds the bridal beauty in the beauty of roses. He says 'Rose is a rose...fragrance makes it tall.' (H, 497) For him, roses are bride's blushing cheeks:

> Blooming roses
> Bride's blushing cheeks---
> Beauty speaks.   (H, 48)

The poet describes the lotus, giving a high status to it for its multi-petal beauty. It is born in the mud to rise above the impure water and shine in sunny glory:

> Multi-petalled lotus
> Above the muddy water---
> beyond the foetus.   (H, 50)
>
> Lotus smiles
> We vaguely travel miles and miles
> To breathe nature's beauty.   (H, 271)

The nature poet in TV Reedy jumps with joy as he looks at the jasmine creeper. The reader visualizes not only the creeper with the bunch of jasmines but also a necklace studded with pearls. It marks one of the most beautiful descriptions in this volume:

> A jasmine creeper
> studded with blooming petals
> fragrant pearls.   (H, 334)

Like T.V. Reddy, Wordsworth finds ecstasy and solace with his contact with nature as described in the poem 'The Daffodils'. He gets engrossed in the beauty of daffodils:

> A poet could not but be gay
> In such a jocund company;
> I gazed---and gazed---but little thought
> What wealth the show to me had brought. ("The Daffodils")

Wordsworth recalls the beauty of daffodils and the beauteous forms of nature 'in vacant or in pensive mood'

> And then my heart with pleasure fills
> And dances with the daffodils.   ("The Daffodils")

T.V. Reddy gets tactile and palatal bliss at the sight of fruits like apples, cherries, mangoes and so on. He enjoys the sight of apples and his description of the woman apple-seller is at once natural and realistic:

> A woman vendor
> with her basket full of fresh apples---
> buyer's eyes were on her fairer apples.   (*H*, 179)

The above haiku echoes the idea of Robert Frost's nature lyric, "After Apple Picking". T.V. Reddy is not just for the sights and sounds of nature but also for observing the human tendency and man's hidden desire to look at the beauty of woman. He enjoys the scents and the sight of the fair apples as Frost enjoys 'the scent of apples' and at the same time he is not blind to the buyer's eyes on her 'fairer apples'.

Wordsworth finds pleasure in birds, as there is joy for him in all objects of nature. He describes birds and wishes to partake in their joy and freedom; for instance in *The Prelude* he says, 'Free as a bird to settle where I will' (9). He expresses the joy and freedom of the bird and believes that there is life, joy and love in nature. In the same way T.V. Reddy also finds pleasure in birds and flowers and so he watches birds like parrots, sparrows, gulls, doves, frogs, and ants etc. as sources of his joy.

> Parrot spreads its feathers.
> Sings as a child in spring weather---
> Wings to the rising sun.   (*H*, 62)
>
> Guava grove---
> parrots perch o bough,
> kiss and bite in love.   (*H*, 285)
>
> Eagle's fairy flight
> racing with warm sunlight
> an aerial survey.   (*H*, 259)
>
> The sight of sea gulls
> adds life to the sea and sandy shore;
> Our minds it lulls.   (*H*, 754)

Apart from birds, he describes domestic animals such as cattle, dogs and bulls and they become an integral part of his rich description of nature:

> Dog's subtle nose
> our foul corrupt deeds knows;
> Our home police force.   (*H*, 189)

Like the Romantics, T.V. Reddy wants to be away from this world of hard realities and bitter truths getting united with the beauty of nature and as such his haiku are excellent descriptions of nature:

> Playing flutes of reeds
> Spell-bound stretches of weeds
> in concrete jungles.   (*H*, 205)
>
> Flowers blossom,
> Add new aura of fragrance
> To my pining bosom.   (*H*, 227)

Nature is not something confined only to greenery abound with leaves and stems. Of course, greenery is green gold in nature and the pleasant sign of life. Nature has boundless attractions and infinite impressions and at the same time it is an incredible teacher teaching lessons and sermons on values to mankind. Ants are there to teach men unity and hard work. Bees are a model for unflinching toil in collecting honey from flowers for the human race. Peacocks and other dancing birds are to teach the art of dancing which involves graceful movement. Cuckoos and other singing birds inspire man to sing as melodiously as they do for the delight of man on the earth. There are many objects of nature to teach man some valuable lesson or other as a great teacher. Nature therefore serves the role of a university on a bigger and wider scale. This is the angle from which both Wordsworth and T.V. Reddy look at Nature.

Like Wordsworth, T.V. Reddy treats nature as the fountain of pleasures. Like Wordsworth, he finds in nature benevolent attitude. He finds solace in nature. It bestows on him what human beings cannot give in this age of advancement:

> Drops of dew,
> Nature's gift, our delight---
> Priceless pearls bright.   (H, 77)
> A walk in the beach
> A pleasant joy within the reach---
> The moon at sight.   (H, 93)

Like Robert Frost and Philip Larkin, T.V. Reddy sees the hostile side of nature too. Nature is a double-edged weapon, for it is both benevolent in its motherly treatment and violent in its wild fury. He finds in nature its scourge and violent nature. That is why, Reddy being a deep observer of the various roles of nature presents its opposite roles of protecting and nourishing angel and destroying and disrupting violent force. Breeze is calm and soothing, but the winds and storms are violent, terrifying and destructive

> Wild forest
> For winds to play games,
> Zooming flames.   (H, 44)
> Deafening thunder---
> clouds and doubts thicken,
> eyes and minds darkened.   (H, 97)

The poet indirectly wishes that man should fight against the hostile forces of nature and cross the hurdles in life to achieve his cherished goal.

The earth is abound with the plenty of nature's immeasurable wealth and beauty and man lives on nature getting the greatest pleasure from the sights and sounds of nature. If Robert Frost opines, 'Earth is the right place for love' in 'Birches', Reddy considers Nature as mother, teacher, guardian and sole protector. It is the place for man's rapture in nature and an adventure for enhancing one's stature. T.V. Reddy echoes the idea -

> We owe to earth this tread,
> With courage, let us raise our head;
> Life is an adventure.   (H, 543)
> I need no Paradise;
> Let us transform our home into a heaven
> and spring a surprise.   (H, 811)

Among Indian poets in English T.V. Reddy as a poet and man is unique in the sense that he has left a stamp of his own in presenting nature and in expressing his love of nature in which aspect he comes closer to Wordsworth the celebrated British poet of nature. For Reddy, nature is the source of joy and multiple pleasures. Nature is a teacher to teach him lessons, a guide to give him its joyous company and mother to offer him protection and loving service and a friend to give cool shade and relief with bower and beauty that rejuvenates his spirit. These one thousand haiku are a rich mine of inspiring poetry expressed in power-packed capsules of miniature form of poetry from the quill of T.V. Reddy who is at once a romantic poet and a satirist, a nature poet and a realist. He is a potential signature in modern poetry in English whose melodious voice has cast a spell across countries and continents. Certainly, he shines as a star in the literary firmament.

Abbreviation: 'H' refers to haiku in *Thousand Haiku Pearls*. Number after the letter H refers to the number of the haiku in the book.

Works Cited

Frost, Robert. *American Literature: An Anthology*. New Delhi, Eurasia Publishing House, 1976. Print.

Reddy, T. V. *Thousand Haiku Pearls*. New Delhi: Authors Press, 2016. Print.

Wordsworth, William. *The Prelude*. London: Penguin Classics, 1850. Print.

24

Social Consciousness in T.V. Reddy's *Quest for Peace*

Neelam K. Sharma

T. V. Reddy (1943) has been a poet and an active educationist who held different positions during his teaching career. He emerges in most of his poetry as a responsible social being concerned with the fall of values in general and he is seen feeling extremely concerned at the progressively rising trends of standards in human life, especially in Indian context. We find in him a lyricist, a romantic and a realist and he has immense love and appreciation for nature. *Melting melodies (1994), Pensive Memories (2005)* and *Quest for peace* (2013) have some of the finest poems to his credit.

Quest for Peace is a long poem consisting of seven sections or cantos with 1665 lines rhymed with different orders. Vices such as dishonesty, too much of greed and selfishness are exposed and the poet skillfully attempts to attack particularly the present day politics and politicians, their greed, cleverness and disloyalty to the society and to the country at large. Depravity among human beings and in the society has been vehemently criticized by T.V Reddy in *Quest for Peace*. Really, the subject matter of the poem is related to corruption, dishonesty and degeneration of values in the society; but we should also keep this in our mind that the above mentioned subject matter by itself is not sufficient to make the poem an epic in the traditional sense. That is why the poet calls it a minor social epic. It is only by virtue of numerous illustrations from history, legend and great epics and books and references to their characters that the poet is able to impart an epical touch to this poem. Usually in an epic, there should be a hero, a plot, a story and a strong subject matter; but here the poet is the hero and the witness at the same time. Whatever it may be called, the credit lies with the poet for writing such a long poem spreading to 52 pages expressing his ideas in a coherent way. Throughout the length of the work it covers mostly the evil and corrupt aspects of the modern society.

Just as Stephen Gill, a great Canadian poet, who in his magnum opus, *The Flame* is on peace mission, so T.V Reddy in this poem *Quest for Peace* also tries to unveil the follies and vices of society and criticizes them to reach peace as the ultimate goal. In *The Flame* Gill opines that, *The Flame* is about peace and peace is the main area of Gill's poetic depiction. Those who promote peace on earth shall enjoy peace after death. It does not make any sense to expect peace after death, by destroying the peace of others." *(The Flame,* 19)

T.V Reddy is very much concerned for restoring social and moral values in the society. To be peace-loving is to be social. The poet wants to reform society through the medium of poetry. Many poets, writers and authors have engaged themselves in making attempts to bring peace to society. Stephen Gill is one among them. Gill's magnum opus is *The Flame* where he starts his journey for peace with this holy flame. This flame is celestial and holy and it will remove the darkness of the world: 'Where the streams of youth/do not cease flowing/and despair does not nail tents/over the constellation of the dreams/under land of yours/calls me to gather pearls/from the ocean of your wisdom'. (*The Flame*)

T. V. Reddy is a highly disciplined person who is at once ethical and practical and though he has been a dedicated teacher for nearly four decades, never does he spare the defects of the system of our modern education on which he aims his satire:

> Now-a-days everything, even education system,
> is a profitable marketable commodity,
> it is simply an open monetary commodity,
> converting the youth to ethical frigidity;
> corporate school expand their greedy wings,
> convert admissions in to financial springs (QP, 590)

T. V. Reddy is deeply concerned at the gradual fading of moral values which are fast disappearing in the society. His sensitive heart feels aggrieved to see tears in the eyes of laborers and this suffering of the poor peasants pierces his heart. In T.V. Reddy we find a true socialist caring for the good of the society. Perhaps he might have drawn inspiration from Lord Krishna, Buddha, Jesus Christ, Guru Nanak, Mahatma Gandhi, Rousseau, Nelson Mandela who served throughout their whole life for the welfare of the society and made great efforts to restore peace.

It is Indian society which he vehemently criticizes from place to place in the poem. Not only does he do it in *Quest for Peace* but also in other poems. In *Melting melodies* (1994), he is at the pinnacle of his satire when a new born baby undergoes vasectomy:

> The unwashed child
> With uncut umbilical cord
> At the theatrical table
> At the rural health centre
> Undergoes vasectomy
> In the congenial company
> Of a skeletal octogenarian
> Upholds the teacher's increment
> Uplifts the state's record
> The black sky roars livid with red triangle
> The Earth quakes. (*MM*, 15)

In some matters T.V Reddy's *Quest for Peace* can be compared with Alexander Pope's mock epic *Rape of the Lock*. Pope (1688-1744) was a representative poet of 18th century England. He vehemently and vividly mirrored the contemporary London life in his satiric poem *Rape of the Lock*. His portrayal of the social follies and frivolities is entirely satirical unsurpassed by any other poet in English:

> No lap dogs give themselves the rousing shake,
> And sleepless lovers, just at twelve awake
> Thrice rung the bell, the slipper knocked the ground
> And the pressed watch returned a silver sound (*Rape of the Lock*)

In the same way, T.V Reddy represents and satirizes the vices and follies like bribery, corruption, dishonesty prevailing in Indian society with equal force and skill in his inimitable style and in satirical portrait there is no other poet in Indian English who can equal him:

> People of all creeds who lived as loving brothers
> during the white Raj now see with hot
> in their eyes in this cruelly corrupt native Raj. (*QP*, 18)

And

> Even to do their routine work and clear a file
> they wait for years till palms are greased in style.(QP, 25)

T.V. Reddy is a lover of nature and he is very much interested in protecting the Nature which is indeed the protector of all living beings. To love Nature is to love mankind. Nature is our mother, our friend and our guide. This has been acknowledged by great Nature poet William Wordsworth (1770-1850). Many illustrations from his poetry prove that T.V. Reddy is a great lover of Nature. T.V. Reddy's socialist self and his sympathy for the poor and the exploited are quite evident in his poems from the beginning of his poetic career:

> All her sweat ensures her a hut
> While her toil enthrones the lust ("The Toiling Woman", MM, 7)

In contrast to Wordsworth's *Solitary Reaper* or *Tagore's Krishnakali* there had arisen no romance in poet's heart as he beheld a reaper in the field in the hard days of financial problems, but his heart overflows with compassion to the poor corn reaper which is not found in the former poets:

> Is there scarcely a heart
> that sighs for your sweat
> and feels for your toil? .....
> you reap the crop
> heap the harvest
> and feed the millions in cities   ("The Tiller", MM, 8)

Reddy's poems lead us to the inference that he is intensely spiritual and he has strong faith in our Hindu scriptures and their legends. The more he gets spiritual, the more he becomes effective in reaching his goal. He mentions Lord Rama, Buddha, and Christ and satirically attacks the corrupt and vicious people of our society:

> Farewell to Sri Ram, Buddha and Christ,
> cheers to Satan and his shining descendants
> who attract with their rich golden pendants
> flying in planes like Ravan in an air of mist; *(QP, 610)*

In the gingerly handling of satire T.V. Reddy comes closer to Jonathan Swift and Reddy might be an avid reader of swift's satiric works. *Gulliver's Travels* is the biggest social satire of Swift. In the first voyage to the island of Lilliputs, Swift satirizes politics and political tactics practiced in England through the picture of Lilliput. Swift mocks at the politics of England, "It is alleged indeed that the high heels are most agreeable to our ancient constitution: but however this be, his majesty hath determined to make use of low Heels in the Administration of Government, and all the offices in the gift of the crown." In the same way, T.V. Reddy assails the politics and politicians of our society ridiculing their weaknesses and corrupt approaches to the society:

> While the poor are denied drugs and medical tablets
> Our poorer MLAs are gifted with electronic tablets
> For their great service in fuelling hate and division
> Never thinking of the people with any vision; (QP)

Quest for Peace is considered a minor social epic by *T.V. Reddy*; "the reason is that the poet has satirized the vices of the society in this poem. The subject matter of the poem is the exposition of the rampant corruption and degeneration of values in the society." *(Writers Editors Critics)* Vol. 5 issue I, p.71-75 print. The poet wants the contemporary society free from crime, corruption and wars and is interested in such an environment that lends the society to the goal of peace:

> Indeed peace is a blessed state of mind
> let us impart liberal moral stories in schools
> let Rama, Buddha and Christ be our models. (*QP*)

The poet has touched almost every sphere of life and has made his remarks about them. Education, Politics, Caste system, Reservation, British rule in India, constitution of India, the economic Policies of the Govt. of India, Indian rituals, *varnas* etc. have been attacked by the poet in the poem. Mark the excerpts:

> Rituals and responsibilities engulf us
> Faith is as strong as a hard mountain rock and high as the snow–capped Mt Everest
> Ever since we got our independence/ air is vitiated with political slogans dense. (*QP*)

Really, the poet might have gone through the Hindu Scriptures, *the Quran, the Bible* and Persian books. Probably the strong impact perhaps of all these books on the poet has made him morally so courageous that he very fearlessly criticizes the rituals of the society and assails Indian politics and politicians; he wants to free the society from the clutches of vices, follies and frivolities. Just as Lord Rama took a vow to uproot the demons of his time and accepted the challenge to kill them during the exile for 14years, the poet also might have learnt a lesson from the sacrifice of Lord Rama to stand against the vices (rakshasas) of the contemporary society. Valmiki composed the *Ramayan* in Sanskrit and before its composition at a heart-piercing scene he uttered in outburst of anger and sorrow:

Maa nishad pratishtham twam gamah Shashwatisamaha
Yatkrauchch mithunadekamvadih Kammohita ("The Eternity", Vol. 5)

Later with the beginning of these two lines Valmiki with his miraculous pen, for the welfare of the society created a historic epic *The Ramayana;* following that another work in Avadhi language *The Ramcharitmanas* came from a great poet of Bhakti Yuga, Tulsidas. He composed it for the masses in a very easy language. These two scriptures are highly divine and adorable for the Hindus. A true spirit of social consciousness and social reform runs through both the poems:

> 'Parhit saras dharma nahi bhai, par peeda nahi sam adhmai.'
> --- *Ramacharitmanas* (" Geeta Press", 2052th edition)

Reddy is sometimes as humorous as Chaucer. Comparatively Chaucer seems to be more gentle and humorous in his approach in dealing with human weaknesses and foibles than T.V Reddy. Chaucer too has been very piercing and penetrating while presenting some situations in some of his passages. In the same fashion, T.V Reddy the poet in *Quest for peace* makes bold efforts to expose the degradation and to restore the moral values in the society with the help of various literary devices:

> Let's focus our mind on Krishna's gospel
> And tread the righteous path in His spell. (*QP*)

And

> Today's children are our health and bulwark,
> Let us guide them with ethics and truth stark.

T.V Reddy's *Quest for Peace* can be compared to the 14th century poet Chaucer's *Prologue to the Canterbury Tales*. T.V Reddy's satire, humor reminds us of Chaucer's satiric and humorous characters portrayed in his famous poetical work mentioned above; both poets have similar purpose i.e. social reform. *Chaucer* also satirized the contemporary society:

> With us ther was a Doctor of phisik;
> In all this world ne was ther noon hym lik,

> To speke of phisik and of surgerye;
> For he was grounded in astronomye.
> He kept his pacient a ful greet deel
> In houres, by his magyk natureel (*Prologue to the Canterbury Tales*, 411-416)

T.V. Reddy feels bitter in his heart at the pathetic social situation. He expresses his anguish as well as inner grief in the following lines:

> Though the road is rough, never straight,
> I will walk and walk with bleeding feet,
> I determined pace an uncertain fight. (*QP, 470*)

Finally, we conclude that *Quest for Peace* by T.V Reddy is a great piece of poetic art containing social satire in it. Every satirist is at heart a reformist. Reddy also wants to reform the society by pinpointing the vices and shortcomings in it with moral responsibility, civic sense and practical wisdom. This long poem is the direct result of the intensity of his feeling heart to bring some degree of healthy change in the present degenerated society by exposing the ills and evils present in the modern world. The poet is in a sense justified in calling this poem a 'Minor Social Epic' as it presents the ideological battle between moral and immoral forces, between virtue and vice. He deserves unreserved admiration for his moral courage and conviction and creative competence in executing this great project and realizing his selfless objective. Undoubtedly he has been very successful in accomplishing this self-imposed mission.

Abbreviations:
MM: Melting Melodies.
QP: Quest for Peace.

Works cited

Arora, Sudhir K. *The Flame Unmasked:* Prakash Book Depot, Bareilly, 2010. Print.

Chaucer. From "Ideas and Forms in English and American Literature", Vol.1. Poetry. Ed. Homer A. Watt & James B. Munn, New York, Scott, Foreman & Co., 1925; 2nd edition, 1932.

Reddy,T.V. *When Grief Rains*. New Delhi: Samkaleen Prakashan, 1982. Print.

---- --- ----*Pensive Memories*. Chennai: Poets Press India, 2005. Print.

---- ---- ----*Quest for Peace*. New Delhi: Authors Press, 2013. Print.

Stephen, Gill. *The Flame*. Canada: Vesta Publication, 2008. Print.

Sharma, Neelam. K. "Peace and Spirituality in Stephen Gill's The Flame", *Labyrinth* vol.3/ No. 04- Oct, 2012. Print.

Sharma, Neelam K. "Mohanty and His Faith in "Prayers to Lord Jagannatha", SRJIS, Sept- Oct 2013. Print.

25   India Seen through the Eyes of T.V. Reddy: A Study of *The Broken Rhythms*

Ramesh Chandra Mukhopadhyaya

India ranks second in farm output in the world. And agriculture is its backbone. True, that the contribution of agriculture and allied sectors to the country's GDP is ever on the wane. It was 17 percent only in 2014. But we must not forget that 49% of total workforce in the country are engaged in agriculture and similar other activities. T.V. Reddy depicts the twenty-first century Indian farmer drawing his weary feet to the field in the morning only. Reddy describes a farmer going to his field:

> With a loin cloth around his waist
> and a soiled towel, the only cover
> for his sun burnt back he drew his wearied feet
> to his field – a still-born child: (*BR*, 91)

This is an instance of perfect word painting. We see the farmer as it were on the canvass of real life. And look at his weary feet plodding towards the field. It seems that he has lost his zest for life. Why? What ails the ploughman? Look at the field. It is like a still-born child with no signs of life—with not a drop in the well. The well stands for endless springing water and grace from unknown depth. But the dry well signifies the waste land or the land that is not great for growing stuff. So does it not speak of want of irrigation in agricultural land? Nearly fifty percent of net sown land in India falls in un-irrigated areas. And mark you the field has seedlings transplanted. It suggests that Indian agriculture is already a slave girl in the hands of the capitalist system. The transplanted field is like transmigrated souls. Does it not remind one of T.S. Eliot watching the crowd of people flowing over London Bridge like zombies? (*Waste Land*. www.bartleby.com) The life of this farmer plodding his way to the field is itself a fallow field.

With Steinbeck, a fallow field is a sin and unused land a crime against their children (*Grapes of Wrath*). Here fallow field is a metaphor for the life of a farmer. It clearly tells us how our country ignored to sow seeds of life in these common men whose lives could have been creative overflowing with milk and honey. The fallow field of the farmer's life is laden with thorns and thistles. Adam and Eve partake of the fruit of the tree of knowledge and are cursed by God. God tells them that their land will henceforth grow thorns and thistles. But the farmer has done no wrong against God's will. Be that as it may, the farmer pulls on like the dumb bull that ploughs looking every day up in to the skies for the deceptive clouds with sighs.

Yes, every one of us is being dragged like a dumb bull by the capitalist system. Both man and animal are being starved and exploited. There is no hope of redressing the ills and abuses in the society. So we look into the skies. But where is God? The clouds are deceptive. Hopes have been turned into dupes. Hope springs eternal in human breasts; Dante's Inferno asks us to abandon all hopes (Inferno, Dante, Wikipedia). Are the Indian farmers denizens of the Inferno upon earth? ("Farmer", *BR*, 9)

With the advent of evening the pensive farmer limps back home. His feet are bare and sore. The famished bulls also accompany him. His wife cooks a morsel of rice with twigs. To eat is also an ordeal. They take rice with tamarind chutney and butter milk. This food habit is absolutely stamped with Telugu culture. Thus Reddy's poetry is charged with the fragrance of regional culture.

He dwells on *Ugadi* or *Yugadi* i.e. the New Year Day (*BR*, 30) for the Telugu people. He dwells on *kavadi* or burden in relation to the worship of Muruga who is essentially a Tamil god or South Indian God. His longing lingering look back to the glory that was Hampi and the marvelous sculptural beauty of the temples at Warangal and Ramappa, reminisces the ancient glories of Andhra Pradesh. The poet is aware of what disaster was done to the images of the temple near Warangal by the Muslim invaders. The poet at the sight of the ruins of the throbbing divinity on stones feels as if thousand swords pierce his spine. The past becomes living present and bleeding present through the medium of the poet ("Thousand Pillars", *BR* 1).

But at the same time Reddy's poetry transcends regionalism. He laments the lost glory of Harappa. Like a realist he dwells on the lasting pain of the fallen India. This is not all. Is not the farmer as delineated by Reddy the representative of the farmers all over the world whose existence is in jeopardy with the advent of expanding capitalism? Is not the fallow life of the farmer comparable with the existence of the hollow men and stuffed men that we are? The farmer and the common man have no other entertainment than sex at their disposal. The farmer and his wife proceed to the ritual of procreation. They have no inheritance and no saving. It is night. The whole village has plunged into the silence of a grave. The farmer coughs in the still of night and the cough become loud and long ("Pensive Farmer" 10).

The farmer lives in a village. Could we visit a village where such farmers do live? But the journey to the village could be a traumatic experience for the reader. Let us share the experience of the poet journeying to a village —

> I got into a state (or stately) bus
> with a sigh of relief
> for at last it came
> amid clouds of dust and din.   (*BR*, 7)

The irony is evident. The state bus has been called stately bus. How stately is the bus? Well it comes amidst cloud of dust and din. And the bus comes after a long wait. Let us smile on the other side of our lips and try to understand the transport system in the country. The roads overflowing with dust are not transport-friendly. The buses do not keep time though stately! Ha! Ha! The bus, the poet observes, has kinship with modern art. There is much crowd and more cargo, a barbarous blend of wood and wooden face. And when the bus starts with a groan the poet is seated on the bus with his heart in his palm. So, that is the state of transport in our country ("Travel by Bus", BR 7).

The bus journey over, let us visit an Indian village. A village is a clustered human habitation in the countryside. As per the 2001 census 72.2 percent of the population lived in about 638000 villages in India. Reddy describes a village as flaccid or pale. His poem 'The Village' (BR 11) describes a typical Indian village. As soon as it is morning the crow caws in triumph. It has made the cow's back bleed. The onlooker exclaims - let her bleed and perish. The Sun reaches the meridian and evokes in them midsummer madness. One of the villagers complains - 'Your buffalo has grazed my crop'. The Sun retires in disgust and they sit under the large peepal tree and whisper to one another. They whisper, conspire and conceal. In short the village society is a veritable hell as it were where backbiting, malicious and spiteful talk, abuse vituperation, slander and quarrelling are the rule. The poet points out that the very hands that were fed by the mango tree have now felled the tree. The poet says:

> Don't turn your eyes
> from the naked tree;

> it is as dry and stark
> as the skeleton of cow
> whose carcass is punctured
> by the steely beaks of vultures.
> Tired of giving life
> the pond by its side
> has become dry;   ("The Naked Tree", *BR*, 4)

Thus rural India is such a place where cows are wounded by the crows. The bullocks starve. The vultures feed on the carcasses of the cows. The wells and ponds are dry. Land is uncultivated. The uncultivated men pass their time in slandering against one another. The readers are apt to ask themselves who the vultures and crows are.

And to crown it all the country is infested with goons. Mark the rhetorical strategy -comparison and contrast among similar things like the dynamite, cyanide, cobra and a goonda all of whom are killers, in the following poem addressing the goon -

> Dynamite
> is less explosive
> than you
> Cyanide
> is less deadly
> than you -
> black cobra
> less pernicious
> than you -
> the lawless goonda.   ("Reign of Terror", *BR*, 20)

The lawless goonda has no scruples. He prowls in the society like a wolf and robs men of their gold, blood and even golden chastity. Thus the society is worse than wilderness even. The wolf robs men of their lives. But neither do they covet gold nor do they rob one of her chastity. These lawless goondas crowned with crimes have ushered in a reign of terror. In other words there is no law and order in the society. The crown might be a synecdoche that stands for the ruler. About thirty-four percent of newly elected M Ps in the present parliament have criminal cases against them ("Reign of Terror", *BR*, 20).

On the roadside there might be a leper. The poet describes him as blemished mass wrapped in rags. This might remind us of Johnsonian style. This is not an affected, stilted and pompous language. In fact such sights as a leper begging on the roadside are quite frequent in India. He is a human. And still does he look like a man? We ignore the unnaturalness of a leper's get up in our everyday life. Reddy, an artist in the right sense of the term portrays a stunning figure of a leper to draw our attention to what man has made of man. And the apparently bombastic language has come to his aid. A few spit at the leper's odious sight. A dog empties the remnants of a leaf and passes by with cherubic contentment. The pleasure of defecation of a dog has been dwelled on with great power and force. But to add to this while the leper scared of the dog reels in living death, the dog scared of the leper flees from him in dread. Thus we are in a situation where man is scared of the domestic animals and domestic animals are scared of man. The very foundation of human civilization trembles ("A Leper", *BR*, 8).

We have witnessed the leper - a blemished mass wrapped in rags. Now there is a beggar - a heap of bones wrapped in skin; his thorny head an inverted hot pan. This is an instance of word picture again. If mellifluous note of poetry is granted for the fashion of the day Reddy is a rebel who revels in anti-poetry and portrayal of the ugly. While Rome burns Nero fiddles. Despite the sight of the beggar the mistress of a house with her bare arms stands by her lover smiling for nothing in the balcony. In other words the wells of compassion and sympathy are dry now. But this is not all. Greater surprise waits for the reader. A wealthy man throws a slice in the cracked bowl of the beggar and lo! A bitch comes in time and devours it. The poet comments---the dusty bowl smiles at a moving monster.

The Upanishads exhorted us to give with fear, to give with heart, to give in a friendly way (Shikshavalli-vedarahasya net). Compare how the wealthy man whose money is dishonestly earned gives alms to the beggar with the mode of giving as prescribed by the Upanishads. And mark, the slice thrown to the beggar is devoured by a bitch. This is happening everyday in India. The government for example gives dole to the poor. And in most cases the money does not reach the poor. It is devoured by the timely appearance of middle men ("Beggar's Bowl", 22).

Earlier gift economics was largely in vogue. In gift economy valuables are not sold but given away without any explicit agreement for immediate or future reward. Gift economics now-a-days has been replaced by market economy where greed is the motivating factor. And the consequence has been described by Dr. Reddy through a parable which could be retold thus: Once upon a time there was a proud lamb or ram. But misfortune befell him. The ram was killed and its flesh was transferred to epicurean tomb. The phrase epicurean tomb puts in our minds the notion of consumerism. A drunken person feasting on the flesh of the ram flings a bone at a beggar. The beggar and a dog vie with one another to possess the prize. Modern market economy encourages competition. What is the competition like? It is like the competition between the dog and the beggar in the parable. Nowadays we always want to possess. We are beggars. Even the richest man is a beggar. Even the richest country under the Sun is a beggar. It wants to possess more and more; this lust for possession has brought about the competition between the dog and the beggar. The war among nations could be symbolically depicted as fight between a dog and a beggar for a piece of flesh.

The sequence of events in the narrative as put forward by the poet Reddy is innovative. It moves forward from present to past. The poem "Bony Reward" (23) opens with a dirty black bitch running a race proud of her prize possession. It is dramatic and photogenic. The reader is apt to ask what the proud possession of the bitch is and with whom does the bitch race. Step by step from present to past do we proceed only to reconstruct the story along the diachronic axis from past to present. In other words Reddy puts forward the narrative in a deconstructed way to be reconstructed by the reader. Thus Reddy often revels in writing text where the reader must exert himself to get at the meaning.

We met a poet in English literature drunk in the milk of paradise (Coleridge in "Kubla Khan", www. poetry. foundation. org). Reddy aware of his poetic art sometimes seems to identify himself with drunken lips from which sparks of truth leap forth. They come to him as easily as the ripe fruits fall from the trees ("A True Drunkard", 12). It reminds us of a hymn to Lord Tryambaka. The hymn reads: "May we be released from life and death cycle just as the cucumber falls from the tree so that we could be free (*Rigveda* 7-59-12)".

Here perhaps the poems fall from the tree of time and space to become timeless reproach against evil. See how Reddy describes the Swamiji -

> They all praise his spiritualism and simplicity
> For he ate only apples, cashew nuts and dried grapes
> Drank pure milk and juice brought by fair sex.   ("Swamiji", 13)

This is a perfect instance of irony where the intended meaning is different from actual meaning. The poet tells us that the potter and clay were his easy victims. This is polite sarcasm and irony reminding one of ladies popping in and popping out of the banquet hall talking of Michelangelo (*The Love Song of J Alfred Prufrock* by T S Eliot, www.poetry.org).

There is a wedding feast held in the hall loud with music radiant with stone-set jewellery and electronic watches and saris; the bins outside the hall overflow with bits and crumbs and sweets and savory. While unbridled revelry is let loose in the banquet hall skeleton shapes with hollow eyes, sunken stomachs and soiled rags shove, gnash and snarl in rage to gain their share of the food left off. The dogs vie with them. Heaps of plenty beside chill penury characterize Indian society. ("Wedding Feast", 29) About 32.7 percent people in India live below the poverty line. There are just 18359 taxpaying people in India.

In this developing society even middle class women can hardly work with honour. The typist girl in the office tries to avoid the prowling lascivious looks at her office. At last with a dry smile she spreads the red carpet of her youthful beauty to the M D. And mark the dramatic irony when the poet exclaims that the MD ensures her rise in status before the sunrise. There is the improvement in the standing of the lady by way of sacrificing herself to the MD. And surely her rise in status is ensured before sunrise in the bed only. With sunrise her elevated position as the beloved of the MD will be descried. To spread the red carpet of youth or to rise in status before sunrise are polite expressions. But the underlying tone has a marked bitterness in them ("The Typist Girl", 34).

So these are a few vignettes of life in India. India once upon a time, famed to be a crucible of religion, is now a cubicle of callous creeds. The conflicting isms here radiating nefarious hues, the weird dance of the tidal waves of caste colour shatters the myth that India offers unity in diversity. The assembly halls here in the land are corrupt, crowded with corpulent ministers, tom-cowards and braggadocios like Bobadils of Ben Jonson, who brag that they are the followers of the great hero of a patriot Subhash Chandra Bose. Here in India righteousness is scarce as sugar or cement. This is apparently a case of bathos. But on another level quality control in economic production of sugar or cement could be achieved by a nation whose members are righteous and honest. According to Reddy, capitalism cannot prosper without some kind of honesty. Truly India is as it were a wild desert burning in the hot Sun of corruption. Widespread dissembling has spread here the carpet woven with myriads of mirages. The mirages promise groves that shelter peace and spiritualism. And a traveler in quest of peace in India is destined to be waylaid. But the poet Reddy cannot but be shocked at this dismal sight. He asks—'Can rains (of compassion and virtue) evade forever/ with elusive clouds?' ("This Sacred Soil", 36-37)

Just as Wordsworth castigates the English nation as stagnant and selfish in the sonnet 'London 1802', so does Reddy castigate the Indian nation. The imagery of Gandhi's ghost being chased till it bleeds and recedes reminds us of Seneca and the revenge drama of Kyd. Revenge is now fast asleep. But when it wakes up, will not revenge upon the corrupt ministers and their cruel aids take place in the shape of showers of inexhaustible compassion pouring upon the country?

While Wordsworth described his contemporary England as stagnant swamp, Reddy condemns flat out the state of Indian nation as a sun-burnt desert. While Wordsworth invokes the spirit of Milton to resurrect, what will Reddy do? No, he will not ape the unknown citizen of Auden or the gentleman of normal degree who pleased boss and the workers, an angel at home an asset to the firm ("The Report", 35).

It is bootless to consult the roadside fortune-teller with a bird in a cage. Can the bird which is itself pent up in the cage light up the winged hope of the poet to float and run in the blue deep of freedom where there is no cruelty, no corruption, no conceit and no dissembling? ("Fortune Teller", 2) There is the gypsy woman walking along the street and crying - 'I can tell your fortunes, hear my *sode*'. Her anklets and bracelets and bangles jingle; mirrors sewn in her sari reflect the piercing Sun. She sells a parcel of sweet dreams in exchange of remorseless morsel for herself. What else could the people do in a country where there is no honesty, creativity, economic activity, where we have to abandon all hope? ("The Gypsy Woman", 33) The poet can see into the futility of consulting the so-called soothsayer.

The poet is carried off by a nap. He is distracted from the nap by the metallic sound, *Om Muruga*. In other words the chant of *Om Muruga* does not delight the poet. The name Muruga itself stands for the *Pranava* or *Om*. Murugan is MukundanRudra and Kamalan, creator, preserver and destroyer in one, and his abode is in the hills. It is said that Murugan relieves one of the burdens or *kavadi* if one journeys uphill to pay homage to Murugan chanting the name Muruga. Murugan is by the by fond of hills as his abode. The poet espies the tipsy steps of the barefoot devotees exposed to the burning Sun carrying mindless and penance- exhausted bodies soaked in sweat as it were. The stony savior Murugan however is unmoved and does not say a word. Hence prayers to gods for deliverance from the encircling waste land are of no avail. ("Quaint Faith", 19).

The so-called rituals, religious or secular, are meaningless to the poet. They are as it were empty sets without any content. They are the agents of degeneration. Hearing the crackers and perceiving the loud pomp and pageantry on the day of *Ugadi* or New Year Day, the poet feels how mindless the society is. It is not joy or happiness but want of joy and happiness that impels the society to burst in sudden revelry, because the society has nowhere to go. And despite that it struts and swaggers. And who knows the society is rushing towards death and destruction? Reddy's euphemism in this context is characteristically thought-provoking -

> This game of endless journey goes on
> till it is arrested by the last milestone ("The New Year Day", 30)

Reddy is a modernist poet. Modern poetry speaks of hyacinth and biscuit in the same breath. T S Eliot measures life with coffee spoons. And Reddy tells us that X-ray report confirms that no alien particle of humanity is in man. The Bible says that God made man in His own image and the Upanishads posit that men are the children of Eternity, but such revelations are belied. Owls hoot at man. Dogs whine at him as if he is an apparition. The ending lines of the poem are quite revealing: 'Are you a beclouded sun/or an ever eclipsed one?' ("Eclipse", 18). The toothless mastiff bitch of Coleridge makes answer to the clock four for the quarter and twelve for the hour. Some say she sees the lady's shroud ("Christabel", by S T Coleridge, www.poetry foundation. org).

Surrounded by apparitions in human shape the poet seeks refuge in sensuousness perhaps. In his erotic poem 'Between the Lines' Reddy seems to be the true heir of Gatha Saptasati of Hala, the illustrious Telugu Satavahana Emperor of 1st century C.E. and Sanskrit erotic poetry. The poet's personal experience with his lady love has been erotically and aesthetically presented in a sequence of shapes and images reminding us of the sculptures of love-making at Khajuraho or Konark. The images in the poem have the solidity and flexibility of figures forged by sculptors. This is no mean achievement for a poet. But presently after the consummation of love making the whole affair seems to the poet a storm in the tea cup. Anticlimax or bathos constitutes the underlying structure of the powerful poem. ("Between the Lines", 28)

The ravishing beauty of a jasmine flower drives the poet to tear it off from her mother's breast in a dream. In a furious triumph the poet finds it shrunken - a piteous sight. Thus any act of possession only robs the beauty of the thing possessed. Hence there is nothing to be possessed in the world. Those who want to possess things are like cows mutilating jasmine flowers and pulling the creeper. The mute agony of the petals of jasmine is heart-piercing:

> 'Nameless and withered though they were
> Their manes cried in mute agony –
> 'Save us from rape and murder, ungrateful wretches' - ("Jilted Jasmine", 32)

In fact the opposites like the beautiful and the ugly, happiness and sorrow are appearances. Child-philosopher-seer best, Lord Krishna as a child put a pinch of dust into his mouth. The child does not distinguish between sweets and dust. Lord Krishna is Time itself. Time is like the child which has no value judgment. It devours everything; everything is dust as if it were having no intrinsic value. In fact in the parole of the poet-- a few quick steps all is earth and dust. Dust we are and to dust we must return after the strut and fret of the existence ("Child", 15). Life and death are two poles of a magnet of a metre long; we move from one pole to another. It is for a short while that we stay. Our experiences within this brief passage of time are vast. And despite that our lease of life is not long enough to unravel the mystery of the infinitude ("Existence", 17).

We travel by the train of time and find the earth moving and in the course of the journey it is felt that the opposites, the Babel created by the passengers and the silence resulting from their exit from the train, merge. Men may come and men may go, but the brook or the train of time goes on forever. The train moves along parallel rails of joys and sorrows of life and death - the two poles of a magnet one metre long. Being passengers of the train, being pent up in time and space, we can never ever decode the mystery of existence ("The Train", 6).

We are in the train. Everything else is in some kind of train. There are myriads of different times and spaces. From our train we look at other trains as it were. From a moving vehicle everything else seems to be moving. And the greatest minds since the days of Sophocles and Vedic rishis have been gazing at the endless Milky Way without beginning and at this amazing existence knowing not what to say. Matthew Arnold in his "Dover Beach" claimed that the ancient Greek writer Sophocles looked upon life steadily and as a whole. But that is not true. Reddy with the spark of a true philosopher says the poets and philosophers and seers have at best culled some shreds from the infinite. They never delineate the totality of existence before us ("The Milky Way", 5).

Hence, there is no point in renouncing the world for a life in the Himalayas and parceling the desires of the flesh into the snow-capped cold storage. Because in the cold storage they might slumber; but they are never killed. The poet wants to be in his own elements. He will not follow any given road to truth. Everybody must find or make his own way to truth: 'real transformation/ flouts all flavored formulae/of our pseudo-Sadhus and Babas;' ("Convert", 16). Now as things stand for the poet, however much the poet might despise the world, he is not given up. On the contrary he will forge arrows from bamboo and shoot at targets backed up by neutron bomb. This is sheer romanticism. Can anyone fight machine guns with sticks? ("Bamboo Arrow", 31).

But the poet prays to God, if any, for strength and grit to face the odds of life and to know the journey's end and its meaning; he is always modest and honest in his expression and that is the strength behind his powerful lines:

> "I exist, but I don't know why,
> Life is too short to know
> That which is infinite;'   ("Existence", 17)

The poet it seems prefers life in death to death in life. The poet finds in the smile of a tribal child the signs of resurrection ("Child's Smile", 14). The poet finds in the ant the message of hard work that might rejuvenate the society ("Toiling Ants", 3). That is how the broken rhythm of existence could be set aright perhaps.

In conclusion, *The Broken Rhythms* is a significant book of poems on many counts. Firstly, it holds out a mirror to life as it is in India. Thousand pages of Indian economics and Indian sociology cannot teach us the truths about the social and economic predicament in India better than the handful of poems in *The Broken Rhythms*. Unlike essays on Economics or Sociology, these poems are the minute observations seen through the personality of the poet. The decadence of the Indian society converts the poet into melting mood and he is flung into the Serbonian bog of contemplation on the meaning of life and time. Finally he picks up bows and arrows made of bamboo to brave a sea of troubles. He finds the rhythms of normal existence with the desired norms of human values broken and this picture of reality is faithfully reflected in these poems. That is the underlying structure of the bunch of poems embodied in T.V. Reddy's *The Broken Rhythms*.

26 Poetic Iridescence of T.V. Reddy

A.K. Choudhary

"Dr. T.V. Reddy is morning star in the firmament of Indo-Anglia poetry. He is a poet par excellence who has profound message to convey."

Dr. Krishna Srinivas

T.V. Reddy who has to his credit 10 poetry collections---*When Grief Rains* (1982), Samkaleen Publications, New Delhi, *The Broken Rhythms* (1987), Poets Press, Madras, *The Fleeting Bubbles* (1989), Poets Press, Madras, *Melting Melodies* (1994), Poets Press, Madras, *Pensive Memories* (2005), Poets Press, Madras / Chennai, *Gliding Ripples* (2008) Publish America, Baltimore, USA, *Echoes* (2012), Gnosis, Authors Press, New Delhi, *Quest for Peace* (2013), Authors Press, New Delhi, *The Rural Muse :The Poetry of T. Vasudeva Reddy* (2014), Authors Press, New Delhi, *Golden Veil* (2016), Authors Press, New Delhi, *Thousand Haiku Pearls*(2016), Authors Press, New Delhi, *Sound and Silence* (2017), Authors Press, New Delhi, two novels--*The Vultures* (1983), Calcutta, India and *Minor Gods* (2008), New York City, USA and three Criticism books--*Jane Austen: The Dialectics of Self-Actualization in her Novels* (1987), Sterling, New Delhi, *Jane Austen: The Matrix of Matrimony* (1987), Bohra Publication, Jaipur, and *A Critical Survey of Indo-English Poetry* (2016), Authors Press, New Delhi, has become a darling of the creative community in Indian English poetry. Indianness is the soul of Indian English literature. Indian ethos, religious doctrines, universalism, spiritualism, morality and guiding spirits run wild across his verses that make him out and out an Indian English poet from the fertile literary soil of India. As a matter of fact the essence of Indianness of his verses makes him a poet of the Pondicherry School of Poetry rather than the Ezekielian School of Poetry in Indian English literature.

His poetic approach, divine notion, captivating thought and sensational social painting has made him a leading literary luminary of Indian English literature. Reddy's poetic order works wonders for literary grandeur on a land of sages and poets ((Menander)) where his mind- blowing thought, lucid expression, visionary ideology, stirring imagination and painterly painting have made him an eminent poet of exceptional creative talent across the world. His description of Kashi, Kedarnath, Tirupati, Chitrakuta and various other temples enlivens the cultural culmination of Indian society in English poetry. Ram, Krishna, Buddha and Christ thrill and enthrall his poetic passages to glow with the spirit of universalism everywhere. These Indian words—*Chaturvarna, pundits, neem tree, sivathandava, darshan, Shraddham, Parandham, avatar, nirvana, karma, sanyasi, tapovan, dharma, Maya, pranayama, pindam, bhagwan, mukti, raj* - and many others establish his poetic career as one of the leading Indian English poets with strong Indian sensibility from the fertile literary soil of India.

Like Syed Ameeruddin, T.V. Reddy has shown his linguistic expertise in using unique word structure that enchants the readers and lovers of poetry reading. These combinations of words— arrange and rearrange, broker and smuggler, ballot and bullet, brier and barrier, crown and frown, creed and breed, crow and sparrow, dark and stark, disrobe and rob, far and near, fear and terror, fear and tear, fume and flame, gaze and rage, glean and gain, heat and hate, low and slow, lip and zip, men and women, move and prove, mirth and death, power and sphere, peace and grace, power and slayer, pseudo and shadow, rock and block, read and breed, right and bright, rustle and bustle, ruing and ruining, struggle and giggle, slip and dip, subways and gateways, tense and distance, tiller and toiler, trick and prick, wear and tear, wine and dine, victual and ritual - and many others speak volumes about his natural talent of creating music and artistic pattern of versification in Indian English poetry. The critics can smell the essence of the Pre-Raphaelite poets across his verses while he versifies the artistic stanza for the verse suitors:

> Their chorus of sounds shrill
> Like a hilly rill fills with thrill,
> Wings spread sunny smiles
> Waves of spring for miles and miles ("Sparrows", *Echoes*)

As a prominent poet Reddy has proved his expertise in using examples of various figures of speech. These examples of alliterations—'Always breeding brazen broken brigades', 'a concrete change, a challenge', 'Cheering chimes and choking movements', 'drink delighting drops of beauty's honey', 'fertile fields of fresh luminous morns', 'Fission, flow and fusion', 'hollow heads and fans heap vanity', 'Offices full of bribe-breathing bloody bugs', 'paints, puffs and powders of varied tastes', 'seeing disease, decay and death sizzle', 'springing from scents, smells and perfumes', 'springs sweet symphonies', 'terminating all termites of terminology', 'to find faint fusion in confusion', 'we are a selfish sullied sinning race', 'we shall sing in sacred solemn lays' and many others that overflow with rhythmic music make him a poet of global repute without dispute.

His proverbial passages pierce the poetic nebulosity that strikes the verse suitors most. Here lie few examples of the proverbial dialogues --

> Never did he foresee Heaven within his reach, /
> This life is the supreme gift of the One Supreme
> to bloom into life divine, not to fade as a bad dream;/ (*QP*, 1660-1661)
> Awake, arise or be fallen in ignorance forever /... (*QP*, 1638)
> Indeed, Peace is a blessed state of mind, .../ (*QP*, 1357)
> None can extend the time of the final call
> however great or tall it tolls the knell of all, .../(*QP*, 1208- 09)
> One who preaches hate and kill is no God,
> for peace and love stands always true God' // (*QP*.1187- 88)

and several such charming lines that enrich the poetic beauty of his verses to its utmost degree abound his poetry.

Peace is the birthright of all living beings in general and the human beings in particular on this strife-torn earth. His keen observation shows not only the mirror to the society but also makes him the guide for Tom, Dick and Harry in India. In his Preface the poet writes: "Search for peace has become a wild goose chase and the modern man makes a vain bid to find it at the horizon's end. Exploitation flourishes with multiple heads in multiple forms and terrorism and extremism reign with blood-thirsty fangs."(*QP*, 6)

Terrorism has become a great threat to the global society. The heinous crimes---Mahabodhi Temple's blast, Madrid and London blast, blasting of Bamiyan Buddha with dynamites, Bali bombings, Norwegian Breivik's mass-killing, Delhi High Court blast, Mumbai carnage and many others create havoc amidst the common masses. The poet warns against the immoralities growing rapidly in the society. The political bankruptcy has become a matter of concern for the countrymen.

Like Nissim Ezekiel, Reddy paints a painterly picture of the ailing society in which all become helpless. The poet versifies this stanza in which he writes:

> Politics is the chosen game of clever guys
> who prefer negative arts and polished lies
> and the crowning act and art of swallowing
> thousands of crores released for nation-building.(QP, 249-252)

As a matter of fact Reddy ridicules the pseudo writers, pseudo professors, pseudo politicians and pseudo secularists who have been misguiding the society for their own sake. The poet paints a sensitive picture in the stanza that speaks volumes about the ongoing immoralities infecting the global society. He condemns those activists who always shed crocodile tears over the death of the innocents but come forward to protect the human rights of the terrorists and the killers. As a result he murmurs melodiously for the celestial message:

> Like Alexander, let us march forward
> With courage and conviction in the noble task,
> Like Asoka, spread the serene peace inward
> And in that inward light let us in delight bask,
> Like Sivaji, oppose the dark negative forces,
> Like Napolean, harness all positive resources,
> Like Vivekananda, tread the righteous path
> Shaking off the beastly slumber and sloth; (QP, 1618-1625)

The poet shows not only the mirror to the society but also suggests some measures to avoid such critical moments. He seeks solace from Alexander, Asoka, Sivaji, Napoleon and Vivekananda and wishes to abide by the righteous path for the sake of the humanity.

> While India groans under endless corrupt greed,
> Egypt bleeds under the violence of a new breed
> When a football match transforms the ground
> Into a senseless violent battle and burial ground;
> Unless leaders with broader vision take the reins
> The pest of the age old dogma kills the brains. (QP, 1528-1533)

Strife of life is better than ever. The chequered career of life makes a man more mature, more sensitive and more conscious than those who have not inhaled the essence of the chequered career. Experience is another name of perfection. Life must go onwards for the better future in the womb of time. Life must be spiritual, magnetic and sublime. It must be fragrant for all those crossing the way of life. Dedication, determination, and devotion are the chief tools of life upon which failure or success depends in the coming days. Life is a crown of thorns rather than a bed of roses. To embrace the challenge of life is the main thing for a man of game person. Life is to blossom, not to extinguish. The path of life is divine and superfine for the spiritual sanctity. The chequered career makes life more mature with the passage of time. Life is a great challenge for a man of conscience. The cultural life that blooms breeds the passage for prosperity and humanity for the races next to come. The religious doctrines that have been running wild from times immemorial guide the course of Indian masses. The cultural heraldry of his verses makes him a disciple of Aurobindonean School of Poetry in Indian English poetry. Imagery, simplicity, capital idea, philosophy, religious philosophy and several other poetic qualities of his verses make him a recognized poet of reputation in Indian English poetry.

His concept of beauty beautifies the face laden with virtuous qualities. Physical beauty is the subject of ravage with the passage of time. He ridicules the physical beauty that exists only for the time being. His concept of beauty bursts forth in this stanza:

> Beauty is as thin as skin, well we know
> Still we run after the vanishing glow.
> Eve enters Paradise fresh and pure,
> With forbidden taste she leaves unsure. ("Beauty Parlor", *Echoes*)

His philosophy of marriage is a noble one that glorifies the sacred bond. Marriage is the union between the opposite sexes. It sends the suitors in the seventh heaven. Love is beyond measure. His concept of love is the living force for the union between the two.

> Love is a living force free from guile,
> Its invisible touch a spring of joy,
> In all seasons never does it cloy;
> With throbbing spirit it spurs the heart
> And pumps the blood with emotive art. ("Love is Light", *Echoes*)

Love is the spiritual right that blooms only in perfect psyche. As and when the lover and the beloved join this world; they lose their identity and become one in all. Life is a crown of thorns rather than a bed of roses for those who possess sensitive mind. Those who possess piggish philosophy are the burden of the society due to their Herod policy for the people in general.

Inheriting the vision of the sage Sri Aurobindo, Reddy asserts his ultimate hope that,

> This life is the supreme gift of the One Supreme
> to bloom into life divine, not to fade as a bad dream. (*QP*, 60)

The thought of gold leads the way to the treasury of misery. This piggish philosophy spreads sophistry in favour of the dark world. As a result the poet shows the mirror to this generation and warns them not to surrender themselves for the dark kingdom of sophistry. His poetic purpose is to embrace the kingdom of wisdom rather than gloom. The thoughts of gold and glory are nothing but an eternal inferno.

Reddy is primarily a poet of the village who has enjoyed the essence of rural sensibility since his childhood. The scenic beauty of the locality thrills his poetic gems for more and more versification for the sake of cultural heraldry of Indian English poetry. Like the Romantic poets Reddy is the ardent suitor of natural iridescence that adds fuel to his poetic passion to its utmost degree. The poet muses melodiously:

> Autumn speaks with a fast fading grace,
> Spring fails to spring surprise or its trace.
> All seasons are richly fertile for corruption
> That grows without reason or correction;
> For corruption most fertile is Indian soil,
> The weed has full growth without any toil; (*QP*, 38)

The plant gives fruits, the flower gives fragrance, the bird gives melodious song and the animal gives milk for our livelihood. Men must have friendship with these objects and make the earth a better place to live in.

In one of his interviews, Reddy comments about his philosophy of nature in these words:

> "I was so much influenced by the British Romantic poets. Right from the good olden days, even when I was a student, I was fond of Romantic Poetry - the poetry of

Wordsworth, Shelley and Keats. Naturally it had made a deep impression on me. Moreover, I was born and brought up in a village - the village which was surrounded on all sides by the beauty of Nature. So the influence of my surroundings was there deeply on me. That is why, I was very much impressed and began drawing so much of pleasure in describing the objects of Nature which I saw". (www.bologi.com/2013)

Nature has remained the guide of several poets from times immemorial that plays a key role in the writings from time to time. The fragrant flowers, the radiant sunset, glittering stars, roaring clouds, sparkling rainbow, running waters of the rivers, bowing trees, melting mountains and several other natural objects fire the poetic imagination to its utmost degree. The cycle of nature is the permanent wealth on this earth where all living beings are expected to abide by this tradition. Nature was the guide of Wordsworth while Keats inhales the sensuousness from its iridescence. The marvelous painting of nature in his poems proclaims Reddy primarily a poet of nature in Indian English literature. Reddy is out and out an Indian English poet because Indianness overflows throughout his poetry with great poetic beauty. Reddy abides by the ingredients of Aurobindonean School of Poetry because the cultural and mythical messiahs flourish in the melodious lines of his verses. Like the romantic poet Reddy is a great lover of natural beauty and its iridescence that fires the flames of the poetic passion of a number of poetry lovers all over the globe. He further adds in his another conversation:

I have tried to present multiple colors and shades of nature in my poems. I love nature and I like to paint nature in most of my poems. Whether we like it or not we have to live in nature and with nature. Therefore, it is our duty to preserve the purity of nature. By harming nature, we would be harming ourselves. Already we have done greater harm and it is time to protect nature so as to protect the human race. We are children of nature and nature is our mother, guide and philosopher. In short, I have tried to present the real life of our villages in my writing.(http://literaryjournal.in)

The satiric tone, humorous poetic passage, free verse, witty satire, masterly painting, exquisiteness of expression, lucidity, focus on burning issues and several other poetic features make him a pupil of Ezekielian School of Poetry in Indian English literature. So far his poems are concerned; T.V. Reddy is close to the Augustans rather than the Romanticists in English literature. Reddy's sensational poetic approach, realistic social painting, impressive poetic style, selection of apt words, uses of mythical, historical and literary names, pigmented poetic passages, mind-blowing captivating thoughts, imaginative imagery, Ezekielean tradition of writing, Augustan's witty satire, Indianized version of presentation, lucidity and expression and lyrical luminosity shape souls of many a promising poet in Indian writing in English. Like Jayant Mahapatra, Reddy makes an earnest attempt in exposing the social and political hypocrisy of the Indian masses that made a treasury of the raw materials for versification in English poetry. The fragrance of his poetic wisdom can be inhaled everywhere in India and abroad, because he is a recognized poet all over the world and his poetry is critically examined by various critics across the globe and he won thunders of applause of the Indian poetry lovers.

His romance with the verse makes poetry his sweet heart because he plays with various concepts of poetry as if they were the erogenous zones of his sweet heart. His poetic purpose that can shape souls of many a committed reader creates sensations amidst poetry lovers in Indian English literature. His central idea that deals with various burning issues of life kindles the imagination of many a poetry lover to strive for perfection in life. Reddy is really a leading literary star from the fertile literary soil of India and the imperishable quality of his poetry always creates ripples of poetic beauty and glory that echoes in the minds of the reading community. His promotion of the up-coming and contemporary Indian English poets through his qualitative critical book viz "A Critical Survey of Indo-English Poetry" is really a golden step in Indian English literature. Many of his everlasting poetical passages with their enduring poetic excellence are sure to become a part of our memory with their inbuilt aesthetic beauty sweet as nectar. His poetic wisdom is really a healthy nourishment to the minds of all those willing to pursue poetry as their career in life. His dedication to the poetic meadows, selfless service to the humanity and promotion of the promising poets make him a superstar glowing in the empyrean of Indian poetry in English. T.V. Reddy is really a great poet of this century who has been propagating the message of universal peace and brotherhood amidst the masses irrespective of the race or religion or region they belong to. The fragrant flower of Reddy's poetry has started to bloom and blossom and will continue to flourish in the womb of time.

It is my privilege to conclude this article with this precious comment of Nissim Ezekiel:

> "T.V. Reddy is always a realist and his poems are reflections of his socio-economic consciousness…Like a gifted sculptor he chisels his poems with the deftness of master craftsman."

Works Cited

Ezekiel, Nissim. "Foreword to T.V. Reddy's *Pensive Memories*". Chennai, Poets Press India. Print.
Boloji.com: www.bologi.com/2013.
Majumder, P.K. *English Poetry in India*. Kolkata : Bridge –in-Making, 2015. 381. Print.
Reddy, T. V. *Echoes*. New Delhi: Authors Press. 2012. Print.
Reddy, T. V. *Quest for Peace- A Minor Social Epic*. New Delhi: Authors Press, 2013. Print.

27 The Vicissitudes of Life: A Critical Analysis of *Fleeting Bubbles*

Prasaja VP

T. Vasudeva Reddy, who belongs to Andhra Pradesh, the rice bowl of India, is a renowned poet, critic and novelist. He served as Lecturer, Reader, U.G.C. National Fellow, Visiting Professor; and retired as Principal of Govt. Degree College in 2001. He has to his credit twelve collections of poetry, two novels, and three critical books. He has amassed multiple awards including International Eminent Poet in 1987, Hon. D. Litt. from WAAC San Francisco in 1988, Best Teacher Award from the Government of Andhra Pradesh in 1990, Best Poetry Award in 1994, the coveted U.G.C. Award of National Fellowship in 1998, and the International Award of Excellence in World Poetry in 2009. He is now holding the dignitary position of the president of GIEWEC (Guild of Indian English Writers, Editors, and Critics).

T.V. Reddy is a poet of unusual variety who is preoccupied with a flood of experiences. He is a persona of great sagacity who is engrossed with his world of poetry. His poems are apparently simple and small. There is no need to read between and beyond the lines as the central idea is perceptible from the surface reading. Reddy's poetry is persistently attentive to details of rural people and places, aspects of human, animal, and plant. Much of his poetry glosses over the vicissitudes of life, its beauty, illusions, hopes, sufferings, and other existential elements. *Fleeting Bubbles* (1989) is the third poetry collection of Reddy. It comprises of thirty-nine poems. The paper attempts to analyze the poets' approach to various forms of life in his poetry with respect to his personal philosophies.

Fleeting Bubbles is a representation of the multifarious lives in this mini world. As the title signifies it is a delineation of the transient and ephemeral nature of life. The lives of the least neglected were carefully etched by his pen. Be it living or non-living, Reddy shows utmost sincerity and elegance in his portrayal. His poems are genuine attempts to find the true meaning of life. Dazed by the fragmentariness of the modern life, the poet seeks the real nature of life to impart a real meaning to the existence. Unlike many of the escapist poets who try to run away from this world of suffering, Reddy is obsessed with life. He wants to enjoy the pleasant illusions of life. Through his poems he emphasizes the need to strive through life. Life in this material world is a tedious voyage, yet he makes efforts to make it a bon voyage.

Humans are highly strung up to seek meaning in life. The gushing of the unending sufferings makes us pessimist and cynical and we start to lead an aimless life. Our fleeting life in this universe compels us to have a sense of meaning in life. We should know our lives and identity, our existence and experience, and have some sense of purpose. This will make us feel happier and more satisfied. In Reddy's poems the speaker is a confused man in the world of suffering who undergoes a philosophical journey to understand the real essence of life.

Life is a continuous struggle and it is part of every individual to face dangers and threats of dangers. Thus human beings are enduring a tormented life. In "Let the Eyes be Shut," the speaker wants to shun all the distractions in life to lead a pleasant life. He wants to close his eyes against alien invasions from the traffic-jammed roads. The speaker hardly wants to have a blurred vision of the pleasant illusions. Here 'eyes' are the metaphors of 'mind', alien invasions are the unexpected tragedies, and the traffic-jammed roads symbolize our problematic life.

In "Flux of Life" the speaker is a vulnerable man with a jubilant spirit and the ability to remain optimistic in the face of personal despair. His mind is overloaded with the pain of his 'deceased dear.' He painstakingly continues his life since he knows none accompanies the dead. Whatever happens in one's life, he must endure everything and has to flow with the current of life. As a result the speaker adopts certain resilience techniques to withstand the tragic invader of life, the death. He understands the philosophical truth-'time alone can heal'. He is aware of the undeniable truth:

> When Time rings the final bell
> unawares we make our exit
> from the stage without a sign' (8).

He is attuned to kill the time and turn to forget the unforgettable, haunting memory. The poet is seasoned to optimize life. The poem "In Tense Flight" is a reflection of the poets' confused state of mind. Here the speaker is an escapist who wants to escape from everyone, and moreover from himself. But he is enchained by the bonds and binds of life. He could not fly away. His self is entrapped in the dark shadow of his body. He is made a captive. His self is the prisoner in the great jail of body. Probably the situation in which he finds himself forces the poet to give expression to this state of confusion as he is bound to the situation by the circumstances.

In "A Forlorn Soul," the poet presents a pitifully sad and abandoned speaker who is forsaken by his selfish relatives. In his prosperous time the speaker was a welcome guest to everyone. The hungry kith and kin extracted everything from him. Now they are crushing him and inflicting never-ending pains upon him. His eyes which were once their leading lamp are 'gnawed by aberration'. His hands that served as the unshakable support are 'shunned as a contagion'. He is surrounded by everyone, yet he feels isolated and tormented. With a desperate will he still tries to appease their needs. He tries to drift their sinking boats to the safe shore. But once they safely reach the shore these disloyal folk mercilessly strangle the 'forlorn soul' and they celebrate his doom. In this thought-provoking poem, the poet reveals that man is the lone animal on earth brooding over life till he reaches his grave.

Reddy's poems are about the daily struggles of everyday men and women. In "The Dark Valley" the poet presents the unending suffering of a man. The speaker is a failure in the riddle of life. During his childhood days he trod over a smooth and clear path. But as he grew up he has to confront the umpteen problems of life. These 'blazing sparks of fire' burns his feet. There is hardly any bridge to cross the 'maze of misery'. The speaker could not withstand and he faints and falls into the valley of night. In the dark unpleasant night he gropes for a ray of light. The dark valley symbolizes the dark and disastrous consequences of human life:

> My heart bleeds, my torpid brain sizzles
> A pigmy cauldron to hold the seething riddles;
> The way that used to be smooth and clear
> Is now strewn with blazing sparks of fire; ...
> I faint and fall headlong into the vale of night
> In vain I grope in the dark to catch a beam of light. (15)

The philosophical aspect of human life gets an elaborate expression in the short poem "Tide". It reminds us of the prominence of our fleeting life. Here the poet appeals to the readers not to be proud. People are blind after attaining material prosperity. In their rat race they even forget to embrace moral values. With the metaphor of tide the poet conveys the message that for every rise there will be a fall:

'Tide/Stop thy pride/and foaming ride/Beware/of your momentous fall/before your heart breaks/at the slid shores.'(p. 14).

The poet's acceptance of suffering as a condition of life stresses the importance of living life as an endless journey. In "The Tedious Voyage," the poet undertakes a cumbersome journey without a proper goal or destination. He is riding his tiny boat, and it batters against the 'gales and whales'. The rising and falling of the waves represents the hopes and despairs in life. The heavy storm carries the boat and it leaves the boat amidst the fathomless sea. He clings to the optimistic thought of safely reaching the shore. The poet's strenuous efforts to control his boat prove to be fruitful. In this poem, Reddy emphasizes the common theme of perseverance. He crafts an ordinary character sinking in the deep depths of life. He often considers giving up. But he rekindles his inner spirit. The speaker who is stuck in a difficult situation develops positive attitude towards life. He still has something to live for. Hoping against hope he expresses - "Still I steer rudderless / gazing at the faint star / vainly hoping to come ashore" (16).

A mood of deep disillusionment is created in the poem "I am Tired." Here the poet broods over the theme of the transience of human life. As the title denotes, in the poem the poet is distressed by the journey of life. His life is filled with sleepless nights. He grieves over the pathetic condition of his wife who is persistently battling for breath. The poet, sitting by her, is praying for her sudden recovery. He does not want to see his children as orphans. He thinks of the uncertainty of life. His comparison of life as a fleeting bubble which is colourful but momentary is emblematic.

The poem "Is the World Beautiful" reminds the readers of an age-old saying 'All that glitter is not gold'. The poet begins the poem by a rhetorical question, raising a query over the beauty of the world. He is attentive to the antithetical way of the world. Everything beautiful has its own face of ugliness. The rose, the queen of the garden and the symbol of love, has its pricking thorns; jack, the king of all fruits has its prickles; pandunus, the sweetest of all the fruits has its mortal asp. The rose, jack, and pandunus are symbolic of the contemporary man. Man has the contradictory nature of vice and virtue. The rich man is destined to starve in the midst of his riches. Cattle provide sufficient milk to man and he prospers with it. But the same man mercilessly slaughters them. Displaying their smiley countenance people kill each other.

Born and brought up in a village, Reddy is impressed by the rural life and so he portrays the virtues of the village and the blessings of the Nature. At the centre of his poems there is usually a representation of rural life and situation. Virtually his characters are raised from the rural soil. He paints the perfect picture of the life and situation of village women, bride, widows, old woman, the corn reaper, housewife, and the snake charmer.

Female characters always occupy a central position in Reddy's poems. The poems "Women of the Village," "The Indian Bride," "A Widow," and "The Corn Reaper" can be analyzed from the trope of feminist criticism. These poems echo varied voices of women in the Indian patriarchal context. In "Women of the Village" the poet presents a typical portrait of the village women folk. In the burning village the women are standing like 'expiring candles.' Their pathetic situation is revealed as the poet described them as 'famished cattle.' They are busy in their activities. They have to cover long distances to fetch a pot of water. Like the drying water in the pond their dreams are also dying. They dream of a life free from misery and suffering. These loyal wives patiently wait for the arrival of their husbands. The realistic representation of the life of rustic women throws light on the status of women in Indian society:

> Catching snaky visages in water
> Weaving desires in the plaits
> Of their cobra-long hair
> They carry pots of sweat ...

> and wait for their men
> with flickers in their eyes. (1)

"The Indian Bride," is a realistic poem that sheds light on the heartrending picture of an Indian bride. The poet used phrases such as 'adorned idol,' 'bedecked doll,' and 'vanishing species,' to show the helpless condition of the bride. In the midst of the crowd the bride feels isolated. The poet also underscores the issue of dowry as he refers to 'the borrowed currency'. For the 'thrice-cursed bride' the '*thali*' is a form of new bondage, a chain that symbolizes slavery. She is the obedient slave who is trained to play to his tunes. The unfortunate situation of every bride is delineated in these lines:

> "Having bought the groom in auction
> As cattle dealers buy their lusty bulls
> she is content to be his slave" (2).

Reddy invites our attention to the plight of the woman who suffers psychologically. In the poem "Old Woman" the poet is pained to see an old woman leading a poverty stricken isolated life. He gives a physical description of the woman which is both sympathetic and horrible. Her unkempt grey hair is likened to clusters of snakes. She wore tattered cloths and her severe condition is heightened when he says the stitches in her cloth outnumbered her wrinkles. She is also lacking the power of sight. She is described as a haunting figure with a soul wrung in agony. Restricting a normative life, she is considered by everyone as an ill-omen: "The Swamiji saw her on his way, spat at her / And went in fury for his ill-luck to see her first" (21). But she hardly pays any attention to their grudge or grumble. She is leading a vulnerable life, yet she puts a faint smile. She accepts only that which is needed for her survival. Her only prayer is to be united with God in His world. By portraying the character of the old woman, the poet spotlights the irrationality and unfounded fear associated with these destitute women.

"The Corn Reaper" reminds us of Wordsworth's "Solitary Reaper". Under the blistering sun the corn reaper is reaping her own life. She is unaware of the lustful gaze of the landlord. She is engaged in her hectic work thinking of her wailing child and her drunken husband. Reddy here paints a miserable picture of a rustic woman whose destiny is to bear the suffering for the sake of her family: 'she cut the corn patiently/sitting like a flower under the foot/thinking of her wailing child at home/and of the volley of blows on her back/given last night by her drunken lord' (22).

Through the poem "The Housewife" the poet presents a stereotypical housewife which every man aspires to have. The housewife leads a 'lifeless life.' The poet sheds light over her poverty stricken life when he describes the empty clay barrels. Her poverty hardly affects her familial bond. She hesitates to feed herself and finds pleasure in feeding her husband and children. In her thatched hut, she is waiting for the arrival of her partner from the field with a ray of hope. Amidst the poverty her mind is full of 'hopes of blank future'.

"The Snake Charmer" delineates the life of a penurious snake charmer. He is described as a 'skinny Skeleton'. This is symbolic of the impoverished life endured by him. He is playing over his gourd-pipe and emits its charm of music. The gourd pipe is comparable to a magic wand. The poet describes the cobra as the 'vanquished captive' that emerges like blind Samson. The grace with which the poet describes the unwanted creature is beautiful beyond description. The snake charmer is undergoing much prick and pang just to satisfy himself with a 'handful of rice'.

As a social critic, Reddy lashes at the hypocritical and selfish politicians. "Democratic Lines" and "In Exile" are the supreme examples of his satirical poems in which he ridicules the meanness of the politicians. They are directed against the corrupt politicians who destroy the prosperity and economy of our nation. They sound honest notes of protest. In "Democratic Lines" the poet mocks at the politicians:

"the greater the degree of hypocrisy
the stronger the asset to be a leader;" (33).

The poet cynically addresses them as the 'matinee idol', 'the black marketer', 'the broker', 'the racketeer', 'the gambler', and an 'unruly student'. The poet continues his criticism. He spotlights the illiteracy of the politicians as he says they are the unruly students to whom the 'academic books are untouchables.' These affluent politicians are blind and deaf to the sufferings of the people. The people are suffering, but at the same time the relatives of the politicians revel in 'ill-gotten wealth.' The politicians are content with the hike in price of 'leaves and loaves, meat and rice' as their favorite is cashew nuts.

In the poem "In Exile" the poet again portrays the brutal picture of the corrupt politicians. The fisherman and the hunters are killing animals to feed the hungry souls. But the politicians ruthlessly kill humans for material gains and prosperity. Politicians who occupy higher positions do so less to perform public service than to obtain private riches at the expense of the state. These material-minded men entrap human values and those precious values are now in exile.

As Reddy is predominantly concerned with human life, Nature also plays a primal role in defining his mode of poetic experience. Man and his interactions with nature is a recurrent motif in his poetry. In "Blessings of Jasmine" the poet zooms in the beauty of a simple flower and how it serves others with its presence. It acts as a curing medicine and healing balm in both the occasions of joy and sorrow. With its 'soothing scent' it energizes the newly wedded couple. It is a divine blessing to mankind. Jasmine flower, the lovely gift of nature, is a thing of beauty and is a joy forever. It symbolizes the healing power of nature. Here the poet glorifies the jasmine flower and celebrates its pure, natural essence, and thereby wishing the readers to follow this naturalness.

To conclude Reddy stands out as a prestigious poet who has made an indispensable position in the realm of Indian English poetry. His poetry is a pleasant blend of the traditional and the modern, the romantic and the realistic trends. The unique feature with him is the fact that melody and his poetry are inseparable and the rhythmic beat flows as an undercurrent in all his poems. In general, his poems are a genuine attempt to trace and track the mysteries of life. Though pain and sufferings permeate his poetry, many of them have a hopeful tone. The speakers of his poems are aware of the daunting problems that overwhelm them. They were all muddled but eventually decide to persevere. Reddy does not camouflage the difficulties of life, yet he encourages his readers to remain hopeful that positive changes are possible.

Works Cited

Reddy, T. V. *Fleeting Bubbles*. Madras: Poets Press India, 1989. Print.

Wordsworth, William. "Solitary Reaper". from *Ideas and Forms in English & American Literature, Vol I. Poetry,* Ed. by Homer A.Watt & James B.Munn. New York, Scott, Foreman & Co., 1925; 2nd ed. 1932. 460. Print.

28   Exploring Paradoxes and Contradictions of Postmodern Life in *Echoes*

Arti Chandel

Introduction

Paradox is "a statement that is seemingly contradictory or opposed to common sense and yet is perhaps true" or "an argument that apparently derives self-contradictory conclusions by valid deduction from acceptable premise" (Paradox). Contradiction is a "statement or phrase whose parts contradict each other", or "logical incongruity", or "a situation in which inherent factors, actions, or propositions are inconsistent or contrary to one another" (Contradiction). Satire is "a literary work holding up human vices and follies to ridicule or scorn", or "trenchant wit, irony, or sarcasm used to expose and discredit vice or folly" (Satire). The postmodern era, begins from 1950s, is remarkable for its "potential for mass destruction and its shocking history of genocide had evoked a continuing disillusionment" (Phutela, 105).

T. V. Reddy, the poet under study, has given expression to the paradoxes and contradictions of postmodern man by using paradox and satire in his collection of poems titled *Echoes*. Poetry to T. V. Reddy is "an expression of one's feelings and an outburst of emotions and thoughts; it is, in general, the expression of one's creative imagination which may be realistic or romantic in its essential spirit." (Re: T.V. Reddy- on Poetry) In this particular work by T.V. Reddy under study there is greater focus on the realistic side of his poetic imagination.

Objectives

The paper aims at a detailed analysis of the poet T. V. Reddy's collection of poems titled as *Echoes*, especially his satirical depiction of the postmodern human situation. It explores the paradoxes and contradictions, incongruities, abnormalities, oddities, and flaws and faults of the man of postmodern era. It is a study of the use of paradox, contradictions and oxymoron too as effective tools to expose, ridicule and satirize contemporary man and his behavior. Of course, the poet offers the realistic picture of contemporary society and his aim behind this satire and ridicule is nothing but correction.

True Side of Human Advancement

Poems in *Echoes* echo many contradictory and opposing notes and ideas that act as satire and thereby expose the vices and wrong practices of postmodern human race and their so-called humanity. The book opens with the poem 'Human Touch', where the poet sarcastically describes the development and growth of human race. He addresses his fellow humans as 'you' and narrates the sad tale of their advancement. He asserts that humans have "travelled a long way" but not to the bright land of happiness. They have reached "into the lonesome land of darkness / leaving a trail of haunting blindness" (9). The poet emphasizes at the seemingly contradictory yet true nature of human race and its journey by expressing that at the beginning humans were "a little human", but now they have "strayed far away" (9). It is shocking that human beings could be called human, when they were uncivilized, uneducated, uncultured and untamed barbarous creatures, but now they have lost all human values and lacked even the slightest trace of humaneness that they possessed earlier. Their road to development is not an easy one, as it is unknown, "untamed and unmapped" (p.9). Also, it is almost impossible for them to take a backward journey, for there is no way back to reconnect them with their past and with their roots, as they "can't keep the track of footsteps / through night's unintelligible silence" (9). The journey of postmodern man is similar to that of Adam and Eve living in the Garden of Eden and their fall from there. The poet draws an allusion to the Utopia of Eden, declaring that the only means of humans' redemption is their reaching "the Utopia of Eden / and breathe the breeze of the garden" (9). The poet concludes on the note that "substance and shadow in right mix / can deliver the man from the fatal fix" (9), which affirms the poet's belief in harmony of body, mind and spirit.

Similarly, 'Organized Violence' emphatically gives voice to the aftermaths of evil, pain and futility of war and violence. The poem has a magnificent beginning in the form of incongruous yet valid sensory experiences: "Often I hear with haunting fear / the volcanic sparks of silence / emitted by ceaseless violence / across the burning borders" (21). Here, the image of hearing the sparks of silence marvelously narrates the sad tale of war across the borders of neighboring nations. The borders are exploded by "imported AK 47s / and inhuman human bombs" (21). The phrase 'inhuman human bomb' depicts the plight and foolishness of the postmodern human race at the use of human body to carry out the most condemnable practice of killing own race.

The perplexing advancement and progress of post-modern man with the march of time finds expression in "The March of Time". The dilemma of contemporary man reaches its height as the "clouded mind struggles / in this hurricane-blasted ship / in its voyage for a ray of light" (25). There seems to be no hope for human race, as it has lost right direction and the base or centre that sustains it only through right values. It has been human nature to destroy what nurtures, which, in turn, leads to their destruction. The self-destructive human temperament is satirically exposed by the poet in these words: "Branches that liberally spread / generous shade are cruelly cut" (25). What can be more foolish than this? Nonetheless, it is absolutely true that postmodern human trend tends to spoil everything that has been sustaining them for ages. True that the 'march of time' can neither be stopped nor reversed, but the symptoms and side-effects of the so-called advancement cannot be ignored too. The poet rightly remarks:

> "How long can we travel with sore feet
> on this aimless pathless unmapped land
> holding a blade of grass as a magic wand" (25).

The obvious irony in the above comment aptly describes contemporary human position and situation. There are many poetic pieces that make fun of the political leaders and the corruption on their part.

The poem "Liberal Leader" confounds the poet "With bags of liberal promises / taller than palms and pines" (78). The poet draws a humorous parallel between the 'liberal leader' and Colossus on the one hand and, side by side, calls him 'a huge road roller "with the crushing sound / on chips of granite gravel" (78). The clarion call of the leader reminds the poet of "a chanticleer on the dunghill" (78). He befools the public so smartly that they easily fall into his trap:

> his words flow like honey
> fill their empty bellies
> with tempting spicy freebies" (78).

What a powerful satire and so humorous and exact, yet sharp! The poet gives the reason for the foolishness of the public, indicating that it is not the fault of the people. They are helpless, as "the instant political magic / creates a halo of illusion" (78).

Misconceptions of Postmodern Man

Paradox prevails all through the poem "An Echo", where the poet challenges the prevalent and widely accepted concept of postmodern individuals being Invincible. He confronts the notion of being all powerful by voicing the truth: "We think we are unconquerable / but we are still so miserable" (10). The misery and suffering of human race haunts the poet to such an extent that a poem likes. "An Echo" is born, where he sarcastically questions his fellow beings about the truth that they are unable to endure and hence they live in the false notion:

> "How long do we see the rehearsal
> of this dull replay of the shadow
> of the bereaved truth, a widow" (10).

In the poem 'On the Borders of Night' the evening tide touches the protagonist's feet, which drives him to "reflect cool and numb", yet it fills his "mind with swarming thoughts dumb" (13). The poet brings here two contradictory images -- one of the coolness and numbness aroused within him with the touch of evening tide; and the other of the swarming thoughts that come to his mind leading to confusion, hence making him dumb. Also, the whole effect of all this on the persona's mind is quite unexpected and contradictory to the commonly accepted belief. Rather than having a head full of cobwebs and heart filled with entangled strings, he is the one with "an emptied head and heart" (13). The title 'So Tall and So Small' itself is a mix of opposing notions presented through the sizes here. Man's vulnerability and instability as well as the unpredictable course of fate and life are depicted in simple yet powerful words:

> How the sudden change
> incredible, so terrible a wide range!
> Yesterday you looked so strong and tall" (16)

But then "a single day, a potent fateful day / could command the entire life with its say" (16). Then the poet firmly declares: "Suddenly you, so tall, look so sullenly little" and all this is nothing but "the ordained result of the cumulative vices" (16). Human abnormalities, pride and shallowness are satirized in "Lord of the Universe". The poet affirms the ancient belief of the *Vedas* and *Upanishads* about the existence of the Supreme Power or Lord of the Universe and ridicules human behavior and foolishness:

> We may think we are highly wise,
> but we are too small and tiny to praise
> the glory of the Lord of the Universe;
> with this little tongue and futile verse.   (100)

Though this is the truth, "man in the peak of pride feels tall" and "this blind man in blinding power / with gold Him he wants to cover" (100). But, "Can we please the One who owns / the entire Universe as his wealth / with gold and wealth got by stealth?" (100)

Past and Present

"Untraced into Dust" pathetically describes the disintegration of the beauty and truth of past, the conversion of a majestic historic monument into a mausoleum. The downfall compels the poet utter that whosoever witnesses the colossal destruction suffers from the hibernation of fancy, as there is no flight of imagination at such a sight. This is quite painful that the "royal palace built heroically a thousand years ago ... stands now in ruthless ruins" (11). The present appearance and condition of the historic capital town of Vijayanagar, now known as Hampi, is beautifully presented by T V Reddy through the juxtaposition of seemingly paradoxical phrases, as the "historic town that is made and unmade everyday" (11). The ironical remark exposes the truth that though the ancient historical monuments and heritage sites are symbols of truth and beauty of bygone era, they are made and unmade each day by the vision and opinions of the people, who presently visit them. Again, Reddy brings paradoxical ideas together, when he declares that "the broken rock-cut entrance / guarded by the sculptured Hanuman / a mute spectator of the havoc inhuman" (11). The sculptured Hanuman, mentioned here, as the guarding agent of the fort, is a Hindu mythological character, who is worshipped as *sankatamochana bhagvan* by the Hindus – one who guards against all evils: yet it remains a silent spectator to the havoc caused by the Muslim intruders and invaders. Also the poet refers to the destruction as 'the havoc inhuman', indicating that though they were human in appearance, yet the cruelty and ruthlessness of their act matches no human act and it makes them inhuman.

In "Search for Peace" Reddy again expresses his feelings on past and present times as in 'Untraced into Dust'. He describes the desolate and "neglected ruined capital / of the long forgotten empire" of Chandragiri, where "sovereign tense is strangled / between presence and absence, / present neglect and past havoc" (22). Thus, the present time, which one must use constructively to act and work, is ironically wasted, spent idle and killed mercilessly between what is present and what is not, that the carelessness of the present and the destruction of the past. While speaking of destruction of time, the poet confesses that "time is smart and sharp / to silence the killer and the killed" (22). "Fond Memories" most likely records poet persona's sweet memories of his separated wife. It begins with the paradoxical images like "Memories rock and block my head" (17). T V Reddy asks the heart-breaking but relevant question: "Does real joy, enshrined in fond memories / with a potential evolving elusive devices, / survive the onslaughts of time and its queries?" (17) Thus, when nothing can survive the damages of time, is it possible for real joy to sustain such mighty blows of time through memories? Memory, though powerful, remains yet an elusive technique.

Dilemma of Postmodern Man

"Life on Wheels" narrates the protagonist's monotonous every day journey between his home and workplace. Reddy calls this journey as "the hot distance to and fro / between two hostile points, dead ends / uncompromising with unbending bends" (19). Here, one finds the use of oxymoron or compressed paradox in seemingly opposing terms used side by side by the poet, such as 'dead ends' and 'unbending bends'. The Oxford English Dictionary defines oxymoron as "an expression [that] in its superficial or literal meaning [is] self-contradictory or absurd, but involving a point" (oxymoron). Again, the poem "Scars Reopen" is replete with the use of oxymoron. It opens with paradoxical lines: "These scars on my physical frame / are simply fun and frolic, a game, / but they leave a livid smarting mark / on my mind, torn by forces dark" (24). The scars on the poet-persona's body represent his adventurous spirit that takes life as a challenge, whereas the same marks on his mind reveal the hardships and agony of his life, as mind is a junction of a variety of dark and warring forces. Thus, while body faces every difficulty of life as a fun, it is mind that is torn between the extremes and is a house of many a negative thought. One has to fight hard with these dark forces in order to live. Quite aptly, the poet voices the ironical and paradoxical truth and informs his beloved: "Let me be burnt with your promises; / or kill me with your cold kindness" (24). Both the treatments and situations appear to be similar to the poet persona, whether he himself catches fire or gets himself burnt with the beloved's passionate but fake promises or she kills him with cold and calculated kindness. There is no difference between these two experiences, as the destined end of both the practices is the same, which is death and nothing else.

The Universal Truth

The concluding poem "Nothing Follows" is full of contradictions disclosing the reality of human life. The poem utters absolute and universal truth through a series of contradictions and inherent paradoxes. Detachment in attachment and attachment in detachment are the two sides of the same coin and both mean the same. Though nothing in this Universe belongs to us, yet one belongs to everything. The same is asserted by T V Reddy: "I pervade the whole Universe / every atom in me is not mine / but I occupy every atom, every line" (101). And how true is this paradoxical declaration!: "This air, this water, this land / nothing is ours, nothing belongs to us / ... / But everything is mine, ours, / the entire Universe is mine" (101). The poet knits a chain of oxymoron and contradictions to peel off the truth layer by layer. He lists the human incongruities line after line and finally, concludes the poem at the only truth of human life:

> Having eyes we don't see, foresee,
> having ears we refuse to hear,
> having mind we don't think, we only blink.
> This world is a vast stretch of illusion
> a fusion of shades, a land of shadows
> allergic to touch, explosive to approach;
> we run to catch or snatch a mirage
> and defame the constructed fame;
> By the time our charmed eyes open
> They are forced to close for ever.   (101)

Despite all these oddities and despite all other differences, the fate of all the humans is indispensably same, as "our last place is pit or pyre" (102). The book ends at a positive note that the only way to live our life is doing whatever good we can do wherever we are, because "When we come we bring nothing / when we leave we carry nothing" (102). Then why are we busy hating each other and damaging everything including environment? Rather than wasting our life on destruction and petty issues, let us before departing "do a bit of good / leaving a trace of fleeting fragrance" (102).

Conclusion

The caravan of paradoxical and oxymoronic statements, images, opinions, ideas and experiences goes on ceaselessly as the poet moves from one poem to the other one. The whole book is replete with beautiful and meaningful paradoxes and contradictions, which result in irony and satire, as the poet remains constantly active and involved in exposing and ridiculing the wrong practices, vices and inborn flaws of human beings. Like his novels his poetry, too, is realistic. It deals with and delineates the prevalent social practices of present times. What is true of his fiction is also true of his poetry. Prof. K. Venkatachari of Osmamia University states about Reddy's fiction that "it is a bold experiment in realistic fiction. I am particularly struck by its sweep and inclusive aspect of our life and it presents a fascinating chiaroscuro of the play of corruption, greed, passion, superstition in our social milieu" (his Letter to T. V. Reddy). The same play of all these evils and many more is found in *Echoes*. Reddy himself confirms: "The guiding principle of presentation should be realism, whose ultimate objective may be probable correction, rectification or a distant vision of idealism." (Re: T.V. Reddy- on Poetry) Thus, the poet reveals the true characteristics of postmodern humans and their eccentricities as well as self-damaging tendency. The purpose of the poet is none other than holding and showing the mirror to society, in which it can see its true image, reflect on what is wrong and take corrective measures.

Works Cited

Contradiction. Web. 19 August 2017. <https://www.merriam-webster.com/dictionary/contradiction>.

Oxymoron. Web. 18 August 2017. <https://googleblight.com>.

Paradox. Web. 19 August 2017. <https://www.merriam-webster.com/dictionary/paradox>.

Phutela, Rohit. Poetcrit. (Jan. 2014): 103-110. Print.

Satire. Web. 19 August 2017. <https://www.merriam-webster.com/dictionary/satire>.

Reddy, T V. "Re: T.V. Reddy- on Poetry" Message to the Author. 16 August 2017. E- mail.

Reddy, T V. *Echoes*. New Delhi, Gnosis, 2012. Print.

Venkatachari, K." Letter to T. V. Reddy". 26 Jan. 1984. Qtd. K. Rajani in Poetcrit. (Jan. 2016): 56-60. Print.

29 Angst and Despair: Existential Concepts in the Poems of T.V. Reddy

Anantha Lakshmi Hemalatha

Jean-Paul Sartre once wrote, "Man is condemned to be free; because once thrown into the world, he is responsible for everything he does". Existentialism is a term applied to the work of a number of philosophers since the nineteenth century who generally focused on the condition of human existence, and an individual's emotions, actions, responsibilities, thoughts and the meaning or purpose of life. It is a philosophy that makes an authentically human life possible in a meaningless and absurd world. Existential philosophers often focused more on what is subjective as opposed to analyzing objective knowledge.

In his first collection of poems *When Grief Rains*, T. Vasudeva Reddy shares the belief along with the Existentialists that philosophical thinking begins with the human subject – not merely the thinking subject, but the acting, feeling, living human individual. A retired Professor of Literature, T. V. Reddy is a renowned poet, novelist, and critic of literature. He is the author of ten collections of poetry, with his most recent collection *Thousand Haiku Pearls* released in 2016. Commenting on his first collection of poems, Rosemary C. Wilkinson says, "…Truly *When Grief Rains* (author's first collection of poems) is an insight into a rare soul longing for the ethereal."

"Life is a Desert" captures the sense of being alone and isolated in the desert of life. He finds himself a 'marooned man' in the midst of his 'kith and kin'. People around him are cautious and careful so as not to entertain or encourage him to befriend them. His poverty-stricken condition worsens and weakens him physically and mentally. The worn out soul questions:

> How long shall I resist the jealousy?
> Envy and ennui of the society? (*WGR*, 14)

Despair in existentialism is generally defined as a loss of hope. As Kierkegaard defines it in 'Either/Or', "let each one learn what he can; both of us can learn that a person's unhappiness never lies in his lack of control over external conditions, since this would only make him completely unhappy". Here, in the poem, it is the external conditions that act upon him and make him feel that life is unbearably agonizing. The sense of reality shatters him and makes him understand the ways of the world resulting in despair.

> I am a lone man in the barren land.
> Dissembling mirage tantalizes me,
> A thirsty man with a parched tongue.
> Life is an elusive endless desert,
> Full of sands and storms, no oases (*WGR*, 14)

The notion of the Absurd has been prominent in literature throughout history. It contains the idea that there is no meaning in the world beyond what meaning we give it. Many of the literary works of

Samuel Beckett, Franz Kafka, Eugene Ionesco, Jean-Paul Sartre, Joseph Heller and Albert Camus contain descriptions of people who encounter the absurdity of the world. Similarly, the poem "At the Cross Road" metaphorically speaks of the life as a street and how he finds himself stranded at the cross-road. His inaction is contrasted with the actions of the moving vehicles:

> Hooting, shouting and howling
> Blinding, deafening, deadening and carrying
> Heaps of stones and broken soda glasses; (WGR, 20)

The usage of the verbs suggests the ongoing action and reminds us of the significance of the verbs as presented by Carl Sandberg in his poem "Chicago". Every part of his body is bruised and there is no medicine to stop the bleeding. His 'present plight' is not acting as the balm that could heal the wounds. The past, in the form of memories, haunts him; but he has to decide the next move in order to avoid being overrun by the racings automobiles.

> A second's hesitation may overrun me;
> One way or the other I must decide,
> To avoid the assault, the racing tsunami;
> But I find cornered – a checkmate? (WGR, 20)

The poem "Transience" is about the seemingly endless attempts of man to do great deeds in life and acquire wealth. The poet laughs at man, who feels eternal and says,

> ... when the end seizes him
> He has no voice to claim
> Even a mere six by two (WGR, 29)

The human body is 'full of punctures' in the long and tiresome journey of life.

> The body, full of puncture,
> In its long tedious journey
> Succumbs to inevitable decay,
> Searches for solace in the dark cradle (WGR, 29)

Death is the only tool of escapism the poet can think of to relieve him from this meaningless existence. It is in relation to this concept of the awareness of meaninglessness that Albert Camus claimed that "there is only one truly philosophical problem, and that is suicide" in his *The Myth of Sisyphus*. In the book, Camus uses the analogy of the Greek myth of Sisyphus to reveal the futility of existence. In the myth, Sisyphus is condemned for eternity to roll a rock up a hill, but when he reaches the summit, the rock will roll to the bottom again. Camus believes that this existence is pointless but that Sisyphus ultimately finds meaning and purpose in his task, simply by continually applying himself to it. The poet comes to a similar understanding when he says that there is nothing to gain or lose in life as well as in death. We have to surrender ourselves to the unavoidable occurrence of death which brings down everyone to the same level. He concludes philosophically,

> Great deeds are writ in water,
> All glories lead only to dust (29)

Futility is an expression of severe mental turmoil, an existential angst. Existential angst occurs when the Self is brought face-to-face with itself as a finite and temporal self. In angst, the world in which the Self finds itself is revealed as groundless and meaningless. The Self becomes detached from its own projects and everything that has hitherto provided base, meaning, and structure. In short, the Self comes face-to-face with its own finiteness; and is forced to come to terms with the full meaning of its finite existence as temporal being. Futility focuses on the theme of ineffectuality of human existence. This meaninglessness also encompasses the futile struggles and sterile efforts taken to make our lives meaningful and the subsequent feeling of nothingness in our existence.

> The Nothingness around me gapes and gasps;
> It hardly breathes – a baneful breeze! (*WGR*, 24)

Even his attempt to smile becomes 'abortive'. When he looks into the 'time mirror' and finds it broken he exclaims,

> Alas! It already broke into hundred odd pieces;
> Million images run away from me in dread,
> A vast tract of vacuum stretches
> To the farthest edge of futility (24)

The past invades the present and takes life into an obscure state.

> Like wisps of receding cigarette smoke
> That blurs the keen camera of vision (24)

In existentialist philosophy, the term 'existential crisis', specifically relates to the crisis of the individual when he realizes that he must always define his own life through the choice he makes. The existential crisis occurs when one recognizes that even the decision to either refrain from action or withhold assent to a particular choice is, in itself, a choice. T.V. Reddy puts across this idea in his poem "I See No Other Way". The persona seems to be a confused man unaware of the techniques to solve the puzzle of life. All types of permutations and combinations fail him in solving the puzzle; still he has to make a choice.

> Still it is the need of the hour
> To settle one way or the other
> 'To be or not to be' is the question:
> Not to be or not to be in being is the fix (*WGR*, 41))

The poet's dilemma reminds him and us of the dilemma faced by Hamlet. Many scholars consider the speech by Hamlet to be one of several existential manifestos in *Hamlet*. Existentialism professes that the past and future are insubstantial; the present is all that humans can be sure of. For humans, being — what **IS** — is the only truth; everything else is nothing and no rest at all?

> Eventually, the puzzle 'acquires a fear complex' from which the poet tries to flee.
> I am quarantined against the iron clasp.
> Racing down the mountain
> I managed to come out of his grip;
> It was not tight, but I am not free either (41)

It is to be noted that once one is out of an existential crisis, one is able to get into another, or is not completely out of it. In anxiety, the self is confronted with death. Death is the possibility of impossibility – the vulnerability of total and complete world collapse; thus, the Self comes to grips with its possibility of having no more possibilities: ceasing to exist.

> The exit of the gasping breath alone
> Shall release me from the lingering pain (41)

This again reminds us of Hamlet's death wish. Hamlet hopes that death is nothingness, that death will "end the heartache and the thousand natural shocks that flesh is heir to," that death will end thinking, knowing, and remembering. But he fears that, in death, he will be haunted interminably by bad dreams of life itself, by dreams heavy with the memory of fear and pain. Ultimately, he says, that's why humans dread death. We fear that our consciences will torment us forever. Thus, human beings choose life, with its torment and burdens, chiefly to avoid death, the great unknown. However, death is, like life, inescapable, and Hamlet curses his luck for having been born at all.

An existential crisis is often provoked by a significant event in the person's life – a life-threatening experience. "Gray Hair" talks about a different crisis, a threat posed to his age. Reaching a personally significant age, usually, provokes the sufferer's introspection about personal mortality. The sight of gray hair on his beard is 'abhorring'. He finds it repulsive as well. Though the silvery line on his temple is uprooted with a spade, the razor, the yet to be born off-springs pose a threat to him. The poet feels that the grey hair is mocking at him. The poet in a lighter vein concludes thus:

> I dread thy yet unborn progeny
> And flee from the reflected agony. (19)

"Realization" is a poem steeped in existential ideas. The poem illustrates an attitude towards man's experience on earth. The opening lines unveil the lack of knowledge on the part of the poet in his futile and hopeless pursuit of an unobtainable goal.

> Life's major part was spent
> Without my being aware of it;
> A vague and obscure career
> Full of futility – a waste land,
> A dreary desert full of sand (33)

The poet recalls his past as a boy and looks into his future – 'a silent cemetery'. The poem examines questions such as death, the meaning or meaninglessness of human existence, and the bewilderment of human experience that can only be reconciled in mind and art of the existentialist. Not only does the Self surrender its sense of an intrinsic or universal meaning to its life – but abandons as hopeless the possibility of ever uncovering such a meaning. Existential angst is not the loss of meaning; but rather, but it is the coming to the realization that there never was any meaning to begin with. Resignation comes to him on realizing that death is the ultimate, inevitable end in the lives of human beings:

> I resign myself to my finale
> And wait for the inevitable moment
> With a foot firmly planted
> Inside the last resting place (33)

But death is not merely the cessation of biological processes; nor is it what we commonly associate with the notion of 'perishing' or 'expiring'. Again, death is not an 'event' that is yet to take place in some distant future; a mere 'not-yet'. Death is the only available choice; there is no moral criteria attached to the choosing. Rather, it is a highly personalized endeavor in which the Self affirms the process of becoming a Self in the face of the absolute emptiness of existence. In all actuality, inauthentic existence is likely far more comforting and pleasurable than existing authentically. Fleeing from one's own recognition that one is going to die – and reverting back to the ready-made meaning provided by others is far more likely to produce a 'happy', or at the very least, a more agreeable life. Therefore, this realization on the part of the poet regarding Death is appreciable.

This acceptance of Death as the only reality is illustrated by the poet in another poem titled "In Memoriam". The poet observes a boy taking a clean slate and writing down the alphabets from A to Z. Then he rubs off the letters and writes and re-writes 'numerous words in the same slate by repeating the action. The poet catches it up in a beautiful image,

> A little world freshly peopled

> Within the structural bounds –
> A creation in its essence! (34)

We may not remember people from our own lineage, those who lived before our age and had paved way for us to walk on. As they are out of sight, they are out of mind.

> Recollection of the ancestors, the departed souls –
> Is as dark as the tomb that hides them
> Our lives, when we depart,
> Are letters swept off the slate (34)

An aphoristic phase comes here in the concluding lines:

> Death in a sense is the only reality,
> And dust, the earth, the only eternity (34)

"The Dying Wick" is a poem of loneliness and desolation. The poem begins with the last flicker of the wick at midnight. In the all-pervading darkness, he is able to feel the leaves bowing to the wind, hear the thunder awakening the child in the cradle and see the lightning that blinds his vision. As a rhetorical device, darkness has a long-standing tradition. As a poetic term, in the Western world, darkness is used to connote the presence of shadows, evil and foreboding, or in the modern manner of speaking, darkness connotes depression.

> I do not know, to be true,
> Where this darkness leads to;
> It invades my desolate spirit
> And saps my sinking soul (27)

The poet expresses his ignorance as to where the darkness is leading him. Man's mind once engrossed with despondency, loses all capacities of hope.

"My Own Shadow" is yet another play with shadow and darkness. The poet wakes up at night disturbed by something. When he attempts to sleep again, he is able to visualize his own 'scorched shadow', appear and disappear momentarily into oblivion.

> My dreamy eyelids shut
> And in the blinding darkness
> I could see clearly
> Against eternity's gory screen
> My own scorched shadow –
> An evanescent shape
> Receding into oblivion (18)

The titular poem "When Grief Rains" is a poem in the affirmative. As always there is the 'death wish' to break away from the misery and pain. Unable to withstand the gale, the storm, and the relentless rain of sorrow, misery and grief, he wants to seek the ultimate end – Death.

> When gales of sorrow
> Wreck my surging spirit,
> Misery storms my being,
> And grief rains incessantly
> I wish to drench myself,
> Depart from these ills
> And enter the pores of the earth
> With drops of rain that seep (25)

Grief is a comprehensive response to loss. While the terms are often used interchangeably, bereavement refers to the state of loss, and grief is the reaction to that loss. Human existence is marked by loss and grief. Despite this, the poet feels that there is an inbuilt mechanism in man that wishes to protect himself from the downpour of desolation and despair.

> Still somewhere in me
> A dim desire creeps unawares
> To possess the instinctive mackintosh (25)

When questioned, "Why is poetry important?" T. V. Reddy replied, "Poetry is the best medium to express one's feelings and emotions. That is why we have identified poetry as the first and foremost literary genre in the history of any literature. Poetry has the ability to make a deep impression on the mind itself. There is little durability with prose. Poetry is the expression of imagination of the deepest feelings of the heart. And that is why poetry has an everlasting quality." T. V. Reddy's poetic art gains everlasting magnitude as it borders on the living conditions of human beings. The mystery of continued existence is permanent and unending. The poet has truly contributed something of enduring value to Indian English poetry for which he will always be remembered.

Works Cited

Cairncross, Andrew S. *The Problem of Hamlet: A Solution*. PA: Norwood Editions. 1975. Print.

Kierkegaard, Soren. *Works of Love*. New York: Harper & Row Publishers, 1962. Print.

Marino, Gordon (ed.) *Basic Writings of Existentialism*. New York: Modern Library, 2004. Print.

Raja, P. and Keshari, R.N. Ed. *Busy Bee Book of Contemporary Indian English Poetry*. Pondicherry: Busy Bee Publications, 2007. Print.

Rao, Rama. *Sensitivity and Cultural Multiplicity in Recent Indian English Poetry*. Jaipur: Aadi Publications, 2014. Print.

Reddy, Vasudeva. *When Grief Rains*. New Delhi: Samkaleen Prakashan, 1982. Print.

Ronald, Aronson. *Camus and Sartre*. Chicago: University of Chicago Press, 2004. Print.

30   Echoes of the Sublime in T.V. Reddy's *Sound and Silence*

K. Rajani

T.V. Reddy needs no introduction to the reading community of Indian poetry in English as he is a reputed poet with eleven poetry books, two novels and three critical works. Numerous articles have appeared on him both as a poet and novelist and the recent critical work on him i.e. *The Poetic Art of T.V. Reddy: New Perspectives* with 24 scholarly articles by reputed writers is an excellent critical study of his poetry from different angles focusing on multiple aspects of T.V. Reddy's poetry spanning over three and a half decades from his first poetry Collection *When Grief Rains* (1982) to the tenth one *Thousand Haiku Pearls* (2016). The present collection *Sound and Silence* is Reddy's latest work (2017) consisting of 80 poems covering a wide range of subject matter from our race and space to birds, hills and seasons, from dog, frog, mouse and glow worm to park, foliage and hurricane and mountain, from love and life to smiles, rivers, and temples, from this body and pubs to the sun and earth. In Reddy, we find reflection of nature in all its colours coexisting with satiric vision which is a rare phenomenon and his poems are best known for the abundance of imagery and human values. The significance of the present book lies in the fact that it makes us feel the echoes of the sublime voice in the midst of sound and silence.

The collection begins with the poem "Our Race" which articulates his disappointment as well as his anger at the slavish attitude of our Indian race in bending and bowing to cruel and aggressive forces. Being very much conscious of the glory of our ancient civilization and culture the poet is fully justified in expressing his angst at the present situation prevailing in the country: 'What is wrong with our ancient race? We stand always last in the race'. He says we need not feel proud of our democracy and for well over thousand years the total number of its staggering numbers has failed to make us bold and on the other hand it has made us 'dumb and numb'; now we are left with haunting memories of the horrible past and what is there for us to read except the sickening pages red with stains of dried streams of blood? Reddy makes a correct analysis and diagnosis of the contemporary situation in India and fearlessly he presents the pitiable plight:

> then we were fleeced by alien wolves,
> now by the ruthless cruel native wolves   (*SS*, 9)

The poem is marked by the bitter reality of the situation. With the same spirit he continues the expression of his anguish in the next poem 'Let Us Rise'. The poet wants that his county men should not lose dignity or courage, but they should rise to protect and preserve the dignity of their motherland; first he would rise and give the clarion call to all others to wake up and rise. The poet says –'I shall rise till my word swells like a tide/ that rides through the world;/ I will rise and raise my fallen brethren/ with my wounded word, still brave' (11). In the next poem 'Stand Erect' he addresses his fellow brethren to stand erect with a heroic heart and moral pride and march forward with a fearless mind. Modern man is like a caged bird and the truth of his actual condition is no better than that of a caged bird. The persona in the poem voices his helplessness: How can a slave sing in the fallow field/though the canopy above is unbounded? It is freedom that gives individuality to man and without freedom he loses both his identity and individuality. The poet projects this meaning in the ending lines of the poem:

> Liberated, my tune floats and flows,
> Kisses leaves and petals that dance
> In woods, groves and wider fields
> And touches strings of heart within   (14)

The poem 'Savage Space' is a direct attack on the heartless activities of the terrorists and the war mongers, because any nuclear war in the present situation is only an act of total destruction of the major part of the world. Savage hands and minds will reduce the boundless space to narrow space and the space for living on the earth gets shrunken. Unless peace is promoted and established there won't be any hope for happy and healthy life. The poet gives the needful call: 'Let us revive and resuscitate the passive land,/bruised and battered beyond recognition,/where the grass is stained with blood'. Still the poet is not totally disheartened and in the midst of hopelessness the poet sees a ray of hope: 'Though the long winter night is freezing/none can arrest the arrival of the dawn/ on the beaming rays chasing the shadows; / children will surely smile as blooming flowers/ and koels won't fail to greet from their bowers.' (16).

Reddy speaks of human dignity in the poem "Dignity in Exile" and expresses that the value of dignity is getting diluted. He deserves all admiration as he has the courage to say that Great Walls, Pyramids and Taj Mahals 'are in fact not great wonders of ancient peace/ or prosperity, people's dignity, glory or grace;/built with whips and cudgels and spears/on pools of sweat, tears, blood and broken bones/ they stand now in veiled shameless gory glory'. Unless we rise above the futile lines of rituals and mechanical gestures we can't rise; if it is not realized, 'solemnity sinks and cleanliness goes in exile'. He goes beyond the vague limits of satire and gives correct prescription for the malady:

> Let all the miracles and wonders of the world
> Revolve round the axis of 'Live and let live.   (18)

The sharpness of his satire can be seen in the poem "Media the Medusa" where he makes a critical dissection of the media such as newspapers and media which are drowned in corruption and he says: 'What is there freely to say or speak/where corruption is at its improbable peak?' Now he expresses his anguish at the degenerated newspapers: What is there gainfully to read/when almost all of us are brought to bleed,/when media is fond of cheap mass masala/spreading wild rumours, cancer tumours/and newspapers become private pamphlets?'(20). The poet is bold enough to express his views and each line hits us as a bullet never missing its target:

> Morning newspaper spreads foul smell
> of pages of rotten material rising in its pitch
> as the sickening smell of a rotten rat
> by the wide roadside with traffic jam
> wet with stagnant drops of stingy rain.
> All these papers are like thrown away leaves
> at the end of a corrupt political banquet. (20)

Reddy aims his satire not only at the media but at the corrupt political leaders and the entire system. What he advocates is cleanliness in life – in thought and act. The ending lines of the poem are at once emphatic and appealing:

> Morally we are nil or lean sans any sheen

> Unless we rise above this filth and foul smell
> we can't rise above the lines of enveloping hell. (20)

The spiritual dimension of Reddy's poetry is clearly discernible in the poem "My Sole Wish" where he thinks of his trapped soul and contemplates on the way to get the soul liberated and to reach the Supreme God who can be reached only with one-mindedness. To do a little good even in a small measure would have its durable impression on the life. With the help of words from the field of commerce he tries to drive home the thought he intends to convey. Though spiritual and commercial subjects are poles apart, Reddy makes an ingenious application of the utility value of one field in enhancing the contextual significance of the other field. He says:

> A little move towards the goal would be great;
> though little, let the closing balance of this life
> open the veiled eyes in the next session. (21)

He continues this thought and extends the thread of spiritualism to the poem "Enigma" which looks like a sonnet with its rhyme scheme but for an extra line. This is a poem where many threads are woven into a single stronger thread as it is at once subjective and objective, realistic and satirical, socialistic and spiritual. The persona in the poem can be taken as a typical modern man in his old age as his hair has turned as white as cotton. He says he couldn't realize all his gloried aims which are now like broken bubbles and pricking thorns. But it is not so with the rich and powerful, because for them right is wrong and wrong is right as they are capable of changing the colour of the act as per their choice. But in truth all our acts, all our pomp and glory are like fading rings of airy puff:

> All the acts and facts we strongly feel central,
> These gloried days and deeds we feel eternal
> are indeed baubles and bubbles ephemeral. (27)

The poem 'Novel Bonds' speaks of multiple earthly bonds such as domestic and familial bonds, societal bonds and other material bonds that bind a man or woman within a tiny sphere of narrow circumference and make us work as bonded slaves deprived of time to think of the right path and move in the right direction. Ultimately it is death that frees us from all this bonded labour. Towards the close the poem moves from material world to the spiritual and the transition is so naturally and deftly designed by the poet that we feel unawares the voice of the sublime: 'All these multiple onerous knotted bonds/thrive and strengthen with growing age,/make us live as croaking frogs in ponds;/these bonds force us to work like bulls/till we gasp for breath and collapse with age;/Unaware we are freed from these ties/as a freed bird with sudden exit from the stage.' (32)

The lines titled as "15th August" are a realistic analysis of the present situation social as well as political because the celebration of the Independence Day is now more a ritual than a moment of the patriotic spirit of hard-won freedom: 'Innocent students with flaming hearts assemble/and stand in front of the blinking flag;/Flags are flatly hoisted by our fat leaders,/strangers to the semantic spirit of the word./ ... Children get chocolates for standing in the sun/while masses free loads of liberal promises' (45). Thus the poet, a hard realist to the core, gives a pen-portrait of the situation.

There are a few fascinating poems on nature such as "Cascading Hills", "Learn from Birds", "The Sun", "The Glow Worm", "Fall Foliage", "Central Park" etc. "Glow-worms", a delightful creation of The Creator, make the dark night glow with their scanty light turning fields into twinkling grounds. The sense of wonder the writer expresses in the concluding lines is beyond the power of ordinary versifiers:

> On blades of grass you turn and twist, glide and glow,
> You dace and play hide and seek as winds blow.

> Are they little stars or has the sky come down to
> Illumine the night and bless this tiny town? (65)

One of the remarkable poems in this collection happens to be 'Fall Foliage' which re-creates the enchanting spectrum of Fall colours at the beginning of the winter season in Northern parts of USA. The poet who had the opportunity of seeing the fall colours with the rare power of his quill re-creates the rare experience of enjoying the most delightful sight of the changing colours of fall foliage:

> Their changing hues shine and steal our enthralled hearts.
> The charm of alchemic change is above the power of arts;
> Green to greenish dark, overnight it turns to light rose,
> then to princely pink and incarnates in pretty purple pose;
> Woods and forests cease to be weary, weirdly and wooden.
> Appear as an enchanting fairy land rosy, green and golden;
> maple leaves change to rosy glow, then to apple red
> gliding from shade to shade, cherry-red, dapple-bred; (80)

Reddy's lines on the Central Park compel our admiration at the memorable blend of word music and natural beauty of the famous Park in New York City. Such minute description of the beauty of nature coupled with the constant flow of melody can hardly be found even in most of the poems written by Americans. See how the poem starts:

> A vast spacious stretch of salubrious majestic sylvan scene
> Spread with canopied sunny sheets of levelled lushier lawn
> in the heart of the human jungle in enigmatic emerald sheen
> The glittering dewy green dons the ravishing robes of dawn. (82)

This is an emerald beauty in the heart of the financial capital of the world and serves as balm to all the tired souls and wearied visitors and travelers.

'Space' is indeed a thought-provoking poem that scans the vast space in the globe and gives a stunning diagnostic report of the crisis of space for the righteous. It begins – 'In this sphere there is ample space/in every field for this wild and corrupt race/for the changing shades of human face,/ but little space for the poor frightened peace'(48). The poet's heart is grieved to see that while there is so much of space for the ever-spreading acts of terrorism, there is little space for peace.

There is the marvelous narrative poem "The Hurricane" with nine stanzas of four lines each with rhyme scheme. It is about the tragic effect and catastrophic result of a massive hurricane that wiped out a fishing hamlet which was bubbling with buoyant life till that hour bequeathing solemn silence at the immediate sunrise. The description of the place, the sudden hurricane and the nature of the ghastly watery tomb is given in such an extraordinary style that it lasts long in our memory:

> Volcano behind and cyclone all around the sea dark and deep –
> When they rose in fury earth did quake with the big wave;
> Life did shake with a helpless cry at the vast yawning grave
> to lie in the midst of dance of danger and death to weep. (91)

The ending is really beautiful expressing the strength of life that has the natural capacity to survive against all odds:

> At sunrise the sea and sky looked blue and calm and beautiful,
> With not a trace of existence the little beach looked clean;
> Soon a few sprawling huts sprang and life was not dull or lean,
> Life is stronger than death and is more varied and wonderful. (92)

Reddy is a born poet of nature as Wordsworth and in his earlier books he re-creates the rural scenes and situations with its beautiful environment full of trees, plants, flowers and agricultural fields. The poem "Cascading Hills" surprises us with its inspiring description of nature rich with hills and rills, birds and animals, flowers and musical notes. It is an enchanting description of the walk through the cascading hills and forests to reach the famous Temple atop the hills at Tirumala-Tirupati which happens to be his native region in Andhra Pradesh. By the by the Temple is nearer to his village and Chandragiri than to Tirupati. The richness of the description of nature in this poem is so great that it is to be read and enjoyed. A few lines are quoted here to have a slice of the taste of the beauty of the poem: 'varied birds, pigeons and parrots, crows and sparrows/perch on boughs and fly to nearby trees in swift rows,/greet us shining in sweat and comfort our wearied feet/ with their full-throated shrill notes of rhythmic treat./various sounds of monkeys, foxes, stags, boars and bears/fill with the melody of mixed notes our receptive ears./Murmuring waters march with a long triumphant smile/hopping down the sloping rocky hills many a mile/ and laugh at the limping steps, a hearty laugh serene' (p.33).

To this group of spiritual poems belong poems such as "Badrinath", "At the River Ganga", "Varanasi", "Amarnath Temple" etc. His love of nature and firm faith in the spiritual coexist in equal ratio in all these poems. Badrinath situated in the higher Himalayan range covered with snow would at all hours be echoing with the soulful prayers of the devotees which is faithfully described here: 'As the waters flow with cosmic music/of chanting of *Ohm* the primordial sound/the echo fills the snowy hills all around' (p.35). The description of nature as well as the freezing cold presented in the poem "Badrinath" is marvelous, while the figure of speech is powerful with patriotic significance:

> chill air vibrates with a cooing tune of low echo,
> that merges with the chant's cosmic echo;
> The Lord, set in solid stone, smiles at the old
> limbs and at the aggressive invading cold;
> pines stoutly stand erect in icy armour
> like heroic soldiers in Leh or Kargil Sector (35).

Reddy unreservedly expresses his faith in the holy river Ganga in the poem "At the River Ganga" and the poem is imbued with pensive charm as he refers to his personal life. He went there with the solemn objective of mixing the ashes of his dear departed wife and the poem is in a way a spontaneous overflow of powerful feelings recollected in tranquility. He says – 'I stand on the slimy step on the Ganges ghat/and watch the deep waters running with the rot.' He continues: 'Ghats are red with flames of burning bodies on pyres/ Speeding waters sing their solemn notes as funeral lyre'. The ending lines are a beautiful expression of the faith of millions of the people of this ancient land:

> People of all creeds and parts of the world make pilgrimage
> to their holy places to reap joys and have long life in any age.
> But to come and die at Kasi people of this ancient land dream,
> to die at the feet of Kasi Viswanath, the soul of the Vedic stream. (94)

The poem "Varanasi" starts with the hoary past of this most ancient city and the thought of the poem described above continues here with greater force:

> The prime ancient city of above ten thousand years old,
> Withstanding battles, gory wreck and havoc stands bold;
> after fierce fall from ruthless fanatics rises like Phoenix,
> from the Lord an eternal gift, a miracle and a divine fix; (99)

The description of the most famed temple is extremely genuine and we do not find an extra word which speaks of the poet's deft handling of diction. Since the temple has been existing from times immemorial on the bank of the Ganges the way to reach the Temple remains the same and one has to walk through narrow lanes and confusing streets overcrowded with pilgrims on one side and on the other with freely moving cattle. See how pictorial is his presentation of the Ghats and the river Ganga at the foot of the Temple: 'While crowds of chanting devotees all the ghats greet, /Harischandra and Manikarnika bear all the burning heat/of the flames of burning pyres for full ten thousand springs/as the sea of Ganga waters carries in her deep womb in rings/the treasures of ten millenniums of ancient culture sublime/and bears the unbearable weight of foul filth and slime/amid sailing boats, chanting lips and slowly moving toes,/grazing goats, jumping monkeys and injecting mosquitoes,/pseudo-sadhus, *bada babus*, and beggars alien to purity,/Himalayan hermits, *aghoras*, yogis and tight security.' (99)

The description of Varanasi would be incomplete without the portrayal of *Ganga Harati*. The music that accompanies the *Harathi* fills the entire area with divine vibrations transporting us to a higher realm. All over the world people go to the religious centres and holy places for the fulfillment of their desires and for the longevity of life; but Varanasi is unique in that respect as people come here, stay and wait for years to die and have their bodies burnt or thrown into the sacred waters of the river Ganga. It is here that the poet has excelled other poets such as Shiv K. Kumar and Keki Daruwalla who too have written on Varanasi but totally failed to reflect the essence of the place. Where the senior poets failed, Reddy succeeds in capturing the spirit of India and presenting it in his poems. The ending lines of Reddy mirror the essential spirit of the place:

> Varanasi is an epic and metaphor of Indian life and heritage;
> A symbol of survival that prepares us to the final stage
> to greet the grisly inevitable end with a bold spiritual smile
> and not to crave with a passionate urge for an extra mile. (100)

The poem "Amarnath Temple" is written in stanza form with seven four-lined stanzas ending with a couplet fully observing the rhyme scheme. A reading of the poem reveals the heights of spiritual consciousness he has reached without which it is not possible to have the vision of sages in the rocks and the garlands of *Rudrakshas* in the place of snowy hills near the Cave Temple. What is particularly remarkable with Reddy is he is at once conscious of the spiritual and the social elements of the pilgrimage to Amarnath Temple including the continuous threat from the terrorists which is focused in his expression 'guarding Jawans' that protect the pilgrims. The rhythmic music of the lines runs on par with the celestial music arising from the chanting of Ohm:

> Ranges of Himalayas continue to cover the rugged land
> Ice-capped peaks compete to kiss the soaring azure sky;
> Pine trees vie with guarding Jawans that protect the band
> who chant the sacred Ohm echoing vales and hills high. (101)

What surprises us in this book is the finding of numerous sonnets and the reader gets a rare opportunity of deriving the great pleasure of tasting the beauty of nearly sixteen sonnets of great quality in metre as well as meaning though occasionally he makes a departure from the traditional sonnet. In him we see the happy blend of Petrarchan and Shakespearean sonnets. Spiritual thought is central to the sonnet "The Voyage" where the proverbial journey of life is metaphorically presented as a voyage. The sonnet on Seven Hills is a beautiful piece of enduring quality portraying the supreme Lord standing amid nature's spell of green glory on the salubrious top of the sacred hills seven. The faith of the people of the land is expressed along with the eternal flow of dharma:

> Countless flowers of varied colours dance at the golden rays

> Blazing camphor vies with sandalwood's fragrant flame.
> Faith flows in this land unbroken by swords of savages
> Eternal dharma shines as the northern star through ages. (58)

In the next sonnet "Remember Him" Reddy like a sage pays a tribute to the glory of the Lord and he says 'No being can creep or crawl without the Almighty's nod' and to understand the truth of God one has to come out of the veil of *Maya* as the spark of divinity is there in all . The concluding lines are superbly penned:

> Every tiny atom in the universe is a Power-packed one
> If it is released well in right earnest, battle is won. (59)

The sonnet 'Prime Source and Seed' states the *Upanishadic* truth that the One Supreme willed and multiplied into countless entities and though He is formless and nameless all these countless forms and names refer to that power only. The last two lines reveal the inexpressible nature of the Supreme One:

> Beyond the vast visible light and immeasurable endless night
> forever It blazes, the Sublime Soul, the flawless Eternal Light. (61)

The sonnet "False Image" is a gem of a piece that can help in the building up of one's character and in arresting the thought of bending and bowing before others. With the deft image of the tree he tries to drive home the nobility of the concept of individuality:

> Of course trees in general grow straight, fairly vertical
> Then what is the wrong with this product, an odd man? (70)

He says in the next sonnet "My Only Shield" that one should not yield to the changing colours and shades of time, but one has to stand against the roaring waves of afflictions and hurdles with patience and forbearance and swim across the tide to win at last. Though things turn awry one should not yield and with a balanced heart and with firm faith in the Lord one has to proceed:

> To the changing shades of frigid fate I should not yield,
> My faith in me and in the One Supreme is my only shield. (72)

His sonnet "The Last Sip of Tea" is one of the most delightful sonnets in English language. Tea has become an essential part of our daily life and in a sense it is the nectar of everyday life of the poor and the rich alike. The sonnet starts with the seductive lines: 'The cup of tea greets with a sweet seductive smile/ with more pure milk, less sugar and lush green leaf/and fumes as perfume cast a spell on nose like a nymph/Beads of winking bubbles shine like rubies for a while.' The mellifluous flow of alliteration with end rhymes and internal rhymes is the hallmark of Reddy's poetry and it wafts our hearts as gentle balmy breeze:

> Unasked, unmasked it inspires us to the poetic pitch,
> a trusted friend of the poor that barely live on bread.
> Fumes as airy visions transport us to feel the liquid bliss,
> The last tasty sip lingers long as the bliss of beloved's kiss. (74)

Within the short scope of the sonnet "On Faith", the poet in right earnestness speaks of the purity of faith in the Lord and finds fault with vicious Missionaries and people who try to convert others and who let themselves to be converted to other religions by becoming victims of lures, bribes and material wealth. The poet also takes cudgels against the idea of terror and the promoters of terror. He says: 'In truth no need to change one's real colour and faith/ Some indulge in the greedy game of collecting wily wealth/Some in the guise of social work convert the poor in stealth/All faiths are truly rooted in one and only one divine faith' (98). The poet has succeeded in articulating the irreversible divine truth in simple and vivid words:

> To be kind and compassionate is the essence of any noble faith
> Hell, if any, is reserved for blood-thirsty promoters of terror
> Transform such cruel beasts from heinous thoughts of horror. (98)

Right from the good olden days there have been many people who hate idol-worship totally ignorant of the spirit behind it. Reddy with his cosmopolitan culture and unadulterated spiritual faith tries to focus on this:

> O worshippers of the abstract impersonal formless Lord,
> hate not form, what shines in it is the same One Infinite ... (104)

Many Holy Wars, Crusades and religious wars took place in the history of the world owing to extreme fanaticism and India became the pitiable victim of the merciless Muslim invaders from the beginning of the second millennium who razed to the ground thousands of sacred temples such as Somnath Temple and great libraries such as Nalanda. Astounding wealth of sculpture at Warangal and Hampi Vijayanagar were totally destroyed and now one sees only a vast expanse of ruin and wreck. All this monstrous activity in the name of religion moves the poet so much that he finds it difficult to express the damage in words and with an aggrieved heart he says:

> Religion can't be a game of spilling blood or a missionary mart,
> No prophet is greater than your kind, pure and righteous heart. (104)

Now let me conclude this article with Reddy's poem "My Poems" where he expresses the plight of a poet who fails to get due recognition in spite of the quality of the poems. We find a bit of introspection on the part of the poet and after initial despair he gathers courage and with confidence he speaks:

> My poems may not be heaven-born,
> but I know definitely they are not still-born;
> There may be a partial egalitarian eclipse,
> But they are alive; to read there are lips;
> One day they can raise their glowing heads,
> smile and sleep contented on healthy beds. (90)

Reddy is at once a poet and critic of repute and as such he has the critical ability to make an assessment of his poetry and with the right spirit of confidence based on the ingrained worth of his poems he has given utterance to the above lines. Though he as a poet may appear to be neglected he is sure to achieve the due recognition in due course of time. While some are always after publicity Reddy is a different person as he appears a little reserved though he is always cordial and compassionate.

Great would be the loss if we fail to mention about the ceaseless music that flows as an undercurrent in all the poems of T.V. Reddy which we long to hear and feel. It is in this melody we hear the echo of the sublime voice. The book begins with music as the first poem opens with rhyming lines springing music full of rhythm and the last four lines are alive with rhyme –sages, ages, /race, lace. We come across rhyming pairs of words and rhythmic words everywhere in his poetry; for instance see –numb, dumb, / mind, behind/ stage, bondage, / hill, thrill, / flowers, bowers etc. Reddy's sonnets are a mine of delectable music springing from the constant beat of the rhythm and such expressions are beyond count in his poetry and in fact music is the breath of his poetry. Reddy's poetry is a marvelous blend of sound and sense springing from profound silence. In his poems that deal with social or satirical theme, nature or spiritual theme we find an undercurrent of the sublime voice whose echo lingers long in our minds.

About the Poet

Dr .T. Vasudeva Reddy, born in Dec. 1943 in a village near the famous pilgrim town Tirupati in Andhra State in India, did M.A in English in 1966 and got Ph. D. for his thesis on the novels of Jane Austen. He worked as Lecturer, Reader and U.G.C National Fellow and Visiting Professor, and retired as Principal of Govt. Degree College in Dec. 2001 and later as Principal of prestigious Post-Graduate colleges. He received the Awards of International Eminent Poet in 1987, Hon. D. Litt. from the WAAC, San Francisco in 1988, Best Teacher Award at the College & University level from the Govt. of A.P. in 1990, Best Poetry award for his third poetry book *The Fleeting Bubbles* from Michael Madhusudan Dutt Academy, Calcutta in 1994 and the prestigious U.G.C Award of National Fellowship in 1998. His biography figures in the American Biographical Institute (N. Carolina, USA), International Biographical Institute (Cambridge), Reference India & Asia (New Delhi) and Sahitya Akademi (New Delhi).

He is a renowned poet, critic and novelist of international repute. His poems appeared in French journals in Paris. M.Phil. and Ph.D. theses have been produced on his works. He received the international Award of "Excellence in World Poetry" in 2009. He is now Hon. President of GIEWEC (Guild of Indian English Writers Editors and Critics). He is an internationally recognized poet in English with 11 poetry books to his credit. His poetic career spans over a long period of three and a half decades from 1982 till now and his creative quill knows no rest. He is at once a realistic and romantic poet, a lover of nature and a poet with social commitment, a lyricist and a satirist aiming at the improvement of ethical standards.

As Prof. David Kerr of Monash Univ. Australia says, "T.V. Reddy is a real poet with a commitment to perfection….His poetry is an outburst of emotion and it succeeds in creating the basic human feelings." In the words of Prof. Nissim Ezekiel, a distinguished Indian poet, "Like a gifted sculptor he chisels his poems with the deftness of a master craftsman."

Other Works

Poetry:

When Grief Rains (New Delhi, Samakaleen Pubs., 1982)
The Broken Rhythms (Madras, Poets Press, 1987)
The Fleeting Bubbles (Madras, Poets Press, 1989)
*Melting Melodies (*Madras, Poets Press, 1994)
Pensive Memories (Madras, Poets Press, 2005)
Gliding Ripples (U.S.A., Baltimore, Pub. America, 2008)
Echoes (N. Delhi, Authors Press, 2012)
Quest for Peace (N. Delhi, Authors Press, 2013)
Golden Veil (N. Delhi, Authors Press, 2016)
Thousand Haiku Pearls (N. Delhi, Authors Press, 2016)
Sound and Silence (N.Delhi, AuthorsPress, 2017)
The Rural Muse: The Poetry of T.Vasudeva Reddy. Ed. K.V. Raghupathi (N. Delhi, Authors Press, 2014).

T.V.Reddy's Poetry: The Pulse of Life - Essential Readings (USA, Modern History Press, Ann Arbor, MI, 2017)

Novels:

The Vultures (Calcutta, Golden Books, 1983)
Minor Gods (New York, 2008)

Criticism:

Jane Austen: The Dialectics of Self-Actualization in her Novels (New Delhi, Sterling Pubs., 1987)
Jane Austen: The Matrix of Matrimony (Jaipur, Bohra Pubs., 1987)
A Critical Survey of Indo-English Poetry (N. Delhi, Authors Press, 2016).

Grammar:

Advanced Grammar & Composition in English (Hyderabad, Commonwealth Pubs., 1996)

About the Poet:

The Poetic Art of T.V.Reddy: New Perspectives (A Collection of 24 Critical articles), ed. by Prof. K.V.Dominic (N.Delhi, Authors Press, 2017)"

About the Contributors

1. Dr. Sheeba S Nair, Assistant Professor, Dept of English, Sree Ayyappa College for Women, Chunkankadai, Tamil Nadu, India. She is an eminent critic whose published work speaks volumes of her outstanding credentials as a critic. She is an expert critic on all genres of literature. An academically active teacher, she is guiding research scholars.

2. Dr. D. Gnanasekaran, Former Professor and Head, Department of English, Kanchi Mamuniwar Centre for P.G. Studies and Research, Pudicherry, India. He has a distinguished academic career and as a critic, his published papers are evidences of his authority over Indian Writing in English. He has put in 39 years' teaching experience; a bilingual writer; authored over 60 published research articles; regularly contributing articles to various journals; Ph.D. research supervisor; evaluating Ph.D. theses from other universities; a poet, short story writer, critic, translator; presented papers at about 50 National and International Conferences and Seminars; resource person in UGC-Academic Staff Colleges and Chairperson in many National seminars; broadcast talks on varied topics and short stories; given several invited talks and keynote addresses; member of PG Board of Studies in Autonomous Colleges; Communication Skills Consultant. His collection of Research Articles titled *Indian Writing in English Today: Insights for the Future* has been brought out by Authors Press, New Delhi recently. *The Madcap* is his English translation of *Piththan*, an anthology of Tamil poems by Kavikko Abdul Rahman. He is currently working on a book on Stylistics to be published soon. His collection of his poems and short stories are ready for publication.

3. Dr. DC Chambial, a retired Professor of English, one of the major contemporary Indian Poets in English and critics writing today. He has been the editor of three decades old biannual journal *POETCRIT*, Maranda, Himachal Pradesh, India. He has ten poetry collections to his credit. He is a widely published poet in anthologies. A master critic, Chambial regularly contributes his critical writings to journals and books. Critical works and numerous articles have been published on him.

4. Dr. Abida Farooqui, Asst Professor of English, PTM Govt College, Perinthallamanna, Kerala, India. She is an eminent critic and has a number of publications to her credit. She delivers keynote addresses and acts as a resource person in seminars and conferences.

5. Dr. C.A. Assif, Associate Professor and Head, Department of English, MGGAC, Mahe, India. A respected teacher and an active researcher, Assif is an eminent critic on poetry. His criticism reflects his command over in-depth understanding of subject.

6. Dr. K. Padmaja, is an Associate Professor of English and In-Charge, Dept. of English at D.K.Govt. College for Women (Autonomous) Nellore, A.P., India. She is an English Language Teacher Trainer Certified by APCCE and RELO in Activity Based Language Teaching) in student-centered teaching methodology and conducted almost 20 workshops for teachers. She is also a Research Supervisor under the jurisdiction of Vikrama Simhapuri University, Nellore. She has published 02 Books and 14 papers in various national and international Journals.

7. Dr. Santosh Ajit Singh, a celebrated teacher and an eminent critic who has published extensively in journals and books. She attends seminars and presents papers at different venues in the country.

8. Dr. Koganti Vijaya Babu, a celebrated critic and an eminent poet in Telugu and English, now working as Associate Professor in English at Govt. Degree College for Women (Autonomous), Guntur, Andhra Pradesh, India. His interests are varied. A bilingual writer, Vijaya Babu is both an academician and a researcher. A language specialist, he has delivered extension lectures on language and its components. He is the recipient of Best Teacher's Award from the Government of Andhra Pradesh, India.

9. Arabati Pradeep Kumar, Associate Professor of English, Anurag Group of Institutions (Autonomous), Venkatapur, Rangareddy, Telangana, India. He is an established critic and regularly contributes papers to journals and books.

10. Dr. Palakurthy Dinakar, Asst Professor, Government Degree and P.G. College, Koratla, Jagtiyal, Telangana, India. He is a translator, book-reviewer and an eminent critic. He delivers lectures on different genres of literature. He is the recipient of Best teacher's Award from the Government of Andhra Pradesh.

11. Dr. S. Karthik Kumar, Asst Professor, Dept of English, Annamalai University, Chidambaram, Tamilnadu, India. A distinguished critic, he has several publications to his credit on diverse branches of literature. He has attended seminars in India and abroad. He successfully organizes seminars and conferences in his institution.

12. Dr. D.C. Chambial: See no.3.

13. Dr. G. Srilatha, Associate Professor of English, P.B.Sidhartha College of Arts and Science, P.G. Centre, Vijayawada, India. A distinguished critic, she has been a regular contributor to journals and books. She is known for conducting seminars and conferences.

14. Dr. Anju S Nair, Asst Professor of English, Tagore Arts College, Puducherry, India. An eminent critic, she contributes her criticism to journals and anthologies. She is known for excellent communicational skills. At present, she is guiding research scholars.

15. Mrs. S. Malathy, Asst Professor of English, Tagore Arts College, Puducherry, India. A distinguished teacher and an eminent critic, she has innumerable publications to her credit.

16. Dr. Lily Arul Sharmila, Asst Professor of English, Tagore Arts College, Puducherry, India. A teacher with two decades of experience, she is an eminent critic on all genres of literature.

17. Dr. V. Suganthi, Asst Professor, Thiruvvalluvar Govt Arts College, Rasipuram, Tamilnadu, India. She is an active academician and a literary critic.

18. Dr. R. Janatha Kumari, Asst Professor, Dept of English and Research Centre, Sree Ayyappa College for Women, Chunkankadai, Tamilnadu, India. She is a distinguished critic on Indian Writing in English and Post-Colonial Literatures. As an editor, she edits a printed journal *Daffodils*.

19. Dr. Candy D Cunha, Asst Professor, Andhra Loyola Institute of Engineering & Technology, Vijayawada. She is an eminent critic on Eco-Literature and has substantial contributions to her credit in the area.

20. Gobinda Sahoo, Lecturer in English, Sarbamangala Degree College, Gollamunda, Kalahandi, Odisha, India. He is an eminent critic on Indian Writing in English. At present, he is the Co-editor of *Rock Pebbles,* Odisha.

About the Contributors

21. JS Divya Sree, Asst Professor of English, Sree Ayappa College for Women, Chunkankadai, Tamilnadu, India. A reputed critic, she contributes her criticism to journals and books.

22. Dr. Poonam Dwivedi, Asst Professor of English, Baba Balraj Engineering College, Balachaur, Punjab, India and Associate editor *Contemporary Vibes*, Chandigarh and a regular contributor to journals and anthologies. A poet with two published collections, Poonam is actively engaged in research.

23. Dr. K. Rajamouli, Professor and Head, Dept of English, Ganapathy Engineering College, Waranagal, Telangana, India. He has eleven books to his credit. He is a poet, novelist, short story writer, critic and writer of language books.

24. Dr. Neelam K Sharma, an eminent critic hails from Surjan Nagar, U.P., India. He is a distinguished critic and has several contributions to his credit.

25. Prof. Ramesh Chandra Mukhopadhyay, M.A. (Triple); M.Phil., Ph.D. in English; sutrapitaka Tirtha; a veteran scholar, researcher, a literary critic, editor and bilingual writer and a prolific writer from Kolkata. He has contributed immensely to journals and books on different areas of literature. He is the pioneering leader and dedicated soldier of the Underground Literature Movement in Bengal and he is the Editor of the reputed journal Platform along with Prof. Mousumi Ghosh of Calcutta University. He has written more than thirty books in English and Bengali. Recipient of Ashutosh Mukherjee Gold Medal for his treatise on modern drama.

26. Prof. A.K. Choudhary:-Arbind Kumar Choudhary, Poet, Editor &Critic, Editor: *Kohinoor* (ISSN 0973-6395) *&Ayush* (ISSN0 974-8075), An eminent poet and critic in English. Many articles have come on him. Research is going on his poetry. Four full length critical books have appeared on his poetry. He is the Universal Ambassador Of Peace From Poetry, Geneva, Honorary Member-International Writers And Artists Association, USA; Associate Prof. &Head of English Department, Rangachahi College, Majuli, Assam, India-785104.

27. Mrs. Prasaja VP, Asst Professor of English, Sree Ayyappa College for Women, Chunkankadai, Tamilnadu, India. She writes regularly to journals and anthologies.

28. Dr. Arti Chandel, Asst Professor of English, Dharmasala, H.P., India. She is the associate editor of *Poetcrit*, a long standing biannual journal from Maranda. She is an eminent critic and a book-reviewer and has several publications to her credit.

29. Mrs. Anantha Lakshmi Hemalatha, Asst Professor of English, Tagore Arts College, Puducherry, India. She is a translator and her works in translation have received accolades from the world. An academically active, Hemalatha is a serious researcher.

30. Dr. K.Rajani, Asst. Professor of English, Govt. Arts College (Degree & P.G.), Chittoor, Andhra Pradesh. A noted writer and critic on Indo-English literature. Her doctoral thesis is on the poetry of I.K.Sharma, D.C.Chambial and R.K.Singh. She is a regular contributor to Journals on English literature. She has published numerous articles and reviews on Indian poets in English.

Typesetting by Victor R. Volkman, Modern History Press (Ann Arbor, Michigan)

About the Editor

Dr. P.V. Laxmiprasad is an active academician, an avid researcher, a literary critic, and a resource person. A teacher with two decades of experience, he is the author and editor of **10** published books in English Literature. He is widely published in journals, books and anthologies. His publications speak of his outstanding credentials and long-standing commitment to English literature. Overall, he has 300 publications to his credit. He has passion for music and literature. He is working in the Department of English, Satavahana University, Karimangar, Telanagana, India.

His published books:
- *Exploring New Horizons: Myriad Dimensions in the Poetry of Manas Bakshi,* Authors Press, New Delhi, 2017
- *The Poetry of I.K.Sharma : New Tracks and Literary Swings,* Authors Press, New Delhi, 2017
- *The Spirit of Age and Ideas in the Novels of PCK Prem,* Authors Press, New Delhi, 2016
- *Critical Readings on the Fictional World of Manju Kapur,* Aadi Publications, Jaipur, 2016
- *The Heterogeneity of Story Writing: A Critical Evaluation of Eight Indian Short Story Writers in English,* Authors Press, New Delhi, 2015
- *Mapping Thematic Variations: The Poetry of DC Chambial,* Authors Press, New Delhi, 2015
- *An Anthology of Criticism on Six Indian English Poets,* Sarup Publications Pvt Limited, New Delhi, 2015
- *Introspective Voyager: A Collection of Critical Essays on the Poetry of K.V.Raghupathi,* Authors Press, New Delhi, 2014
- *The Philosophical Muse: Perspectives on the Poetry of K.V.Raghupathi* (Critical Book of Essays), APH Publishing Corporation, New Delhi, 2012
- *Universal Witness* (Poetry Collection in English) Thematic Publications, Latur, M.S., 2012

Index

A

A Heart Unbowed, 20
A Poem, 32
A Violent Winter, 23, 24, 35
adharma, 14
Ageing Smiles, 23, 24
Aim High, 19, 54
Alone as a Bird, 54, 119
Amarnath Temple, 210, 211
Ameeruddin, S., 183
amrita, 1
Andhra, 215
Andhra Pradesh, iv, 19, 66, 69, 75, 112, 177, 189, 210
Arnold, M., 9
Assembly of Quadrupeds, 25
At the Cross-Road, 101
At the Field at Noon, 18
At the River Ganga, 210
Atharva Veda, 119
Aurobindo, S., iii, 50, 54, 109, 134, 186
Austen, J., 13, 112, 183

B

Badrinath, 132, 210
Bamboo Arrow, 182
Bankrupt Clouds, 19, 51
Beauty Parlor, 186
Beggar's Bowl, 179
Bhagavad Gita, 46, 47, 48, 54, 134
Bharathiar, 115
Bhatia, H.S., 56
Bird in the Cage, A, 54, 119
Biting Breeze, 35
Bleeding Words, 107
Blessings of Jasmine, 37, 97, 193
Bradley, A.C., 32
Broken Life, A, 109
Bubble, A, 24, 79

Buddha, 11, 31, 109, 133, 134, 145, 155, 172, 173, 174, 183, 184
Byron, iii, 125, 151

C

Calcutta, 102, 183
Carson, R., 125
Cascading Hills, 208, 210
Caudwell, C., 32
Central Park, 208, 209
Chambial, D.C., iv, v, vi, 33, 217, 218, 219, 220
Chandragiri Fort, 69, 75
Change, 28, 101, 129, 133
Char Dham, 9, 151
Chariot of Jagannath, 76
Child's Smile, 182
Cholas, 10
Choose the Right Path, 2, 15, 54, 114, 115
Civilization, 28, 102
Clifton, L., 27
Cloud, The, 66, 70, 71, 72
Coconut Tree, iv, 25, 66, 69, 70
Cold Foe, The, 19
Comfort Zone, 134
Corn Reaper, The, 191
Corn Reaper. The, 96, 192
Countryside, 107
Crow, The, 25, 36, 138
Cry in the Jungle, A, 132

D

Dark Valley, The, 190
Das, K., iv, 33, 135
Democratic Lines, 192
Derozio, H.L., iii, 15
Dharmasala, 22, 23, 66, 67, 68, 74
Dignity in Exile, 207
Dover, 18, 21, 35, 40, 182
Dreams, 101
Dubey, B.K., 119

Dull Evening, The, 137
Dumb Toys, 16, 122
Dutt, T., iii, 50
Dying Wick, The, 29, 103, 204

E

Echo, An, 196
Eden Garden, 19
Eliot, T.S., iii, vii, 27, 66, 153, 154, 158, 176
Empowered Woman?, 134
End of Arch, 4
End of the Arch, 19
End the Dynastic Rule, 20, 52, 53
Endless Night, 29
Enigma, 208
Erase the Borders, 109
Erstwhile Farmer, 19, 52, 120
Eternal Ethics, 14, 47, 54
Existence, 182
Ezekiel, N., 101, 135, 188
Ezkiel, N., 33

F

Fall Foliage, 208, 209
False Image, 212
Farmer, 31, 122, 128, 176, 177
First World War, 142
Flowers Shall Bloom, 20, 53, 123
Flux of Life, 190
Fond Memories, 197
Forget Me Not, 3, 16, 53
Fort, The, iv, 23, 66, 69, 75
Fortune Teller, iv, 30, 180
Frost, R., 2, 3, 15, 16, 74, 114, 162, 168, 169, 170
Futility, 28, 102, 201

G

Gandhiji, 31, 132
Ganges, 35, 132, 147, 149, 150, 210, 211
GIEWEC, 215

Gill, S., 142, 171, 175
Glow Worm, The, 208
Grand Mother's House, 33
Gray, T., 79
Green Canopy, 18, 54, 119
Grow Old We Must, 5
Gypsy Woman, The, 180

H

Hamlet, 202, 205
Hazare, A., 147, 150
Healing Echo, The, 138, 139
Himalayas, 35, 67, 68, 131, 132, 151, 182, 211
Hippocrene, 32
Hope, 20, 54
Housewife, The, 38, 97, 192
Human Touch, 194
Hurricane, The, 209

I

I am Tired, 191
I See No Other Way, 202
Idols for the Idle, 108, 109
In Memoriam, 22, 30, 203
In Tense Flight, 98, 190
In the Shell of Solitude, 1, 13, 41, 53, 112
Indian Bride. The, iv, 191, 192
Interview, An, 25, 78
Is the World Beautiful, 191
Iyengar, K.R., 103, 130

J

Jilted Jasmine, 181
Journey in the Jungle, A, 131, 132

K

Kalyani Dam, 22, 34, 66, 67, 74
Karmakar, G., 40, 100, 104
Kedarnath, 8, 132, 151, 183
Kerr, D., 101, 215
Kipling, R., 10
Kith and Kin, 81, 82, 83
Krishna, 14, 47, 104, 105, 109, 126, 133, 154, 172, 174, 181, 183
Kundera, M., 45

L

Lake at Night, The, iv, 34
Lake Serbonis, 45
Lakshman Bridge, 131, 132
Lal, P., 102
Last Sip of Tea, The, 212
Learn from Birds, 208
Learning is Life, 54, 123
Leavis, F.R., 107
Leper, A, 178
Let Me Stand Erect, 5, 122
Let Us Rise, 206
Life is a Desert, vi, 28, 81, 102, 200
Life on Wheels, 197
Listen to Our Song, 52
Look at the Stars, 19, 54, 122
Lotus, 37, 140, 167
Lotus Palace, The, 140
Love is Light, 186

M

Mahapatra, J., iv, vii, 135, 187
Make This Life Real, 17
Mansion in Ruins, 121
March of Time, The, 195
May, R., 7
Meaning of Love, 16, 53
Middle-class Man, The, 20, 44
Migrating Birds, 23, 38, 138
Milky Way, The, 128, 182
Mortal Frame, The, 29
Mukhopadhyaya, A., viii, 123
My Father's School Days, 20
My Only Shield, 212
My Own Shadow, 204
My Poems, 213
My Sole Wish, 208
My Soul in Exile, 94
My Soul's Plea, 32

N

Naidu, S., iii, 33, 50, 56, 73
Nair, S., v
Naked Tree, The, 30, 37, 127, 178
Nature, 118
Nature's Play, 34, 37, 130
Need of the Hour, 14, 53
New Year Day, The, 181
Nietzsche, 127
Night of the Scorpion, The, 33
Night Watch, 18, 54
No More Tears, 3, 16, 123
Nothing Follows, 135, 198
Novel Bonds, 208

O

Ode to the West Wind, 6, 21, 100, 105
Old Napkins, 2, 13, 54, 113
Old Woman, An, iv, 95
Omniscient Teacher, 25
On Faith, 212
On the Borders of Night, 196
On the Sacred Hills, 66, 73, 78
Organized Violence, 195
Our Leader, 25, 77
Our Race, 206
Our School Days, 120
Our Thirsty Land, 17, 18, 51, 116, 119

P

Pair of Doves, A, 24, 36, 37, 138, 139
Pair of Sparrows, A, iv, 36, 66, 69, 79
Paramathma, 11
Parandham, 9, 183
Patel, S., 132
Path of Life, 110
Pensive Farmer, 31
Plants, 131
Power of Love, The, 24
Prem, P.C.K., iv, 33, 220
Prime Source and Seed, 212
puranic time, 1
Pyres and Fires, 4, 53

Q

Quaint Faith, 181
Quest for Peace, 56–65, 142–58, 171–75

R

Raghavan, T., 39, 40, 51
Raghupathi, K.V., iv, 13, 33, 40, 105, 220
Rainbow, v, 66, 73
Realization, 30, 104, 203
Reddy, P.B., 39
Reign of Terror', 178
River, The, 25, 35, 66, 72, 73
Riverside, 17, 18, 54, 120
Rose, The, 37
Ruins of a Great House, 75

Index

S

Sabari, 26
Sacred Soil, The, 31
sanatana dharma, 50
Sanatana Dharma, 14, 47, 54, 158
Sandberg, C., 201
Savage Space, 207
Scars Reopen, 197
Search for Peace, 197
Second Coming, The, 15, 21, 47, 48
Seeded Soil, 19, 52, 122
Seminar, 25
Seven Hills, 211
Shakespeare, 21, 29, 140, 153
Shelley, iii, 2, 9, 20, 28, 71, 74, 98, 100, 115, 187
Singh, T.D., 126
Smile, the Saviour, 15, 42, 114
So Tall and So Small, 196
Solitary Reaper, The, 96, 104
Soyinka, W., 27
Sparrow, The, iv, 36
Sparrows, 36, 184
Star is a Star, 123
subjectivity, 1
Summer Sizzles, 121
Summer Trip, A, 131, 132
Sun, The, 177, 208
Supreme Being, The, 98
Supreme Lord, The, 24, 66
Swamiji, 31, 179, 192
Sweet Scar, 27, 100
Sylvan Scene, 17, 54, 119, 120
Syntax of Love, 16, 53

T

T.S. Eliot, 142–58
Teacher, The, 97
Tedious Voyage, The, 191
Tell Me What He Is, 42, 52, 53
Tennyson, 6, 72
That Thing Money, 25, 78
The Fair Sex Centre, 22
The Taj, 22, 25, 75
Thirst, 25, 76
Thirsty Field, iv, 29, 35, 103
Thiruvalluvar, 76, 80
This Dull Evening, 22, 24
This is the City, 23
Thousand Haiku Pearls, 85–93, 159–70
Thousand Pillars, 30, 177
Thy Echo, 17
Thy Loving Grace, 24
Tide, 190
Time Spares None, 108
Tirupati, 215
To India—My Native Land, 15
To Love, 28
To My Other Half, 138, 139
To Rest in Peace, 5, 19, 54
Today's Rural Life, 18, 52, 121
Toiling Ants, iv, 128, 182
Train, The, iv, 30, 31, 182
Transience, 29, 103, 201
Travel by Bus, iv, 30, 177
True Drunkard, A, 179
Tryambaka, 179
Tsunami, 25, 140
Two Plus Two is Two, 79
Typist Girl, The, 180

U

Ugra Narasimha, 47
Ultimate End, 19, 52, 53
University Units, 77
Unpredictable Man, 23, 24
Unsolved Mystery, 53, 113
Upanishad, 13

V

Varanasi, 147, 210, 211
Veil of Death, 24, 138, 139
Vernal Love, 24, 79
Vijayanagar, 69, 140, 197, 213
Village Girl, The, 24, 38
Village Song, 33
Village, The, 24, 31, 38, 177
Vision Four Two's, 25
Voyage, The, 24, 211

W

Waiting, 15, 24, 46
Waiting for an Avatar, 15, 46
Walcott, D., 75
Watching the Field at Night, 18, 119
Watching the Sea, 35
Water is Dearer than Blood, 17, 51, 115, 122
Water Is Dearer than Blood, 53
When Grief Rains, 28, 204
Widow, A, 191
Wings of Dragon, 134
Women of the Village, iv, 96, 191
Wordsworth, iii, 9, 18, 19, 74, 96, 98, 104, 107, 118, 123, 125, 159, 160, 161, 162, 165, 167, 168, 169, 170, 173, 180, 187, 192, 210
Wounded Sky Frowns, 35

Y

Yeats, 47

The Pulse of Life: Essential Readings is a representative collection of the poetry of T. Vasudeva Reddy, a luminous star shining in Indian English poetry. His poetry is a pleasant blend of the traditional and the modern, the realistic and the romantic, the symbolic and the imagist, the urban and the rural, satirical and lyrical streams of poetry.

His poems cover a wide thematic pattern ranging from the remote village to the global level, a bewildering blend of rural and global life. Whoever wishes to have a glimpse of the reality of the Indian rural scenario and see the struggles and sufferings of poor farmers can go through the poems of T.V. Reddy. Poems, spread over eleven volumes till now, and spanning 35 years, are now collected for the first time ever in this Essential Readings edition.

"In the vast desert of Indo-Anglian poetry, it is quite refreshing to see the life-giving oasis of Reddi's poetry which at once resuscitates and invigorates even a slumbering mind. His poems are as immortal as the frescoes of the famous Ajantha caves in India."
--Dr. Edith Rusconi Kaltovich, N.J.

"My attention is sometimes arrested by the striking imagery and phrasing. The poet has a keen eye to mark the exceptional whether in life or nature."
--Dr. K.R. Srinivas Iyengar, Madras

"In his poetry we find concrete examples of poetic excellences that distinguish him from other Indian poets and reserve for him a permanent place on the Indian Parnassus. Every poem is a nugget of thoughtful fancy studded in the fabric of the poet's pageant of poetic filigree."
--Dr. D.C. Chambial, Editor, Poetcrit, H.P.

"Like a gifted sculptor he chisels his poems with the deftness of a master craftsman."
--Prof. Nissim Ezekiel, Mumbai

ISBN 978-1-61599-344-4

Learn more at www.ModernHistoryPress.com

www.ingramcontent.com/pod-product-compliance
Lightning Source LLC
Chambersburg PA
CBHW082118230426
43671CB00015B/2726